Growing up COMMUNIST and JEWISH in Bondi

JOHN DOCKER is a writer and cultural historian who lives in Sydney with his wife the historian Ann Curthoys. He researches and writes in a number of fields, including Australian literature in international contexts, Jewish identity and diaspora, genocide and massacre studies. In exploring cultural theory, he has written on Edward Said, Gandhi, Derrida, Mikhail Bakhtin and Walter Benjamin. He contributes essays to the *Journal of Holy Land and Palestine Studies*. With Ann Curthoys he published *Is History Fiction?* (2005, 2010) as well as essays in genocide studies and cultural studies, for example, 'Stuart Hall and Cultural Studies, circa 1983' (2017). He is currently writing a book entitled *Sheer Folly and Derangement: Disorienting Europe and the West, from the Enlightenment to Modernity*.

VOLUMES IN THIS WORK:

Volume 1: My Father, Ted Docker
Volume 2: My Mother, Elsie Levy
Volume 3: I am Born

ALSO BY JOHN DOCKER

Australian Cultural Elites: Intellectual Traditions in Sydney and Melbourne, Angus and Robertson, 1974

In a Critical Condition, Penguin Books, 1984

The Nervous Nineties, Oxford University Press, 1991

Postmodernism and Popular Culture: A Cultural History, Cambridge University Press, 1994

1492: The Poetics of Diaspora, Continuum, 2001

The Origins of Violence: Religion, History and Genocide, UNSW Press, 2008

Race, Colour and Identity in Australia and New Zealand, edited with Gerhard Fischer, UNSW Press, 2000

Rethinking Gandhi and Nonviolent Relationality: Global Perspectives, edited with Debjani Ganguly, Routledge, 2007

Growing up COMMUNIST and JEWISH in Bondi

An Ego Histoire, a Dictionary of Modernity, an Autobiography, a Romance

My Father, Ted Docker

Volume 1

JOHN DOCKER

KERR
Melbourne, Victoria

First published 2020
Kerr Publishing Pty Ltd
Melbourne, Victoria
ABN 64 124 219 638

ISBN (volume 1) 978-1-875703-33-3 (Print on Demand, PoD)
ISBN (set) 978-1-875703-32-6 (Print on Demand, PoD)
ISBN (volume 1) 978-1-875703-37-1 (eBook)
ISBN (set) 978-1-875703-36-4 (eBook)

BIC Category: Biography & Autobiography
BISAC Category 1: BIO006000 BIOGRAPHY & AUTOBIOGRAPHY/ Cultural, Ethnic & Regional/General
BISAC Category 2: BIO006000/Historical; BIO037000/Jewish; BIO10000/ Political
BISAC Category 3: HIS004000/Australia & New Zealand

Cover photograph: Ted, Elsie and John Docker

Cover and book design: Paul Taylder of Xigrafix Media & Design
Typeset in Verdigris MVB Pro Text 10.5/14pt

Print-on-Demand and eBook distribution: ebookalchemy.com.au

National Library of Australia PrePublication Data Service:

A catalogue record for this book is available from the National Library of Australia

For Ann, Ned, Shino and Leo

Contents

Prologue

Dear Reader, a traditional prologue for a play would list the *dramatis personae* in a vertical column, with the names of characters next to the actors who play them. Instead, I will be discursive, and will introduce key figures and places: mother, father, uncles, Jewish, Irish, Communist, Bondi.

As I have understood my family history, my father Ted Docker, born in Sydney 26 November 1894, descended from an Irish Protestant family in County Clare in the west of Ireland, followed an Irish cultural convention (which I might have wrong, or maybe I'm making this up) that as the youngest son he could not marry until his mother Susan Nash died. Susan lived in Sydney's eastern suburbs, in South Coogee, near a little cemetery, close to the Pacific Ocean. My father, when he wasn't travelling for the Communist Party of Australia, of which he was a foundation member from 1920, lived in his mother's house.

My mother, born in the East End of London in 23 Alfred Street, Bow, migrated to Sydney with her Jewish family, with her parents Rose and Philip Levy and her two younger brothers Lew and Jock in 1926. Then 14, my mother began working in a clothing factory.[1] She, also a member of the Communist Party from the 1930s, lived with her family in a semi-detached house in O'Brien Street, Bondi, not far from Six Ways, which via

Hall Street led directly to the famous beach. (As immigrants and refugees, Jewish families often came to live in Bondi, which still attracts successive waves of new migrants from many nations over the generations. Bondi is a palimpsest of layer upon layer of newcomers.)

My mother and father must have met in the late 1930s in the Communist Party. I don't know exactly when, and I don't know how: there are no family stories I know of to help me. Many decades later, after my mother died in 1986, I visited my uncle Jock and aunt Jeannette (known in the family as Awky). They said my mother was highly valued in their migrant family because she had been the first to gain employment. Also, that she was a very stylish dresser when young. I know my father was a smart dresser from security documents available online. He was under surveillance by the Commonwealth Investigative Bureau, forerunner of ASIO, from 1930. They once recorded his appearance when he reached London by ship in 1934; he was on his way to Moscow to attend the Comintern's Seventh Congress that took place in 1935, where the new policy of the Popular Front was established for all Communist Parties. At Tilbury Dock in London, my father was described, as he came off the ship, wearing a 'dark grey mixture suit with black stripes'. I think this was the suit I inherited after he died. He is also noted as having blue eyes and fair hair. In the late 1930s, then, so I hazard, Ted Docker, well dressed with blue eyes and fair hair, and Elsie Levy, stylishly dressed, of dark hair and brown eyes, were attracted to each other.

To marry my father, however, my mother would have to 'marry out'. Perhaps, I'm now guessing, my mother was the first in her Jewish family stretching back to late eighteenth century London to marry out. I've just looked at the genealogy of my family – drawn up by Ann Curthoys' mother Barbara for me in my 2001 *1492: The Poetics of Diaspora* – and I see no indication there that anyone in that long history married out.[2] Ann and I have been together since early 1969 (what we call our living together anniversary, 10 January 1969), and Ann appears more than once, indeed increasingly so, in this ego histoire.

Every afternoon, my mother visited her parents in O'Brien Street (42 O'Brien Street just flashed up in my mind, maybe it was 42), and after a primary school day, often after playing touch football or tennis, I would make my way there. My father rarely joined us, which was puzzling for a child. Perhaps he wasn't fully accepted because my mother had married out, had married a *goy*, a non-Jew, a Communist, a godless man, a man much older than their daughter.[3] My mother was committing a rebellious act. She sometimes said that she didn't feel comfortable mixing with my father's Protestant family, felt they were anti-Semitic, hostile to her. In terms of his Protestant family, my father marrying my mother was also a rebellious act.

I find the age disparity between my father and mother startling. My father was very high up in the Communist Party, and almost 18 years older than my mother. My mother was part of an eastern suburbs Jewish group in the Party, and in the middle to late 1930s she and her brothers helped create the Sydney Jewish Youth Theatre, of which a lot more in subsequent chapters.

My father had a reputation in the Communist Party for being formidably hard line. Ann tells me that her parents Barbara and Geoff, part of a younger generation of radicals who had joined the Party in World War II, considered Ted Docker to be old school, stern and unrelenting, severe. I don't remember him like that as a child. He was an amiable presence in the family, but of course, both things could be true.

My mother and father married 4 February 1941. Two sisters were born before me, and my mother more than once told me that her mother told her, 'if you fall now, it will be a boy'.

In any one street in Bondi there were many single standing houses, but also many apartment blocks, including art deco buildings and some in what I think of as a Californian Spanish style. We lived in a little red brick block of apartments, Flat 2, 48 Edward Street, Bondi. Perhaps it was built in the 1920s, neither art deco nor Californian Spanish, but perhaps something in between. Edward Street in south Bondi was and is a long street that roughly ran parallel to Bondi Road where the trams rattled along from the city to the beach. (Wondering how long the Bondi tram existed, I just googled, it began in the late nineteenth century and ceased in 1960, to be replaced by double decker buses.) The block of eight apartments, on two levels, was on a sort of hillock; as you faced it, our apartment was on the right hand side on the ground floor; above us lived the landlord, who would occasionally bang on the ceiling if we kids made too much noise. The apartment was small. A kitchenette, my mother's domain, opened on to a living room where family conversations bubbled along. Occasionally my mother ventured from the kitchenette holding a large kitchen knife to make a point. (Much later, when reading Philip Roth's *Portnoy's Complaint*, I came across something so unnervingly similar I had to stop reading).

It was in the living room that we three children did our homework, though I can't remember doing any in primary school. In winter we crowded around a little heater (I think it was a kerosene heater) which my father would attend to, filling it up, getting it to work. I think my parents had decided not to get a TV because it would disturb our homework, but suddenly, in my final year of high school, they purchased one. We would sit and watch the ABC (modelled on BBC TV). My father always wanted to look at the news. Before that, family entertainment came from the radio, which nestled on a shelf which my father, trained in his early life as a carpenter, made and placed on the wall. It was beautifully crafted from dark wood, and presumably placed with the landlord's permission. Our parents' bedroom next. Then a closed-in verandah where we children slept, one bed and a double bunk; my bed was on the top bunk. The verandah room looked north over Rose Bay (where our uncle Jock and aunt Awky lived), with Sydney Harbour beyond. Whenever there was a blackout in the apartment, we rushed to the verandah room to see if it was general, if the whole area between us and Rose Bay was also blacked out. It often was: blackouts post-war and into the 1950s seemed quite common.

In the living room, next to the window, was a Singer sewing machine that my mother would expertly sew on. Her sewing would lead to shopping expeditions involving going from Bondi into the city, and she often took me along. We would catch the tram which laboured its way up Bondi Road then proceeded – for ages, it seemed – along Oxford Street, turn into Elizabeth Street and then, where Elizabeth Street met Market Street, there was David Jones, the landmark large department store on the corner. This was the women's store (David Jones men's store was nearby on another corner). We would catch a lift (there was a lift operator in uniform, Ann says he would likely be a TPI, Totally Permanently Incapacitated, war veteran) up to a higher floor, maybe the fourth or fifth, where my mother would choose a length of material from a large roll and a paper pattern. For lunch, we would catch the lift to the cafeteria on an upper floor, specialising in meat pies with gravy and mashed potato and peas, my first eating experience outside the family: 1950s Anglo-Australian food one might truly say.

When we got home, my mother would cut the pattern into pieces and make clothes. My memory as a child was that my mother dressed well, especially when she would go into the city (she always said 'town' as in 'let's go into town').

One time my mother said, 'Come on, we're going into town'

and we caught the tram into to a large city department store, possibly Anthony Hordens. We visited a floor where my mother wished to buy lino for the living room floor, honey-coloured from memory, and a carpet to go in the centre of the room. My mother chose very carefully, this was obviously important to her. In my *1492: The Poetics of Diaspora*, in the chapter where my uncles Lew and Jock reminisce about their early London life in the East End, they recall that their father Phil eked out a precarious existence as a taxi driver while their mother Rose was a skilled cigar maker. Jock recalled that in the house they grew up in, 'The furniture was very primitive – sufficient chairs to go round the table but nothing elaborate in the way of lounge or any of the various things that go to make what I think is a cultured home'.[4]

My feeling is that the three children, as they became adults in Australia, wished by contrast to their London upbringing to create living spaces that were stylish and where visitors could gather and enjoy conversation.

Dear Reader, now my ego histoire – defining ego histoire in a preliminary way as family histories that intersect with wider histories – begins its various journeys.

1 John Docker, "Genealogy and Derangement", in Vanessa Castejon, Anna Cole, Oliver Haag and Karen Hughes (eds), *Ngapartji Ngapartji In Turn, in turn: Ego-histoire, Europe and Indigenous Australia* (ANU Press, Canberra, 2014), pp.173–188.

2 John Docker, *1492: The Poetics of Diaspora* (Continuum, London and New York, 2001), ch.2, 'Genealogy and diasporic memory: searching my family tree'.

3 John Docker, 'A Space for Self-Fashioning: An Antipodean Red-Diaper Baby Goes to University in the Sixties', in Dee Michel, Jacqueline Z. Wilson and Verity Archer (eds), *Bread and Roses: Voices of Australian Academics from the Working Class* (Sense Publishers, Rotterdam, 2015), p.60.

4 John Docker, *1492: The Poetics of Diaspora*, pp.152, 160.

Preface and Acknowledgements

In my mind's eye a tableau is taking shape, of the occasion when Ann Curthoys and I first heard the term ego histoire. In 2008 we attended a conference entitled Myth, Memory and History at the Centre for Australian Studies, University of Barcelona, convened by the Director of the Centre, Sue Ballyn. In a break between sessions, we were delighted to see the historian, filmmaker and historical anthropologist Anna Cole. Ann had supervised Anna as a doctoral student at Sydney's University of Technology in the early 1990s when its humanities and media and cultural studies programs were the most innovative and experimental among Sydney universities, and Anna became a lifelong friend of ours. We look forward to meeting up with her on visits to the UK where she lives. Anna was based in London for many years before moving south to Lewes (associated with Virginia Stephen and Leonard Woolf, Lews will loom large in this book's narratives).

Anna was accompanied by her friend Vanessa Castejon, who teaches and researches in Paris and had written a doctoral thesis on radical Indigenous politics in Melbourne. There were beaming introductions all round.

The conversation went something like 'Ann and John,' Anna said, 'we're eager to talk to you, Vanessa and I want you to become interested in something we're involved with, ego histoire. Have you heard of it?' No, tell us about it. Anna said, 'It's associated with the well-known historian of contemporary France, Pierre

Nora. He's usually known for his work on memory and place, but in 2001 he published an essay on ego histoire that we're excited by. We wish to relate it to Indigenous Australia. We would love you two to take an interest in it.' We said yes, yes, count us in, but we hesitated for a moment. We said we were writing other things for a while, especially because we're still very much involved in genocide and massacre studies, and Ann was working on her project on Paul Robeson (Ann's paper at the Barcelona conference was entitled 'Remembering Paul Robeson's tour of Australia, 1960'). But we'll get to it, we will! Vanessa said she would email us Nora's 2001 essay, with its intriguing title, '*L'ego-histoire est-elle possible?*'[1]

In fact, an opportunity to engage with ego histoire came quite quickly, also as a result of that conference. Attending was our friend Frances Peters-Little, the Indigenous historian, film-maker and musician. After Barcelona, Frances, Ann and I met and became excited by the thought of editing a volume of essays inspired by the theme of the conference, Myth, Memory and History. We contacted Sue Ballyn and remain grateful to her for supporting our proposal to produce a volume of essays focussing on Indigenous Australian history. Plotted over many a coffee in Sydney's inner-west Glebe and Balmain when we returned to Australia, *Passionate Histories: Myth, Memory and Indigenous Australia* was published in 2010. The famous swimmer and social activist Ian Thorpe contributed a Foreword, a moving speech lined with anger entitled 'Australia's dirty little secret', that he gave at the 'Beyond Sport Summit' in London on 9 July 2009, where he draws attention to appalling health conditions experienced by Indigenous Australians, and tells of his advocacy on behalf of 'Fountain of Youth' and 'Close the Gap'. The volume is dedicated to Frances' father, the singer James Oswald Little, descendant and elder of the Yorta Yorta and the Yuin/Monaro peoples. Each contributor provided a biographical note for the List of Contributors, which was at the head of the volume.[2]

In the Introduction, Frances writes that a concern that kept emerging in the essays was 'the role of passion – engagement, commitment, compassion, emotion'. Frances wonders about those who declare that historians can be completely dispassionate: 'As an Indigenous woman and historian who spends much time writing about Aboriginal history and Australia's colonial past, I find this discussion of whether one ought to be compassionate or not somewhat bewildering. It is a luxury I have not been afforded.... The whole basis for wanting to become a historian in the first instance comes from a place deep inside me, from a desire to understand, acknowledge and come to terms with what has happened to my ancestors, my culture and my land.'[3] Frances' chapter, 'Remembering the referendum with compassion' concerned the 1967 Referendum (giving the federal Commonwealth government powers to legislate on behalf of Aboriginal people and to include them in the census).

We invited Anna Cole and Vanessa Castejon to contribute ego histoire chapters to *Passionate Histories*. In her note, Anna wrote she 'works in the area of historical knowledge, embodied knowledges, and the gendered politics of colonialism', her life moving between Australia and the UK. Anna's chapter is entitled 'Making a debut: myths, memories and mimesis'.[4]

Vanessa is part of CRIDAF: Centre de recherches interculturelles sur les domains anglophones et francophones, Université Paris 13. For many years she has been working on the recognition of Indigenous rights on an international scale, and belongs to the United Nations Working Group on Indigenous Peoples and the creation of a global Indigeneity. Vanessa's chapter is entitled 'Identity and identification: Aboriginality from the Spanish Civil War to the French Ghettos'.

From the 2008 Barcelona conference, then, there emerged a confluence of ego histoire and passionate history, drawn to each other, speaking to each other. *Ego histoire* as a methodology, a way of exploring histories, combines powerfully with what Frances in the Introduction so strikingly refers to as 'the role of passion – engagement, commitment, compassion, emotion'. *Ego histoire*, as does passionate history, foregrounds the I who writes, and reflects on the ego historical question, Why did I engage with such a topic at such a time, and why and how did I become interested? In ego histoire, the writing of history is genealogical; it starts from urgent concerns of the present.

We very much admired Anna and Vanessa's project – shared with a friend and close collaborator of theirs, Oliver Haag, who we would later meet – that, as a group of young scholars situated in Europe, they wish in an anti-Eurocentric spirit to extend Nora's notions of ego history, with its own interest in French colonialism, towards a conversation between Europe and Australia, with its history of colonialism. Ann and I hoped to be able to contribute, but after the 2008 conference we found ourselves occupied with other writing, and put off reading Pierre Nora's essay until we were ready.

After some years, ego histoire's moment for us personally did arrive. We read Nora's manifesto-like essay, and mulled over its implications for history writing.

In 2012, Ann published an essay, 'Memory, History, and *Ego-Histoire*: Narrating and Re-enacting the Australian Freedom Ride'. Here Ann sees ego histoire as tracing personal and family histories that are both intensive and lead outwards into wider and longer perspectives. Ann evokes the multiple ways that the 1965 Freedom Ride through NSW towns, in which she participated as a young University of Sydney student, has been remembered and commemorated, discussing the role of the participant-historian as a keeper of memory, suggesting there is a relationship between professional history and popular memory. Because of her 2002 book *Freedom Ride: A Freedom Rider Remembers*, for many years now she has been asked to speak to school children; to assist with requests for photographs; her 1965 travel diary which is online has helped participants in two re-enactments of the Freedom Ride; her book has inspired a play; and American Freedom Riders, black and white, are keen to meet up with her when they happen to visit Sydney. As Ann says, it is rare that a week goes by without her being contacted to provide various kinds of information on, or to speak about, the 1965 Freedom Ride.[5]

Anna and Vanessa, along with Oliver Haag, have proved to be inspiring in attracting scholars to their vision of ego histoire, so much so that ego histoire has become an expanding transnational movement. In 2011, Anna and Vanessa and Oliver as Europe-based scholars, along with Australian-based historian Karen Hughes, organised a conference in Paris, Researching the Other, Transfers of Self: *Ego-histoire*, Europe and Indigenous Australia, which led to the preparation of the wonderfully entitled collection *Ngapartji Ngapartji, In turn, in turn: Ego-Histoire, Europe and Indigenous Australia*. They invited Ann and me to contribute chapters. Ann however demurred: she felt she had nothing to contribute at that time. I said I would like to offer an essay, 'Genealogy and Derangement', though it would be tangential to the theme of Indigenous Australia, so you may not want it. Fortunately, they accepted it. Like Ann in various essays and her 2002 book *Freedom Ride: A Freedom Rider Remembers*, I had long been interested in mixing personal and family history with intellectual and cultural history, as in 'How I became a Teenage Leavisite and Lived to Tell the Tale' (1981), an essay first published in the literary journal *Meanjin* in 1981 which I reproduce as a chapter here. In 2001, my book *1492: The Poetics of Diaspora*, mixing genealogy, diasporic history, personal observations, and literary and cultural history reflections, for example, concerning Spinoza in the seventeenth century and Leopold Bloom in Joyce's *Ulysses*, each interpreting the story of Exodus in heretical ways, was published.[6]

I couldn't, however, just rush into writing 'Genealogy and Derangement', I first had to do some sustained reading of the papers Ann and I had deposited in the early 1990s in Mitchell Library in Sydney, part of the State Library, on Macquarie Street, opposite the Botanic Gardens. In the early 1990s Ann and I were living in Sydney, but in 1995 we had moved to Canberra, Ann becoming Professor of History at the Australian National University (later, Manning Clark Professor of History) there, while I found a home in the Humanities Research Centre, for the first few years as an Australian Research Council fellow. In 2008 we returned to Sydney, first living in Bondi and then in Glebe near the University of Sydney, where we found a home in the History department. For months in late 2010 and into 2011, I travelled every day into the city to Mitchell Library to look at our papers, taking lots of notes which I still extensively draw on, mainly for the writing of *Growing Up Communist and Jewish in Bondi*, but also for other associated talks and writing. In 2011 I felt honoured to be asked by Ann and my friend Zora Simic of the Sydney Feminist History Group to give a talk. Every year, Zora said, they invite a man to speak, this year you have been chosen; in preparing for the talk, entitled 'Men and Women's Liberation', I read the relevant notes I had taken on our papers in Mitchell Library. I gave the talk on 25 August 2011, and it went, I dare to think, gratifyingly well, giving me confidence that I could 'do' ego histoire at book length; I later worked it up as a chapter for 'I am Born', this book's final section.

I drew on Ann and my notes in Mitchell Library to write 'Genealogy and Derangement' for *Ngapartji Ngapartji, In turn, in turn: Ego-Histoire, Europe and Indigenous Australia*, which was published in 2014; by coupling 'genealogy and derangement' I was thinking that my father and mother gifted me wildly divergent diasporic family histories, Protestant Irish and London Jewish, and that I feel equally intensely about both of these histories. I agree with Pierre Nora in '*L'ego-histoire est-elle possible?*' that the I who writes is always off-balance, as are the texts the ego-historian produces, always close to vertigo. Genre in ego histoire tosses about like a drunken boat, to adapt a famous image of Rimbaud, an important figure for my 1960s generation who appreciated his sentiment in a letter of 1871 that we strive to reach 'the unknown by the derangement of *all the senses*' (*Il s'agit d'arriver à l'inconnu par le dérèglement de tous les sens*). In the same letter, Rimbaud writes *Je est un autre*, a captivating thought I take as a key to ego histoire in its desire to foreground the narrator. I interpret Rimbaud's phrase in the plural: I am an other, or others.[7]

Dear reader, I hesitate to say more here in this Preface about ego histoire as vertigo and drunken boat. I will save a fuller account for my Introduction.

The title *Growing Up Communist and Jewish in Bondi* seemed to arrive of itself as natural and right, and in any case, people find it amusing, 'Bondi' is supposed to represent the famous beach and mindlessness, maybe for the whole settler nation, but here was a title indicating very different histories.

I should mention that I did write a couple of essays in the spirit of Nora's ego histoire around the time I wrote 'Genealogy and Derangement' for *Ngapartji Ngapartji*. I wrote 'Troubled reflections on my father' for *What Did You Do in the Cold War, Daddy? Personal Stories from a Troubled Time*, edited by Ann Curthoys and Joy Damousi (2014), and I must thank Ann and Joy for giving me this opportunity to write what is indeed a troubled text. I also wrote a kind of companion essay, 'A Space for Self-Fashioning: An Antipodean Red-Diaper Baby Goes to University in the Sixties' for *Bread and Roses: Voices of Australian Academics from the Working Class*, edited by Dee Michell, Jacqueline Z Wilson and Verity Archer (2015). I still recall the occasion when Verity visited Sydney and Ann and I had dinner with her in downtown Thai Town at the Chat Thai, followed by Asian flavoured icecream in an arcade across the road, and she asked me if I would like to contribute. (Coming from a venerable academic family, Ann couldn't be called upon.)

It was my son Ned Curthoys who particularly urged me to write a memoir. We recently had a chat, and recalled that we enjoyed a number of conversations about the idea though I can't remember the exact dates, we would bring pen and paper with us and throw around suggestions, Ned would jot them down. I especially remember coffee in a café in Sydney in the inner-west suburb Annandale, on Booth Street, sitting out the front, though Ann recalls that Ned and I also had a coffee shop conversation in Bondi somewhere. I was delighted and relieved to find the notes Ned took on these occasions in a rather battered folder entitled Preface and Acknowledgements and Contents Page, alongside an assortment of old family photos, a brochure put out by the NSW Department of Education honouring teachers for serving in World War I (this relates to one of my father's brothers), plus stray scribbled preliminary ideas. Ned and I felt that after *Growing Up Communist and Jewish in Bondi* the sub-title could be something like Adventures of Identity, A Memoir, a notion I have always liked, since Gerhard Fischer and I convened a conference in 1998, held at the Goethe-Institut in Sydney in leafy Woollahra, entitled 'Adventures of Identity – Constructing the Multi-cultural Subject'. The conference title surprised us by attracting scholars from across the world; a selection of papers was published in 2001 by Stauffenburg Verlag, Tübingen, under the title *Adventures of Identity: European Multicultural Experiences and Perspectives*. Another sub-title Ned and I tossed around was Memoirs of a Non-Australian Australian, a nod to Isaac Deutscher's essay 'The Non-Jewish Jew'.

Themes for the memoir we thought of included: I was a Red Diaper baby; I was a teenage Leavisite; the Sydney Libertarians and the New Left; continuing Sydney and Melbourne differences; opposing film censorship; discovery of popular culture (after my 'high literature' training as a literary critic); discovering Australian literature (after the demented Anglophilia of the Leavisites); internationalising and cosmopolitanising the study of Australian literature (an approach I deployed in my doctoral thesis, Literature and Social Thought: Australia in an International Context 1890–1925, awarded 1981, and in *The Nervous Nineties: Australian cultural life in the 1890s*, published 1991); postmodernism; how the poststructuralism of Foucault and Derrida is insufficient, we need Mikhail Bakhtin's wealth of ideas about literary form; *Bildung* (here as sensibility – Ned's own intense interest, as in his 2013 book *The Legacy of Liberal Judaism: Ernst Cassirer and Hannah Arendt's Hidden Conversation*); and rebutting Zionism.

We also decided to include an Epilogue: Father and Son, a Conversation between John Docker and Ned Curthoys.

On another slip of paper, a shopping To-Do note paper from Kikki, Ned jotted down our further ideas for chapters: My Father, Ted Docker and the IWW; Ted Docker, the CPA and Intellectuals; Ted Docker and Walter Benjamin in Moscow; A revolutionary's bookshelf; My Mother, Elsie Levy, in Bondi, her books; for Elsie Levy, history could be optimism and catastrophe; WWII and Jewish Communists and the Holocaust; and my childhood in Bondi. On the back of the note paper was another list organised into periods: Wobblies; CPA; Elsie Levy/Docker; adolescence (arguments with my father over Stalinism); 60s – Push; 70s – Australian Studies; 80s – postmodernism, popular culture; and 90s-2000s – Israel/Palestine.

Throughout these chats with Ned there is no mention I can see in the notes of ego histoire, perhaps because the idea had fallen into abeyance for Ann and me after the 2008 Barcelona meeting. Yet, remarkably, most of what we listed at this early stage does appear here.

Ned has read and valuably commented on many of the chapters in this book, and we enjoyed staging our dialogue.

I come now to acknowledging Ann Curthoys. It's difficult to remember a time in my adult life when, except for conferences and fellowships elsewhere, we have not been together, in Australia or other parts of the world where we have travelled, taught and researched. Soon after we started living together in Sydney in early 1969, Ann, an early member of the highly active Women's Liberation movement stationed at 67 Glebe Point Road, Glebe, told me of her admiration for Simone de Beauvoir, which I'll talk about now, because I quickly came to share her admiration and it became crucial to our relationship, and remains so.

In 2002, Ann contributed a chapter, 'Autobiography and Cultivating the Arts of the Female Self' for *The Politics of Moralizing*, edited by Jane Bennett and Michael J Shapiro. It is a beautifully crafted and complex essay.[8] I'll reflect here only on how the essay relates to the beginnings of our relationship. By stressing individual action and historical agency, de Beauvoir, Ann considered, offered an alternative to the victimology apparent in some strands of feminism. Ann compares de Beauvoir's thinking here with the Foucault of *The Use of Pleasure* and *The Care of the Self*, the second and third of his books on the history of sexuality in the classical world, where Foucault draws attention to the task of making a life, of questions of choice and self-realisation, and individual responsibility.

Ann writes that for her generation de Beauvoir was the epitome of a woman concerned to care for, control, and transform herself as she chose, adding that this idea came less from her most famous text, *The Second Sex*, than from her autobiographies such as *Prime of Life* and *Force of Circumstance*, and novels such as *She Came to Stay* and *The Mandarins*: 'As a young woman in Australia in the 1960s and 1970s... the autobiographies and some of the novels meant everything to me', providing 'a guide for the fashioning of a new kind of feminine self', for in them de Beauvoir's life 'as an intellectual, a writer, and a woman' was spelled out 'in painstaking and fascinating detail', to be pondered and explored 'for clues as to how we might live differently from our parents' generation and from most of the society around us'.[9]

Ann was interested in every aspect of de Beauvoir's evocation of her life, the clothes she wore in her own individual way, the food she ate and where she ate it, de Beauvoir saying in *Prime of Life* that in Paris her lunch was a bowl of borsch at Dominique's, and supper a cup of hot chocolate at La Coupole, and also how much walking featured in de Beauvoir's life. When she was a teacher in Marseille, she walked and walked by herself. Walking was important in how her relationship with Sartre was created, especially in its early stages. In *Prime of Life* de Beauvoir recalls that she and Sartre would meet each morning in the Luxembourg Gardens and walk the streets of Paris talking until late at night, about themselves, about their future life, their yet unwritten books.[10]

Ann discusses the importance of reading for young Australian girls like herself. In their school years in the 1950s they read novels like *Anne of Green Gables* and *Little Women*, providing strong role models. In their university years, de Beauvoir took the place of these novels, Ann also pointing out that in *Memoirs of a Dutiful Daughter* de Beauvoir herself discussed how important *Little Women* had been to her, especially the character of Jo March, who had in *Little Women*'s fictional world of the 1860s sought to express her creativity, personal autonomy and economic independence. Ann feels that to these significant novels for teenage girls could be added Ethel Turner's *Seven Little Australians*, with its key character, Judy, significantly killed at the threshold age of 13, as if her wildness and daring could belong only to childhood, never to womanhood: 'It was as if in *Little Women* Jo, rather than Beth, had died at puberty. We wanted to be like Jo; we wept over Judy.'[11]

I was inspired by Ann to read *The Mandarins* as well as the autobiographies that had come out so far. I felt I had to catch up as quickly as I could, then we could try to work out how de Beauvoir's writings might help shape our lives as intellectuals; we talked about the importance of the art of conversation and how to practise it; and the high place of friendship. We took long walks, reflecting on what our lives together could be. We sought out nearness to water as always magically stimulating new ideas, new perspectives, trying out a half thought, a what do you think. I remember one night we sat on a low wall in Birchgrove, a kind of extension of Balmain, overlooking a pocket park, alongside a dark Sydney Harbour, near the Dawn Fraser Swimming Pool. We would drive in our ancient little black VW beetle to the beach at Bondi and lie on the sand talking. Ann suddenly said we should think of having a baby one day; we stared out to sea, beyond the waves. We still like walking, usually in the morning before breakfast, still try out tentative ideas, admit to troubling knots in our thinking that maybe we could untie; and we comment on each other's writing. I don't want to send anything out into the world unless Ann has read it and made suggestions. She is a wonder at what I can't do: structural editing. When I read Ann's work, I'm a kind of miniaturist, questioning the placement of a comma here or there, perhaps suggesting a phrase.

I can't remember that we were ever as interested in Sartre as in de Beauvoir, though I think we both read *Nausea* as students. Later, we liked Sartre's notion on method: of going into a text and then outwards. When Ann and I wrote 'Defining Genocide' for *The Historiography of Genocide*, edited by Dan Stone, first published in 2008 – the same year we learned of ego histoire from Ann and Vanessa and the same year I published *The Origins of Violence: Religion, History and Genocide*, we discussed Sartre's essay 'On Genocide', written on behalf of Bertrand Russell's International War Crimes Tribunal, investigating whether there were actions by American forces during the war in Vietnam 'which can be legally called acts of genocide'. Sartre's 'On Genocide' report was adopted by the Russell Tribunal in 1967, the Tribunal then unanimously declaring 'the United States guilty of the crime of genocide' in terms of the 1948 UN Convention on Genocide.

Sartre's essay is important in the history of genocide studies, especially in its linking of colonisation and genocide. Taking the French conquest of Algeria as his primary example of settler colonialism, Sartre argues that colonisation is 'by its very nature an act of cultural genocide': 'For the subject peoples this inevitably means the extinction of their national character, culture, customs, sometimes even language'. In Algeria French troops maintained their authority by 'terror', by 'perpetual massacre', which Sartre saw as 'genocidal in character' since it aimed at the destruction (and here he alludes to Article II of the 1948 UN Convention) of a part of an ethnic, national, or religious group, in order to terrorise the remainder and to 'wrench apart the indigenous society'.

Nonetheless, Sartre argues, the French colonizer's desire to destroy and replace indigenous society was tempered by the perceived necessity to use Algerian labour. The Americans by contrast had no direct economic interests in Vietnam and felt no inhibition in envisaging a 'total genocide': the methods used by the Americans included in the South massive bombing, ruining of crops, murder, rape, looting, and 'concentration camps'; and in the North systematic destruction of the economic base, deliberate attacks against civilians and targeting of hospitals, schools and places of worship, leading to serious psycho-social 'mental harm' among children. Sartre concluded that there was a global aim of the American policy makers, they intended the genocide of Vietnam to serve as a warning to humanity as a whole to be submissive: 'The group which the United States wants to intimidate and terrorize by way of the Vietnamese nation is the human group in its entirety.'[12]

De Beauvoir's novels and autobiographies, her evocation of

the formative years of her relationship with Sartre, her stressing the importance of self-fashioning and the art of conversation, her urging that intellectuals should always heed the young, have stayed with us all our lives; they form part of what Ann Genovese has explored as a long Australian feminist tradition, especially focused on and radiating out from de Beauvoir, that continues to the present.[13]

Fancifully, I think now of Simone de Beauvoir's *Adieux to Sartre* (1981, translated 1984), the first part concerns the last 10 years of Sartre's life, 1970 to 1980, the second part her 'Conversations with Jean-Paul Sartre' in 1974, I asked Ann to gift it to me for Christmas 2018. Inside, Ann has written: 'De Beauvoir, whom we've admired all our lives'.

So many more acknowledgements suggest themselves. Not least is Ann Genovese, who along with her fellow jurisographers Shaun McVeigh and Peter Rush invited me to take part in a panel of the 'Lives Lived with Law' symposium held at the Melbourne Law School in December 2014; the talks were then published in the journal *Law Text Culture*, volume 20, 2016. As I understand it, jurisography, a wonderful concept created by Ann, Shaun and Peter, performs a way of writing jurisprudence that calls attention to itself as writing, where the jurisographer foregrounds herself or himself as narrator, as persona. For the issue of the journal, Ann Genovese and I wrote together an essay, 'Places Lived: An Ego-Histoiriste and Jurisographer Discuss Living with Law in Sydney', and I also wrote an essay, 'Of Pearls and Coral: Jurisography and Ego History'. Ann Genovese feels, like I do, that jurisography and ego histoire, while in very different intellectual fields, are companionate concepts, and perhaps I could add that both jurisography and ego histoire are drawn to and interact with passionate history.

Ann Genovese, once a doctoral student of Ann's at UTS in

Sydney in the early 1990s who moved to the Melbourne Law School, became a lifelong friend for both of us and for our son Ned Curthoys, along with her family, Paul Ronfeldt and their sons Samuel and Joseph. Qnly a year or two ago, during a visit to Melbourne, Ann and Samuel and Joseph cooked a beautiful Ottolenghi dinner for me, amid much laughter and telling of stories. I owe Ann huge thanks for being such a great supporter over so many years of my ego histoire writing project, and I look forward to reading her book on jurisography that she is writing.

When Ann Curthoys and I returned to Sydney in 2008 after 14 years at the Australian National University in Canberra, living for the first two years in Bondi, we gratefully found an institutional home at the University of Sydney in SOPHI (School of Philosophical and Historical Inquiry) where we attended the weekly history department seminars. In April of 2009 I gave a talk for one of these seminars, 'Rejecting England: Sir Walter Scott's *Ivanhoe's* Rebecca and George Eliot's Daniel Deronda'.

When we moved in December 2010 from Bondi to live in Glebe (to which we hoped to return at the end of 2019), my daily life continued as before, going to the Mitchell Library every day for months well into 2011, then beginning to write chapters for *Growing Up Communist and Jewish in Bondi* as well as essays on genocide and settler colonialism, especially for the London journal *Holy Land Studies* (now *Holy Land Studies and Palestine*) edited by the Palestinian historian Nur Masalha.

Instead of my going to the Mitchell Library every morning as before, our days now invariably involved a morning visit to our favourite coffee shop in Glebe, Badde Manors, on Glebe Point Road, at the Parramatta Road end.

I've just asked Ann, when do you think coffee shops came to be such a feature of Sydney life? In her essay 'Autobiography and Cultivating the Arts of the Female Self', Ann reflects that for young students and graduates in the 1960s, the Paris of Simone de Beauvoir was 'at once somewhat like our own society, and yet so very different from it': 'We did not "take a cup of chocolate at La Coupole", or drink decent coffee, or frequent the same café day after day.'[14] Ann googled, and it appears that Badde Manors was established in 1982, one of the first cafés to open on Glebe Point Road, and the longest lasting. So I'm guessing coffee and cafés as a mass phenomenon came to Sydney in the 1980s and 1990s, spreading rapidly, always accompanied by imported Italian coffee machines; in a longer and wider view, part of the Mediterraneanising of Australian cuisine since the Italian and Greek migrations of the 1920s and 1930s, and the Lebanese migrations of the 1970s.

Our lives in Glebe settled into a daily rhythm. In the morning, before breakfast, we would make our way from our little terrace house, perched on a hill, to Sydney Harbour's Blackwattle Bay where there was a walk around the shoreline, a favourite of Glebe residents.

After breakfast, Ann and I would drive to Derwent Street, a quiet street which is parallel to busy Glebe Point Road, walk down a lane to Glebe Point Road and cross the road to enter Badde Manors, on a corner of Glebe Point Road and another street whose name I can never remember. Badde Manors was not far from 67 Glebe Point Road where Sydney Women's Liberation had begun meeting in the early 1970s, and a short distance along from Gleebooks, my favourite bookshop; on its street side, Badde Manors' large windows are open to the northern sun. It has particular features; it is vegetarian in a Middle Eastern way (also now has vegan dishes as we know from annual visits from Perth to Sydney); in the front section it has a number of booths, while out in the narrower back section it has lots of small tables so someone by herself or himself could comfortably find a place to sit and read; it has a fairly wicked range of rich Viennese style pastries, next to a display fridge with colourful gelato offerings; going there every morning, the staff would recognise us and knew that we always ordered a piccolo.

On entering from the street, we would either find a booth in the front section, or if not a small table out in the back part, sit, take out reading material, position the piccolo, sip, then settle in and read and scribble on an article or in the margins of a section of a book we felt we needed for the day's writing, then, feeling content, pay, then go to Harris Farm's fresh food and delicatessen in Broadway the nearby large retail centre, then walk back through the lane to Derwent Street and drive back home. It used to be in a little white car and now for some years we drive a little red car. At home we would write for the rest of the day. Sometimes we would go back to Badde Manors for lunch with colleagues and friends.

I might add here that since the 1980s coffee has spread exponentially across Australia; in Perth a regional coffee culture has developed centred on multiple variations of a macchiato that Ann and I are somewhat mystified by, even after being in Perth for three years. Coffee Australian style is now making its way internationally; I was struck by a reference in a *Guardian* article, Tuesday 16 July 2019, by Wendell Steavenson who wrote that when he returned to Paris in 2014 after a four-year absence, 'Australians had established Italian coffee bars and you could finally get a decent cappuccino'. The genus 'Australian makers of flat whites' is known to have forged a presence in New York City; in the UK the flat white is now a standard offering. I should record that there is some dispute whether or not the flat white is an Australian invention. Our friend Charles Ross, who has sadly died, lived for a while at 17 Berwick Street in London's Soho, above the Flat White Café. From the play of accents, I judge it to be run by both New Zealand and Australian baristas. When visiting Charles, we would enjoy a coffee there. I've googled, and it appears that in New Zealand the flat white, like the pavlova before it, is firmly held to be a New Zealand creation.

Returning from Canberra to Sydney in November 2008 to live first in Bondi then in Glebe enabled us to resume more regular contact with friends we had only seen intermittently on visits. I must thank Mairéad Browne, a colleague of Ann's from UTS days, and David Browne for responding so warmly to my desire to know more about my father's family history in Ireland's County Clare before my Irish grandmother Susan Nash migrated to Sydney in the latter nineteenth century. I recall a party chat around Christmas time in Glebe, Mairéad and David tell me of, and afterwards find for me, a transcribed song about Clare by Andy Irvine which I then deployed as an epigraph for the chapter, 'The impossibility of being Irish'. When visiting Ireland, their diaspora home, they tried to track down any remaining trace of the Nash family including visiting a cemetery; they assisted in the delicate matter of extracting genealogical information from the Clare Heritage Centre; and David, the doctor, has been helpful in urging us at our age to 'keep moving', something we often say to ourselves, David says, keep moving, keep moving.

In the spacious cafeteria of the NSW Art Gallery, overlooking on its north-eastern side the wharves of Woolloomooloo crowded with cafés and behind them Sydney Harbour and the naval base of Garden Island and behind it glimpses of little yachts and busy yellow and green ferries, we would have regular chats with historian Desley Deacon. These conversations, on a Saturday or Sunday, stretched over a substantial part of the day, coffee before lunch, lunch, talking all afternoon till about four, when we might hurriedly see what was on display at that time in the Gallery, perhaps a special travelling exhibition; no topic was rushed, there was ample time to talk about and explore what we had been doing. Desley had been at the talk I gave in 2011 on 'Men and Women's Liberation'. She would ask: how is your ego histoire going, John? I would mention things that had come up I found difficult to explain, and Desley, the biographer of the American anthropologist Elsie Clews Parsons and latterly the actor Judith Anderson, would make wise suggestions. On many tables nearby and across the whole area could be seen other groups of families and friends talking for long periods, or friends with laptops working intently together.

I've just asked Ann what are your memories of these times.

> Ann: Many friends have been interested in your ego histoire project, and ask about it when we meet, but it was probably with Desley that you have had the most extended and detailed discussions. She has been expert at drawing out what you were working on, what the issues were, and often made helpful and insightful comments.

Our friend Rosemary Pringle, like Desley, was at my 'Men and Women's Liberation' talk. I recall that in discussion she asked why there had been no Men Against Sexism groups in Australia comparable to the British and American movements. I couldn't answer, I remember looking embarrassingly blank. For many years Rosemary has lived in south Bondi, in a small block of apartments looking directly over the beach at a point where the Pacific's waves form their shape and rhythmically sweep towards the beach. On a weekend morning, usually on a Sunday, Ann and I would drive to Bondi beach from Glebe, walk to the northern 'family' end, near one of the flags, always the same one, while Rosemary would walk from her apartment, passing the southern end of the beach where the board riders are. We would swim, hoping the waves were catchable that day (though not too big), then make our way round the historic Pavilion and over a little old concrete bridge and cross Campbell Parade and go along a path next to the Bondi Hotel to the Sonoma artisan bread shop, find a small table with stools and have coffee and toast. Conversation would range widely, we would often have a second coffee, Rosemary would always ask questions about the ego histoire, what are you talking about now, John? I would say I'm coming across things from the past that puzzle me, for example, at the end of primary school my unfortunate encounters with IQ tests, and why the male teachers were so devoted to caning, and Rosemary put forward insightful reflections that inform the chapter 'I emerge disgruntled into the world'.

We also talked about ego histoire with old friends Jock Keene and Judith Keene, who live in Glebe. Jock is a maritime scientist who now looks after vegetable gardens for the public benefit near the Glebe Library. Judith a historian of modern Europe – a participant with Ann in the Alchemists, the writing group in the history department at Sydney University – who has in recent years given talks on a Picasso painting about the Korean War, which we attended at the NSW Art Gallery, and researches on the Cold War more generally, in all sorts of international contexts. In Sydney, we would meet Jock and Judith at Miya's, a tiny Japanese café on Glebe Point Road near Bridge Road, or we would visit their holiday house in Bulli, south of Sydney, north of Wollongong, close to the ocean and swimming. Judith had worked as a research assistant for Henry Mayer in the politics department at Sydney University in the late 1960s, early 1970s. I told her of the essay I wrote on the Sydney Libertarians for his journal *Politics* in 1972. Judith asked could she see it, I sent it to her and she reminisced about the undoubtedly eccentric Sydney University professor of political theory Henry Mayer.

I would like to thank literary critic Gavin Edwards, who we have known from Sydney University days in the 1960s, for sharing with us through the decades, in Sydney, Cardiff and London, an ideal of intellectual life as the adventure of ideas; in a recent lunch together at the British Library café, Gavin mentioned that he had once shared a lunch table at the café, the very table we were sitting at, with a descendent of the Gore Booth family. I was quickly able to direct attention to my ego histoire interest in the Irish Protestant tradition and in particular the Gore Booth sisters, Eva and Constance, who became Countess Markievicz. Each sister was radical in her own way. I said how much I disliked the poem Yeats wrote on Eva after her death in 1926. (I reveal my irritation in my early chapter on 'The Impossibility of being Irish'.)

I would like to thank colleagues at the University of Western Australia for their warm support in the last several years for my project. In July 2016, Ann and I moved to Perth to be near our son Ned Curthoys, his partner and our dear friend Shino Konishi, and our grandson Leo, though we had been visiting Perth from Sydney for a year or two before that. For the 2015 Day of Ideas – Reviving the Flâneur, 16 October 2015, I gave a talk on 'The Flâneur, Modernity, Tradition, History' in relation to Walter Benjamin, T S Eliot, and Hannah Arendt, my thanks to Susan Takao, then director of the Institute for Advanced Studies at UWA and a Walter Benjamin enthusiast herself, for inviting me to participate in this very lively event. The talk was subsequently published by *Westerly* in May 2016, its editor Catherine Noske, under the title, 'The Flâneur under Water, the Flâneur as Dancing Star'.

Soon after Ann and I moved to Perth in July 2016, I was invited by Jane Lydon to give a talk to the UWA history department, which I presented on 24 August 2016; the talk, which drew on chapters I was writing for *Growing Up Communist and Jewish in Bondi*, was entitled 'Ego histoire as interdisciplinary methodology – reflections on T S Eliot as Ridiculous Parvenu, Vicious

Anti-Semite, and an Architect of the Holocaust', and I must thank everyone who attended for a wide range of spirited questions.

At UWA we were fortunate to be able to resume an old friendship with literary and cultural critics Philip Mead and Jenna Mead who had been in Perth for some years. We would meet at Gesha's coffee bar on Queen Victoria Street, as you drive into Fremantle, Gesha's having its own coffee-bean roasters and brand of coffee, which one can buy in stylish bags to take home. Over coffee and lunch, we four exiles from the distant east would affectionately catch up on what each was writing and future projects we were considering. Philip kindly read my chapter 'A Week in the west coast of Ireland: 14–21 June 2014'. Alas, it is now some 18 months since Philip and Jenna returned to Melbourne.

A final, essential acknowledgement. I remember a conversation at a gathering where the Adelaide historian Margaret Allen asked what was I writing these days. I said an ego history. She asked how was it going, how much had I written. I said quite well, I'd written 100,000 words on my father. 'Well, then, John,' Margaret said, 'you must at least write 100,000 words on your mother.' I took Margaret's challenge to heart.

Perth 27 September 2019

1 Pierre Nora, 'L'ego-histoire est-elle possible?' *historein* 3, 2001, pp.19–26.

2 Frances Peters-Little, Ann Curthoys and John Docker (eds), *Passionate Histories: Myth, Memory and Indigenous Australia* (ANU E Press, Canberra and Aboriginal History Inc, Canberra, 2010).

3 Peters-Little, Curthoys and Docker (eds), *Passionate Histories: Myth, Memory and Indigenous Australia*, Introduction, pp.1–2.

4 See also Anna Cole (2019), '"The History that has made you": Ego-histoire, Autobiography and Postcolonial History', *Life Writing* 16:4, 527–538.

5 Ann Curthoys, 'Memory, History, and Ego-Histoire: Narrating and Re-enacting the Australian Freedom Ride', in Antoinette Burton (ed.), *Historical Reflections/Reflexions Historiques* 2012 38/2.

6 John Docker, *1492: The Poetics of Diaspora* (Continuum, London and New York, 2001).

7 John Docker, 'Genealogy and Derangement', in Vanessa Castejon, Anna Cole, Oliver Haag and Karen Hughes (eds), *Ngapartji Ngpartji In turn in turn: Ego-histoire, Europe and Indigenous Australia* (Australian National University Press, Canberra, 2014), pp.173–74.

8 Ann Curthoys, 'Autobiography and Cultivating the Arts of the Female Self', in Jane Bennett and Michael J. Shapiro (eds), *The Politics of Moralizing* (Routledge, New York and London, 2002), pp.93–111.

9 Ann Curthoys, 'Autobiography and Cultivating the Arts of the Female Self', pp.95–96.

10 Ann Curthoys, 'Autobiography and Cultivating the Arts of the Female Self', pp.98–99.

11 Ann Curthoys, 'Autobiography and Cultivating the Arts of the Female Self', pp.103–104.

12 Ann Curthoys and John Docker, 'Defining Genocide', in Dan Stone (ed.), *The Historiography of Genocide* (Palgrave Macmillan, London and New York, 2008), pp.23–26.

13 See Ann Genovese, 'An Australian feminist tradition: three notes on conduct, inheritance and the relations of historiography and jurisprudence', *Journal of Australian Studies*, Vol.38, No.4, 2014, pp.430–444.

14 Ann Curthoys, 'Autobiography and Cultivating the Arts of the Female Self', p.105.

Introduction

Dear Reader, there are a number of ideas, notions, concepts, tropes, cultural figures, which I very much admire and help shape the writing of *Growing Up Communist and Jewish in Bondi.*

Above all, the great German-Jewish cultural theorist Walter Benjamin (1892–1940) influences *Growing Up Communist and Jewish in Bondi* throughout, not only in reference to particular ideas of his but also in a kind of general, diffuse, intangible, over-arching, pervading way. I can precisely date my interest in Benjamin. In the early 1980s I was part of a small media and popular culture studies group in Sydney. We were pooling our intellectual resources – there was a philosopher, a film theorist, a sociologist and I was there as a cultural historian – and decided to discuss what were usually considered key essays. I had never read any Benjamin, but when we read his 1936 essay 'The Work of Art in the Age of Mechanical Reproduction' (reproduced as the penultimate essay by Hannah Arendt for her selection of Benjamin's writings, *Illuminations*, published in 1968), I was immediately entranced by his way of writing and manner of thinking, so idiosyncratic, so eccentric, so independent of any orthodoxy. I felt that Benjamin stood in opposition to a long twentieth-century tradition of cultural theory, given prominent expression in Theodor Adorno and Max Horkheimer's Frankfurt School that was contemptuous of mass culture from the detective novel to jazz, seeing as it as securing mass conformity. What I came to regard as the left-pessimism of the Frankfurt School was rapidly becoming orthodoxy to the point of dogma in the fast-developing field of cultural studies. Dear Reader, I have to confess to intensely disliking the Frankfurt School!

In an early sally inspired by Benjamin, in *Arena* 60, 1982, in an essay 'In Defence of Popular Culture', part of a group of essays in this issue of *Arena* that came out of the early 1980s discussion group, I suggested that in the 'Work of Art' essay Benjamin returns a positive verdict on the relationship between film, audience response and psychoanalysis; I ventured my own suggestions concerning the character of popular culture, that it was dominated not by a socially binding realism but by fantasy, myth and symbolism; social exploration; and populism.[1]

These early formulations were certainly preliminary and crude. After many years of subsequent intensive reading in cultural history, especially the writings of the Russian cultural theorist Mikhail Bakhtin as well as Natalie Zemon Davis, and teaching media and cultural studies in the 1980s and into the 1990s, I published in 1994 *Postmodernism and Popular Culture: A Cultural History*. It includes an early chapter, 'The Frankfurt School versus Walter Benjamin', where I dissect at length Adorno and Max Horkheimer's essay 'The Culture Industry: Enlightenment as mass deception' in their *Dialectic of Enlightenment*, an essay which had become foundational to left-pessimist culture theory.[2] Biographically, I noted that with the rise of Nazism in the early 1930s, German Jewish intellectuals such as Adorno and Horkheimer and Herbert Marcuse became exiles in the US, re-establishing their Frankfurt Institute of Social Research in New York. Benjamin had settled in Paris in the 1930s. He and Hannah Arendt were in the same friendship circle when she came to Paris after the Nazi accession to power in 1933.[3] While Arendt and her husband Heinrich Blücher managed to escape through Spain and Portugal to reach New York, Benjamin tragically took his life in the Spanish border town of Portbou when refused entry on 26 September 1940.[4]

In a final section, of 'The Frankfurt School versus Walter Benjamin' chapter, 'Who was Walter Benjamin?', I confide that what intrigues me about Benjamin is that he was not really a firm member of any set school of thought, or certainly not for long or without introducing dissolving doubts. There is, I considered, no single unified 'Walter Benjamin', throughout his life he could be seen trying to work through contrary and competing positions, from nihilism and anarchism to surrealism to Brecht's Marxist theatre to Jewish mysticism to mainstream Frankfurt School theses. From work to work, essay to essay, he often reveals quite opposed attitudes, to progress, cultural tradition, technology, mass society, the city. Benjamin's writings accept neither a linear narrative of pessimism nor of optimism, of bleakness or of hope. What dazzles in Benjamin's playful textuality is his theatrical staging of arguments, questioning any magisterial presumption of knowledge of history and humanity's true needs; Benjamin permits competing contradictory voices, discourses, writings, moods, to speak to each other, to unsettle, jostle, joust and duel.[5]

There are many reasons why I feel an affinity with Walter Benjamin. One concerns failure. After completing my doctoral thesis, 'Literature and Social Thought: Australia in an International Context 1890 to 1925' in 1980 I tried but failed to gain an academic position teaching literature. I then turned to a different future, occupying myself with an assortment of book reviewing, Literature Board grants, part-time university teaching in media and cultural studies including TV Studies, and over the years venturing into many other fields: Australian literary and cultural history; contemporary theories of culture, identity, colonialism and diaspora; Orientalism and exoticism; monotheism and polytheism; historiography (especially co-exploring with Ann Curthoys); autobiographical essays; genocide studies in relation to the Enlightenment, religion and settler colonialism; massacre studies. For many years now, since 2010–11, I've journeyed into a new and challenging field: the research for and writing of this ego histoire.

Benjamin never secured an academic position. After World War I he worked his doctoral thesis into *The Origin of German Tragic Drama*, published in 1928. He chose the ever-precarious freedom to write in any way and on any topic he considered interesting and urgent to be talked about. On the island of Capri he met Asja Lacis, and they cooperated together in the writing in 1925–6 of *One-Way Street*, joining a centuries-old literature of fragments (I'm thinking of Montesquieu's *Persian Letters*) made famous in modernity by Nietzsche, and crossing such fragment literature with a Dadaist attack on the institutions of culture and the notion of cultural hierarchy, of a hierarchy of forms and genres. *One-Way Street* sets out to destroy any conventional notion of literature. 'Filling Station', its opening section, declares that in the present age 'true literary activity cannot aspire to take place within a literary framework – this is, rather, the habitual expression of its sterility'; instead of continuing 'the pretentious, universal gesture of the book', writing now 'must nurture the inconspicuous forms' revealed in 'leaflets, brochures, articles, and placards' (here reminding me of Rimbaud).[6]

The pages of *One-Way Street* are broken into placard-like sections, of parables, miscellaneous reflections, lists, aphorisms ('To great writers, finished works weigh lighter than those fragments on which they work throughout their lives' – Standard Clock).[7]

I first read *One Way Street* many years ago. I'm looking now at my copy, with its scribbled marginal comments and underlinings, it's starting to fall apart. But as I write this ego histoire one particular question interests me: does Benjamin in *One Way Street* deploy the I voice, and if so, how? In the early section 'Breakfast Room', Benjamin thinks of a dream he has had, 'A visit to Goethe's house. I cannot recall having seen rooms in the dream... The curator requests us to sign the visitors' book lying open on a desk at the farthest end of a passage. On reaching it, I find as I turn the pages my name already entered in big, unruly, childish characters.'[8]

In *One Way Street*, I'm hazarding, Benjamin does use I but it is not necessarily the I of consciousness, rather the placard-fragments will at times trace the journeys of an I into surreal dreamscapes.

There is another affinity I feel with Benjamin: we share an interest in children's writing, and also, in my case, with children's television. Ann Curthoys and I watched a lot of popular television with our son Ned Curthoys, who was born in 1974, which quickly led us into thinking about children's enjoyment of images and narratives that mock the power and authority of the parental world.[9]

I recall contributing articles about children's television for The Guide, the 'pink pages' section of the *Sydney Morning Herald*. How this came about, I can't remember. I'll try to find what I wrote. I've just riffled through boxes of old folders, and happily came across one of these contributions, dated 6 January 1986. Here I stage a mildly fractious conversation that I say took place at a literary studies conference, where I accuse my colleagues of being cultural authoritarians for preventing their children from watching popular TV shows. We know, they robustly reply, that you've taken to defending popular television, but really how can you defend such rubbish, it's grotesque, bizarre. I explain, rather loftily, in something like the following way:

What it boils down to, I think, is this: If you let kids have their head and let them watch what they want to, you can learn a lot about the cultural history of fantasy. You begin to realise that the forms of fantasy children enjoy haven't changed that much for centuries.

In early modern Europe, for example, so-called World Upside Down broadsheet illustrations were extremely popular.

These pictures showed a cat being chased by mice, a wolf at the mercy of sheep, a fox being attacked by rabbits, hunters being pursued by the animals they usually kill or horses in a carriage being pulled along by humans.

These pictures obviously related to folk literature, with clever rabbits outwitting traditional foes, and to carnival and festive practices in which usual relations of authority, power, status, age and gender were mocked and inverted.

We usually assume that nineteenth – and twentieth – century 'mass culture', because it's commercialised, is a different creature, a new monster, when compared with the popular culture of pre-industrial times. But I don't agree.

Compare these broadsheet illustrations with the fantasy world of TV that kids enjoy, the cartoons of Tom the cat being outwitted by Jerry the mouse, or the Coyote being outsmarted by the Roadrunner.

Think of the cartoon *Inspector Gadget*, where the true heroes, clever, resourceful and wise, are not idiotic adults like Gadget, but the little girl and the dog.

Think of all the comedies, from *Robin's Nest* and *Bless This House* to *Kingswood Country* and *Home Sweet Home*, where the blustering claims to authority by the father – 'patriarchy' – are derided.

Think of that children's perennial favourite *I Dream of Jeannie*, where Jeannie, a tiny genie in a bottle, emerges to outwit her master and his military superiors.

Then think of Phillis and Aristotle, a subject popular in stories,

> paintings, and household objects from the thirteenth through to the seventeenth centuries.
>
> In this story youth overthrows age; sexual passion triumphs over dry, sterile philosophy; nature surmounts reason, and the female, the male.
>
> Aristotle and Phillis, Jeannie and Inspector Gadget... perhaps the kids can educate us.

In venturing these thoughts I was drawing on my recent reading of Natalie Zemon Davis' wonderful essay 'Women on Top', Mikhail Bakhtin's *Rabelais and His World*, and David Kunzle's chapter 'World Upside Down: The Iconography of a European Broadsheet Type' in the collection edited by Barbara A Babcock, *The Reversible World: Symbolic Inversion in Art and Society*.

From such reading in the 1980s emerged my 1994 book *Postmodernism and Popular Culture: A Cultural History* (fittingly dedicated to my son Ned Curthoys).[10]

On 4 November 2014, I can see from the inside cover page, Ann Curthoys gave me as a gift a large book, *Radio Benjamin*, edited by Lecia Rosenthal, published in that year. I learn from the cover flyleaf that Benjamin, from 1927 to 1933, wrote and presented something like 80 broadcasts using the new medium of radio; the surviving transcripts appear in *Radio Benjamin* for the first time in English. When Ann gave me *Radio Benjamin* I quickly glanced at the list of contents for Section I: Youth Hour, Radio Stories for Children, which, the editor tells us, were broadcast from 1929 to 1932 on Radio Berlin and Southwest German Radio, Frankfurt.[11] One day, I thought, I would read these properly.

Looking at these broadcast stories now, I note that Benjamin very much used the I voice in directly addressing his young listeners in a relaxed and witty speaking voice, sometimes parodying himself as the narrator. I'll evoke two of his stories, one a kind of Grimm Brothers fairy tale, the other concerning the characteristics of dogs.

I see I put a pencil mark alongside two stories about toys, 'Berlin Toy Tour I' and 'Berlin Toy Tour II'. Benjamin begins 'Berlin Toy Tour I' (broadcast on Radio Berlin, March 15, 1930) with 'Sister Tinchen', and I notice that it includes images of danger, threat and death. 'Sister Tinchen', Benjamin tells his young listeners, was popular in the last 30 years of the previous century: 'it could be found in many a nursery, including the one in which the man speaking with you now spent his earliest days'. On the second page of 'Sister Tinchen', Benjamin relates, there is a 'sombre' picture showing 'five children miserably huddled together next to a dilapidated hut'. Their 'mother died that morning, and it's been quite some time since they had a father'. However, peril looms. In the background of this picture 'one sees a fairy, delicate and doll-like, holding a lily'. Her name is Concordia, harmony, she promises the children she will protect them as long as they always get along. An evil wizard, the fairy's enemy, promptly throws the children a pile of gifts which the boys in the family stupidly quarrel over, allowing the wizard and his devils to ensnare them in a sack.

However, their sister, the 'heroine' of the story, is not so snared, and she sets out to free her brothers from the 'wicked sorcerer's lair where the devils have taken them'. The evil sorcerer sets traps for Tinchen, including toys and 'magnificent doll-houses', but if she utters the words that she would like to stay with the toys, she will never be able to find and free her brothers; over and over, just as she is about to say the fatefully wrong words, a 'small blue bird suddenly appears, sits on her shoulder', and sings a reminder, 'Tinchen, dearest Tinchen mine, Think about your brothers thine!' Thus, says Benjamin, Tinchen successfully makes it through all sorts of enchanted lands, with the little blue bird appearing just in time. Benjamin then adds, making fun of himself: 'We could follow her everywhere if this weren't the radio station's Berlin Hour and I didn't have to zip back to Berlin through secret underground tunnels while Tinchen stays in the magic kingdom.'

Benjamin concludes 'Sister Tinchen' by adding that perhaps his audience will 'remember this fairy tale in a few years when, in the higher grades at school, you hear some of Goethe's greatest dramas, *Faust* in particular'. Faust, he tells them, makes a deal with the devil, who has to do 'whatever Faust wants, and in return he gets Faust's soul'. But eventually Faust breaks with the terms of their pact, and unfortunately 'there's no little blue bird' to save him, with the result that 'then and there he drops dead'.[12]

Dear Reader, I'll have to neglect talking about 'Berlin Toy Tour II', and rush on.

In Section I: Youth Hour – Radio Stories for Children, I note there a number of disaster stories for the children to learn about: 'The Fall of Herculaneum and Pompeii', 'The Lisbon Earthquake', 'Theater Fire in Canton', 'The Railway Disaster at the Firth of Tay' and 'The Mississippi Flood of 1927'. What really caught my eye, however, was the next story, 'True Dog Stories'. When I was young I had an unfortunate experience with a nasty dog, so I'm suddenly very interested in this particular radio broadcast by Benjamin. I'm reading it now; it was broadcast on Radio Berlin, 27 September 1930.

Benjamin opens 'True Dog Stories' by calling on Linnaeus's famous description of dogs, 'the very same Linnaeus you all know from botany and the man responsible for the system we still use today to classify plants'. Here, Benjamin continues, is what the 'great scientist' has to say about dogs, and then he starts quoting a long passage from Linnaeus, This is the first part:

> Feeds on meat, carcasses, farinaceous grains, but not leaves; digests bones, vomits up grass; defecates onto stone: Greek white, exceedingly acidic. Drinks by lapping; urinates to the side, up to one hundred in good company, sniffs at its neighbor's anus; moist nose, excellent sense of smell; runs on a diagonal, walks on toes; perspires very little, lets tongue hang out in the heat; circles its sleeping area before retiring; hears rather well while sleeping, dreams. The female is vicious with jealous suitors; fornicates with many partners when in heat; bites them; intimately bound during copulation...

Benjamin next addresses the question, does each dog have its own individual character? Yes, he assures his listeners, each has its peculiarities which give dog owners precious conversation material. Humanity's close association with dogs began thousands of years ago with their great victory over the wolf and the jackal; these wild animals then became dogs; however, the fierce characteristics of ancient wild animals have resurfaced, for example, with the half-wild dogs of Inuit which resemble the Arctic wolf. There are also some domestic dogs, especially mastiffs, that are more dreadful and bloodthirsty 'than they had been in their primitive state'.

Benjamin then tells the story of 'the most famous of all bloodhounds', Bezerillo, who the 'Spaniards of Fernando Cortez came upon while conquering Mexico, and then trained most hideously' to attack 'the Indians'. Bezerillo's 'audacity and intelligence' were extraordinary. Yet, while 'so cruel and so fierce, he sometimes showed himself to be much more humane than his masters'. One morning, a Captain Jago de Senadza desired to have some 'barbarous fun by letting Bezerillo rip to shreds an old captive Indian woman'; he gave her a letter and ordered her to deliver it to the governor of the island; the letter instructed that the dog be let loose to attack and kill the old woman. When the poor, defenceless Indian woman saw the ferocious dog storming after her, she fell to the ground in fear. In desperation, she showed the dog the letter, explaining that she had brought it to the commander on orders. Bezerillo hesitated at these words, and after a moment's contemplation 'approached the old woman tenderly'. This incident astounded the Spaniards, appearing to them as something mystical, or supernatural, which is probably why the governor set the old Indian woman free. Bezerillo met his end in a skirmish with Caribs, who felled him with a poison dart. It's easy to see, Benjamin said, bringing the story to a close, 'how the unfortunate Indians saw such dogs as four-legged abettors of the two-legged devil'.[13]

In June of 2001 my friend Subhash Jaireth and I organised an international symposium, 'Adventures of Dialogue: Bakhtin and Benjamin', at the Humanities Research Centre, Australian National University, Canberra. We formed the idea to hold a conference on two of modernity's greatest literary and philosophical thinkers, who were born almost at the same time, and in the late 1920s published two of the last century's most challenging, brilliant, speculative works, *Problems of Dostoevsky's Poetics* and *The Origin of German Tragic Drama*. Theorists came in from the US, Scotland, Hong Kong and Singapore, as well as the Australian cities of Newcastle, Sydney, Melbourne and Canberra itself. Proceedings were entertainingly visual, with much showing of slides, movie excerpts, photos, postcards. Subhash and I could not have been more pleased; we felt we had helped to create a symposium performed in the mischievous, irreverent, daring spirit of Bakhtin and Benjamin's own writings. Papers from the symposium subsequently appeared in two special issues of *JNT: Journal of Narrative Theory* in 2002 and 2003.

The issue of *JNT: Journal of Narrative Theory*, 2003, is entitled

'Benjamin and Bakhtin: Vision and Visuality'. Subhash and I introduced the essays. I'll focus here on what we said about Benjamin and his thinking about the city of modernity. In 'A Berlin Chronicle' (1932), we suggested, Benjamin creates a complex intricate artful text, far from an innocent autobiographical chronicle. Benjamin says he is not writing autobiography if we understand autobiography to be concerned with time, that is, with sequence and an assumed continuous flow of life; rather, he is talking of 'a space, of moments and discontinuities'. Sometimes the very syntax of 'A Berlin Chronicle' is quite broken. The city is translated into text calling attention to itself. Text becomes labyrinth, of memory, space, time, dream and consciousness. The modern city is a labyrinth, with Ariadne, the Lady of Labyrinth, its Muse. She can possibly rescue the wanderer (child and youth), just as in myth Ariadne had rescued Theseus. But then, as we know from the mythological story, Theseus betrays Ariadne: woman is betrayed by man; and in the labyrinth of the city more generally, there will always be betrayal and 'mistaken identity' as well as neighborhood, family relationships, school comradeship, companions who travel with one, masters and teachers one learns from.

Neighborhood, companions, mistaken identity and such like, says Benjamin, are the primal acquaintances that we need, enabling the wanderer to find an individual voice, reflect on the differences between individual lives. Yet the wanderer is also drawn to patterns and repetitions that shape, haunt, and harm. Referring to Nietzsche's remark that experiences keep recurring, Benjamin writes of 'paths that lead us again and again to people who have one and the same function for us: passageways that always, in the most diverse periods of life, guide us to the friend, the betrayer, the beloved, the pupil, or the master'.

There is another labyrinth that figures in 'A Berlin Chronicle': the I, the elusive self that might reside in the interior of the subject, its 'enigmatic centre, ego or fate'. But the wanderer is not so much interested in finding a possible centre as in exploring the many entrances and passageways themselves. The wanderer looks for entrances that might lead into the interior of city and psyche, but realises that he can only seek and explore the mysteries of the labyrinth by becoming lost. The art of becoming lost is indeed an art of urban existence he must learn and school himself in, just as with the café he must learn that the art of waiting is as important as any activity one engages in, in that space that offers both sociability and solitude as desired. Benjamin refers to a time in his later life, more in Paris than Berlin, 'when the frequenting of cafés was a daily need'; in time he will 'possess that passion for waiting without which one cannot thoroughly appreciate the charm of a café'.

In 'A Berlin Chronicle' Benjamin registers the city as shadowed by 'disaster', as in a local flood he once comes across while roaming. The city is the scene of such unpredictable 'extraordinary events', yet almost alongside are sights and places of utter banality. The city is also the scene of unwelcome changes, as with the Berlin café he takes to frequenting, the Princess, where he writes, close to a jazz band, discreetly consulting slips of paper, *The Origin of German Tragic Drama*. One day the Princess Café is renovated and becomes the Café Stenwyk, sinking to the level of a beerhouse, and Benjamin has to give up going there.

In writing about the city he comes to realise the complexities of memory, the 'mysterious work of remembrance'. Memory is 'not an instrument for exploring the past but its theatre'. We dig into our 'buried memories' and find images like 'precious fragments or torsos in a collector's gallery'. He thinks of Proust: memory throws up images, but each image unfolds like a fan, and 'only in its folds does the truth reside'. Memory is also braided with fetishistic objects, like a ring he associates with an ex-fiancée, the most fascinating ring he has ever seen, a dark garnet, portraying a Medusa's head. Memory is the pleasure of looking at cherished postcards kept in albums. Memory attaches itself to childhood dreams half remembered from sleepy evenings, when, in a wonderful image, the 'dream ship' came to fetch the children.

In 'A Berlin Chronicle' then, the city as theatre of modern space and visuality is associated with a bewildering variety of images, musings, states, contrasts: liminality and familiarity; companionship of friends, assistance, and betrayal; prizing of lostness; thresholds; the grotesque and bizarre; the usual and disaster; extraordinary events and banality; memory as inhering in folds; waiting; pauses; silence; clairvoyance and prophecy; fetishistic objects; ghosts; fragments and body parts; adulthood trying to remember childhood; the poetic and the profane; the ordinary and domestic along with the exotic and fantastical; eros; cross-dressing; fear and violence, robbery and murder; treasured postcards; man as distant secretive father who tells frightening stories of death from sexual disease, stories that have to be repressed and release themselves later to memory as in trauma; woman as kindly grandmother (a great traveler from whom he believes he inherits his own 'love of travel' as well as his 'delight in giving presents'), reproving practical mother, Ariadne, prostitute, Medusa, ex-fiancée; meeting places vibrant and then lost, irrecoverable, mourned. The city as too much and too little; as efflorescence and blankness, excess and desolation, illumination and blindness. Each city is individual and distinctive, yet always recognisable as part of a general urban modernity in its technologies and hierarchies. The city is where thought works by image as well as touch, sound, smell. The city is where the dead are ever-present, where vision meets the invisible.[14]

Oddly, I forgot about this frenzy of semi-colons in Subhash and my introduction to 'Benjamin and Bakhtin: Vision and Visuality' in 2003. Years later, writing this ego histoire, Ann Curthoys urged me to become interested in Virginia Woolf and I was delighted to find her enthusiastic use the semi-colon; I found myself irresistibly using it again.

As promised in the Preface when referring to ego histoire as vertigo and drunken boat, I will now try to make clear why I was and remain so enchanted with Pierre Nora's 2001 essay 'L'ego-histoire est-elle possible?'[15]

Soon after reading Nora's essay I felt inspired to write a fragment, 'Notes on reading Pierre Nora, "L'ego-histoire est-elle possible?"' (rather I hoped in homage to Walter Benjamin's fragments 'Theses on the Philosophy of History', exploring its literary and philosophical associations. These notes remained as an unpublished manuscript, until in 2016 I wrote an essay for the journal *Law Text Culture*, at the invitation of the Melbourne Law School jurisographers Ann Genovese, Shaun McVeigh, and Peter D Rush; my essay is entitled 'Of Pearls and Coral: Jurisography and Ego History', and I extensively drew on my notes on reading Nora for it. I will now plunder my *Law Text Culture* essay.[16]

In 'L'ego-histoire est-elle possible?' Nora offers reasons for why he considers that ego histoire made its appearance in French intellectual life when it did, in the late twentieth century.[17] One relevant development, Nora tells us, was the return of the subject to the centre of action and thought, which came after the great period was over of what he refers to as structuralism, semiology and textology. The return of the subject-influenced historians to be more aware of the freedom, will and desires of the thinking and acting individual. The late twentieth century, Nora reflects, was the moment of a new interest in writing biography, which had specific French associations, including the powerful historical image of de Gaulle. Another epochal trait was the rise of historiography, Nora observing that in France historiography was for a long time slow to impose itself on historical practice, yet when it did its effects have been almost subversive, dismantling traditional national grand narratives. Nora feels that both historiography and ego histoire evince a capacity to de-familiarise that which we feel we live spontaneously, such as memory, a well-known interest of Nora, as in his collection on places of memory. Inflected by historiography and ego histoire, memory has to become self-conscious and self-questioning. Yet another development was that one now felt one lived in a reflexive or epistemological age, where theoretical reflection was being integrated with historical practice. In Nora's view, historiography and ego histoire, along with theoretical reflection and self-reflexive memory, are part of the same constellation.

As you read 'L'ego-histoire est-elle possible?' you quickly realise Nora intends the question to be taken very seriously: ego histoire may not be possible, it may be a failure, or half-failure. But is failure failure? For ego histoire to succeed as a single, unified, coherent project would be to destroy ego histoire, to return it to conventional historical writing, which ego histoire wishes to make strange. In our *Is History Fiction?* Ann Curthoys and I refer to what we conceive as the double character of history, that it both works through a rigorous scrutiny of sources and partakes of the world of literary forms.[18] What literary affiliations does ego histoire move one to think about? When Nora invokes the notion of ego histoire defamiliarising conventional empirical history, I think of theories of defamiliarisation in literary theory and dramaturgy, in the Russian Formalists and Brecht. I also think of theorists of modernity such as Walter Benjamin and Hannah Arendt.

Nora regards the ego historian in ways that remind me of Hannah Arendt's book *Men in Dark Times*, where intellectual personality is discussed in terms of biography, anecdote, vignette, and social genealogy (as in her chapters on Rosa Luxemburg and Karl Jaspers). We might also think of Deleuze and Guattari in *What is Philosophy?* regarding philosophers as 'conceptual personae' or 'thought figures', engrained with ambivalence, contradictoriness, and idiosyncrasy.[19] There is also the important notion of sensibility, that can be explored in terms of image, metaphor, and story, and in terms of cultural figures. Nora himself is drawn to the figure of the outsider. He tells us that for a long time ego histoire existed outside of conventional academic history; an existence that was clandestine, subterranean and uncategorisable, exciting and fascinating by its intensity and passion.

Nora, however, doesn't claim to be a complete or absolute outsider to the history profession. Rather, he positions himself as 'marginal central'. It is, he says, his intellectual nature to be always inside and outside at the same time. He is marginal to academic life in that he cannot be clearly defined as an academic, or editor, or writer. He is central in belonging to higher studies and as part of the publisher Gallimard. But his higher studies institution is eccentric (giving shelter to what he jokes are sheep with five feet), even if – or hence – lively and creative. His chosen field of memory is not history in a traditional sense. In moving across various fields and sectors of intellectual life, his journey appears to him like the lateral movement of a crab, which in turn reminds me of familiar images from T S Eliot's poem *The Love Song of J Alfred Prufrock*. 'I should have been', laments Prufrock, 'a pair of ragged claws' scuttling across the 'floors of silent seas'.[20] Prufrock's apparent passivity, timidity and self-contempt does not, however, characterise the sensibility of Nora's ego historian. Rather we might think of a marrano-like figure I talk about in my book *1492: The Poetics of Diaspora*, the stranger as evoked by Georg Simmel; I will return to Simmel's great essay near the end of this Introduction.[21]

Nora tells us that his own troubled feeling of being for as long as he could remember at once inside and outside French society was intensified by his experience of being a teenage Jewish boy surviving by hiding during World War II. He feels a distance from people who have not experienced how tragic history and life can be. He realises that he is fascinated by the history of contemporary France, *this strange country*. He wants to ask of France fundamental questions that were born for him during the war, in the stupor of defeat, the experience in France of Jews like himself, the Resistance; and after the war, the conflict between communism and Gaullism, and further questions posed by France's colonial wars. He regrets that the Annales school in its interest in the long view made it so difficult for historians to study contemporary France. Nora turns to memory and ego histoire as ways into contemporary history, which he believes has been neglected by French historians.

I find particularly interesting Nora's conception of the ego historian as a distinctive intellectual personality of an unsettled, fragmented and contradictory kind. At one point Nora asks of the ego historian, who is she or he? As I interpret this question, Nora is hazarding the thought that, as he puts it, the ego historian is neither, or rather might be all of, the autobiographer, the writer, the friend, the psychoanalyst and the confessor.

Here is what so attracts me about Nora's essay. Nora insists that the ego historian is not to be encapsulated as an autobiographer, though she or he will draw on autobiography. Furthermore, the ego historian is not necessarily to be identified with historians, with the history profession. Yet if ego history represents various failed efforts in terms of identity and coherence, its failures, or half failures, are of immense interest. Indeed, its half-failures, as he phrases it, are perhaps ego histoire's true success. I'm reminded of Walter Benjamin when in his essay 'Some Reflections on Kafka' in *Illuminations* he observes that to understand Kafka we must never lose sight of his being a failure: 'One is tempted to say,' Benjamin writes, that once Kafka 'was certain of eventual failure, everything worked out for him *en route* as in a dream. There is nothing more memorable than the fervor with which Kafka emphasized his failure.'[22] In her beautiful introduction to *Illuminations*, Arendt suggests that Benjamin and Kafka are in this respect very much alike. Kafka, Benjamin, and the ego historian as a failure or half-failure: here surely is an interesting lineage for the genealogy of ego histoire.

In the spirit of Pierre Nora's essay, then, I regard ego histoire as an adventure of ideas, free to mix and juxtapose genres, texts, media, modes, perspectives, and narratives in unpredictable and surprising ways.

Nora's 'L'ego-histoire est-elle possible?' brings to mind Herodotus. In Ann Curthoys and my *Is History Fiction?*, in our chapter 'Herodotus and World History', we argue that Herodotus' *The Histories* helped establish historical writing in antiquity as cosmopolitan, internationalist and transnational. What characterises *The Histories* is its doubleness, where the concern for history as a discipline, with associated research protocols, is combined with the interest in storytelling. *The Histories* provides an exemplar of expansiveness and inclusiveness, that historical narrative can be written in any genre-, or variety of genres. Herodotus does not confine history to any area or field or focus, rather establishing historical writing as freely economic, political, diplomatic, social, cultural, sexual, religious, military, naval.

In its recognition of doubleness, Ann and I suggest, *The Histories* anticipates contemporary literary and cultural theory in many ways. The frame story of *The Histories* tells of how the Persian empire came into being, how it came to invade Greece in the early part of the fifth century BCE, how its attacks were finally repulsed, followed by how the Athenians, victorious at Salamis, immediately set about creating an empire themselves. Yet *The Histories* also relates a proliferating number of stories that record the everyday, curious, fantastical, exotic or marvelous. The effect is similar to what we can observe of the mode of storytelling in *The Thousand and One Nights*, where the frame story concerning the perilous relationship between King Shahriyar, who lived in the lands of India and China, and his new wife Shahrazad under threat of death, is always in tension with the multiple stories that lead to more stories that lead to more stories that have only an indirect or indeed no relationship to the frame story involving Shahriyar and Shahrazad: the stories exceed the frame story and the frame story can never rein them in. Ann and I note that in the Enlightenment, from early in the eighteenth century, the *Nights* influenced narrative towards a delight in decentredness and the mixing of heterogeneous genres, from the erotic to the cosmological. In the nineteenth and twentieth centuries, the *Nights* influenced Dickens, Wilkie Collins, Conrad, Joyce, Borges.[23]

Ann and I feel that the doubleness of *The Histories*, as both disciplined enquiry and proliferating stories, anticipates the notion of modern allegory in Walter Benjamin's prologue to *The Origin of German Tragic Drama*. Benjamin argues of the kind of allegory that developed in the sixteenth century in baroque art and theatre, that there is a constant tension between the apparent clarity of an idea or emblem, and the profusion of images, often almost chaotic, used to illustrate or personify the idea or emblem. Benjamin says that in *The Origin of German Tragic Drama* he is writing a kind of philosophical history. His method will be like constructing a mosaic, which represents a fragmentation into capricious particles, emphasising the distinct and separate. Philosophical history always works by digression so that in the search for truth what might be most valuable to investigate, Benjamin suggests, is the most singular, eccentric and extreme of examples, the most unusual and isolated; examples to be found in the merest fragment, the minutest detail. In these terms, Herodotus' *The Histories* in its digressive method establishes history from its beginning as philosophical history.[24]

If the frame story for *The Histories* is the war of the Persians and Greeks, and the frame story in *The Thousand and One Nights* concerns the perilous relationship between King Shahriyar and Shahrazad, the frame story for my ego histoire is family history and autobiography that converge on 27 November 1974 when our son Ned Curthoys was born in Sydney, yet where, while the frame story is certainly not lost to view, stories go everywhere, in time and space.

For my birthday in October 2016, Ann bought for me from Gleebooks a book – I can't remember now how we came to know of it, perhaps Ann saw it in the Gleebooks Gleaner, the bookshop putting out a regular news sheet of new publications – by Shihāb Al-Dīn Al-Nuwayrī, *The Ultimate Ambition in the Arts of Erudition: A Compendium of Knowledge from the Classical Islamic World*, edited, translated, and with an Introduction by Elias Muhanna.[25] Reading the Introduction gave me an idea. Muhanna explains that *The Ultimate Ambition in the Arts of Erudition*, one of the most important collections of Arabic-Islamic literature and thought, was written in Egypt in the first part of the fourteenth century at the time of the Mamluk Empire; the compendium was heir to the classical Islamic humanistic tradition that had formed the basis of learned culture in the Middle East for centuries; it was constituted in an encyclopedic gathering together of several centuries of poetic, historical, religious, and scientific writings; and as well as the great archive of classical Arabic-Islamic thought, it drew on materials from Ancient Greece, Persia and India; it conversed with a contemporary culture of the elite that can be characterized as cosmopolitan and intellectually omnivorous in its outlook, in what, Muhanna says, has been described as a veritable Age of Encyclopedias.

Al-Nuwayrī's encyclopedia, Muhanna explains, was enormous, containing 33 volumes, which he has distilled into a single volume. As the back cover indicates, the compendium contains entries on everything from medieval moon-worshipping cults, sexual aphrodisiacs and the substance of clouds, to how to get the smell of alcohol off one's breath, the deliciousness of cheese made from buffalo milk, and the nesting habits of flamingos. Its concerns venture across the cosmos, universal history, the human being (including physiology, genealogy, music, wine, amusements and pastimes, and political rule), the animal world, and the plant world.

I'll quote the passage in the Introduction that really caught my eye:

> The Arabic title of the work (*Nihāyat al-arab fī funūn al-adab*) tells us that its subject is the cultivation of *adab*, a multi-faceted concept which, in its classical formulation, denoted a standard of polite behavior and corpus of literary materials that formed the basis for a well-rounded education. By al-Nuwayrī's time, the range of topics that fell under the purview of *adab* had grown. What we would call literature today was still the heart of this corpus: poetry, proverbs and parables, exemplary orations and epistles, and other examples of belletristic prose. But it now also included medical remedies and other forms of practical science, technical discussions of financial accounting and legal practice, enormous quantities of history, and other fields. While *adab* had always had an encyclopedic aspect, al-Nuwayrī's text represents a maximally expansive and disciplinarily agnostic vision of this ideal of humanistic education.[26]

I sat at the Flinderz coffee shop in Hillarys, northern Perth, mulling over this passage. In terms of historical writing, what Muhanna refers to as the encyclopedia's heterogeneity of material reminds me of Herodotus's *The Histories*, especially when Muhanna tells us that al-Nuwayrī was inclined to record many viewpoints on a given subject rather than a single one.[27]

As in Al-Nuwayrī's encyclopedia, in Herodotus' *The Histories* we see a plethora of stories that record the everyday, curious, fantastical and marvellous, for example, famous courtesans in ancient Egypt or the evocation of how the Amazons join up with the Scythians.[28]

What also got me thinking in the quoted passage concerns the notion of *adab*, which Al-Nuwayrī, Muhanna says, deployed as a method of composition of his text as a kind of personal project of self-edification; al-Nuwayrī regarded *adab* as the mark of the most enlightened minds of his time. Here, I thought, could be a connection to ego histoire. The notion of *adab* as Muhanna describes it got me thinking of the German Enlightenment notion of *Bildung* as my son Ned Curthoys evokes it in his 2013 book *The Legacy of Liberal Judaism: Ernst Cassirer and Hannah Arendt's Hidden Conversation*, suggesting its importance for the German-Jewish intellectual tradition stretching from Moses Mendelssohn in the late eighteenth century to Hannah Arendt in the twentieth. Ned Curthoys writes that for Mendelssohn *Bildung* is a 'dynamic self-cultivation' that seeks to be 'counter-historical'.[29]

What I would like to think now is that my ego histoire as I have been writing it since 2011, along with being influenced by Herodotus and *The Thousand and One Nights*, pays homage to the medieval tradition of Arab-Islamic heterogeneous writing and the cultivation of *adab*. I hope so. I hope so.

A note on genealogy, which figures everywhere in *Growing Up Communist and Jewish in Bondi* as ego histoire (as it had in my 2001 *1492: The Poetics of Diaspora*). In the fifth fragment of his 'Theses on the Philosophy of History' in *Illuminations* Walter Benjamin reflects that 'every image of the past that is not recognized by the present as one of its own concerns threatens to disappear irretrievably'.[30] Genealogy is absorbing not to say fascinating because it does bring up images and flashes of the past. Genealogy brings history close, yet in no ordered way. It goes anywhere, it is spasmodic, it leaves so much unknown, it is always difficult to decipher and interpret, it is like chaos in action.

I mourn the death of Walter Benjamin.

In 2005 I published an essay on a journey Ann Curthoys and I took in Spain, 'The Chorizo and Genocide: Travel Notes on Barcelona, Granada, Cordoba, and Portbou, June-July 2005', in *Sephardic Heritage Update* (Number 176, 25 September 2005, editor David Shasha). I will include the long account as one of the final fragments of this ego histoire. Here I will record our northward journey from Barcelona:

> 5 July: early in the morning Ann and I catch the train that goes from Granada to Montpellier (there we will catch another train to Marseille). The train moves northwards alongside the Mediterranean, and then arrives at the border town of Portbou. I had particularly wanted to see Portbou as the place where Walter Benjamin died on 26 September 1940, almost certainly by suicide. As the train slowly negotiates the border, I bitterly scribble in my diary: *Tuesday 11.10 am – the train to Montpellier has stopped at Portbou – from the train seems no more than a desolate railway town, with bare hills surrounding the station on the left. The station is grimy. Ann takes a photo of the 'Portbou' sign. Various men, French-speaking, are laughing on the platform, then get on the train, which is now creaking, moving. Vale Walter Benjamin. I'll see how far the French border is from here, how far you got into Spain as you tried to escape.* When we return to Australia I read in Momme Brodersen's biography that Portbou officials, assuming that Benjamin was a Catholic, had on 28 September given him extreme unction, a requiem mass and burial in the town's Catholic cemetery. His grave was paid

> for out of the money in his possession, but only covered 'rental' for a period of five years. Brodersen adds that after that time, in December 1945, his remains were transferred, probably to the common grave in the cemetery. (Also back in Canberra I take down *Reflections* from my shelves and read again Benjamin's two essays 'Marseilles' and 'Hashish in Marseilles'.)

In their biography *Walter Benjamin: A Critical Life* (2014), Howard Eiland and Michael W Jennings offer detailed research findings on what might have happened to Walter Benjamin in Portbou in late September 1940, for what exactly happened is unclear. Benjamin was attempting an illegal crossing into Spain as had other exiles. From there, he hoped to make his way through to Portugal and then on to the US. He was accompanied by three companions from Marseille, Henny Gurland and her teenage son Joseph, and Lisa Fittko. After arduous walking through the Pyrenees, Benjamin and his companions reached Portb only to find that the Spanish government had recently closed the border to illegal refugees from France. Benjamin and his companions were told they would be returned to French soil, where they would face almost certain internment and transfer to a concentration camp. At some point during the night of 26 September, Benjamin composed a note for Henny Gurland that she later reconstructed from memory:

> In a situation presenting no way out, I have no other choice but to make an end of it. It is a small village in the Pyrenees, where no one knows me, that my life will come to a close.
>
> I ask you to transmit my thoughts to my friend Adorno and to explain to him the situation in which I find myself. There is not enough time remaining for me to write all the letters I would like to write.

Sometime later that night, Benjamin died after taking a massive dose of morphine. Unaccountably, the next day the border was reopened.[31]

In *Hannah Arendt: For Love of the World* (2004), Elisabeth Young-Bruehl writes that the last time Walter Benjamin saw Hannah Arendt and Heinrich Blücher in Marseille, he entrusted to their care a collection of manuscripts, including 'Theses on the Philosophy of History', which he hoped they would be able to deliver to the Institute for Social Research in New York. While they waited for their ship in Lisbon, Arendt and Blücher read Benjamin's 'Theses' aloud to each other and to the refugees who gathered around them.

Young-Bruehl records that several days after arriving in New York in 1941, Hannah Arendt took the suitcase containing Benjamin's manuscripts to the office on West 117th Street where Adorno and his colleagues had reestablished the Frankfurt Institute for Social Research. However, not long after she received a letter informing her that one of the manuscripts had been lost; distressed and incredulous, Arendt feared the manuscript had been suppressed; she also now suspected that the Frankfurt institute members were not going to do what she thought they were morally obliged to do, publish Benjamin's manuscripts.

Young-Bruehl observes that Hannah Arendt had never wanted to give Benjamin's manuscripts to Adorno, but felt bound by Benjamin's instructions. And she felt grateful to Adorno for arranging Benjamin's emergency visa to the US. She bitterly recalled that Benjamin was afraid of Adorno and the institute on whom he depended for financial support to survive, and that Adorno had highhandedly edited and cut in 1938 an essay by Benjamin on Baudelaire, the institute considering Benjamin a bad Marxist, not sufficiently dialectical.

In the fall of 1942 Arendt and Blücher read newspaper stories from Europe that the Germans had built extermination centres, and that they were using gas to kill Jews. They were brought close to despair. Arendt wrote a poem for her dead friend, entitled simply 'W.B.', its final verse:

Distant voices, sadnesses nearby.
Those are the voices and these the dead
Whom we have sent as messengers
Ahead, to lead us into slumber.

As it turned out, Benjamin's work remained uncollected until 1955. In 1968, out of continued loyalty to her dead friend, Arendt edited an English volume, *Illuminations*, and wrote the introduction for it. She was at work on a second volume, *Reflections*, at the time of her own death in 1975.[32]

Like Benjamin, Hannah Arendt deeply believed in friendship, for which I honour her and I honour him.

I come now to genocide studies, in which Ann and I have been involved since the late 1990s. A key ego histoire question is, how does one become involved in a particular intellectual endeavour, a field, a discipline, an area, what leads one to it, why was it urgent that something be investigated? Also, could there be an element of chance, of serendipity, involved?

In 2001 Ann Curthoys and I edited for the Australian journal *Aboriginal History*, olume 25 2001, a special series of essays entitled "Genocide"?: Australian Aboriginal history in international perspective'. Its contributors, exploring a variety of perspectives, were Colin Tatz, Tony Barta, Andrew Markus, Anna Haebich, A Dirk Moses, Rosanne Kennedy, Larissa Behrendt, Deborah Rose and Bain Attwood.

In our 'Introduction – Genocide: definitions, questions, settler-colonies', Ann and I explain that the idea for a collection of essays on 'Genocide?' came originally from our reading of a comment by the Indigenous scholar Marcia Langton in *Australian Humanities Review* in mid-2000, that Aboriginal writing, scholarship and research are taking on the feel of Holocaust studies in the sense that Aboriginal people write, read, and research to 'try to understand the terrible, inexplicable past'; she expressed disgust at 'those who do not want what happened to us and our ancestors remembered into "history"'; she did not use the word 'genocide'.

Ann and I thought the questions Marcia Langton raised, of how to come to terms with terrible pasts, and how can we use insights from one history to interrogate another, deserved sustained further thought. The unresolved issue for us was whether the notion of genocide could be fairly applied to Australian history. The Human Rights Commission's *Bringing Them Home* report of 1997, which investigated the history and effects of Aboriginal child removal in the nineteenth and twentieth centuries, had controversially argued that Australian child removal practices fell within the definition of genocide used in Article II of the Convention on the Prevention and Punishment of the Crime of Genocide, United Nations, 9 December 1948: 'In the present Convention, genocide means any of the following acts committed with intent to destroy, in whole or in part, a national, ethnical, racial or religious group, as such…'. One of those acts listed was 'Forcibly transferring children of the group to another group.' In these terms, the *Bringing Them Home* report concluded that Australia had its own history of genocide. This aspect of the report horrified many Australians of varying political views; many people, including historians, rejected the notion that child removal could reasonably be described as 'genocide'.

Ann and I did not know where to stand in this debate. We found ourselves issuing a flurry of questions: Was the term genocide applicable to Australian history in relation to the Stolen Generations? Did it apply to other aspects of the past, such as Australia's history of massacres and violence on the frontiers of settlement? Ought not Australians, as a way of clarifying thinking, be more aware of the international debates around concepts such as genocide, Holocaust, trauma, guilt and apology, and their applicability or otherwise in the Australian context?

At this point in writing our introduction, serendipity made its move. Somehow we knew that the originator of the concept 'genocide' was the great twentieth-century Polish-Jewish jurist Raphaël Lemkin (1901–59), who had defined the term in his 1944 *Axis Rule in Occupied Europe: laws of occupation, analysis of government, proposals for redress*; and that his definition became the basis of the 1948 UN Convention. However, relative newcomers to genocide studies, we had not read *Axis Rule in Occupied Europe*. Could it, we wondered and hoped, be somewhere in the ANU library system, in one of its libraries on campus, and yes it was, in Chifley Library, the main humanities undergraduate library, a 100 yards or so away. We found the call number. I walked over, entered the library holding the call number on a slip of paper, walked about, found the shelves where it should be, stopped, and there it was, gazing at me, as if waiting for this moment. I borrowed it, brought it back, and Ann and I had it in our hands.[33]

Ann had mostly written the first historiographical sections of the introduction; now she urged me to read *Axis Rule in Occupied Europe* immediately, to absorb myself in it, this might be important for gaining our own independent sense of what Lemkin meant by genocide, especially as many of the contributors to the raging debate that accompanied the 1997 Human Rights Commission's *Bringing Them Home* report equated genocide, as in the Holocaust, with mass murder, the mass killing of an entire people.

As I plunged into reading *Axis Rule in Occupied Europe*, especially its preface and the all-important chapter IX, 'Genocide', it soon became apparent, as I told Ann later that day, that Lemkin did not equate genocide with mass murder. Rather, for Lemkin, genocide involves wide-ranging processes that may include, and usually do include, mass killing, as was occurring, Lemkin pointed out, in the present world war. Ann and I agreed that I should, as carefully and precisely as possible, outline in the remainder of the introduction how Lemkin conceives of genocide, beginning with how in chapter IX Lemkin proposed his new concept of genocide as a two-fold process.[34] I have to confess that I took liberties for reasons I can't now remember, I clumsily brought together a sentence from the preface and another from chapter IX:

> Genocide has two phases: one, destruction of the national pattern of the oppressed group; the other, the imposition of the national pattern of the oppressor. Genocide meant that one national pattern was to be destroyed, to be replaced by the imposition of another.[35]

I could see that Lemkin's definition as it went on folded in colonisation, but I decided to defer that aspect until later in the introduction.

I explain that for Lemkin in chapter IX genocide signified a 'coordinated plan' of different actions 'aiming at' the destruction of the essential foundations of the life of national groups, with the 'aim' of annihilating the groups themselves. Genocide was to be considered as a composite of actions rather than one single defining act or mode by which the destruction of a group or nation's foundations of life were to be secured. It involves consideration of political, social, legal, intellectual, spiritual, economic, biological, physiological, religious and moral aspects. It involves considerations of health, food and nourishment in relationship to genocide and as part of genocide. It involves consideration of family life, care of children, and birth as well as death. It involves consideration of the honour and dignity of peoples, and the future of humanity as a world community.

I won't summarise, even briefly, our quite lengthy exposition of Lemkin's detailing of these different considerations that constitute how wide-ranging genocide can be; they include many examples of German actions in the occupied territories of World War II.

In the next section of the introduction, I point out that Lemkin in chapter IX considered that practices of colonialism were important for the German occupiers and constituted the second phase of genocide, the imposition of the national pattern of the oppressor during or after the destruction of the national pattern of the oppressed group. Here I completed Lemkin's definition: 'This imposition may… be made upon the oppressed population which is allowed to remain, or upon the territory alone, after removal of the population and the colonization of the area by the oppressor's own nationals.'[36]

In the following section of the introduction, I turned to the American historian Ward Churchill in his 1997 book *A Little Matter of Genocide: Holocaust and denial in the Americas 1492 to the present*. While working on the introduction, our friend Debbie Bird Rose, who has sadly died, lent us her copy of *A Little Matter of Genocide*, which is dedicated to the memory of Lemkin. In its impassioned, bitter, mordant way, *A Little Matter of Genocide* takes up Lemkin's challenge to study the possible relationship of genocide to settler colonialism in modern world history. Very briefly, Churchill argues that settler colonies around the world that were established following European expansion post-1492 in the US, Canada, Australia, New Zealand, South Africa and Argentina, are inherently genocidal in terms of Lemkin's definition of genocide as a two-fold process involving settler colonialism; in Churchill's words, a settler colony to be a settler colony requires 'wholesale displacement, reduction in numbers, and forced assimilation of native peoples'. Churchill feels that Sartre, addressing the war crimes tribunal established by Bertrand Russell in 1967, went a long way towards restoring Lemkin's original notions of genocide by equating colonialism and genocide. In Churchill's view, settler colonies involve genocide in their very being.[37]

I agree with Churchill in *A Little Matter of Genocide*. There is indeed an inherent relationship between genocide and settler colonialism.

Looking back on my rather clumsy contribution to the latter parts of Ann and my introduction to *Aboriginal History* volume 25 2001, I simply should have spelt out the full definition of genocide as a two-stage process as Lemkin formulated it in *Axis Rule in Occupied Europe*:

> Genocide has two phases: one, destruction of the national pattern of the oppressed group; the other, the imposition of the national pattern of the oppressor. This imposition, in turn, may be made upon the oppressed population which is allowed to remain, or upon the territory alone, after removal of the population and the colonization of the area by the oppressor's own nationals.[38]

For many years now, decades, this passage has become iconic in genocide studies. Tony Barta, in two important essays in the 1980s, 'After the Holocaust: Consciousness of Genocide in Australia' (1984) and 'Relations of Genocide: Land and Lives in the Colonization of Australia' (1987), which Ann and I discuss in our essay 'Defining Genocide' in Dan Stone's collection *The*

Historiography of Genocide (2008), challenged a view that had become common in genocide studies, that genocide should be defined as systematic and state-directed. In both essays, Tony Barta called for renewed attention to Lemkin's two-phase definition of genocide in chapter IX of *Axis Rule in Occupied Europe* linking genocide with colonisation.[39]

Ann and I have quoted Lemkin's *Axis Rule* chapter IX passage more than thrice in subsequent writings, including in the 'Defining Genocide' essay in *The Historiography of Genocide*, for it so clearly, lucidly, far-seeingly entwines genocide and settler colonialism in an inherent, constitutive, relationship. Such a perspective is important to *Growing Up Communist and Jewish in Bondi*.

In 2003–4 Ann and I lived in Washington DC, staying in Georgetown. Ann was the GO8 Visiting Professor of Australian Studies at Georgetown University and taught various classes; I took a class in Australian literature. On Tuesday 9 December 2003 we catch a train from Union Station to New York. We go to 15 West 16th Street. There we do research at the American Jewish Historical Society in their Lemkin archives. Then we catch the uptown underground to the New York Public Library to look at the Lemkin archives there. We wished to find out as much as we could of Lemkin's thinking about the entwinement of settler colonialism and genocide. This research led to a great deal of conceptualisation and new writing on our part for many years, and continues still. I gave a seminar talk, 'Raphael Lemkin's History of Genocide and Colonialism', for the United States Holocaust Memorial Museum, Center for Advanced Holocaust Studies, Washington DC, 26 February 2004.[40] For *Empire, Colony, Genocide: Conquest, Occupation, and Subaltern Resistance in World History* (2008), edited by A Dirk Moses, Ann wrote a chapter, 'Genocide in Tasmania: The History of an Idea', and I wrote a chapter, 'Are Settler-Colonies Inherently Genocidal? Re-reading Lemkin'. We wrote our chapter 'Defining Genocide' for Dan Stone's *The Historiography of Genocide*, where in our concluding section we note that historians like Jürgen Zimmerer, A Dirk Moses and Wendy Lower are exploring how much previous European colonising inspired Nazi genocidal practices including colonising projects in the land mass east of Germany.[41]

Ann Curthoys, Ann Genovese and Alexander Reilly, in their *Rights and Redemption: History Law and Indigenous People* (2008), quote Lemkin's passage on genocide as a two-fold process of destruction and replacement that entwines genocide and colonisation. Curthoys, Genovese and Reilly discuss at length the actions, brought in the wake of the *Bringing Them Home* report of 1997, of *Nulyarimma* and *Buzzacott* initiated in the Australian courts in 1998. The applicants of *Nulyarimma* and *Buzzacott* were an alliance of Aboriginal elders, the 'Aboriginal Genocide Prosecutors'. They saw their actions as an opportunity to determine the unresolved question of whether genocide had been, and continued to be, perpetrated by the settler community in Australia. The *Nulyarimma* application first came before Justice Crispin of the ACT Supreme Court on 17 July 1998. The applicants' submissions focused on their experience of genocide in Australia.[42]

Given the sensitive nature of the claim concerning genocide, the judge and the government lawyers were clearly of the view that the applicants should have their day in court. The applicants then sought to put before the court additional material documenting their personal experiences, and asked the judge to visit the Tent Embassy. Justice Crispin acceded to this request. At this hearing, some of the applicants addressed the judge in relation to the effect of colonisation on them personally and of the trauma still suffered by Indigenous Australians as a result of their treatment by whites. Curthoys, Genovese and Reilly detail how the genocide cases of *Nulyarimma* and *Buzzacott* failed in law because, while Justice Crispin concluded that genocide against Aboriginal communities 'had most probably been committed in Australia', there can be no legal consequences since 'genocide did not (and continues not to) exist in Australia as a crime under statute or under the common law'.[43]

The authors leave the last powerful words to Wadjularbinna Nulyarimma:

> I just wanted to say… that it does not matter how many judges, white lawyers are here to help in this case, I would like the judges to keep an open mind that the victims of genocide are the experts in the facts of what has happened and how genocide is affecting them. You know, it is not only in the past, it is affecting us today and we want to put that point across and I hope we are taken seriously because we mean to move forward with the times. We are pushing for change and change is inevitable. And we do not want to come to the courts wasting our time, having to repeat painful experiences, having to bring up things that we would rather forget and coming here then going back to my community in the Gulf of Carpentaria and seeing our children who do not have a future. They do not have a future. They are already suffering from the effects of the legal system in this country and the policies in this country. And I do not want the legal people to think that the judges and the lawyers have a handle on this thing. It is our case. We are bringing it forward and this is only the beginning of a long struggle…[44]

In the Introduction to their 2018 book *Taking Liberty: Indigenous Rights and Settler Self-Government in Colonial Australia, 1830–1890*, Ann Curthoys and Jessie Mitchell quote Lemkin's definition of genocide as a two-phase process, arguing that it enables us to recognise both the enormity of the human destruction that occurred in the wake of colonisation as well as give full recognition to the histories of survival and transformation that followed, testament to human resilience and adaptability. They point out that many Indigenous scholars have embraced the concept. Larissa Behrendt, for instance, has commented on 'the conviction that Indigenous communities feel about "genocide" being the word and the concept that describes the colonial legacy inherited and still pervasive'; these convictions, she continued, 'form part of the legitimate contest over the writing of Australia's colonisation'.[45]

There are further ideas, notions, concepts, tropes, cultural figures which help shape the writing of *Growing Up Communist and Jewish in Bondi*. As promised, one concerns the German sociologist Georg Simmel's great 1908 essay 'The Stranger', which I found illuminating for my chapter, 'Strangers amongst the nations: Mr Bloom and Spinoza' in my *1492: The Poetics of Diaspora*. As I explain there, Simmel conceives the stranger as a figure who, simultaneously and disturbingly, fuses features of both wandering and fixity. The stranger, says Simmel, is the wanderer who comes today and stays tomorrow. While he belongs to a spatially defined group, he always remains a potential wanderer. His position in the group is defined by the fact that he has not belonged to it from the beginning, that he imports qualities into it which do not and cannot stem from the group itself, and that he is always considered as not an owner of soil. He is an element of the group itself, in his interactions with it both a full-fledged member yet outside it and confronting it. His relations with it are contingent, exhibiting a kind of abstraction. Towards the group the stranger feels a certain kind of objectivity, a particular structure of feeling composed of nearness and distance, involvement and indifference, though such is not to be confused with passivity. Such objectivity gives him a kind of freedom, in terms of perception, understanding and evaluation of what others in the group take as given, qualities which he also brings to his close and intimate relationships.[46]

In the darkest days of the Holocaust, Hannah Arendt drew urgent attention to a dissident Jewish lineage, a genealogy that she felt was of great importance for humanity. At the end of her 1943 essay 'We Refugees', Arendt refers to a 'thread of Jewish tradition' centred in the figure of the 'conscious pariah', the 'tradition of Heine, Rahel Varnhagen, Sholom Aleichem, of Bernard Lazare, Franz Kafka, or even Charlie Chaplin'.[47]

In her 1944 essay 'The Jew as Pariah: A Hidden Tradition', Arendt takes up and expands on the story of 'those bold spirits who tried to make of the emancipation of the Jews that which it really should have been – an admission of Jews as *Jews* to the ranks of humanity, rather than a permit to ape the gentiles or an opportunity to play the parvenu'. Out of their 'personal experience Jewish poets, writers, and artists' were able to 'evolve the concept of the pariah as a human type – a concept of supreme importance for the evaluation of mankind in our day'. Arendt selects four of these poets, writers and artists, who represent different types of the pariah: Heinrich Heine's schlemiel (fool figure) and 'lord of dreams'; Bernard Lazare's 'conscious pariah'; Charlie Chaplin's grotesque portrayal of the suspect (in an endnote Arendt records that 'Chaplin has recently declared that he is of Irish and Gypsy descent, but he has been selected for discussion because, even if not himself a Jew, he has epitomized in an artistic form a character born of the Jewish pariah mentality'); and Franz Kafka's 'poetic vision of the fate of the man of goodwill'.[48]

Arendt's methodology here is to focus on individual biographies, teasing out similarities and differences in ideas and contexts, a methodology she also later deploys in *Men in Dark Times*.

Like Arendt, I very much admire the figure of the conscious pariah, which I draw on at various points in this ego histoire.

Also important for me is the figure celebrated in Isaac Deutscher's essay 'The Non-Jewish Jew'. Tamara Deutscher, in her Introduction to the collection of his writings on Jewishness, *The Non-Jewish Jew and other essays* (first published in 1968) where 'The Non-Jewish Jew' is the lead essay, tells us that as a child growing up in the small Polish town of Chrzanow, Isaac was destined by his father Jacob to become a rabbi. Nonetheless, Isaac and Jacob would enjoy reading Spinoza together: 'Spinoza the rebel, the atheist, the heretic, the excommunicated Jew, proved an all too successful mentor for the very young rabbi who was already abandoning religion for good and all'; father and son also read Heine together, his prose and lyrics and satirical verses, which could not lead Isaac 'back to the Synagogue' from which he was already moving away. Tamara Deutscher comments that the 'father himself, indirectly and unwittingly, sowed all the seeds of doubt and planted in Isaac that respect for heresy which remained characteristically his till the end'.[49] (Isaac Deutscher, born 1907, died while visiting Rome in 1967.)

In 'The Non-Jewish Jew' Deutscher argues that the 'Jewish heretic who transcends Jewry belongs to a Jewish tradition', as we can recognise in 'those great revolutionaries of modern thought Spinoza, Heine, Marx, Rosa Luxemburg, Trotsky, and Freud'. They all found 'Jewry too narrow, too archaic, and too constricting'. They all went 'beyond the boundaries of Jewry', and they 'represent the sum and substance of much that is greatest in modern thought, the sum and substance of the most profound upheavals that have taken place in philosophy, sociology, economics, and politics in the last three centuries'. Yet, Deutscher continues, 'in some ways they were very Jewish indeed', for they were 'born and brought up on the borderlines of various epochs'; they 'dwelt on the borderlines of various civilizations, religions, and national cultures'; their 'mind matured where the most diverse cultural influences crossed and fertilized each other'; they 'lived on the margins or in the nooks and crannies of their respective nations'. Each of them 'was in society and yet not in it, of it and yet not of it'. It was this that enabled them to 'rise in thought above their societies, above their nations, above their times and generations, and to strike out mentally into wide new horizons and far into the future'.[50]

In her Introduction, Tamara Deutscher reflects that Isaac Deutscher 'belongs, and saw himself belonging', to the tradition of non-Jewish Jews he evokes in his famous essay.[51]

Dear Reader, I'll close this Introduction by circling back to its beginning. The stress on the agency of certain figures in Simmel, Arendt and Isaac Deutscher's essays, pointing to the ways the stranger, the conscious pariah, and the non-Jewish Jew act on the world, challenge the world, resonates with Pierre Nora's reflections on how in ego histoire there is a return of the subject to the centre of action and thought, influencing historians to be more aware of the freedom, will and desires of the thinking and acting individual.

Herodotus' *The Histories* creates historical writing in antiquity and for the future as international, cosmopolitan and transnational, at the same time establishing the I voice at the beginning of history conceived as world history.[52]

Elias Muhanna, introducing Shihāb Al-Dīn Al-Nuwayrī's *The Ultimate Ambition in the Arts of Erudition: A Compendium of Knowledge from the Classical Islamic World*, written in Egypt in the fourteenth century, writes of the importance of *adab* as an ideal of humanistic education, of sensibility and self-cultivation actively engaged with world knowledge.

The multiple stories of *The Thousand and One Nights* reveals Shahrazad's wonderful creativity of narrative, defying the threats and desire for total control and domination and the domestic violence that mark the patriarch in history, here Shahriyar, her husband the king.[53]

1 John Docker, 'In Defence of Popular Culture', *Arena* 60, 1982, pp.72–87.

2 John Docker, *Postmodernism and Popular Culture: A Cultural History* (Cambridge University Press, Melbourne, 1994), pp.36–50.

3 See Elisabeth Young-Bruehl, *Hannah Arendt: For Love of the World*, second edition (Yale University Press, New Haven and London, 2004), p.116; Hannah Arendt, *Men in Dark Times* (1968; Harcourt Brace and Company, New York and London, 1993), chapter on 'Walter Benjamin, 1892–1940', p.173.

4 Walter Benjamin, *Illuminations*, edited by Hannah Arendt (1968; Schocken Books, New York, 2007), Introduction, p.18.

5 John Docker, *Postmodernism and Popular Culture: A Cultural History*, pp.46–50.

6 Walter Benjamin, *One-Way Street and Other Writings* (1978; Verso, London, 1992), pp.45–104.

7 Benjamin, *One-Way Street and Other Writings*, p.47.

8 Benjamin, *One-Way Street and Other Writings*, p.47.

9 John Docker, 'Antipodean Literature: A World Upside Down?' *Overland* 103, July 1986, pp.48–56.

10 John Docker, *Postmodernism and Popular Culture: A Cultural History* (Cambridge University Press, Melbourne, 19940.

11 Walter Benjamin, *Radio Benjamin*, edited by Lecia Rosenthal (Verso, London and New York, 2014).

12 Walter Benjamin, *Radio Benjamin*, pp.37–40.

13 Walter Benjamin, *Radio Benjamin*, pp.182–185.

14 John Docker and Subhash Jaireth, 'Vision and Visuality', *JNT: Journal of Narrative Theory*, Volume Thirty-Three, Number One, 2003, pp.3–7; Walter Benjamin, 'A Berlin Chronicle', *One Way Street and Other Writings* (Verso, London, 1992).

15 Pierre Nora, '*L'ego-histoire est-elle possible?*' *historein* 3: 19–26.

16 John Docker, 'Of Pearls and Coral: Jurisography and Ego History', in *Law Text Culture*, vol.20, Lives Lived with Law, edited by Ann Genovese, Shaun McVeigh and Peter D. Rush, pp.18–32

17 In Vanessa Castejon, Anna Cole, Oliver Haag and Karen Hughes (eds), *Ngapartji Ngapartji In turn, in turn: Ego-histoire, Europe and Indigenous Australia* (ANU Press, Canberra, 2014), Appendix, pp.289–296, Stephen Muecke provides a translation of Nora's 'L'ego-histoire est-elle possible?'.

18 Ann Curthoys and John Docker, *Is History Fiction?* (University of Michigan Press, Ann Arbor, 2010), p.11.

19 Curthoys and Docker, *Is History Fiction?* p.10.

20 T.S. Eliot, *Selected Poems* (Faber and Faber, London, 1961), p.14

21 John Docker, *1492: The Poetics of Diaspora* (Continuum, London, 2001), pp.86–87.

22 Walter Benjamin, 'Some Reflections on Kafka', in *Illuminations*, pp.144–145.

23 Ann Curthoys and John Docker, *Is History Fiction?* p.30.

24 Ann Curthoys and John Docker, *Is History Fiction*, pp.31–32.

25 Shihāb Al-Dīn Al-Nuwayrī, *The Ultimate Ambition in the Arts of Erudition: A Compendium of Knowledge from the Classical Islamic World*, edited, translated, and with an Introduction by Elias Muhanna (Penguin, New York, 2016).

26 Shihāb Al-Dīn Al-Nuwayrī, *The Ultimate Ambition in the Arts of Erudition*, p.xviii..

27 Shihāb Al-Dīn Al-Nuwayrī, *The Ultimate Ambition in the Arts of Erudition*, p.xix.

28 Curthoys and Docker, *Is History Fiction?*, pp.30–32.

29 Ned Curthoys, *The Legacy of Liberal Judaism: Ernst Cassirer and Hannah Arendt's Hidden Conversation* (Berghahn, New York and Oxford, 2013), p.36; also 112.

30 Walter Benjamin, *Illuminations* (1968; Schocken, New York, 2007), p.255.

31 Howard Eiland and Michael W. Jennings, *Walter Benjamin: A Critical Life* (The Belknap Press of Harvard University Press, Cambridge, Massachusetts and London, England, 2014), pp.670–675.

32 Elisabeth Young-Bruehl, *Hannah Arendt: For Love of the World*, second edition (Yale University Press, New Haven and London, 2004), pp.162–163, 166–167. See also Ann Curthoys and John Docker, *Is History Fiction?* second edition (University of Michigan Press, Ann Arbor, 2010), p.109, and Ned Curthoys, *The Legacy of Liberal Judaism: Ernst Cassirer and Hannah Arendt's Hidden Conversation* (Berghahn, New York and Oxford, 2013), p.171.

33 Raphaël Lemkin, *Axis Rule in Occupied Europe: laws of occupation, analysis of government, proposals for redress* (Columbia University Press, New York, 1944).

34 *Aboriginal History*, Volume 25 2001, Curthoys and Docker, 'Introduction – Genocide: definitions, questions, settler-colonies', pp.1–15.

35 Ann Curthoys and John Docker, 'Introduction – Genocide: definitions, questions, settler-colonies', p.5.

36 Lemkin 1944: 79; Curthoys and Docker, 'Introduction – Genocide: definitions, questions, settler-colonies', pp.10–11.

37 Ward Churchill, *A Little Matter of Genocide: Holocaust and denial in the Americas*

1492 to the present (City Lights Books, San Francisco, 1997), pp.52, 84–88; Curthoys and Docker, 'Introduction – Genocide: definitions, questions, settler-colonies', pp.11–14.

38 *Axis Rule in Occupied Europe*, pp.xi, 79–80.

39 Ann Curthoys and John Docker, 'Defining Genocide', in Dan Stone (ed.), *The Historiography of Genocide* (Palgrave Macmillan, London and New York, 2008), pp.28–29.

40 In *borderlands* e-journal, Volume 4, Number 1, 2005, I published a series of fragments, 'Is the United States a Failed Society?' In fragment VI, I evoke Ann and my trip to New York to the American Jewish Historical Society and the New York Public Library to research Lemkin's archives. In fragment XXIII, I briefly evoke the seminar paper at the Center for Advanced Holocaust Studies at the Holocaust Museum on Thursday 26 February 2004; I mention that I had been kindly invited by Wendy Lower, then of the Center, an historian who is an expert on Nazi colonization in Ukraine and Russia; I add that the original title I had offered was, 'Are settler colonies inherently genocidal? Re-reading Lemkin', however, a couple of weeks before I give the paper, I am informed that there has been some unease within the Museum at the title, and a new one is given to me, 'Raphaël Lemkin's History of Genocide and Colonialism'; in my preamble, I say that, 'The term "settler colony" which I will be deploying today does not seem to be a term often used in the US, in any case its mention often seems to elicit a puzzled look."

41 Ann Curthoys and John Docker, 'Defining Genocide', pp.33–34; Wendy Lower, *Nazi Empire Building and the Holocaust* (University of North Carolina Press, Chapel Hill, NC, 2005), p.19.

42 Ann Curthoys, Ann Genovese, and Alex Reilly, *Rights and Redemption: History, Law and Indigenous People* (UNSW Press Sydney, 2008), pp.111–112, 118–120.

43 Curthoys, Genovese, and Reilly, *Rights and Redemption*, pp.121–133.

44 Curthoys, Genovese, and Reilly, *Rights and Redemption*, p.133.

45 Ann Curthoys and Jessie Mitchell, *Taking Liberty: Indigenous Rights and Self-Government in Colonial Australia, 1830–1890* (Cambridge University Press, Cambridge, 2018), pp.15–16; Larissa Behrendt, 'Genocide: the distance between law and life', *Aboriginal History*, Volume 25 2001, pp.146.

46 John Docker, *1492: The Poetics of Diaspora*, p.86.

47 Hannah Arendt, *The Jewish Writings*, edited by Jerome Kohn and Ron H. Feldman (Schocken Books, New York, 2007), 'We Refugees' (1943), p.274.

48 Arendt, *The Jewish Writings*, 'The Jew as Pariah: A Hidden Tradition' (1944), pp.275–277, 297.

49 Isaac Deutscher, *The Non-Jewish Jew and other essays*, edited and with an Introduction by Tamara Deutscher (Oxford University Press, Oxford, 1968; Merlin Press, London, 1981), Introduction, pp.17, 20.

50 Isaac Deutscher, *The Non-Jewish Jew and other essays*, pp.26–27.

51 Tamara Deutscher, Introduction, p.22.

52 Ann Curthoys and John Docker, *Is History Fiction?* Second edition (University of Michigan Press, Ann Arbor, 2010), pp.19–20; see also Ann Curthoys and John Docker, 'The Boundaries of History and Fiction', in Nancy Partner and Sarah Foot (eds), *The Sage Handbook of Historical Theory* (Sage, London, 2013), pp.202–203.

53 Ann Curthoys, 'Family Violence and Colonisation', *Australian Historical Studies*, vol.51, no.2, 2050. pp.145–164.

My Father, Ted Docker Volume 1

1

Ted Docker, the Communist Party and Intellectuals

Dear Reader, this is not the first time I've tried to write about Ted Docker, my revolutionary Communist father born in 1894, who was a member of the anarchist, syndicalist and Marxist IWW (International Workers of the World) during World War I; a founding member of the Communist Party of Australia in 1920; and a paid functionary of the Communist Party for decades in the twentieth century, one who attained very high positions, including the Central Committee, the Political Committee, and, perhaps most notoriously in the history of Australian Communism, especially in relation to intellectuals and writers, a member of the Control Commission, responsible for discipline within the Party and expulsions from it.

After World War II, around 1948 or perhaps 1949, the year of the New South Wales coal strike, he fell from these high positions, and became an ordinary member in his local Bondi branch. Family lore, as I absorbed it as I was growing up, suggested that my father, apparently in charge of Party members in NSW active in the trade unions, was held responsible by the Party leadership for the disastrously 'hard line' taken against the Federal Labor government, which helped prolong the strike until its breaking by government intervention when Prime minister Chifley famously sent in the troops. This was when the Party was in one of its recurrent 'social fascism' moods, decreed by the Soviet Union-dominated international body, the Comintern (or its post-World War II equivalent the Cominform), demanding hostility to social democratic parties like the Australian Labor Party.

Now, however, I'm not so sure that my father was demoted because of the coal strike. A declassified document, stamped N49056 and dated 29 November 1948 of the Commonwealth Investigative Bureau, forerunner of ASIO, quotes from the newsletter of the right-wing journalist Frank Browne's 'Things I Hear, No.107' to the effect that Ted Docker and Jock Miles, then both senior members of the Communist Party, had lost their positions, My father had been taken off the Party payroll, and had had to go back to work at his original trade, as a carpenter. It may, then, have been a question of a generational change effected by a younger generation keen to assume power.

In 1949 I was four years old. My father was in his mid-fifties, his political career over. He had married late in his life, when he was 46, and he was 51 when I was born. So, I think I can declare with confidence that I have no direct knowledge of my father, of his personality and sensibility, of his tastes and style, when he was at the height of his power within the Party. Ted Docker participated in one of the twentieth century's momentous political events, the worldwide rise of the Communist movement following the 1917 Russian Revolution, and its decline and fall in the second half of the century. As in the TV show *Who Do You Think You Are?* in its British and Australian versions, with its genealogical tree of significant ancestors put on screen who might illuminate the present, I am in search of this pre-1949 figure, this man Ted Docker who was born into the late nineteenth century *fin de siècle*; who had his own ethnic histories, and his own mother and father, brothers and a sister; who was young and made choices.

Rebels to Family and History

I know this search will not be easy. I do, however, have nagging questions in mind that loosely guide this journey, and which I fear I won't be able to answer. Why is it that in some families there are rebels, as was my father in relation to his family, who go against the grain, or much of the grain, of that family's historical existence? Why does this happen? Can it be explained? Am I also a rebel in this way, or in any way?

Think of Jane Austen's *Pride and Prejudice*: why is Elizabeth Bennet so different from all her other sisters, even Jane her favourite and confidante? Why is she so independent, so wild? In chapters 7 and 8 Elizabeth appalls Mr Bingley's fashionable sisters Miss Bingley and Mrs Hurst by 'crossing field after field at a quick pace, jumping over stiles and springing over puddles with impatient activity, and finding herself at last within view of the house, with weary ankles, dirty stockings, and a face glowing with the warmth of the exercise', in order to see Jane when she is ill at Netherfield. Mrs Hurst declares that Elizabeth on arrival 'looked almost wild', while Miss Bingley acidly adds that Elizabeth walking alone, 'quite alone', with her 'ankles in dirt', revealed an 'abominable sort of conceited independence'. As far as I can recall, Elizabeth never reflects on why she is so different from her more socially conforming sisters. It is, of course, a given of the novel. Yet it's also a feature that fascinates us in modernity, one of the reasons why *Pride and Prejudice* is so loved.

Think of Gandhi (1869–1948), one of my heroes of history. (In the conclusion to my 2008 *The Origins of Violence: Religion, History and Genocide*, I suggest that 'Gandhian thought provides hope for the world'; perhaps its only hope.)[1] A beautifully written essay by Leela Gandhi, '*Ahimsa* and other animals: The genealogy of an immature politics', can help us here. Leela Gandhi tells us that her great grandfather's sojourn in London from 1888 to 1891 to study law, had been authorised by the elders of his community in

India only on condition that he not engage in sex or touch meat or drink liquor. Through eating in London's spreading vegetarian restaurants, the young Mohandas Karamchand Gandhi sees on sale in one of them a copy of Henry Salt's *Plea for Vegetarianism*, introducing him to a world of dissident thinking, in what were then very lively if marginal circles in late Victorian and *fin de siècle* England. Such thinking would prove formative, Leila Gandhi argues, for his later anti-colonial and anti-imperial ideas centring in his notions of *ahimsa*. The opposition to kreophagy or meat eating in animal welfare thought and vegetarianism revealed for Gandhi a wealth of connected ideas, where *zoophilia* as love of animals opened out into *xenophilia*, an openness to and hospitality towards outsiders, aliens, strangers and foreigners, including the British Empire's dispossessed indigenous subjects.[2]

For these English radicals, as for the young Gandhi, vegetarianism, challenging imperial notions of meat-eating masculinity, created conversations and affinities with ideas of anti-vivisection, cosmopolitanism (including 'culinary cosmopolitanism', the enjoyment of different world cuisines), cooperative sociality, mutual aid and anarchism, with its opposition to the state. And anarchism, as Leela Gandhi phrases it, influenced Gandhi's 'last, unfulfilled dream of India as an ungoverned society'. This constellation of ideas was associated with thinkers and figures such as Oscar Wilde, Kropotkin, Tolstoy, Edward Carpenter and a particular reading of Darwin's ideas of sentient life as an inextricable web, a kinship of all life forms. Such ideas, Leela Gandhi writes, helped inspire Gandhi's willingness to be idiosyncratic and eccentric, his courage to entertain and live with contradiction. Such ideas influenced the mature Gandhi to define *ahimsa* in a variety of ways, as passive resistance, boycott, non-cooperation and civil disobedience.[3] And such ideas, I think Leela Gandhi is rightly implying, through Gandhi's deployment and interpretations of them, moved from the fringes of late Victorian thought to become central to world thought and world history.

(Leela Gandhi stressing the importance of idiosyncrasy and eccentricity in Mahatma Gandhi reminds me of an essay by Janet Abu-Lughod that Ann Curthoys and I in our *Is History Fiction?* very much like and have learnt a lot from, Abu-Lughod suggesting that world history as a field needs the idiosyncrasy and eccentricity that are entwined with personal vision to suggest new insights and perspectives, inspiring major transformations in how we think about the world.)[4]

Katharine Susannah Prichard, in her gently and affectionately written autobiography *Child of the Hurricane*, pauses for a moment to wonder why she was the only rebel in her large middle-class professional family, the radical who was keenly interested in socialist ideas and joined the Australian Communist Party in 1920 when it was created. Prichard herself can't think of any easy explanation, or any explanation.[5] Families can intrigue with their egregious differences between family members, as we know from the notoriously politically divided Mitford family in mid-twentieth century Britain. Think of Jessica Mitford growing up in her aristocratic English family, with a racist and anti-Semitic father, and two sisters, Unity and Diana, who would become Nazi sympathisers and personal acquaintances of Hitler. Jessica, as she so memorably and wittily relates in her autobiographies *Hons and Rebels* and *A Fine Old Conflict*, ran away from home with her cousin Esmond Romilly and after his death in World War II married an American Jewish civil rights lawyer Bob Treuhaft and joined the Communist Party with its large African-American membership, then worked for a long period for the Civil Rights Congress (CRC), a Communist-led organisation that fought for African-American rights after World War II in a time of terror for American Blacks.[6] Because her husband was Jewish, Jessica feared that when she visited England with him, her splenetic father might shout at him. She never saw her father again.

Think too of the Irish sisters Countess Markievicz (1868–1927), born Constance Gore-Booth, and her sister Eva Gore-Booth (1870–1926), almost exact contemporaries of Gandhi, raised in the late nineteenth century in a prominent Protestant Anglo-Ascendancy family in County Sligo, their father Sir Henry Gore-Booth (an Arctic explorer who tried to find the North West Passage). The sisters would lead rebellious and remarkable lives, lives of courage, achievement and sadness; reference to and exploration of their lives and views will be a thread in the tapestry of the following chapters.

Elizabeth Bennet, Mohandas Gandhi, Katharine Susannah Prichard, Jessica Mitford, Countess Markievicz, and Eva Gore-Booth (more on them soon!) make me think about my father in relation to his family. And they make me think about myself in relation to my father.

I'll now briefly reprise the previous occasions when I searched for my father in memoir-essays I wrote in 1984 and 2011. In each the feeling came strongly through to me that there were a number of Ted Dockers, before and after his fall from power. Also, in each there are anecdotes about my father that are undoubtedly painful and confronting to revisit.

1984: Old Left and New Left

On 26 November 1983, amongst other writers, I was invited to contribute an autobiographical talk on the theme of 'Growing Up in Australia' to the Salamanca Arts Festival in Hobart, and to this day I retain happy memories of Salamanca Place, where we all performed. I entitled my talk 'Father and Son: From Old Left to New' and it was published along with the talks by the other contributors in a special section 'Growing Up in Australia' in *Island Magazine* in 1984.[7] As I record in my opening sentence, my father had died early in 1983, the last surviving founding member of the Communist Party of Australia, formed in October 1920 when he was 26. My talk focused on the political differences that developed between my father and me, especially in my late teens when, still living at home in the parental Bondi flat, I was a young student at Sydney University and becoming part of a New Left intelligentsia that was singularly uninterested in all that my father and his generation of Communists held dear: the Soviet Union as humanity's ideal future, or the necessity of a left political party with a tight organisation and hierarchical structure where intellectuals and writers should know their place: low.

For reasons that I think have to do with my mother's side of the family, with their cultural, theatrical, and film interests, I did not share my father's overriding absorption in the political and economic. Rather I was drawn to literature and literary criticism, had tried to become a poet – a rather sad episode of my teenage years I will revisit later in this ego histoire – and was mainly doing English literature at university. In these late teenage years I also tried, as part of my desire to conceive of myself as a poet, to read Baudelaire and Rimbaud in French, without much success but certainly with fascination, though I must confess that my French pocket edition of Baudelaire's *Les Fleurs du Mal* (a 1961 Gallimard edition with a preface by Sartre), with its striking cover of a painting of two naked ladies with prominent breasts, also rather unhealthily stimulated the kind of erotic fantasies that teenage boys are all too prone to dwell on. (I've just taken it off my book shelves and have it before me; the cover painting is by Gustave Courbet, 'Bathers or Two Nude Women', 1858.) Decades later, a distant memory of Rimbaud's *Le Bateau Ivre* inspired me to describe the unruly carnivalesque Australian literary magazine the *Bulletin* of the 1890s as 'contrary as ever, a heady contradictory cocktail, a drunken boat, a ship of witty fools.'[8]

My life was something of a drunken boat. At university I read works of the Cambridge critic F R Leavis like *New Bearings in English Poetry*, *The Common Pursuit*, and *Revaluation* as obsessively as my father would read Marx, Lenin and the *New Times* from Moscow. At the same time I enthusiastically read the radical American sociologist C Wright Mills who was contending that the traditional working class had become part of the enemy in history, infected with all the ideological features – sexism, racism, anti-homosexuality, anti-hedonism, acceptance of industrial society, obedience to social rules – to which the New Left was opposed. In this view, so formative for my generation in the 1960s, the New Left was an intelligentsia that should seek to unite not with the traditional working class but with the marginal in society, with women, blacks, gays, the unemployed and the oppressed Third World. For C Wright Mills, the working class was sunk in the decay of 'mass culture' and here was a connection, an affinity, with Leavis, though where Leavis and the Leavisites pursued a curious kind of utopian romance with traditional pre-industrial English society with its supposed finer values, the New Left was attempting to bring back into the radical political agenda the importance of participatory democracy, anti-hierarchy, and a libertarianism and anarchistic style that looked back to the Industrial Workers of the World – the IWW, the Wobblies – that the Communist movement felt had been superseded in history by the Russian Revolution; though, as I will later explore, my father retained a vibrant syndicalism, with its ancestry in nineteenth-century anarchism, well into the 1920s.

At the same time again, I was still sort of in the Communist Party because I was born into it and I think I must have gone along to the occasional local Bondi branch meeting with my parents, would read with interest about Togliatti and the supposed independent line of the Italian Party from Moscow, and attend meetings of the tiny Sydney University Party branch, its young students children of members of the Party. There I saw Ann Curthoyshough I can't recall talking to her. I think we must have been in different sub-groups, stirred by obscure ideological differences. I do recall a Party official, Joyce Stevens, coming along once from head office, who told us what the correct Party line was on whatever was happening in the world. What struck me was that she was clearly not university-educated, yet she was telling us young students what to think in our university existence. As it turned out, I left the Party at the grand age of 20. In these student years before my final honours year in English in 1966, when I studied so hard I rarely went out, I was a rather pathetic kind of Friday-night drunk, a beardless youth drinking at the bohemian pub The Royal George near the docks, close to what is now the city side of Darling Harbour. After a party which people at the pub always seemed to know about, I would make sure I left enough money in my pocket to catch a taxi home. Sometimes my father, who didn't drink, smoke or swear throughout his life, and was a habitual early riser from his years working as a carpenter, would find his son passed out on the floor of the flat, the front door still open.

It is painful now to reflect how almost vulgarly, compulsively, cruelly Oedipal I was towards my father in these late teenage years. As I said in my Salamanca Place talk, my father and I would be sitting in the flat in Edward Street in south Bondi, a half mile from the beach, when an Oedipal squall would suddenly burst upon us. I'd accuse my father of complicity with 'Stalinism'. I'd say Stalin put people in forced labour camps, and I'd scream 'Stalin *killed* people! How can you defend someone who killed people?' My father would respond by talking about the greatness of the Russian Revolution, about how the Soviet Union had been invaded by 14 armies, about how the Revolution had changed the course of history (the first revolution to wrest power from capitalism), and about how easy it is to be misled by the capitalist press. My mother would try to intervene and say, 'Don't argue with your father. Why do you do it?' as if the Oedipal drive could be stopped. Our arguments were long and bitter and grinding. I remember once my father suggested that I leave home. He also accused me of using my university education against him, of throwing names at him he didn't know.

In that talk of 1983 in Hobart which became an essay in 1984, I tried to look back on both the Old Left and the New Left and reflect on their historical strengths and weaknesses; I didn't want these reflections simply to celebrate the New Left, or simply to dismiss the Old Left. I would, after all, come to critique the Frankfurt School theorists, who many in the New Left were enthused by, for their contempt of mass or popular culture. I had been upset by my father's death, and upset for a very long time. I ended the essay affectionately. I said that when I look back over my father's life I see a generation of very capable and enterprising people, who in 1920, with little resources except their own energy and vision and a small base in the trade union movement, dared to challenge history. I saw a generation that dedicated itself to a single task with extraordinary imagination, resourcefulness and sacrifice. The members of the 'old left' Communist Party were, I went on, indeed very capable people. In mainstream society they probably could have become mayors and parliamentarians, entrepreneurs and business people. But they had no social ambition or desire for wealth. At times my father was jailed and ordered out of towns by police. He told me that if I were ever jailed, I should make a political statement from the dock. He never owned a house or a car. I concluded the essay by saying that in his role in the history of the Communist Party he may be seen as a stern, unrelenting Stalinist, whereas I saw him as someone who, when I was growing up, was never petty or nasty, who was loyal to his family, who had a mischievous sense of humour and was always making jokes. My final sentences were: Throughout his adult life he was unwaveringly radical. In my adult life I've tried in my own way to follow him.

Thinking about Ted Docker in 2011

In the years between 1984 and 2011, my father gained an unenviable historical reputation for authoritarianism in his attitude to intellectuals and writers in the Communist Party. In my 1984 essay, I had myself anecdotally referred to a memorable moment involving the ANU historian Bob Gollan which occurred after I returned to Sydney after working on an MA on T S Eliot's *Four Quartets* at the University of Melbourne for two years, in 1967 and 1968. In 1969 Ann Curthoys and I were living together in Balmain, rapidly becoming a low-rent abode for intellectuals and writers, and at a party I was introduced to Bob, who was visiting from Canberra. Bob Gollan had been a Communist Party intellectual who left after 1956, the traumatic year of the Soviet invasion of Hungary and but a year after Khrushchev's secret speech concerning Stalin's crimes. On hearing my name, he immediately began denouncing my father's treatment of intellectuals in the Party. 'Docker, that Ted Docker... An expeller, he expelled people.' Later Ann and I became friends with Bob, and his writing on late nineteenth-century American utopians and dystopians like Edward Bellamy and Ignatius Donnelly influenced my conception of the 1890s in Australian literary and cultural history both for my PhD thesis at ANU in the mid-1970s and my *The Nervous Nineties: Australian Cultural Life in the 1890s* (1991).

2011 was the anniversary of the 1951 Communist Referendum, and Ann Curthoys and Joy Damousi convened a conference at the University of Melbourne in September of that year to revisit the Cold War attempt by prime minister Menzies to outlaw the Communist Party, as Menzies had succeeded in doing a decade or so before, from 1940 through to 1942, prompted by the Hitler-Stalin pact early in World War II. For the conference Ann and Joy decided to include a memoir section, with talks by Sheila Fitzpatrick, who had recently published *My Father's Daughter* (2010), Ann's and my old friend Lyndall Ryan, and myself.

In my talk, entitled 'Ted Docker 1951: A Memoir Concerning Three Families', I sketched in contrasting views of my father. There was, for example, Katharine Susannah Prichard's warm evocation of Ted Docker in *Winged Seeds*, part of her goldfields trilogy, published in 1950. Like my father, Prichard was a founding member of the Party; in 1943, she became a member of the Central Committee, with my father also a member. In *Winged Seeds*, set on the Kalgoorlie goldfields, Ted Docker is admired for his anti-racism, internationalism and courage during the race riots in Kalgoorlie in 1934 of Australian-born miners against immigrant communities, mostly Yugoslav and Italian mining families. A sympathetic character Dinny tells us that 'a little bloke name of Docker' got out a 'leaflet urgin' the workers to have nothing to do with the demonstrations against foreigners who were workin' men like themselves', and that Docker and Tom, a local Party member, were 'out all that night, helpin' foreign women and children to get away from their burning houses'.[9]

I also referred to the kindly 'family' Ted Docker I knew as a child, when he returned to his trade of carpenter and then retired. About him in the Bondi flat were a younger wife and a lively young family. Certainly, loss of power and ageing can often be accompanied by a certain degree of mellowing. He had fallen from power in his mid-fifties, and perhaps there were subtle changes in my mother and father's relationship; her activities as a Communist could perhaps receive more attention now, and she was indeed active in the local Bondi and eastern suburbs area, in the Mother's Club of my primary school Bondi Wellington Street, in helping to bring into being a local municipal library, and in the Parents and Citizens Association of my high school. My father, who had married so late in his life, was surrounded by young and talkative children, and he even accepted with very little protest the presence of a modernist painting, a Modigliani print, I and one of my sisters gave to the flat, perhaps as a birthday present for my mother.

It's worth pondering at this point a conversation about art in Prichard's *Winged Seeds*. In her introduction to the 1984 Virago edition, Drusilla Modjeska, while admiring the novel as of great historical value, quite rightly points out how flat, not to say tedious, much of the novel is in its social realist narrative mode.[10] Nevertheless, there is a moment I found very interesting in relation to Communist Party aesthetic debates, so often held to be blindly supportive of realism and dismissive of modernism. The novel introduces into the goldfields two young female characters, twins Pam and Pat, who arrive in the latter 1930s from Britain. In London, Pam and Pat, full of life and passion, had mixed in left-wing Bohemian circles, with Pam's fiancé Shawn, a modernist artist, going to Spain to fight with the International Brigade, where he is badly wounded. Shawn had previously fought against the 'Mosley black shirts' in the East End, being jailed for six weeks. Pam herself is a modernist artist, and paints people and scenes in Kalgoorlie in a modernist mode. There is, however, no authorial voice condemning modernist art. Dinny, a sympathetic character, friend of Sally Gough, the main character of the trilogy, befriends the two young women, who lend him colour reproductions of the work of artists like Kandinsky, Braque and Picasso. When Sally sees the reproductions, she thinks they are crazy, and Bill the Communist, who falls in love with Pat, is at first suspicious, but is impressed when Pam and Pat tell him how many young leftwing artists, writers and intellectuals had gone from London to help the Spanish government, including the Australians Ralph Fox and Aileen Palmer. Dinny learns from Pam that what the modernist artists seek are 'new conceptions of form and light, dramatic reactions to familiar objects, interpretation of the fantasia of memory and subconscious emotions',[11] ways of conceiving a modernist aesthetic that could perhaps be considered in relation to Prichard's striking novel *Coonardo* (1929).[12]

While there are varying responses to Pam and Pat's invocation of modernism, there is no authorial voice in the novel condemning it as a departure from realism: the varying responses are left to stand, and if anything, modernist art is evoked admiringly. Perhaps my father and his rather flinty generation were challenged and softened by this sequence in the novel questioning an absolute belief in realism, especially coming from Prichard, a contemporary of theirs in a lifelong struggle to establish a Communist society. In any case, my father quietly accepted the Modigliani print being installed on a wall in the Bondi flat. I think he was rather amused by the stylized portrait, influenced by African art, of a woman with elongated neck and blank eyes, gazing eternally at a fallen world; a signature image from the Italian-Jewish artist who had been part of the early twentieth-century Paris Bohemia. The Modigliani remained on the wall in the Bondi flat long after I left home, Ann noticing it when we visited together from Balmain sometime later.

(Interpolation! 15 January 2016: while writing a later chapter for Section II on T S Eliot as an Architect of the Holocaust, I was at the same time reading Virginia Woolf's *To the Lighthouse*, set on Skye before and after World War I. Reading into the opening section 'The Window' I pause over a passage where the young artist Lily Briscoe is trying to explain to the elderly scientist Mr Bankes a 'triangular purple shape' on her canvas, which he finds puzzling. Lily says it refers to Mrs Ramsay reading to her small son James; she had, however, she continues, made no attempt at a likeness. The endnote suggests that Lily is painting in a post-Impressionist way.[13] I also think that 'triangular' and a non-representational mode might tell us that Lily is interested in Cubism, which shook world art between 1907 and 1914, beginning with Picasso's *Les Demoiselles d'Avignon* in 1907 and Braque's 1908 *Maisons à L'Estaque*. I think back on Pam and Pat in *Winged Seeds*, invoking Kandinsky, Braque and Picasso, Pam saying that modernist artists seek 'new conceptions of form and light, dramatic reactions to familiar objects, interpretation of the fantasia of memory and subconscious emotions': I'm still reading *To the Lighthouse*, but how well, I think, Pam's evocation of modernism could relate to the cinematic method of the novel. I'll go fancifully further: Pam in *Winged Seeds* on modernism and *To the Lighthouse* could create a triangular relationship with Walter Benjamin when, in his 1936 essay 'The Work of Art in the Age of Mechanical Reproduction', he suggests that film does for optical and acoustical perception what Freud's *Psychopathology of Everyday Life* did for perception of hidden depths in ordinary conversation; the camera introduces us to unconscious optics as does psychoanalysis to unconscious impulses, bringing about a general deepening of apperception for film audiences.[14])

In my talk 'Ted Docker 1951: A Memoir Concerning Three Families' in 2011 for Ann Curthoys and Joy Damousi's conference, I also had the melancholy duty of reporting the very different portrait of Ted Docker that was emerging in histories of the Communist Party and in comments in biographies. In his book *The Reds* (1998) Stuart Macintyre quotes Ted Docker in 1931 saying that the new line being imposed by visiting Comintern agent Herbert Moore, also known as Harry Wicks, that social democrats were now to be perceived as social fascists, had to be accepted. 'There is no room,' Ted Docker said, 'in the Communist Party for slight differences of opinion – we must be on the line completely.'[15] In her biography *Jean Devanny: Romantic Revolutionary* (1999) Carole Ferrier notes that a Party member, Joy Barrington, was 'temporarily expelled in April 1930 for flippantly comparing Ted Docker to Mussolini', though she was reinstated in May after recanting; an example, as Carole says, of the 'self-criticism' introduced by the Comintern agent Herbert Moore. Carole also reports that Ted Docker had once scoffed: 'You don't think we are going to take advice from a writer.'[16]

In his biography of Guido Baracchi, *Communism: A Love Story* (2007) Jeff Sparrow refers to a stormy clash between the revolutionary intellectual Guido Baracchi and Ted Docker, indicating how harsh my father had been in denouncing those he considered dissidents. Baracchi had been summoned to attend a meeting with Party leaders who demanded to know if he was friendly with Trotskyists, and Ted Docker was particularly truculent in the exchanges that followed. On 21 February 1940 Baracchi was found guilty of adherence to Trotskyism and associating with Trotskyists, and was expelled.[17]

In my 2011 talk I also found myself being critical of my father for a reason that concerned the entwined histories of the Docker, Ryan and Curthoys families, histories that stretched back to the 1920s and 1930s.[18]

I had found very disturbing the reading I had done for the talk, particularly as it concerned Lyndall's father Jack Ryan, who in 1930 had been expelled from the Party for not accepting the new Comintern line of 'social fascism'. Yet, as David Lovell and Kevin Windle point out in their book *Our Unswerving Loyalty*, Lance Sharkey and Ted Docker only a few years later brought back from the Comintern's Seventh Congress in Moscow in 1935 yet another new policy, the Popular Front, the reverse of 'social fascism', which was adopted by the Party in Australia later in that year.[19] What Jack Ryan had been expelled for, practising a kind of inclusive radical politics, was now the new line. I was particularly disturbed by an essay, 'The Comintern, the CPA, and the Impact of Harry Wicks', by Ann's mother Barbara Curthoys, who writes warmly of Jack Ryan as a very impressive figure, an able journalist and orator who spoke against the White Australia policy, and was prominent in a trade-union body established by the Comintern in 1921 to coordinate trade unions in countries bordering the Pacific, including China, India, Russia, Japan, Canada, America and Australia. When he was expelled in 1930, he also lost his job as acting editor of the *Pan Pacific Worker*. What struck Barbara was that the case for Ryan's expulsion 'was so weak that today it appears absurd'.[20]

In my Melbourne talk, I said how shaken I was by the implications of Barbara's essay. In my 1984 essay in *Island Magazine*, I reflected that 'my father benefited a great deal from his life in the Communist Party. It gave him friendships, social life, and eventually marriage. As a full time functionary he travelled constantly around Australia and New Zealand,' as well as travelling to England and then to Moscow for the Communist International's Seventh Congress. Now, I said, I think of Jack Ryan being expelled so brutally by a newly ascendant group that included my father. Barbara herself was expelled from the Communist Party in 1970, and we can see her essay as a critical exploration of the culture of expulsion associated with a new line, often a complete reversal, that had to be obeyed. My father participated in that culture; in different generations Jack Ryan and Barbara Curthoys, among countless others, were victims of it.

The memoir session with Lyndall and Sheila was the last one of the day. When it was over, I couldn't join the other conferencees milling about talking in groups. I sat by myself, consumed by a strange kind of misery.

1 John Docker, *The Origins of Violence: Religion, History and Genocide* (Pluto Press, London, 2008), pp.217–218.

2 Leela Gandhi, '*Ahimsa* and other animals: The genealogy of an immature politics', in Debjani Ganguly and John Docker (eds), *Rethinking Gandhi and Nonviolent Relationality: Global Perspectives* (Routledge, London and New York, 2007), pp.17–18, 24.

3 Leela Gandhi, '*Ahimsa* and other animals: The genealogy of an immature politics', pp.19–20, 24, 31–32

4 Ann Curthoys and John Docker, *Is History Fiction?* New edition (UNSW Press, Sydney, 2010), p.249.

5 Katharine Susannah Prichard, *Child of the Hurricane* (Angus and Robertson, Sydney, 1963), p.58.

6 See Ann Curthoys and John Docker, 'Defining Genocide', in Dan Stone (ed.), *The Historiography of Genocide* (Palgrave Macmillan, London, 2010), pp.15–20.

7 John Docker, 'Father and Son: From Old Left to New', *Island Magazine* 18/19, 1984, pp.77–80.

8 John Docker, *The Nervous Nineties: Australian Cultural Life in the 1890s* (Oxford University Press, Melbourne, 1991), p.69.

9 Katharine Susannah Prichard, *Winged Seeds*, with an introduction by Drusilla Modjeska (1950; Virago, London, 1984), pp.30–31; also Ted Docker and Rolf Gerritsen, 'The 1934 Kalgoorlie Riots', *Labour History*, no.31, 1976, pp.79–82.

10 Drusilla Modjeska, Introduction to Prichard, *Winged Seeds*, pp.ix, xi.

11 Prichard, *Winged Seeds*, pp.64–70.

12 See Delys Bird (ed.), *Katharine Susannah Prichard: Stories, Journalism and Essays* (University of Queensland Press, St. Lucia, 2000), Introduction, p.xii. See my analysis of *Coonardoo* in John Docker, *In a Critical Condition* (Penguin, Melbourne, 1984), pp.30–33, 96.

13 Virginia Woolf, *To the Lighthouse*, edited and introduced by David Bradshaw (Oxford World's Classics, Oxford and New York, 2006), pp.45, 182.

14 John Docker, *Postmodernism and Popular Culture: A Cultural History* (Cambridge University Press, Melbourne, 1994), pp.46–48.

15 Stuart Macintyre, *The Reds: The Communist Party of Australia from Origins to Illegality* (Allen and Unwin, Sydney, 1998), pp.164, 178.

16 Carole Ferrier, *Jean Devanny: Romantic Revolutionary* (Melbourne University Press, Melbourne, 1999), pp.2, 66.

17 Jeff Sparrow, *Communism: A Love Story* (Melbourne University Press, Melbourne, 2007), pp. 247–253.

18 For a more detailed account, see my essay 'Troubled Reflections on my Father', in Ann Curthoys and Joy Damousi (eds), *What did you do in the Cold War, Daddy? Childhood, Family, and Friendship in the Cold War* (UNSW Press, Sydney, 2014), pp.87–113.

19 David W. Lovell and Kevin Windle (eds), *Our Unswerving Loyalty: A documentary survey on relations between the Communist Party of Australia and Moscow, 1920–1940* (ANU Press, Canberra, 2008), p.277.

20 Barbara Curthoys, 'The Comintern, the CPA, and the Impact of Harry Wicks', *Australian Journal of Politics and History*, Vol.39, 1993, pp.24–25.

2

A Wobbly: My Father, World War I and the IWW

My father seems to have been the only member of his family who in his generation was an out-and-out rebel, although his brother George, to whom he was close also, seems to have been quite radical. Why, for example, did my father not enlist in 1914 or later in World War I to fight overseas, as many other young men at the time had done? In 1914 my father was in his twentieth year; many men younger than 20 had enlisted.

I do know that two of Ted Docker's brothers enlisted in World War I, both older than him. Once when still living at home, I was on the long hilly walk back with my father from South Coogee to Bondi. We'd gone to Coogee to visit his brother George (whose son Norman Docker would become a prominent figure in the Communist-dominated Waterside Workers Federation). My father suddenly said, 'Two of my brothers died in the First World War.' I always remembered my father saying this, and when I began thinking about writing this ego histoire, I asked Ann the computer whiz (well, certainly relative to my embarrassing lack of prowess) and family genealogist to see what we could find out; I'd make a cup of tea, I said helpfully. Ann googled various sources, including the Australian War Memorial and AIF Project at the Australian Defence Force Academy (ADFA) in Canberra, and there on screen was the information about his brothers Norman

Docker and Henry Docker, my uncles.

In this and other chapters on my father, I will make use of reminiscences that my father related to Ann and me in the early 1970s, when we asked him to talk about his early life. I still have these reminiscences, a little yellowing, in my scrawled handwriting as my father talked, trying to remember events and personalities from 50 to 60 years before. Re-reading them now, they appear to me like a memoirist's gold, giving all sorts of insights and leading me to all sorts of reflections.

I also draw on a family genealogy, 'From Potato Famine to Gallipoli and Beyond', written by Mrs Holmes, the daughter-in-law of my father's sister Alice (now on the family's website maintained by my cousin Einar Docker). Mrs Holmes had invaluable access to Norman Docker's war diary and from both Norman and Henry postcards, letters, photographs, papers and memorabilia. She also drew on conversations with her mother-in-law Alice Docker/Holmes. In 'From Potato Famine to Gallipoli and Beyond', Mrs Holmes tells us that Norman, consequent upon landing in Gallipoli on 25 April 1915, was taken to a hospital ship and then transferred to a hospital in Birmingham UK, where he spent six weeks. He was then entitled to leave and a railway warrant to any town in the British Isles – he chose to go to Ireland, to Kilrush where his mother Susan had come from. In a letter home dated 29 July 1915 he sent to his sister Alice from the Australian and New Zealand Base Depot, Monte Video Camp, Weymouth, Dorset, Norman says that in Kilrush he met cousins and other relations and had a very enjoyable time.

Death of My Uncles

According to the Australian War Memorial files Norman Docker, at the age of 22, embarked from Sydney on 20 October 1914. Unmarried, his occupation was electrical mechanic, his religion Church of England, and his mother lived in Coogee, Sydney. His rank on enlistment was as a Private, 3rd Battalion, Australian Imperial Force, regimental number 916. His war service included Egypt and Gallipoli, and he earned a number of medals (the 1914–15 Star, British War Medal, Victory Medal). It appears that on 6 June 1915 he was wounded at Anzac Cove, and spent some time recovering in England, in a hospital in Birmingham, before rejoining his Gallipoli unit on 11 September 1915. He was killed in action on 11 October 1915 near Pope's Ridge. He is buried in Shell Green Cemetery, Gallipoli, Turkey. There was a witness statement, recording that Norman 'was killed in a listening post when changing relief. He looked around and said: "Well, boys, it's just about time we were changing." He had just said this when he was shot through the head by a rifle bullet and killed instantly.' He left a will, dated 11 November 1914, that stipulated: 'In the event of my death I give the whole of my property and effects to Mrs Susan Docker of Long Bay Rd. Coogee.' His effects are listed as a testament, prayer book, belt, letters, post cards, photo, diary and hymn book. On a Thos. Cook and Son consignment form from Egypt, Susan Docker acknowledged receipt of her son Norman's effects in 1916 (there are two receipts for a package received, one dated 20 May 1916, the other dated 18 August 1916; I think it's 18 August, the handwriting is unclear). Norman's 1914/15 Star and other war medals were delivered to Norman's father Henry James Docker on 9 December 1920.

Four months before Norman died at Gallipoli, on 15 May 1915, Norman's older brother Henry J Docker had also embarked from Sydney. His age at embarkation was 27, his religion Church of England, his occupation school teacher, his rank on enlistment a Private, his regimental number 4376. His unit name was the 3rd Australian General Hospital, 6th Field Ambulance, Australian Medical Corps. The Australian War Memorial has a studio photo of Henry, a good-looking man in a plain private's uniform, holding a kind of cane, taken in Cairo, Egypt. His height was five feet and five and a half inches. The War Memorial also has a photo, dated 13 July 1916, an outdoors portrait of seven men in long tennis trousers holding racquets, which included Henry. The men are taking part, we're informed, in a friendly tennis competition at the courts of the Gezirah Sporting Club, between club members and members of the Australian Army Medical Corps. (When I was telling my son Ned about this photo, he remarked that maybe his and my interest in tennis came from Henry Docker.) He appears to have had bouts of illness, including jaundice, being hospitalised in Lemnos on 8 November 1915. He went to England, and on 25 January 1917 to France. He was wounded in action in Belgium, and died there of his wounds on 4 October 1917. He left a will that stipulated: 'In the event of my death I leave all that I have to my mother.' Concerning his effects, his mother Susan Docker wrote to the army informing them that her son had been presented with a watch by state school officials. Susan received his effects on 16 September 1918, described as: 'Metal watch (damaged) and chain, purse, letters, photos, penknife, cards.' Among his records there is a receipt for his Victory medal, received by his father H J Docker on 6 December 1922, who testified that his son was not married and had no children.

The death of her sons Norman and Henry must have been a dreadful blow to my grandmother Susan, as to so many parents in the First World War, a time of mass death. In his reminiscences, my father says: 'My mother had a belief in education, got her eldest son to become a schoolteacher... he was eventually killed at Gallipoli... so was my other brother, an electrician, killed at Gallipoli – blame Churchill for it.' My father was misremembering here, since the military records show that Henry the schoolteacher died in Belgium in 1917.

Looking at the military records and correspondence, there's something odd going on. There seems to be a three-way tussle between the mother and the father and the Australian Army over who would receive Norman and Henry's war medals. Susan clearly felt that she, not Henry's father H J Docker, should receive any medals and decorations earned by Norman and Henry in their war service, and she refused to cooperate with the army in their efforts to locate the father, even though, it would appear, he was living the whole time in their house in Coogee. I'll focus on the files and correspondence concerning Henry. Susan's position appears to have been that since Henry's will stipulated that 'all that I have' should go to 'my mother', she should receive any medals and decorations. Susan may have taken legal advice about the will in an attempt to persuade the army to agree with her. In the files, there is a letter from Susan Docker, of 'Long Bay Road, near Cemetery, Coogee', dated 26 August 1918, to the Officer in Charge, Base Records, Victoria Barracks, Melbourne, asking for a certificate of death for her son: 'This certificate is required in connection with the obtaining of probate of his will, in order that I may be able to collect all the assets in connection with the Estate.' The army, however, was determined that Henry's Victory medal should go to the father, however long it took. A major who was Officer in Charge, Base Records, Victoria Barracks, Melbourne, addressed a letter, dated 16 November 1920, to Mrs S. Docker. 'Dear Madam', began the major. He pointed out that under the 'Deceased Soldiers Estates Act 1918', the 'provisions of a Will have no bearing upon the distribution of Medals unless they are specifically mentioned therein'. Such mementoes, the major continued, are handed over in a strict order of relationship: 'Widow, eldest surviving son, eldest surviving daughter, father, mother, eldest surviving brother, eldest surviving sister, eldest surviving half-brother, eldest surviving half-sister.' The Major conceded that Susan was registered on the records of Henry Docker as 'next of kin', but he would be 'glad to know' if there are 'any nearer blood relations than yourself to the above-named'; for instance, if Henry's father were still alive, could Mrs S. Docker furnish his name and address at her earliest convenience.

The major's letter sounds like one of those particularly absurd moments in Erich Heller's *Catch* 22. How, one thinks, can a father be a nearer blood relation to a son than his mother? I'm not privy to the mysteries of the military mind, but it would appear that for the Australian Imperial Force during World War I and afterwards, a deceased soldier's effects could go to the mother, but the father should have precedence in receiving the far more important medals and decorations. Fathers are more important than mothers, this woman Mrs S Docker of Coogee, NSW, should recognise, and she should hand over any information she has about how to contact the father. The major ends his *Catch* 22 letter on a polite and hopeful note: 'Thanking you in anticipation of the favour of an early reply.' My feisty grandmother clearly didn't hand over any such information (nor had she in relation to Norman).

The major wrote to his Sydney counterparts, in a letter dated 11 January 1921, complaining that since Mrs Susan Docker had not replied to his request in his letter of 16 November 1920 that she furnish the father's name and address, could they endeavour to find out. And indeed a Special Inquiry Officer from the Provost Marshall's Office, Victoria Barracks, Sydney, in a letter to his Melbourne colleagues dated 3 March 1921, begged to report that he had interviewed the father, Mr Henry James Docker, 'who resides at Long Bay Road, Coogee, and he stated that the deceased soldier was not married, and had no children, and did not especially bequeath the War Medals etc. in his will'. The father had signed a form that the medal could be disposed to him. In the files, there is a receipt for Henry Docker's Victory medal signed by the father, H J Docker, dated 6 December 1922.

Now I think: did this go on all over Australia during and after World War I, well into the 1920s? The army denied mothers the war medals of their dead sons, while insisting on giving them to the fathers, whatever the state of the relationship between them, justifying this action by a bizarre fantasy of a closer blood relation. In her book *The Labour of Loss* (1999), on mourning and wartime bereavement in Australia, Joy Damousi writes in her chapter 'Grieving Mothers' that the 'possessions of soldiers were treasured in retaining memories of the deceased and were important in the gradual process of accepting death'.[1] Something like 60 000 Australian men died in World War I. How much distress did the army bureaucrats cause in Australian families by their stipulation of the superior rights of the father?

On 17 March 2011, on the afternoon of the day that I finished reading the cache of documents that Ann Curthoys and I had deposited in Mitchell Library, I walked down the hill from Mitchell Library towards the Quay, and, acting on an impulse of curiosity, entered the Department of Education building by its back entrance, in Farrer Place. I said to a lady inside that one of my father's brothers was a schoolteacher and that he had died in the first world war. She kindly conducted me to a World War I memorial board to soldier-teachers, and left me alone while I looked at it. There in a list of names was my uncle, H J Docker. On top of the board was etched the British crown, with rays of the sun spreading out from it. The board was dedicated to: 'The memory of the Public School Teachers of New South Wales Who Fell in the Great War 1914–1919 Erected by Their Fellow Officers' – 'For God and Country'. (The reference to officers is a little puzzling; Henry Docker is elsewhere referred to as a private.) H J Docker was also on a longer list of names on another memorial board: 'New South Wales Teachers of Public Schools. Who Served Abroad in the Great War: 1914–1919.'

The Education department lady came back and I thanked her for allowing me to look at the memorials. She said that every Anzac Day there is a service there in honour of the soldier-teachers.

The Australian Soldiers in Egypt

In an essay I published in *History Australia* in 2011, 'Storm Troopers of empire? Historical representation in *Breaker Morant*, Naguib Mahfouz's *Palace Walk* and other war histories', I boldly suggested that since the latter nineteenth century, the psyche of the white Australian settler community is the theatre of a curious tension, between a self-image of white Australians as independent and irreverent and fiercely egalitarian, and an equal and opposite impulse, a desire to be craven towards power, to serve ruling imperial interests, whether the wars of the British empire in the past or, for many decades now, the post-World War II wars of the US. The essay included a critical discussion of the behaviour of Australian troops stationed in Egypt in World War I. In a personal 'final note' at the end of essay, I wrote: 'I do not discuss lightly Australian involvement in World War I. Two of my uncles died in that horrific war, Norman Docker in October 1915 in Gallipoli, and Henry Docker in October 1917 in Belgium. Both had previously been stationed in Egypt. Like many other Australians, I am connected to these histories.'[2]

In my essay I reflect that both Egyptian and Australian writing in the last several decades have seen little to admire in the Australian troops in Egypt. In Nobel Laureate Naguib Mahfouz's novel, *Palace Walk*, there are sharp glances at the Australian military presence in Cairo. The novel, published in Arabic in 1956 and in English in 1990, is set during the First World War and immediately after it, entwining the gathering movement for Egyptian independence, and its crushing by British imperial forces, with stories of a particular middle-class family dictatorially controlled by the husband and father, the merchant al-Sayyid Ahmad Abd al-Jawad, who elsewhere in his life enjoys a reputation amongst his male carousing companions as a witty conversationalist, a refined lover of wine, songs and formidable courtesans and chanteuses.[3]

Here is the relevance of the Australian soldiers in Cairo. Early in the novel we see al-Sayyid Ahmad returning home, after a night of song and laughter, to his wife. Mentioning the war, he began 'cursing the Australian troops who had spread through the city like locusts, destroying the land'. The narrator then drily comments:

> The truth was that he had a special reason for resenting the Australians. Their tyranny separated him from the Ezbekiya Garden entertainment district... He could not stand to expose himself to soldiers who openly plundered people of their possessions and took pleasure in abusing and insulting them without restraint.[4]

Throughout *Palace Walk* the Australians are referred to as an occupying force that arrogantly interfered in Egyptian lives, disturbing public order, a barbarous horde.[5]

A number of historians have also highlighted the misbehaviour of Australian troops in Egypt during World War I. Suzanne Brugger, in *Australians and Egypt 1914–1919* (1980), observes that from late 1914, along with other dominion and colonial troops such as Indian soldiers, the Australians were brought in to maintain the British occupation of Egypt and to safeguard the canal. In Egypt, Brugger notes, the Australian soldiers delegated all menial tasks to their Egyptian underlings who, 'as white men, as Britons', they regarded as an 'inferior race'. They enjoyed being imperial overlords, at all times insisting on their 'personal superiority', a collective consciousness Brugger relates to pre-1914 Australian racial attitudes towards Aborigines and evident also in the White Australia policy.[6]

Their letters and diaries, Brugger writes, indicate that the Australian troops habitually referred to the Egyptian people as 'niggers' and were routinely offensive towards them, their actions ranging 'in seriousness from the vulgar accosting of women, to arson, looting, and rape'. Nothing was beyond the Australians in terms of physical violence or outraging Egyptian sensibilities. They mocked the local religion with derisory parodies of the Muslim call to prayer; if an educated Egyptian expressed indignation at being insulted by an Australian, he would, as Brugger puts it, be reminded of his inferiority when the 'soldier "sunk the boot into him"'; neither old age nor infirmity, including blindness, could protect people from insult and abuse. The practical jokes they played against Egyptians often revealed 'cruelty' and 'sadism'. Drunken Australian soldiers 'wandered in a stupor for days' through Cairo, fighting each other and attacking civilians. And just as characters in Mahfouz's *Palace Walk* regarded the Australians in biblical terms as locusts destroying the land, so also Brugger suggests that the Egyptians saw them as a 'latter-day plague which had befallen them'.[7]

Brugger's general argument is that the Australians placed their convictions of racial superiority, which they felt must be defended in every circumstance by violence, over any wider considerations, to the detriment of the empire they saw themselves as so loyally serving. Indeed, the racism, contempt and cruelty of the Australians were perceived by observers in Egypt as a contributing factor to the March 1919 rebellion.[8]

More recent scholarship supports Suzanne Brugger's critical observations of the Australians in Egypt, in particular their racism. Richard White observes that it is 'surprising how readily ordinary Australians assumed the imperial voice… Private soldiers saw it as only proper that they should have native servants or get "issued with niggers"'; the Australians tended to defend what they saw as 'civilized values with their fists'. White comments that the 'Australians were in Egypt as acknowledged representatives of the imperial power' and that 'part of their role was to enforce Egypt's colonial status'; the Australians were 'armed and made ready to put down' any Egyptian nationalist protests.[9] In

Bad Characters (2010), Peter Stanley writes that many Australians in the AIF in Cairo behaved with the disdain 'white men' felt for what they saw as inferior races. Victor Ault of the 23rd wrote candidly of how 'we thrash the black fellows with whips... Every nigger who is impudent to a soldier gets a hiding... I can't say how many I've belted and knocked out.'[10]

My uncles Norman and Henry were both in Egypt. I don't know why they went to war in the first place, nor how they behaved in Egypt. Whether they participated in such attitudes and behaviour, or quietly resisted or openly criticised such attitudes and behaviour, I do not know.

The Effervescent Wobblies

Reading my father's early 1970s reminiscences it's now clear to me why my father hadn't enlisted to fight overseas as his older brothers Norman and Henry had done. My grandmother Susan felt that two sons going to war was heartbreak enough. 'My mother', said my father, 'thought with my two brothers killed, and I was helping round South Head guarding etc', that he should not go. My father said he was 'about 20 when the war started', and that there was 'compulsory military training'; it was called, he said 'boy transcription', at least, that's what I've written down. My father explained that he was in the 'Citizens Military Forces'. He didn't yet 'have a knowledge of imperialism' concerning the war, but, 'like large sections of the working class', he was 'against conscription and compulsory military training': 'though I think it was a Labor government which brought in the compulsory training'. After a couple of years 'I threw away my uniform'.

Another reason why my father didn't enlist, his reminiscences suggest, is that he was becoming attracted to and then joined the Wobblies, who were famous – or notorious – for opposing the war. His reminiscences chart their rise and fall. 'My brother George used to go to the Domain – he told me of the various platforms, religious people and so on; also, he told me of the IWW.' My father then began going to the Domain, Sydney's equivalent to London's Hyde Park; it was the weekly venue of marginal voices and diverse eccentrics, often drawing large crowds; a kind of alternative public sphere for radical ideas, oratory and wit, as well as, in Michel Foucault's terms, offering ideas for self-fashioning. I sense that the Domain was important to my father's self-fashioning, or refashioning, when he was young, away from his family's inherited Irish Protestant values, which became in Sydney loyalty to the Church of England and reverence for the British Crown. He himself later spoke as a Communist at the Domain, and I recall that he hoped that one day I also would become a speaker there.

My father said that the 'main speakers' for the IWW were Donald Grant, J B King, Tom Glynn, and Peter Larkin, and that he 'knew Peter well'. He was 'carried away' by the IWW position that 'it was the most scientific organization in existence'; the IWW would say they were 'scientific' because they 'organized workers at the point of production'; they were 'against parliamentary action' and 'considered that by the workers being organized industrially they could achieve anything'. My father continued: 'I definitely heard one IWW speaker say we don't believe in all the works of Marx. We only believe in the first six chapters of Volume I of *Capital*, which didn't raise the question of political action.'

The IWW, my father recalled, had 'very good speakers' and a 'big following down the Domain'. He 'got to know' the IWW speakers. The IWW also had a 'hall in the city' and every Sunday night held a lecture there; they would first hold a street meeting in 'Bathurst Street between 7 and 8' and then would sing songs walking along the street towards their hall; my father particularly recalled the singing of 'Hallelujah I'm a Bum'. Like all the other radical organisations, the IWW put out plenty of pamphlets; the IWW 'got a lot from America'. My father explained how the IWW was destroyed and the aftermath. 'After the IWW was smashed up by the Unlawful Associations Act, by Billy Hughes, jailing anyone who said they were in the IWW, we formed and built the Industrial Labour Party, in place of the IWW... we held meetings down the Domain... we issued a paper, and I used to sell it at the Domain... "Industrial Solidarity"... people knew we were the IWW... we couldn't sell IWW literature, we would have been arrested under the Unlawful Associations Act... we sold our newspaper.'

(It was not only in Australia that radicals like the Wobblies were being persecuted by the state. After seeing Ken Loach's film *Jimmy's Hall* while in London in mid-2014, I did some reading in the British Library to try and find out more about the historical figure of James Gralton, and came across a 1991 book by Margaret Gralton, *My Cousin Jimmy*, charting his adventurous life as an Irish social activist, including in the US, Gralton having joined the US Navy in 1909, and so automatically becoming an American citizen. Margaret Gralton records that radicals were under a great deal of persecutory pressure in the following years in New York, with Joe Hill, 1879–1915, being framed and murdered, and Jim Larkin, Peter Larkin's brother, prosecuted for an alleged crime: 'Jim Larkin was in the United States, and was sent to jail for "criminal anarchy" for his part in publishing "The Left Wing Manifesto"'. Jim Larkin was found guilty in 1920, and was 'sentenced to from five to ten years in Sing Sing Prison; Jimmy Gralton was active in the Larkin Defence Fund, working hard for his release, and Larkin was freed after two and a half years'.)[11]

We can register something of the historical drama in Australia created by the IWW during World War I in a near-contemporary text, *How Labour Governs* (1923). Its author, Vere Gordon Childe, later became a famous archaeologist in Europe, but was then a young historian, graduate of the University of Sydney and Oxford. Terry Irving and Rowan Cahill, in *Radical Sydney: Places, Portraits and Unruly Episodes* (2010), in their chapter on 'Vere Gordon

Childe and the Pacifists', tell us that Childe had been secretary of the Oxford branch of the anti-war Union of Democratic Control.[12] Returning to Australia, he joined the Australian Union of Democratic Control in 1916 and helped defend civil liberties against assaults on them by the Hughes federal government; he also opposed the introduction of conscription for military service outside the Commonwealth.[13] Childe himself would not escape persecution for his anti-war beliefs and was denied university positions.[14]

(The Australian Union of Democratic Control was an offshoot of the Union of Democratic Control in Britain, which had a long life. In his *Memoirs from the Left*, John Saville writes that as an unemployed young graduate of LSE in late 1937, he did voluntary work for the Union of Democratic Control, which had been 'founded in the very early days of the First World War by a group of radical liberals'. Its secretary was Dorothy Woodman, and she and the UDC were 'at the centre of the anti-fascist and anti-colonial struggles', including organising the 'China Campaign Committee' following the outbreak of large-scale war by the Japanese against China in 1937. In most of the big cities in Britain there was 'support of the boycott of Japanese goods'; also, the China Campaign Committee booked the 'Queen's Hall in early November 1937 when Paul Robeson sang to a packed audience'.)[15]

In *How Labour Governs* Childe points out that the IWW was a world phenomenon, from its beginnings in the US in 1905.[16] After a split in Chicago in 1908, there were competing tendencies, between those who believed in persuasion, and a more militant wing, called 'extremist' by Childe, who believed in a strategy of direct action in the workplace, including the go-slow, sabotage and strikes. In Sydney by 1913 the militant wing had become the dominant force. The IWW, Childe argues, appealed especially to nomadic unskilled workers who, self-reliant and with no family ties, roved about the countryside to work in mines and railway construction, or harvesting cane, picking fruit, and gaining casual employment in meat works or shearing sheds. Comradeship in the hardships of their working life engendered solidarity with fellow workers. IWW membership in Sydney and Australia generally developed very quickly, so that by 1916 there were locals in Adelaide, Sydney, Broken Hill, Port Pirie, Melbourne, Brisbane, North Queensland, the West Australian goldfields and Fremantle; locals in Australia were reinforced by exiles from elsewhere, including New Zealand and South Africa. Ideologically, Childe feels, the IWW's practices of go-slow and sabotage drew on the 'teachings of Bakunin and Netchaieff', and they were not afraid to admit 'members of the so-called criminal classes'. The IWW were revolutionaries, and techniques like go-slow, sabotage and the strike were necessary in order to make capitalism unworkable.

In a slight tone of superiority, Childe chides the IWW for following the example of the Salvation Army, enlivening their street meetings with 'crude songs with catchy tunes', the songs 'remarkable for their coarseness and brutality'.

Yet Childe also writes admiringly of the IWW's enthusiasm and unflinching energy, their carelessness of personal safety, and their free-speech fights, where members were not afraid to go to prison in numbers; the IWW, he records, 'secured the right to sell literature in the Sydney Domain by simply exercising it in defiance of the existing regulations'. Childe also praises IWW journalism for its brilliance, as in their paper *Direct Action* (established in Sydney in 1914), its editor Tom Barker. Just as they defied the law, so too did IWW members face 'mobs of soldiers and patriot roughs undismayed'. The IWW led the way, far in advance of the vacillating Labor Party, in their unflinching denunciation of militarism and opposition to conscription. The IWW had no respect for conventional political institutions. *Direct Action* exhorted the working class not to put their trust in princes and to struggle against their slave-status; workers should see themselves not as passive consumers of ruling ideas, but as active producers. *Direct Action* vigorously denounced nationalism; if capitalism knew no boundaries of space or race, neither should the international proletariat. The IWW were particularly disgusted by the Labor Party which in their view pandered to nationalism and, in its support for the White Australia policy and the jingo imperialism of Great Britain, actively fomented race prejudice; in the view of the IWW, the Labor Party was calling on the workers of Australia to murder their fellow-workers of Central Europe.

IWW hostility to World War I and later to conscription, Childe records, drew upon it harassment by military authorities, acting in the name of the Australian War Precaution Act, for prejudicing recruitment. In terms of these regulations, several IWW men went to prison, including *Direct Action*'s Tom Barker, who was sentenced on three occasions. Childe now mentions what has become a familiar observation about the IWW, that the organisation turned to incendiarism as a means of intimidating the authorities to release Barker.

There are features of Childe's argument about the rise of the IWW, which he regards as a momentous event in Australian political and labour history, that intrigue me. Childe's reference to 'soldiers' attacking IWW meetings in the Sydney Domain makes me think: what if my uncles who supported World War I were among those who attacked the IWW in the Domain? And what if my father was there on these occasions, either as a member or someone attracted to their views, and helped defend them? Was brother divided against brother? I know this is a wild and fanciful thought, but politics divides families to the point of gulfs and chasms, as in Jessica Mitford's family. However, my father does not mention any such family tensions in his early 1970s reminiscences, and at least in the early part of the war he was, as he says, in the Citizens Military Forces helping guard South Head, the entrance to Sydney Harbour.

I had another thought: while the Australian government was outraged by the acts of arson actually committed by, or alleged to be committed by, the IWW, it appears not to have said a reproving word about acts of arson committed by lawless Australian soldiers in Egypt.

Childe also contends that in general the IWW were not philosophically opposed to violence, since they saw violence, albeit a defensive violence, as necessary in the revolutionary transformation from capitalism to socialism; they would have to defend themselves against the aggressive violence of those in power.

Here I'll leave Vere Gordon Childe and dig some things that interest me out of Ian Turner's 1967 history of the IWW, *Sydney's Burning*.[17] Turner was a Marxist historian of a flamboyant kind, especially well known in the 1960s, who had once been in the Communist Party and was now part of a considerable diaspora of ex-Party intellectuals.

Vere Gordon Childe, discussing in *How Labour Governs* the famous, or infamous, trial of 12 IWW men on a charge of sedition and conspiracy to commit arson, notes that the Crown's case rested exclusively on the evidence of informers who were entirely in the hands of the police; nevertheless Childe was reluctant to concede that the police case was a frame-up.[18] It is this issue that Turner explores at length.

Turner presents his narrative rather laboriously as a kind of mystery thriller with many episodes, revealing near the end that in his view the Crown case was indeed a frame-up, the police concocting and planting incriminating evidence and using informers who lied. Nothing about this is particularly surprising. As a Gandhian, what interests me in Turner's book are various observations about whether the IWW supported violence or non-violence. Where Childe presents violence, even if defensive, as central to the IWW, Turner regards the IWW as more contradictory, with some members given to violence including arson, while others philosophically espoused a mixture of defensive violence and non-violence. In an episode entitled 'Backdrop 1916–1917', Turner evokes a trial, in Perth in December 1916, of two veteran IWW men, Monty Miller and Mick Sawtell, charged with conspiracy. Miller and Sawtell conducted their own defence, using the court-room, Turner says, as a kind of Brechtian stage. In a remarkable speech, Sawtell, asked by his 'Fellow-worker' Miller to explain his philosophy, informs the court:

> The IWW did not believe in violence or the destruction of life and property, although it recognized circumstances – for instance if they were attacked by scabs – when the workers would be justified in using violence. Revolution did not necessarily mean violence; its primary meaning was a total change, as in the Wagnerian revolution in music, Oscar Wilde's revolution in aesthetics. It did, however, mean force; but force could be passive as well as active, as Tolstoy had shown with his teaching of non-resistance. To secure justice for themselves, the workers had to oppose the master class; had not great thinkers like Emerson and Socrates urged that opposition to law and government was the pre-condition of progress?[19]

What caught my attention here was the fascinating invocation of Tolstoy for his 'teaching of non-resistance', which reminds me of Gandhi's admiration for Tolstoy when he was living in South Africa and working out his ideas about soul force, or *satyagraha*, which inspired his great manifesto *Hind Swaraj, or Indian Home Rule* (1909).

Gandhi tells us how overwhelmed he was by reading Tolstoy's *The Kingdom of God is Within You*, admiring its independent thinking, profound morality, and truthfulness. He felt it gave a permanent form to his own notion of *satyagraha*. In 1909 he wrote a long letter to Tolstoy, who noted in his diary that he had received 'a pleasant letter from a Hindu of the Transvaal'. In April 1910 Gandhi sent another letter, enclosing a copy of his recently published *Hind Swaraj*. On 15 August 1910, Gandhi wrote again to Tolstoy, who replied on the day he received it, telling Gandhi of the great importance he placed on the notion of 'passive resistance', which Tolstoy felt was 'in reality nothing else than the teaching of love uncorrupted by false interpretations'. Gandhi received the letter some days after Tolstoy's death on 21 November 1910. During that year, Gandhi had established a *satyagraha* ashram called Tolstoy Farm near Johannesburg. This information about Gandhi and Tolstoy I draw from the text and notes of the Grove Press's *The Gandhi Reader*, a book that is particularly precious to me, which I bought on 11 November 2003 while exploring the Kramer Bookshop in the Dupont Circle, Washington DC.[20]

The next history I read was *Revolutionary Industrial Unionism: The Industrial Workers of the World in Australia* (1995), with its impressive depth of research, written by Ann's and my old friend Verity Burgmann. Verity writes of the difficulty in defining exactly the IWW's ideas in relation to other late-nineteenth-century and early-twentieth radical movements: guild socialism, anarchism, syndicalism, Marxism. In particular, Verity is wary of identifying the IWW as anarchist or syndicalist. She is impatient with the idea that the IWW could be regarded as anarchist for the IWW, she observes, while they possessed a 'real hostility to hierarchical and bureaucratic forms of organization', nonetheless 'emphasised collectivity, unity, organization and centralization'. The IWW's nearest 'political relatives' were probably the syndicalists, who 'eschewed parliamentary strategies and emphasized struggle at the point of production'. Like the IWW, the syndicalists believed socialism 'could only be achieved by workers acting in their capacity as workers' and 'not by proxy either through representatives in parliament or a revolutionary seizure of state power'.[21]

Nevertheless, Verity suggests, the IWW were always ambivalent about the syndicalists, who still retained a belief in the old craft unions. The IWW considered that the craft unions encouraged a kind of elitism, 'a hierarchy of unionists, with skilled workers jealously guarding their status and privileges in relation to unskilled and semi-skilled workers', so creating divisiveness within the working class and 'hindering solidarity'. The IWW believed that the craft unions in any case were becoming obsolete and should be displaced by industrial unions, a new kind of unionism which might one day culminate in the One Big Union which could assume control of the means of production and so overthrow capitalism. Furthermore, Verity points out, the syndicalists 'favoured highly decentralized, even disorganised patterns of protest', a 'decentralized, spontaneist approach' which the IWW rejected in favour of the notion of a 'disciplined proletarian army' which could usher in 'the IWW's new, intricately centralized and highly organized world order'. In contrast, 'syndicalism had no use for government of any sort'.[22]

Verity Burgmann seems herself to share the IWW's disdain for syndicalism and its most famous figure Sorel, author of *Reflections on Violence*: 'The ramblings', she writes, 'of syndicalist "theorists" such as Georges Sorel have little coherence when compared with the very concrete programme of the IWW'. In Verity's view, the IWW should be viewed as quite strictly Marxist in its principles and positions: 'it affirmed an orthodox Marxist critique of capitalism'. Nonetheless, Verity immediately qualifies this statement. The 'Wobblies were not Marxists, pure and simple'; they deserve, she feels, a 'more obscure nomenclature', one which they deployed themselves, as 'revolutionary industrial unionists'. Furthermore, Verity notes, part of the novelty and distinctiveness of the Wobblies was how much they emphasised 'humour, denunciation, iconoclasm'.[23]

Verity highlights some extraordinary examples of the IWW's anti-racism and internationalism.[24]

The IWW, Verity observes, were always critical of nationalism, arguing, for instance, that the leaders of the 1916 Easter Rebellion in Ireland were interested only in emancipation from British domination, rather than working-class emancipation. The IWW, Verity stresses, supported the organisation of all workers, whatever their race, colour, creed, sex or calling. Verity points out that the IWW's striving for the One Big Union would not be complete without the workers of all nationalities and races; she gives examples of their protests against racism, including racism in the labour movement and Labor governments as well as in the press. When the Western Australian Labor premier John Scaddan proposed legislation to exclude Italians from the mining industry, the IWW's Sydney Club wrote a public letter of protest. The IWW's opposition to racism, Verity notes, influenced various socialist organisations also to make a stand. The IWW supported militancy in Australia by Spanish, Italian, Russian, Bulgarian and Chinese workers; since at least September 1914, the IWW had been in communication with Chinese anarchist communist groups. In turn, the IWW gained a significant following among non-English-speaking immigrants. In Western Australia, IWW members were especially active amongst Italian and Slav workers; IWW pamphlets in Italian were imported from the American IWW for distribution in Australia. The IWW consistently opposed the White Australia policy, and they achieved some success organising 'coloured workers' in tropical Australia, who included Chinese, Malays, Filipinos, Japanese, and Shingalese.[25]

Verity is critical of the IWW for its relative neglect of Aboriginal issues, which she believes stemmed from the assumption, widespread at the time, that Aboriginal people were dying out. Verity does, however, quote *Direct Action* when it referred to the 'original possessors of the soil' as having been 'driven off, exterminated by war and decimated by famine or disease, or enslaved…'.[26]

What I concluded from these books by Childe, Turner and Burgmann was how multifaceted the Wobblies were. In effect, they were wonderfully contradictory. Vere Gordon Childe felt their industrial actions were influenced by the powerful Russian anarchist tradition in figures like Bakunin and Netchaieff. Ian Turner quotes the Western Australian Wobbly Mick Sawtell explaining his philosophy in terms of his admiration for Wagner, Oscar Wilde, Tolstoy, Emerson and Socrates. Verity Burgmann insists on the primacy of Marx and Marxism in IWW thinking, but also agrees there is much overlap between the IWW and the syndicalists and suggests that the question of their precise identity must remain 'obscure'. In my view, the IWW can be described as belonging to a broad stream of radical thought that includes the anarchistic and syndicalist as well as the Marxist, jostling together. The Wobblies influentially lived on in historical memory because they were a kind of fearless carnivalesque political and cultural force, fertile in political courage, utopian visions, humour, rhetoric, journalism, poetry and song.

In Arthur Rimbaud's phrase, they were a drunken boat, sunk during the First World War by Australia's cravenly empire-serving federal government; Australia, a supposedly newly independent nation, was a risible entity in international eyes then, and remains so to this day. The IWW was a failure yet not a failure. The IWW as drunken boat, irreverent and enchanting, sailed on, in idea, imagination and inspiration.

Thoughts about Rimbaud

The IWW's anti-racism and internationalism were rare indeed in the latter nineteenth century and into the twentieth. I think there remains, for example, a shadow over Rimbaud's early 1870s poem concerning 'race'. Having just re-acquainted myself with *Le Bateau Ivre*, I can't quite recover from my shock and disappointment at images and phrases in its opening stanza, when the drunken boat who speaks the poem says it is no longer being towed by haulers, for they have been captured by '*Peaux-rouges criards*'. I'll quote the opening stanza from the bilingual edition I have just bought at Sydney's Gleebooks.[27]

> As I was going down impassive Rivers,
> I no longer felt myself guided by haulers:
> Yelping redskins had taken them as targets
> And had nailed them naked to colored stakes.

Here is the banality of European racism in one of its most disingenuous motifs, a reverse narrative where European invaders and colonisers are victims, never victimisers and perpetrators.

Rimbaud is one of my heroes. Reading Andrew Robb's biography *Rimbaud* (2000) reminds me why. There is Rimbaud's interest in a 'derangement of all the senses', which also means a derangement, we might say, of all the genres. Rimbaud wished to dismantle accepted or conventional literary and aesthetic hierarchies. Robb quoted a passage from the prose poem *A Season in Hell* ('Alchemy of the Word') where the poet, in a spirit of intellectual parricide I rather like, says that he finds 'the celebrities of painting and modern poetry derisory', and reveals how much he prefers 'idiotic pictures, decorative lintels, theatre sets, fairground backdrops, shop-signs, popular prints' to art gallery or museum art, making me think of Walter Benjamin and Asja Lacis' *One Way Street* and my own interest in popular culture. Robb feels that *A Season in Hell* is infused with Rimbaud's sense of his life and literary projects as failure.[28]

I'm reminded of the conclusion of Walter Benjamin's essay in *Illuminations*, 'Some Reflections on Kafka' (as I note in my Introduction):

> To do justice to the figure of Kafka in its purity and peculiar beauty one must never lose sight of one thing: it is the purity and beauty of a failure. The circumstances of this failure are manifold. One is tempted to say: once he was certain of eventual failure, everything worked out for him *en route* as in a dream. There is nothing more memorable than the fervor with which Kafka emphasized his failure.[29]

Failure is a sentiment to which I'm very much drawn in relation to my own so-called career.

Robb calls attention to Rimbaud's declaration that Descartes is wrong, there is no stable I, for 'I is somebody else', *Je est un autre*. Robb proposes that a possible key to Rimbaud's universe is a sense of humour. I think here of my own interest in carnival, especially the masking of carnival, concealing identity, creating many identities, playing with identity. Robb observes that Rimbaud saw the world as a kind of theatre, and here I think of Walter Benjamin saying of Kafka, in an earlier essay written on the tenth anniversary of the novelist's death: 'Kafka's world is a world theater. For him, man is on the stage from the very beginning.'[30] Robb refers to a character in *A Season in Hell* wondering about 'secrets for *changing life*' (*secrets pour* changer la vie), a phrase which has resonated through the decades since, not least in the 1960s and 1970s, with those interested in history beginning again with a new consciousness.[31]

Yet Robb also refers to Rimbaud's unsavoury life as a trader in Africa, after he had abandoned poetry in his early twenties. In Abyssinia, Rimbaud joined with other Europeans in the infamous scramble for Africa, trading in ivory and guns.[32] In the Enlightenment, Diderot, in his interpolations in Reynal's *The Two Indies* (in the edition of 1780), warned non-Europeans to beware of colonising and invading Europeans, for they came only to plunder and ravage.[33] In my view, Rimbaud, both in the opening verse of *Le Bateau Ivre* and in his life as a European trafficking in ivory and guns, was a betrayer of Diderot and the Enlightenment at its best.[34]

Rimbaud died in 1891, not that long before the IWW became an international movement. Verity Burgmann concludes her chapter on the IWW and 'race' by arguing that 'the IWW issued the first effective challenge ever to working-class racism in Australia'.[35] The IWW can stand proudly in history, inheritors across the centuries of Diderot's vibrant Enlightenment challenge to imperial Europe's racism, violence and colonialism. The IWW shared with Gandhi a goal of *changing life* by de-centring Europe, attempting to create a worldly consciousness.

Bertrand Russell

Internationalism and opposition to war were singularly unpopular stances during the First World War, when populations on both sides, the British and French as well as the Germans and Austrians, including intellectuals, academics and writers, rushed to enlist or at least declare their fervid support. Some intellectuals did, however, oppose the war, including Walter Benjamin, as we read in Eiland and Jennings' biography. Very early in the war, on 8 August 1914, Benjamin's friend the poet Fritz Heinle committed suicide, an act which was seen by his friends as a war protest and which deeply upset Benjamin himself then and for a long time afterwards. Heinle's suicide was followed in the same year by what Benjamin considered was betrayal by his former high-school teacher, Gustav Wyneken. Benjamin had been attracted to the anti-hierarchical and co-educational pedagogical philosophy of Wyneken, a teacher at a boarding school in Haubinda in Thuringia, central Germany, where Benjamin spent two formative years, in 1905–1906. Influenced by Wyneken, Benjamin argued for a pedagogy that would be critical of conventional schooling, and called for open conversations between students and teachers.

Later, however, Benjamin was outraged when Wyneken embraced nationalism and in November 1914 made a speech declaring that young people should dedicate themselves to the German war effort. In March 1915, Benjamin wrote to his old teacher that by this declaration Wyneken was sacrificing 'young people to the state'. Benjamin considered that Wyneken's new-found nationalism betrayed his earlier, cosmopolitan and Nietzschean ideal of the *good European*. During 1915 Benjamin became friends with Gershom Scholem, and Scholem would remember that Benjamin in that year stood wholeheartedly on the side of the radical leftist and war opponent Karl Liebknecht. On 17 April 1917 Benjamin and Dora Pollak were married in Berlin, and in July 1917 they moved to neutral Switzerland, where they spent two years of exile and isolation from their friends in Germany. The biography also mentions that in Switzerland during the war there was a German pacifist community in exile.[36]

In his chapter on the First World War in his autobiography, Bertrand Russell, then a pacifist (he modified his pacifism during World War II, believing that Gandhi's passive resistance could not work with a regime as brutal as that of the Nazis), reports on his surprise and dismay when he realised how few there were in Britain prepared to speak up against the war.[37] Russell tells us that in the years 1910–14, after the publication of *Principia Mathematica*, he felt his interest in mathematical logic had become stale. He turned more to social issues, becoming increasingly prominent as a public intellectual. Fearful in mid-1914 that war might be looming, he collected the signatures of a 'large number of professors and Fellows' to a statement which appeared in the *Manchester Guardian*, urging that in the event of war England should remain neutral. To his astonishment, the day the war was declared, 'almost all of them changed their minds', including some of his best friends, not least Evelyn and Alfred North Whitehead, A N Whitehead being his collaborator on the *Principia Mathematica*;

in the first days of the war the Whiteheads, he observed, became 'savagely warlike'. There were exceptions, including his friend and lover Ottoline Morrell and her husband Philip, who made a pacifist speech in parliament. A few pacifists began to hold meetings at the Morrells' house in Bloomsbury, which led to the formation of the Union of Democratic Control.[38]

Russell realised, with horror at human nature, that as war came nearer the 'anticipation of carnage was delightful to something like ninety per cent of the population'. Struck by bitterness and despair, he was beset by apocalytpic images of disaster:

> After seeing troop trains departing from Waterloo, I used to have strange visions of London as a place of unreality. I used in imagination to see the bridges collapse and sink, and the whole great city vanish like a morning mist. Its inhabitants began to seem like hallucinations, and I would wonder whether the world in which I thought I had lived was a mere product of my own febrile nightmares.

In a footnote, Russell confides that he spoke of these visions to T S Eliot, who put them into *The Waste Land*; Russell and Eliot were friends, Russell during the war having lent one of the two bedrooms of his London flat to Eliot and his wife, who were then desperately poor. Meanwhile, Russell's colleagues at Trinity College at Cambridge showed their sterling qualities by depriving him of his lectureship.[39]

Russell was, nevertheless, determined to protest throughout the duration of the war, however futile such protest might be. He joined the No Conscription Fellowship; when its original committee was imprisoned, a new committee formed, and Russell became its acting chairman. He remained very busy with the affairs of the No Conscription Fellowship from the middle of 1916 until he was sent to prison in May 1918 for writing an article on 3 January for *The Tribunal*, the No Conscription Fellowship's little weekly newspaper. Russell had insouciantly written that with the continuation of the war he foresaw England and France being occupied by what he called the American Garrison who, 'whether or not they will prove efficient against the Germans, will no doubt be capable of intimidating strikers, an occupation to which the American Army is accustomed when at home'. Russell then continued: 'I do not say that these thoughts are in the mind of the Government. All the evidence tends to show that there are no thoughts whatever in their mind…' Russell was sent to prison for six months, though in the 'first division', meaning that he could read and write as much as he liked, as long as he penned no pacifist propaganda. In prison, Russell read enormously, wrote *Introduction to Mathematical Philosophy* and began work on his *Analysis of Mind*.[40]

We learn more of this event from another autobiography. Dora Black, then a young research scholar at University College in London exploring connections in the eighteenth century between French and English writers, and later to live with and then be married to Bertrand Russell (and thence become Dora Russell), has given a lively description of the hearing when Russell was sentenced. In the first volume of her autobiography, *The Tamarisk Tree: My Quest for Liberty and Love* (1975), in her chapter on 'The Years of War', Dora Black, along with other pacifist sympathisers, attended the trial to lend their support. Black says she already admired Russell for being, great mathematical philosopher or no, a 'mischievous sprite'. She recalls that Russell had been prosecuted under the Defence of the Realm Act, whose offences included writing or acting in a way that might cause alarm and despondency or offend England's allies. In her view, Russell had been sent to goal for his wit, 'because the Government could not bear being made fun of'. When the Prosecutor read out the offending sentences about the American troops as strike breakers and the mindlessness of the government, all Russell's friends and sympathizers burst out laughing. After being hushed by the ushers, the Prosecutor read the sentences out again 'with the utmost pomposity', at which 'we, naturally, laughed all the louder'.[41]

Dora Black's evocation of how Russell's hearing became a theatrical scene, a trial between irreverence and the pomposity of the state, reminds me of Ian Turner's comment in *Sydney's Burning*, that the IWW stalwarts Monty Miller and Mick Sawtell converted their trial in Perth on charges of conspiracy into a Brechtian stage.

In *Eva Gore-Booth: an image of such politics* Sonja Tiernan tells us that while Russell was in prison, Eva Gore-Booth sent him handwritten poems to lift his spirit.[42] Gore-Booth had made public anti-war statements from the onset of the war, and, during Christmas 1914, signed, along with 100 British and Irish pacifist women, an open Christmas letter, written by Emily Hobhouse, addressed to the women of Germany and Austria. Within two months, 155 German and Austrian women responded. On 12 December 1914, Gore-Booth at a meeting of the National Industrial and Professional Women's Suffrage Society gave her first anti-war talk, entitled 'Whence Come Wars?', in which she depicted the horror of war and made it clear that it is male politicians who were to blame for the outbreak of the Great War. Not long afterwards, a Dutch pacifist, Aletta Jacobs, Holland's first female doctor and a champion of birth control, called for an International Congress of Women to be held at The Hague in the Netherlands.[43]

The idea of an international congress quickly gained momentum, and it was arranged that women on both sides of the conflict would meet in April 1915; two main objectives of the conference were to be that international disputes should not be resolved by war, and that women should have a voice in the affairs of nations. Now often referred to as the Women's Peace Congress, thousands of women signed up to attend; there was support for the congress from across North America and Europe, including Britain, Germany, Hungary, Italy, Poland and Belgium. In all 180 women, including Eva Gore-Booth, from Britain and Ireland applied for travels permits, most of which were denied by the British Home Secretary. On 28 April, just before the congress was to meet, the British Admiralty closed the North Sea to passenger shipping, preventing the British delegates from travelling. A key resolution of the congress, which closed on 1 May 1915, made by the delegates who could attend, including from the US, was that women should be granted the vote at general elections, since it was women who were the most powerful force for preventing war.[44]

On 8 and 9 July 1915, Eva Gore-Booth and Russell both attended the Pacifist Philosophy of Life Conference at Caxton Hall in London. Eva gave a paper on 'Religious Aspects of Non-Resistance' where she described the Great War as the most destructive conflict that humanity had ever witnessed. Her speech was later published as a pamphlet for the League of Peace and Freedom, an organisation which grew out of the London pacifist conference. Russell's address to the conference was applauded by the gathering there, some 400 people, as a brave and insightful view of war.[45]

Verity Burgmann intriguingly tells us that since at least September 1914, the IWW had been in communication with Chinese anarchist communist groups, and that on 1 July 1915 *Direct Action* had published a 'heartfelt obituary... to a Chinese anarchist communist, Sifo, who had translated much IWW literature into Chinese'.[46] I'm still not sure what the phrase 'anarchist communist' means; it seems so contradictory, but I was surprised and pleased to note that Bertrand Russell in his autobiography, when describing his visit in 1920 to China with Dora Black, includes a remarkable letter from Johnson Yuan in Shanghai, Secretary of the Chinese Anarchist-Communist Association, dated '6th Oct. [? Nov.] 1920'. I'll quote part of the letter:

> Dear Sir,
>
> We are very glad to have the greatest social philosopher of world to arrive here in China, so as to salve the Chronic diseases of the thought of Chinese Students. Since 1919, the student's circle seems to be the greatest hope of the future of China; as they are ready to welcome to have revolutionary era in the society of China. In that year, Dr John Dewey had influenced the intellectual class with great success.
>
> But I dare to represent most of the Chinese Students to say a few words to you:
>
> Although Dr Dewey is successful here, but most of our students are not satisfied with his conservative theory. Because most of us want to acquire the knowledge of Anarchism, Syndicalism, Socialism, etc.; in a word, we are anxious to get the knowledge of the social revolutionary philosophy. We are the followers of Mr Kropotkin, and our aim is to have anarchical society in China. We hope you, Sir, to give us fundamentally the thorough Social philosophy, based on Anarchism. Moreover, we want you to recorrect the theory of Dr Dewey, the American Philosopher. We hope you to have the absolute freedom in China, not the same as in England. So we hope you to have a greater success than Dr Dewey here.[47]

Johnson Yuan's ironic reflection on Bertrand Russell's lack of freedom in England makes me think of a comment in Dora Russell's chapter on their visit to China in *The Tamarisk Tree*, that the 'Chinese had been deeply shocked to see the Europeans, who constantly sought to impress with their superior morality, engaged in savage warfare'. Dora Russell writes that she 'found the superior attitude of the Europeans towards the Chinese intolerable', and that in the case of the British, such blind belief in their own superiority clearly prevented them from working out a 'more intelligent' policy towards 'the Chinese question'.[48] I'm tempted to comment here that perhaps Dora Russell meant to write 'the British question'.

The climax of Naguib Mahfouz's *Palace Walk* involves British troops in Cairo in 1919 machine-gunning Egyptian students who were peacefully marching in a demonstration against the British presence in their land; the students, the novel suggests, were a leading force in the movement for Egyptian independence.[49] So I was interested to see in Johnson Yuan's letter his belief that the students of China were its greatest hope for the future. It was not a belief that the imperial British wished to encourage; in his chapter on China, Bertrand Russell tells us that in 1926, 'on three separate occasions, British troops fired on unarmed crowds of Chinese students, killing and wounding many'. Russell says that he wrote a 'fierce denunciation of these outrages, which was published first in England and then throughout China', thus incurring the hostility not only of the British in China but of the British Government.[50]

Such was the ceaselessly brutal nature of the British Government and Empire that Bertrand Russell opposed, and which the Australian government, ever keen to report for imperial duty, duly supported.[51] During the First World War the government attempted to crush all internal opposition to Australia's participation, while later in 1919 Australian troops helped destroy Egypt's hopes for independent nationhood.

Conclusion

The IWW's courageous opposition to Australian participation in the First World War was met with such frenzied persecution by the wartime federal government that they were destroyed as an organisation by 1917. Yet they remained influential in historical consciousness. Verity Burgmann reflects that ex-Communist Party intellectuals and historians like Ian Turner and Bob Gollan became interested in the IWW for its anti-authoritarianism and anti-hierarchy, in contrast to the Party and movement that had proven so historically disappointing to them.[52] In *Communism: A Love Story*, Jeff Sparrow writes that Guido Baracchi, in the 1960s and 1970s, lived to see in the New Left a rebelliousness that reminded him of his own youthful involvement with the IWW: 'The exuberant sexuality of the new rebels, their experimentation and relentless bohemianism resembled much more closely the iconoclasm Guido had found around the IWW than the stuffy puritanism of post-war communism.'[53]

Dear Reader, it won't surprise you to know that while doing the research for this chapter and reading about the IWW, I rather fell in love with them as well, though my interest had to some degree been previously piqued by the anarchistic and pluralist Sydney Libertarians, one of whom, Ian Bedford, wrote enthusiastically about the Wobblies from the 1950s onwards.[54] Of the Sydney Libertarians, more later, when I wonder about men and women's liberation.

As for my father, I'm proud that he became part of the IWW. Also, I don't think that IWW attitudes and thinking were simply left behind by the new Australian Communist Party when it was formed in 1920. As we shall see in the following chapter, in relation to Georges Sorel's syndicalism and the IWW critique of craft unions, my father in the 1920s was still very much part of an ongoing heterogeneous radical history, a history that, on the other side of the world, was also shared by Walter Benjamin.

In 'From Potato Famine to Gallipoli and Beyond', Mrs Holmes talks of Susan Nash's life after the war, when she and her husband Henry Docker were devastated by the loss of their sons Norman and Henry. In 1919, she writes, Susan Nash went to Ireland to visit Kilrush and was re-united with members of her family, though she found the visit disappointing. (As far as I can recall, my father never mentioned his mother visiting Ireland after the war.) Susan settled back into the cottage in Long Bay Road; it appears that after the death of two of her sons, she was allowed to live in the cottage for free, as long as she lived. Her husband died in 1933. Because Edward (Ted Docker) was away for much of the time for his work for the Communist Party, including going to Russia, Susan was left on her own, so two of the grandchildren, her daughter Alice's sons James (Jimmy) and Richard (Dick) went to live with her to keep her company. Jimmy was the first to stay, in the early 1930s, and then Dick, when he was 10 years old, went in 1936, and stayed until the end of 1937. Every morning he was required to light a Primus and make a cup of tea and take it to his grandmother, and as he went down the corridor he had to sing 'The Minstrel Boy to the War has Gone'.

According to Wikipedia, 'The Minstrel Boy' is an Irish patriotic song written by Thomas Moore (1779–1852), who set it to the melody of *The Moreen*, an old Irish air; it is widely believed that Moore composed the song in remembrance of a number of his friends, who he met while studying at Trinity College, Dublin, and who had participated in (and were killed during) the Irish Rebellion of 1798.

The Minstrel Boy to the war has gone
In the ranks of death you will find him
His father's sword he has girded on
And his wild harp slung behind him
'Land of song,' said the warrior bard,
'Though all the world betray thee
One sword at least thy rights shall guard
One faithful harp shall praise thee.'

The Minstrel fell but the foeman's chain
Could not bring his proud soul under
The harp he loved ne'er spoke again
For he tore its chords asunder
And said, 'No chains shall sully thee
Thou soul of love and bravery
Thy songs were made for the pure and free
They shall never sound in slavery!'

1 Joy Damousi, *The Labour of Loss: Mourning, Memory and Wartime Bereavement in Australia* (Cambridge University Press, Cambridge, 1999), p.142.

2 John Docker, 'Storm Troopers of empire? Historical representation in *Breaker Morant*, Naguib Mahfouz's *Palace Walk* and other war histories', *History Australia*, Vol.8, no.1, 2011, pp.67–88.

3 Naguib Mayfouz, *Palace Walk*, translated by William Maynard Hutchins and Olive E. Kenny (1956; Black Swan, London, 1994), pp.219, 226–227.

4 *Palace Walk*, pp.11–12.

5 *Palace Walk*, pp.39, 86, 243, 310, 318, 326.

6 Suzanne Brugger, *Australians and Egypt 1914–1919* (Melbourne University Press, Melbourne, 1980), pp.29–30, 69.

7 Brugger, *Australians and Egypt 1914–1919*, pp.36, 42–43, 59, 96.

8 Brugger, *Australians and Egypt 1914–1919*, pp.82–83, 95–96, 113, 116, 120, 126–8, 136–8.

9 Richard White, 'Sun, Sand and Syphilis: Australian Soldiers and the Orient, Egypt 1914', *Australian Cultural History*, no.9, 1990, pp.56–57.

10 Peter Stanley, *Bad Characters: Sex, Crime, Mutiny, Murder and the Australian Imperial Force* (Allen and Unwin, Sydney, 2010), pp.33–34.

11 Margaret Gralton, *My Cousin Jimmy* (Drumlin Publications, Co. Leitrim, 1991), p.13.

12 Terry Irving and Rowan Cahill, *Radical Sydney: Places, Portraits and Unruly Episodes* (UNSW Press, Sydney, 2010), p.133.

13 F.B. Smith, Foreword to Vere Gordon Childe, *How Labour Governs* (1923; Melbourne University Press, Melbourne, 1964), p.v.

14 Irving and Cahill, *Radical Sydney*, pp.133–135.

15 John Saville, *Memoirs from the Left* (Merlin, London, 2003), pp.26–27; also pp.141–43.

16 *How Labour Governs*, pp.131–150.

17 Ian Turner, *Sydney's Burning* (1967; Alpha Books, Sydney, 2000).

18 *How Labour Governs*, p.148.

19 Turner, *Sydney's Burning*, p.73.

20 Homer A. Jack (ed.), *The Gandhi Reader* (Grove Press, New York, 1956), pp.37, 87, 92, 136, 500.

21 Verity Burgmann, *Revolutionary Industrial Unionism: The Industrial Workers of the World in Australia* (Cambridge University Press, Cambridge, 1995), pp.41-43.

22 Burgmann, *Revolutionary Industrial Unionism*, pp.41-43, 49-51.

23 Burgmann, *Revolutionary Industrial Unionism*, pp.42, 44, 51.

24 Burgmann, *Revolutionary Industrial Unionism*, pp.79-91.

25 Burgmann, *Revolutionary Industrial Unionism*, pp.80-91.

26 Burgmann, *Revolutionary Industrial Unionism*, p.85.

27 Arthur Rimbaud, *Rimbaud: Complete Works, Selected Letters*, translated with an Introduction and Notes by Wallace Fowlie, Updated, Revised and with a Foreword by Seth Whidden (The University of Chicago Press, Chicago and London, 2005), Foreword, p.xviii, *Le Bateau Ivre*/The Drunken Boat, pp.128–129.

28 Graham Robb, *Rimbaud* (Picador, London, 2000), pp.xiv, 80, 86, 150, 275, 146-7, 180.

29 Walter Benjamin, *Illuminations*, edited and introduced by Hannah Arendt (Schocken, New York, 2007), pp.144-145.

30 Benjamin, *Illuminations*, essay entitled 'Franz Kafka', p.124.

31 Robb, *Rimbaud*, pp.83, 181.

32 Robb, *Rimbaud*, pp.xiii, xvi, 83, 326-7, 333, 396, 422.

33 See Peter Jimack (ed.), *A History of the Two Indies. A Translated Selection of Writings*

from Raynal's Histoire philosophique et politique des éstablissements des Européens dans les Deux Indes (Ashgate, London, 2006).

34 Cf. Sankar Muthu, *Enlightenment Against Empire* (Princeton University Press, Princeton and Oxford, 2003), ch.3, 'Diderot and the Evils of Empire: The *Histoire des deux Indes*'.

35 Verity Burgmann, *Revolutionary Industrial Unionism*, p.91.

36 Howard Eiland and Michael W. Jennings, *Walter Benjamin: A Critical Life* (The Belknap Press of Harvard University Press, Cambridge, Mass., 2014), pp.23-27, 31, 69-70, 75-77, 92, 106.

37 Bertrand Russell, *The Autobiography of Bertrand Russell*, one volume edition (George Allen and Unwin, London, 1975), chapter eight, 'The First War', pp.238-325.

38 *The Autobiography of Bertrand Russell*, pp.238-240.

39 *The Autobiography of Bertrand Russell*, pp.240-243, 255.

40 *The Autobiography of Bertrand Russell*, pp.240, 247, 254-56, 309.

41 Dora Russell, *The Tamarisk Tree: My Quest for Liberty and Love* (1975; Virago, London, 1977), pp.47, 53, 61–2. My thanks to our friend Colleen Chesterman for lending me her copy of *The Tamarisk Tree*.

42 Sonja Tiernan, *Eva Gore-Booth: An Image of Such Politics* (Manchester University Press, Manchester, 2012), pp.162-63.

43 Sonja Tiernan, *Eva Gore-Booth: an image of such politics*, pp.148-150.

44 Sonja Tiernan, *Eva Gore-Booth: an image of such politics*, pp.150-151.

45 Sonja Tiernan, *Eva Gore-Booth: an image of such politics*, p.157.

46 Verity Burgmann, *Revolutionary Industrial Unionism*, p.88.

47 *The Autobiography of Bertrand Russell*, p.369.

48 Dora Russell, *The Tamarisk Tree: My Quest for Liberty and Love*, pp.117-119.

49 Naguib Mahfouz, *Palace Walk*, pp.492, 496; John Docker, 'Storm Troopers of empire?', p.79.

50 *The Autobiography of Bertrand Russell*, pp.361-2.

51 See Greg Lockhart, 'Race Fear, Dangerous Denial: Japan and the Great Deception in Australian History', *Griffith Review* 32, 2011.

52 Verity Burgmann, *Revolutionary Industrial Unionism*, pp.9-10.

53 Jeff Sparrow, *Communism: A Love Story* (Melbourne University Press, Melbourne, 2007), pp.290-291.

54 See Ian Bedford, 'The IWW in Australia', *The Libertarian* (1958), and 'The Industrial Workers of the World in Australia', *Labour History*, 13, 1967, pp.40–46.

3

The Impossibility of Being Irish: Genealogy, the Great Famine and Irish Protestantism

You may travel far from your own native land
Far away o'er the mountains, far away o'er the foam
But of all the fine places that I've ever been
Sure there's none can compare with the Cliffs of Dooneen

Take a view o'er the mountains, fine sights you'll see there
You'll see the high rocky mountains o'er the West coast of Clare
Oh the towns of Kilkee and Kilrush can be seen
From the high rocky slopes round the cliffs of Dooneen

It's a nice place to be on a fine summer's day
Watching all the wild flowers that ne'er do decay
Oh the hare and the lofty pheasant are plain to be seen
Making homes for their young round the cliffs of Dooneen

Fare thee well to Dooneen, fare thee well for a while
And to all the kind people I'm leaving behind
To the streams and the meadows where late I have been
And the high rocky slopes round the cliffs of Dooneen

'The Cliffs of Dooneen'[1]

In the town of Scariff the sun was shining in the sky
When Willie Clancy played his pipes and the tears welled in my eyes.
Many years have passed and gone since the times we had there
But my heart's tonight in Ireland in the sweet County Clare.

CHORUS

My heart tonight is far away across the rolling sea
In the sweet Miltown Malbay, it's there I'd love to be
So long ago and far away but nothing can compare
My heart's tonight in Ireland in the sweet County Clare.

That August in Kilrush when the rain was lashing down
And our hotel was that hay barn on the outskirts of town.
We were all sick and feverish and Dolan had the flu
But Johnny produced some whiskey and the sun came smiling through.

Those nights in Sixmilebridge when the songs and music flowed
And when it came to closing time sure the lights were turned down low
And the sergeant from Kilkishen he would buy us all one more
And we never left that pub before the clock was striking four.

Lahinch and Ennistmon, Liscannor and Kilkee
But best of all was Miltown when the music flowed so free
Willie Clancy and the County Clare I'm ever in your debt
For the sights and sounds of yesterday are shining memories yet.

CHORUS

My heart tonight is far away across the rolling sea

In the sweet Miltown Malbay it's there I'-d love to be
So long ago and far away but nothing can compare
My heart's tonight in Ireland in the sweet County Clare.
In the days of Sweeney in the sweet County Clare.

'My Heart's Tonight in Ireland',
words and music by Andy Irvine[2]

In this piece of the messy mosaic I've been constructing on my father, I try to retrieve through genealogy his Irish ancestry through his Irish-born mother Susan Nash, the grandmother I never knew who yet became a luminous presence for me from my father's evident affection for her. My father's genealogy intersects with that mid-nineteenth-century catastrophe of Irish history, the Great Famine.[3] The genealogy also involves a marriage in Ireland in the 1860s between a sister of Susan in her Protestant family and a man in a Catholic family, which suggests intriguing questions for me. What did Susan's Protestant family think of her sister marrying a Catholic, marrying out as it were? Did his mother's family speak Irish? Why did one of Susan's sisters die in a workhouse? Did Susan's family in Kilrush share so-called typical values of the Anglo-Irish Protestant Ascendancy, and did those in the family who migrated to Australia bring such values with them? Were there alternative traditions within Anglo-Irish Protestantism, conforming to the Protestant community, or questioning of it, which might have taken new forms and inflections in Australia, where Anglo-Irish Protestantism was a diaspora within a much larger Irish Catholic diaspora?

And another question, for this and the following chapter on the Irish diaspora: Was it, either in Ireland or in diaspora, an easy and simple thing to be Irish, in religious or political terms, or was it always almost infinitely, intensely, complicated and torn?

Death is a constant companion of my father's genealogy,

accompanied by the witnessing of the death of loved ones, especially babies and little children in a family. And mass death featured in the Famine. Despite some lighter moments in getting hold of the genealogy in the first place, much of this chapter has been saddening to write.

In this essay I'll again be calling up my father's reminiscences he related them to Ann and me in the early 1970s, before we went overseas to the UK in 1973–4 and made our own trip to the west coast of Ireland, homing in on County Clare and Kilrush. He was deeply pleased that Ann and I made this visit.

From the South West Coast of Ireland to the Far Antipodes

I know very little about the relationship between Susan and her husband Henry James Docker, my grandparents on my father's side who had both died before I was born. There does seem to be a cloud over the father in family references, or non-references, to him. I cannot recall while growing up that my father ever said one word to me about his father. However, in his early 1970s reminiscences, he told Ann and me: 'My father was a carpenter; my father was English', also that for 'long periods my father was out of work'. On quite a few occasions, however, my father said how much he liked his mother Susan; and, as we have seen in an earlier chapter, both his brothers Norman and Henry who died in World War I dedicated their effects in their wills to their mother as their next of kin. The family seemed to treasure its Irish ancestry; I only ever heard Susan's husband being referred to as 'the Englishman'. My father's mother was spoken of as Susan Nash, not Susan Docker. For his reminiscences, Ann and I asked my father what he remembered of his mother talking about her life in Ireland.

My father said that Kilrush was located near the mouth of the River Shannon, that his mother and her family were Protestant, and were possibly the 'only Protestant family in Kilrush'. The family was 'extremely poor' and had 'no land'. His mother 'got on well with the Catholic children' at school and in the street. She 'would bathe in the River Shannon'. The Nashes apparently had the biggest cat in the district; his mother would remember a fair and 'spruikers'. Susan's 'mother's mother had a dressmaking establishment', and Susan's mother was 'a dressmaker'. Susan would also recall that 'the pigs in Ireland would run in and out of the houses'. (At another time, my father said that his mother was surprised that pumpkin was eaten by people in Australia; in Ireland, she had said, pumpkin was only food for the pigs.) His mother was 'probably about 19 or 20 when she emigrated to Australia'; she was a 'very good singer', sang a song to a social evening on board ship, and was complimented by a man for her singing, who said, 'Miss Nash, I thoroughly enjoyed your song, it gave a thrill to my heart'. Most of the family, my father said, emigrated; one uncle, George Nash, 'became high up in the NS-W Education Department'. When he was growing up, my father became aware that his mother 'supported Home Rule for Ireland'.

I wonder now about the song that the young Irish woman Susan Nash sang on board the ship making the long voyage to Sydney, wonder too if it was anything like 'The Cliffs of Dooneen', which Ann and I listen to over and over in a version sung by the Irish folk singer Annalisa Kerrigan. I respond to it as a song of migration and exile, sad, nostalgic and tender, addressing a land never to be seen again, always remembered as it eternally was, always mourned.

In our visit to Ireland Ann and I visited Kilrush, but we stayed in the nearby seaside resort town of Kilkee for a few days, the hotel allowing us to have a room there even though it was out of season; the hotel was being painted all around us and we ate in the kitchen. Or rather, I cruelly ate huge meals in the kitchen, different ways of cooked potato, deliciously fresh, while Ann, pregnant with our son, lay upstairs in our room, unable to eat, except for some fresh fruit I bought for her from a shop across the road. Your wife is not coming down for dinner, they asked; no, I said, as I tucked into my meal, she's upstairs resting. From Kilkee, we would visit Kilrush. Both towns are in the south of County Clare.

For this ego histoire, Ann did some wizardry on Ancestry.com and we pieced together tentative information on dates concerning my father's parents, both migrants in the early 1880s, one from Ireland, the other from England. On 23 June 1881 Susan Gertrude Nash arrived in Sydney on the *Clyde* with her sister, Harriet; Susan and Harriet's ages were recorded as in their very early twenties. There appears to have been a sister already in Sydney, a Mrs Humphries of Watson's Bay; the writing on the relevant document is a little difficult to decipher. Five years later, on 18 June 1886, Susan married Henry James Docker at St Peter's Church, Sydney, according to the rites of the Church of England. At the time of their marriage, she was living in Woolloomooloo in Sydney.

Henry James Docker was born in March 1861 in Dallington, Northamptonshire, England; his parents were Henry James Docker and Mary Ann Orton. From 1871 his family was residing in Birmingham, Warwickshire. On 28 October 1883 he arrived in Sydney, aged 22, his occupation carpenter and cabinet maker.

From the records, it appears that Susan and her husband the Englishman lived in inner areas of Sydney until 1895, when they moved to the Randwick area of Sydney, near the sea, sometimes in Long Bay Road, sometimes in Elphinstone Street, referred to in the electoral roll records as Maroubra North, though the family always spoke of living in South Coogee; my father said that when he roamed as a boy he would come across Chinese market gardens, and that a son of a Chinese market garden family was a boyhood friend of his. Susan Nash and Henry James Docker had six children: Henry James Docker (1887–1917), George (born 1889), Alice (born 1890), Norman (1893–1915), Edward John my father (born 1894), and Robert (born 1896).

Henry James Docker died in 1933. Susan Nash died in 1940.

Because of my father's warm references to his mother Susan, I was always interested in finding out more about her. In the early 1990s Mairéad Browne, a friend of Ann's at the University of Technology, Sydney, was visiting Ireland and kindly went to Kilrush to look for traces of Susan Nash's family. When she returned to Sydney, Mairéad gave us the notes she wrote down when she and her husband David visited an old Protestant/Catholic cemetery, and a deserted Protestant church, in the town. The scale of the old church, she considered, indicated that there once had been a substantial Protestant community in Kilrush. One particular tombstone had the names of many Nash family members. The inscription on the tombstone suggested to Mairéad that the Nash name was common in the late nineteenth and in the early twentieth centuries, and that there were probably Catholic as well as Protestant families with the Nash name. Mairéad and David also made contact with the Clare Heritage Centre, bringing back information leaflets from the Centre for us. The Clare Heritage Centre is situated in Corofin, a town north of Ennis, the provincial capital of County Clare.

In a folder that I have kept for years entitled John's Genealogy, I've stored a leaflet put out by the Clare Heritage Centre, which informs its readers that the Centre houses a Genealogical Research Centre, as well as an Interpretive Museum that presents a microcosm of nineteenth-century Ireland. The leaflet has various boxes with information. One box concerned land tenure: 'Did you know? Some Landlords held as much as 25,000 acres in Co. Clare, while more than 16,000 Clare families had no land at all!' Another box concerned the famine: 'Did you know? In 1841 there were Eight Million people in Ireland, but by 1861 this had dropped to Five Million!' There was a box that concerned emigration: 'Did you know? That 100,496 people left Co. Clare between 1851 and 1881!'

I wanted to know what the Clare Heritage Centre genealogical records could tell me about Susan's family in the nineteenth century. Contacting the Centre from Australia, however, turned out to be no simple matter, though I did eventually succeed. Dear Reader, I'll tell you how. In a letter dated 27 July 1992 Antoinette O'Brien of the Clare Heritage Centre wrote to me at the School of Humanities at the University of Technology, Sydney, that on receipt of my enquiry (I must have sent a letter) about my Clare ancestry, the Centre had carried out a preliminary search of their records and they had located information about the Nash family. Could I now forward the 'full search fee' and my enquiry 'will receive our full and immediate attention'. I recall that with the help of our Irish friends Mairéad and David we sent a cheque, for a considerable amount, to the Centre, followed some time later by a phone call to them, when I was told that I should not now have long to wait. No information, however, on the Nash family arrived from the Clare Heritage Centre. A long silence set in. I became a little anxious and fretful, not to say irritated. Meanwhile, a year or so later, it was announced that the then prime minister of Australia, the honourable Paul Keating, would be visiting Ireland in search of where his ancestors lived. An article, 'Irish eyes smile on Keating' in the Sydney newspaper the *Sun-Herald*, 22 August 1993, reported that Mr Keating thought his Irish forebears came from Ennis in County Clare. The Irish President Mary Robinson said the *Sun-Herald*, enlisted the help of the Clare Heritage Centre, whose director, Ms Antoinette O'Brien, revealed that Mr Keating's forebears came not from County Clare but from a little village called Tynagh in nearby County Galway. It was now believed, the *Sun-Herald* reported, that a Keating ancestor, John Keating, had been a farmer who was unable to make a living after the great potato famine that began in the 1840s; family members left Ireland for Australia in 1855.

Enraged that such information had so quickly been unearthed

for Keating, who wasn't even from County Clare, I faxed a letter the next day to the *Sydney Morning Herald* (actually, I can't recall now if I simply prepared the fax, or actually sent it, though I'm certain no such letter appeared):

> Dear Sir/Madam,
>
> I was pleased to notice that the Clare Heritage Centre, nudged by Irish President Mary Robinson, took less than a month to research Mr Keating's ancestors (*Sun-Herald* 22.8.93). On 20 August 1992 I contacted the Clare Heritage Centre, sent a cheque for 100 Irish pounds, and followed up a few months later with a phone call, to be reassured that the information was imminent. I'm still waiting.
>
> Now I know what to do. Write to Mary Robinson.
>
> John Docker

Also on 23 August 1993, listing my address in Petersham in Sydney (on the outer edge of the inner west) and including my home phone number, I fired off a letter to the director of the Clare Heritage Centre.

> Dear Antoinette O'Brien,
>
> It has been reported in Australian newspapers that in preparation for the Australian Prime Minister Mr Keating's forthcoming visit to Ireland, the Clare Heritage Centre took less than a month to trace his ancestors. For Mr Keating's sake, I am delighted.
>
> On 20 August 1992 I contacted the Clare Heritage Centre, sent a cheque for 100 Irish pounds, and then some months later rang the Centre. I was reassured that the Centre would be very shortly sending the information.
>
> Since then I have heard nothing.

I'm beginning to wonder if it will ever arrive.

I've enclosed a copy of a faxed letter I've just sent to the *Sydney Morning Herald.*

Yours sincerely, John Docker

I'm happy to report that in the middle of the night, of Friday 27 August 1993, I was woken by the loud ringing of the phone. It was the Clare Heritage Centre; a female voice from Ireland excitedly shouted down the phone that they will have the information for me shortly. Could I get the newspaper not to print my letter, it will be bad publicity, and please could I not write to President Mary Robinson! They had mislaid my file, they thought it was completed when it wasn't, the information is coming. I growled a reluctant acceptance.

When the report came, dated 7 September 1993 and signed by Antoinette O'Brien, Ann and I poured over it with great interest. According to the report, the 'Nash surname was relatively strong in Co. Clare' during the nineteenth century, with 'our Master Index of Baptisms recording 136 families' of that name, including 15 families in Kilrush. After an extensive search of 'all available Marriage Registers for the County', the entry for Susan Nash's parents John Nash and Jane Quilty was found, revealing that they were married in 'the Church of Ireland (Protestant) Church in Kilrush' on 11 August 1841. The Baptismal Registers for the Parish of Kilrush recorded the following children to John Nash and Jane Quilty: William, Sarah, Jane, Catherine, Harriet, Ellen, Susan and George. At the baptisms of the children John Nash's occupation was listed as shoemaker.

According to the Baptismal Register, Susan's birth date was given as 23 December 1855, while Harriet was born on 16 March, 1857. Antoinette O'Brien comments: 'This would make her [Susan] considerably older than you suspected. However, from doing research down the years we find that the vast majority of emigrants falsified their ages for a number of reasons i.e. cheaper passage to Australia, better employment opportunities, marriage prospects etc.' Hhhmmm, I think. This would make Susan and Harriet arriving in Sydney on the *Clyde* on 23 June 1881 in their mid-twenties, Susan 26½Harriet 24. From Ancestry.com, however, we had previously surmised that Susan had been 22 on arrival, Harriet 20. My father in his reminiscences had said that Susan was 'probably about 19 or 20 when she emigrated to Australia', which is perhaps what she told her family.

But back to County Clare. Antoinette O'Brien records that a search of Land Records in the Griffith Valuation Books of 1855 'failed to uncover any listing for John Nash holding property at that time'. This, Antoinette O'Brien comments, 'would not necessarily mean that he did not reside there', for he may 'simply have had no ratable property': 'Here it is important to remember that in Co. Clare in 1859 there were 16,000 families living on less than 4 acres of land while another 16,000 families had no property whatsoever.'

Antoinette O'Brien also points out that the family was composed of Catholics as well as Protestants, recording of Sarah, the oldest sister of Susan Nash, that on 23 July 1867 she was 'baptised in the Roman Catholic Church in Kilrush'. This must have been a kind of re-baptism, because the report had already mentioned that Sarah was baptised on 7 June 1844 in the Church of Ireland (Protestant). Now, in 1867, Sarah chooses to become 'an adult convert', and on the 'same day that she joined the Roman Catholic Church she was shown to have married one Joseph Garry in Kilrush', a Catholic man who was then 26 and was a harness maker, while Sarah was '20 at the time of her marriage'. Over the next 20 years they had 14 children; four of the children died in their first year and another child died at the age of nine.

The report records that Joseph Garry 'could read and write

and speak both Irish and English'. This makes me wonder: did Sarah the ex-Protestant and her still Protestant Nash/Quilty family including my father's mother Susan, speak Irish as well as English? I don't know of any family stories that suggest Susan did. John Nash, who died in 1880, was born in 1815; could he have known Irish when he was growing up early in the nineteenth century?

Startlingly, the report records that also in 1867, some months before Sarah's marriage, her and Susan's sister Ellen 'died at the Workhouse in Kilrush' on 13 March 1867: 'Her age was given as 9 years. "Phthisis and Diarrhea" were cited as the cause of Death.' I stare at this stark entry in the genealogy, and think: why did she die in the workhouse? (My *Shorter Oxford English Dictionary* defines Phthisis as a 'progressive wasting disease', 'pulmonary consumption'.)

On 12 May 1880 John Nash, father of Susan and her siblings, died in Kilrush aged 65. Antoinette O'Brien records, however, that the Clare Heritage Centre's research 'failed to uncover any mention of your great-grandmother Jane Quilty Nash's Death in the Civil Death Register… this would not necessarily mean that she didn't die in Kilrush, her Death may simply have gone unrecorded. In fact it is estimated that there is up to a 20% omission rate in the Civil Registers.' Antoinette O'Brien notes that Church Registers in the nineteenth century 'did not record Deaths', which were 'not recorded until the commencement of Civil Registration in 1864'. As we shall shortly see, Jane Quilty died in Sydney in 1904.

Talking it over with Ann, we surmise that the death of John Nash in May 1880 may have led to immediate economic collapse for the family. Susan's mother Jane Quilty was a dressmaker, but we don't know if she could support the family. More generally, famine revisited Ireland during the winter of 1879–80, recalling the Great Famine of the 1840s and leading to a new wave of evictions, hardship and threat of starvation in the western counties.[4] In any case, it would appear that after the death of their father, Susan and Harriet emigrated, landing in Sydney in June 1881. There they were to join up with another sister, Mrs Humphreys, living in Watsons Bay, who would have been their sister Jane, baptised in Kilrush in 1847, so was considerably older than Susan and Harriet. It looks like the Nash children – including, Ann and I think, George – were coming to Sydney in a kind of chain family migration, supporting my father's view that most of the family emigrated.

Ann and I speculate that George, their younger brother, John Nash and Jane Quilty's last-born, was also on board the ship that landed in Sydney in 1881, and is the brother mentioned in family lore as being high up in the NSW Education Department. More on this interesting brother – my great uncle – in the next chapter.

In 'From Potato Famine to Gallipoli and Beyond' Mrs Holmes writes that Susan and Harriet were sponsored in their migration by their elder sister Jane Humphries; also that their mother, Jane Quilty, believed to be born in 1818, migrated in 1886 from Kilrush to Sydney. Jane Quilty lived for another 18 years and died in 1904; at the time of her death she was living in the cottage in Edgecliff Avenue, off Long Bay Road Coogee, that Susan Docker was living in. Jane Quilty/Nash is buried in Coogee (Randwick) cemetery.

By 1901 it would appear, the family name had disappeared from Kilrush. Antoinette O'Brien notes that the 'oldest official Census in Ireland dates back to April 1901': 'We failed to uncover any mention of "your" Nash family residing in Kilrush at that time.'

What struck me in general about the genealogy is that the marriage of the family parents John Nash and Jane Quilty on 11 August 1841 preceded by only a few years the Great Famine of 1845–50. Their marriage and the consequent birth of their children from first-born William in 1842 to last-born George in 1863 were coincident with the Famine and its long aftermath in Irish history and historical consciousness as well as in the worldwide Irish diaspora. That aftermath includes an ongoing debate among historians and legal scholars which I will touch on in a postscript to this chapter, whether or not the Great Famine should be considered a genocide, its perpetrator imperial Britain. This is of great interest to me as a genocide scholar.

Kilrush on the Shannon

What was Kilrush, the place of origin of the Nash/Quilty family, like in the nineteenth century? I'm grateful to Antoinette O'Brien for including in the large envelope she sent me additional material beside the genealogy, in particular, excerpts from two works that specifically talk about Kilrush. Its history seems to have been split between prosperous pre-Famine early decades of the nineteenth century, and calamitous decades during and after the 1840s.

Antoinette O'Brien had kindly photocopied a section on Kilrush from Samuel Lewis's 1837 *Topographical Dictionary of Ireland*. Kilrush, we learn, a 'sea-port, market and post-town', is '21 miles (s.w.) from Ennis, and 130¼ (s.w.) from Dublin'; the town, 'neatly built', owes its 'present importance' as a trading town to its being 'pleasantly situated on the northern shore of the Shannon, about 15 miles from its mouth'; the chief trade is in 'corn, butter, cattle, pigs, and agricultural produce'. The town pier is protected by a 'sea wall of great strength', which is 'very commodious both for commercial uses'. Steam vessels move regularly between Kilrush and Limerick, and during the 'bathing season at Kilkee' vessels ply daily. In the harbour, ships of war and 'Indiamen' anchor, vessels in distress find asylum, and boats are repaired. The harbour's proximity to the mouth of the Shannon means vessels can put out to sea at any time, and 'therefore it must be considered the best position for an American packet station'.[5]

Antoinette O'Brien had also helpfully included a photocopied excerpt focusing on Kilrush from Sean Spellissy's *Clare: County of Contrast*. Its tone, at times caustic and bitter, is very different from the 1837 work. Spellissy observes that Kilrush, virtually owned by the Vandeleur family, Protestants of Dutch origin, began to develop as a town from the late eighteenth century and prospered in the next century, especially when the Napoleonic Wars led to an improvement in agricultural prices. In 1795 John Ormsby Vandeleur was the richest landlord in the district, his wealth augmented by a 'financially beneficial marriage' and a 'successful piece of political skullduggery with a pocket borough vote in favour of the Act of Union' of 1801. Vandeleur decided to develop the town, and was assisted in this project by a Scots businessman, James Patterson, an ex-gunboat lieutenant who had entered the 'oats trade' in West Clare and then expanded into the shipping business. By 1817 Patterson owned a steamboat, *Lady of the Shannon*, which operated between Limerick and Kilrush and his business also benefited from the increasing popularity of Kilkee as a bathing resort.[6]

Spellissy then evokes the horror, devastation and mass death of the 1840s that ended the 'boom time'. The Kilrush Workhouse, Spellissy writes, opened in December 1841 and was built to accommodate 800 people, but, as the 'Great Hunger' sharpened, extra refuges were built, including a 'fever hospital'. The Famine worsened in its social effects when 'tenant farmers and cottiers' unable to pay their rents, were evicted, some '20,000 people' being 'driven from their homes' between 1847 and 1849. The majority of those evicted died of starvation. Thousands of people poured into the workhouse as a last resort; at one stage, '5,000 people were enrolled as inmates'. With famine and eviction came 'fever and cholera'. Even in 1851, 'fifty people or more' were 'dying each week' in Kilrush. At the height of the 'Great Hunger the Fever Hospital had become known as the "slaughterhouse"'. Starvation, fever and cholera reduced the 'population of south-west Clare to such an extent that it never attained its pre-famine number'. From the 1840s until the 1960s emigration also 'drained the inhabitants out of the region'.[7]

The Clare Heritage Centre genealogy report records that in 1867 Susan Nash's sister Ellen, nine years old, 'died at the Workhouse in Kilrush' from consumption and 'diarrhea'. I think: did she die in the fever-hospital section of the Kilrush workhouse, die there because she was too infectious to die at home with those who loved her?

There are intriguing aspects to Spellissy's evocation of the history of Kilrush and County Clare, in particular of its society becoming increasingly radicalised in opposition to the domination of the town by the Vandeleur family. Most of those evicted in Kilrush and surrounds were Vandeleur tenants, but in '1848 there was little resistance', the tenants were unorganised and had little or no legal help; those evicted were 'wretchedly poor and their houses generally were mud cabins'. However, the Vandeleur evictions of the late 1880s were resisted. Spellissy observes that evictions in Kilrush and other evictions throughout West Clare that began in October 1887 continued until the end of July 1888. Those evicted 'would have been well-off in normal times' and their houses were solid buildings; those doing the evicting were compelled to use a 'battering ram' in order to force an entrance and 'then destroy the house'. These evictions now drew large crowds, the tenants had able legal representation and were organised by the National League and Plan of Campaign. Eventually, Spellissy observes, the 'power of the Vandeleurs' would be broken, along with that of the Pattersons.[8]

In the final sentence of his pages on Kilrush, Spellissy makes an enigmatic reference to 'the Kilrush Soviet'. I was not a little astonished by this, and immediately googled. It appears that between 1919 to 1923, the years of the War of Independence and the Civil War – the time when on the other side of the world my father was helping establish the new Australian Communist Party – there were soviets all over Ireland. Spellissy says no more than that the Kilrush Soviet is now 'all but forgotten'.[9]

Irish Protestant Historical Consciousness

I was so intrigued by Spellissy's reference to a Kilrush Soviet – that I decided to try to find out more about south-west Ireland in the early twentieth century. I was pleased to see that the focus of David Fitzpatrick's *Politics and Irish Life 1913–1921: Provincial Experience of War and Revolution* (1977) is on County Clare, though as far as I can detect it doesn't mention the Kilrush Soviet. County Clare, Fitzpatrick notes in his prologue, has been 'subjected to more intensive sociological and anthropological analysis than any other part of rural Ireland'; in his book he hopes to illuminate, through study of a particular county, Ireland's early twentieth-century history as a period when its rural society rose up against continued British rule. What is distinctive about County Clare, he feels, is that it is something of an 'island, unusually isolated from its neighbours', and an island in another sense, relatively uninterested in Dublin, as if Dublin were the 'spiritual capital of Ireland'. Instead, Clare people either looked inward or outwards, centring their hopes and dreams in what they could achieve in Clare itself, or emigrating, mostly across the Atlantic. The 1911 census, Fitzpatrick's prologue adds, confirms that Clare was mainly an agricultural society; the county was 98% Roman Catholic; its rate of emigration was high; and one third or more could speak Irish.[10]

What caught my eye in Fitzpatrick's book was its portrait of Protestant social values and sensibility in County Clare. In his second chapter, 'Protestants and Unionists' Fitzpatrick argues that by the early years of the twentieth century the Protestant 'Clare Ascendancy' had come to an end, the Church of Ireland had long been disestablished (during 1868 to 1874, by Gladstone), much of Protestant-owned land 'surrendered to former tenants' and its political influence diminished by democratic reforms. The 'old social pre-eminence' of the Protestants, who in their own view had brought 'civilization' to the 'barren west of Ireland' and indeed 'defended civilization and Empire throughout the world', was fast receding. Furthermore, Fitzpatrick notes, Clare's proportion of Protestants in the nineteenth century, even in the towns, was in any case small, and had been declining rapidly in the latter part of the century and into the new.[11]

Clare Protestants in the nineteenth century, Fitzpatrick reflects, had enjoyed 'economic importance' and social prestige, as 'landlords, employers, large consumers and ratepayers, and even cottage industrialists'. They formed a community of their own, their own world, largely insulated from the 'much larger… community of Catholic Nationalists'. Wherever possible, the Protestant landowning gentry dealt with their co-religionists; the gentry were served by Protestant doctors, bankers, engineers and surveyors as well as clergymen, civil servants, domestic servants and shopkeepers. Politically, Protestants were Unionists in relation to Britain: 'Rejection of Unionism by a Protestant was socially as suicidal as that of Nationalism by a Catholic.' Even to 'espouse the Home Rule cause was considered foulest treachery'.[12]

Protestants' sense of community and solidarity was also fostered and strengthened by the Church of Ireland, which, Fitzpatrick feels, often revealed a 'slightly ridiculous institutional arrogance', in relation not only to Catholicism but also to other Protestant denominations. Clare Protestants clung tenaciously to membership of the Church of Ireland, so much so that to leave the Church was to 'repudiate one's membership of the Protestant community' and the 'sense of status that went with it'. Conversion to Catholicism could bring shame and scandal to a Protestant family, who would have to protect their other children by letting her or him pass out of their lives.[13]

Reading Fitzpatrick's evocation of Clare Protestant social,

political and religious consciousness, I wonder about my father's family in Kilrush. My father in his reminiscences said that the Nash family did not own any property, which is confirmed by the genealogy sent by the Clare Heritage Centre. He also said that they were 'extremely poor'. But now I wonder about this. John Nash was a shoemaker according to the genealogy report, and Jane Quilty like her mother a dressmaker. Their circumstances must have been modest, even extremely poor – for Protestants. John Nash and Jane Quilty in their separate occupations could have served the Protestant community; such could have been a buffer between their having continuing livelihoods and the homelessness and starvation that devastated so many in Clare in the mid-century during the Famine.

Yet, they must have been poor. Wouldn't continuing poverty help explain why nine-year-old Ellen, ill as she was, died in the workhouse? Sometimes you feel like shaking the Genealogy Tree, pleading and beseeching, tell us more, tell us more. I'm reminded of Ann Curthoys and my chapter on Herodotus in our *Is History Fiction?*, where we talk about the Pythia in the ancient Greek world created in *The Histories*, who delivers to those seeking knowledge from the oracle a riddling answer always in need of interpretation, and so often misinterpreted.[14] Am I misinterpreting the genealogy here in regard to nine-year-old Ellen?

Then there is Sarah, Susan's sister, the Catholic convert. As the genealogy records, on 23 July 1867, Sarah Nash was baptized in the Roman Catholic Church in Kilrush and then married Joseph Garry, a Catholic. How was Sarah then treated by her Protestant family? Did they feel they had to lose contact with her, since her action may have brought shame and dishonour upon the family in the eyes of their fellow Church of Ireland Protestants? If they defied their Protestant community in this regard, they might have risked ostracism and the loss of the economic basis of their lives during desperate times.

Nonetheless, maybe David Fitzpatrick makes too sharp a distinction between the Protestant and Catholic communities in nineteenth-century County Clare. In his reminiscences, my father says that Susan Nash got on well with Catholic children at school and in the street; also, my father adds, his 'mother supported Home Rule in Ireland'. My father must have heard his mother say this when he was growing up in the early twentieth century when so much had happened and was happening in Ireland for the diaspora to think and talk about. Susan Nash may have been an independent-minded young woman in County Clare before she migrated in 1881, and had supported Home Rule then, despite David Fitzpatrick's certainty that for Clare Protestants even to 'espouse the Home Rule cause was considered foulest treachery'. Her support for Home Rule may have been longstanding, as was her Protestantism. My father recalled that his 'mother was religious' and 'stayed religious all her life'.

David Fitzpatrick himself points out that Irish Protestant political consciousness was not necessarily unified in the late nineteenth century and early twentieth century. Even if very few Protestants followed it, there was a dissident Protestant tradition of 'supporting and attempting to remould according to their own vision the separatist movement'; he mentions famous examples like W B Yeats, Maud Gonne and Constance Gore-Booth.[15] He could also have mentioned Eva Gore-Booth, Constance's younger sister.

Constance and Eva Gore-Booth

I mentioned in Chapter 1 the Irish sisters Countess Markievicz (1868–1927), born Constance Gore-Booth, and her sister Eva Gore-Booth (1870–1926), raised in the late nineteenth century in a prominent Protestant Anglo-Ascendancy family in County Sligo, who would lead remarkable lives. In Chapter 2 I mentioned Eva Gore-Booth sending handwritten poems to Bertrand Russell to lift his spirit while he was in prison, Eva sharing his anti-war stance and pacifism.

Constance married a Polish count and became a famous Irish feminist and republican; an expert markswoman, she participated in the 1916 Easter Rising which proclaimed an Irish Republic, imprisoned for her prominent part in it. Although persecuted by the British, an Irish republican parliament, the Dail Eireann, was inaugurated in January 1919 with Constance an elected member though she was still in a British jail. Constance opposed Irish military service for the British Empire. In 1909 she had given a lecture, 'Women, Ideals and the Nation', where she asked the women of Ireland to 'discourage their boys from enlisting in the British Army', which she referred to as a 'mercenary army', the 'most immoral army in the world'. When Constance was released from prison in England in March 1919 she returned to Ireland. During that year the 1909 anti-enlistment speech was reprinted. In December 1921 Dail representatives at a conference in London agreed to a compromise with the British prime minister Lloyd George, a treaty establishing not a republic but an Irish Free State which would have the same status within the empire as Canada and Australia. The treaty, which demanded that members of the parliament of the Free State be required to take an oath of allegiance to the crown, was the cause of bitter divisions in Ireland. In her speech to the Dail Constance opposed acceptance of the treaty, telling the assembly she would 'sooner die than give a declaration of fidelity to King George and the British Empire', because 'if we pledge our allegiance... this is treading down the people of Egypt and India'.[16]

Eva Gore-Booth also rebelled against her inherited Protestant Ascendancy values in Ireland, becoming a poet, dramatist, feminist, political radical and a gender and sexual visionary. In a 2011 essay 'Challenging Presumptions of Heterosexuality: Eva Gore-Booth, A Biographical Case Study', Sonja Tiernan argues that Eva, who published 19 volumes of poetry, drama, and philosophical prose, and was a significant figure in the Irish literary revival, has been unfairly slighted in literary and political history, in large part because of biographers' heterosexist unwillingness to accept that she had been in a life-long lesbian relationship with her partner Esther Roper. Tiernan writes that shortly after Eva and Esther met in Italy, where they were both recuperating from illness, Eva rejected her aristocratic life at Lissadell House in Sligo and in 1896 moved to the industrial quarters of Manchester to set up house with Esther, and they remained inseparable until Eva's death 30 years later in 1926. In England Eva proved an 'influential and vibrant political activist', orchestrating the electoral defeat of Winston Churchill, then a Liberal Party MP; campaigning for pacifism, Irish freedom from Britain, women's suffrage, trade unions for women, and animal rights; and becoming an inspiration for previously marginalised women workers, including 'barmaids, circus performers, and flower sellers'.[17]

In her biography *Eva Gore-Booth: An image of such politics* (2012), Sonja Tiernan presents a detailed evocation of Eva's life as a life-long rebel, her literary, theatrical, religious and political interests intersecting with many histories: Ireland and England, Celtic mythology and the Celtic Twilight, mysticism and the occult, feminism including in relation to the Celtic Twilight and Irish theatre, cosmopolitanism and internationalism, and vegetarianism and anti-vivisection. There are sharp gender differences with W B Yeats in literary interpretations of the Celtic Twilight, which I will touch on. In Eva Tiernan discerns features of a life as controversial as that of Constance, but in different ways, in particular that Eva unlike Constance was a pacifist and believed in non-violence; the sisters, however, were very close and assisted each other in crises whenever they could.

Tiernan's biography creates a portrait of Eva and Constance's upbringing in the Gore-Booth family home in County Sligo.

Lissadell House and its surrounds help explain Eva and Constance's later lives of feminism and radicalism. At Lissadell, the sisters became expert horsewomen while riding and hunting. When in 1908 Winston Churchill, then a Liberal, stood for the seat of Manchester North-West on a platform that included restricting barmaids' right to employment, a controversial issue of the day, Eva, who had established the Barmaids' Political Defence League, launched a determined campaign in opposition to Churchill. She invited Constance to Manchester to help with electioneering, Constance driving a coach around holding a whip, drawn by four white horses. At a subsequent public meeting, Constance was heckled by a man in the crowd, who cried out, 'Can you cook a dinner?' 'Certainly,' Constance replied, cracking her whip, 'can you drive a coach and four?'[18]

For the sisters, Lissadell, as they grew up, became associated with a cultural geography infused with mythological suggestions of female power. On their horse rides the sisters often stopped to talk with the local tenant farmers, learning from them Celtic legends local to Sligo, in particular, stories and legends of Maeve, the High Queen of Connacht, who was reputedly buried on the cairn of Knocknaree Mountain, which was not far from Lissadell House. Later, Constance, who felt a special affinity with the warrior queen, would name her only daughter Maeve Markievicz, while Eva would write plays which, Tiernan says, partook of the Celtic literary revival style but interpreted Celtic themes in feminist terms by turning upside down conventional gender hierarchies, exploring and presenting female characters from Celtic mythology such as Maeve as central to the drama.[19]

Her first play, *Unseen Kings* (1904), for example, its subtitle 'the enchantment of Cuculain', was radically different from the interpretations of the Cuculain story by male authors, as in W B Yeats' play *The Death of Cuculain*, where Maeve, Cuculain's main adversary, never appears on stage. In 190, Eva's play *The Triumph of Maeve: a Romance*, was published, one that Tiernan suggests, values pacifism and highlights the brutality and inhumanity of war. All the main characters are female: Maeve, her daughter Fionavar, and the female warriors; the mother-daughter relationship of Maeve and Fionavar becomes central to the story, creating consternation in the Irish Literary Society in Dublin some years later when she chose to read from the play. (When, however, Eva's Irish song cycle *Maeve* was set to music and performed in public in 1910, the performance was acclaimed in reviews in the *Manchester Guardian*.)[20]

Eva's various life-interests, I think, sustain a hidden conversation with Mohandas Gandhi, which I will draw out of Tiernan's biography. Like Gandhi in his intellectually formative years in London from 1888 to 1891, Eva in 1900 became a lifelong vegetarian, the English vegetarian movement having its roots in Manchester, and supported animal welfare and the anti-vivisection cause. As with Gandhi, such interests were associated with questioning conventional gender categories and distinctions of masculinity and femininity in vibrant ways, in Eva's case associated with many entwined threads: Celtic Twilight mysticism; spiritualism, the occult and astrology; and theosophy and its interests in Eastern especially Indian religions and beliefs in reincarnation and karma. In 1916 Eva and Esther Roper helped establish a journal entitled *Urania*, Tiernan describing it as remarkable, and indeed remarkable it is, anticipating as Tiernan remarks the radical gender questioning of postmodernity. The journal explored the idea that humanity should eliminate gender as a category of difference, for ideally in Urania there would be no 'men' or 'women' as immutable categories.[21]

Urania, which spanned three decades and was subscribed to by colleges in Britain such as Girton, Newnham and Lady Margaret, and Vassar and Wellesley in the US, wished to highlight that innate differences do not exist between the sexes. In internationalist and cosmopolitan spirit, witty and adventurous, the journal would reprint articles from newspapers worldwide, western and eastern, England, India and Japan, that featured or referred to cross-dressers, individuals who transgressed gender roles, and examples of transsexuality. The journal contested the institution of marriage as supporting conventional gender distinctions. Instead, the editors of *Urania* proposed female same-sex life unions as a superior alternative to heterosexual marriage. *Urania* included stories of famous women in history who loved other women, including in the seventeenth and eighteenth centuries Queen Christina of Sweden, and the Empress of Russia, Elizabeth Alexeievna, and in antiquity Sappho on the island of Lesbos. *Urania* reported on cases where women lived lifelong as men, including the Irish-born James Barry, who in the mid-nineteenth century became an inspector-general of hospitals and during his career fought several duels.[22]

Urania, Tiernan says, was welcomed by New Age groups including the Theosophical Society. Eva and Esther had moved from Manchester to London in 1913, and in 1919 Eva joined the Hampstead branch of the Theosophical Society, her membership certificate personally signed by its president, Annie Besant, though she had been in sympathy with their ideas for many years before. Theosophy's headquarters were in Adyar, India, and its principles were internationalist, hoping to bring into being a universal brotherhood without distinction of race, creed, sex, caste or colour. *Urania* and the Theosophists shared many ideas on feminism and gender, for example, the Theosophical embrace, derived from Eastern religions, of the law of karma and reincarnation. Theosophy entertained notions of gender and sexuality as fluid. The soul, for instance, does not necessarily remain the same sex through its multiple incarnations; in a next life, men might find themselves in female bodies. Furthermore, the division of society into male and female was only provisional, and one day could transform into androgyny. In her play *The Death of Deirdre* exploring the fluidity of gender and identity, Eva establishes a link between theosophical ideals and ancient Celtic religions. The play rewrites the ancient Celtic myth of Deirdre of the Sorrows, the most beautiful woman in Ireland, so that Deirdre is to be recognised as the reincarnation of a male Irish king.[23]

Eva Gore-Booth's health began to decline in the middle 1920s, and in 1925 she was diagnosed with cancer. Yeats, a lifelong friend of Eva, both participants in the Celtic literary revival, visited Eva in her final illness and was shocked when he saw her looking weak and old, remembering the beautiful young woman in Lissadell House to whom he had once contemplated proposing marriage. Eva and Esther had agreed not to tell anyone about Eva's illness, and Yeats blamed her demanding political activities through the decades for the decline of her youthful beauty.[24] Yeats communicated his negative judgement on Eva's life in his poem 'In Memory of Eva Gore-Booth and Con Markiewicz', one of its lines being 'An image of such politics' to suggest what radical politics did to Eva's looks, the line that is used ironically by Tiernan as her sub-title, given that her biography is a wholly positive evocation of Eva's vibrant and energetic political life.

Eva, just 56 years of age, died in 1926. Constance died the following year. Tiernan tells us that a Catholic bible – Constance had converted to the religion she felt was the true religion of the Irish people[25] – was found by her bedside and inside it Constance had inscribed, 'to Mother and Eva 1927 – They are not dead, they do not sleep. They have awakened from the dream of life'.[26] Esther Roper chose an inscription from Sappho's poetry for the headstone of Eva's grave in Hampstead: 'Life that is Love is God'. As Tiernan movingly phrases it, as in life, Eva and Esther (who died in 1938) are together in death, their bodies lying under a stone adorned with a line from the ancient poet from the island of Lesbos.[27]

I suppose what I'm saying is that Irishness, how to be Irish, both in Ireland and the worldwide diaspora, in the nineteenth century and into the twentieth, must have been exceedingly difficult to negotiate in the middle of contrary pressures, viewpoints and ideals, and in times so often experiencing political turbulence and crisis. Irish identity could always have been unpredictable and contradictory. Irish identity, perhaps, was always an impossibility, its only defining feature passion and intensity.

A Yeats poem I particularly dislike

I'll now make a somewhat fevered literary excursus. I want to make a swinging attack on Yeats' poem 'In Memory of Eva Gore-Booth and Con Markiewicz' (Yeats's rather careless spelling of Markievicz). Yeats admired Constance and Eva in particular in the 1890s when he used to visit Lissadell House and they were all young. His admiration for Constance and Eva, however, did not last. Eva died in 1926, Constance in 1927, and it was in that year Yeats wrote the poem It is the reverse of being gently valedictory and affectionate. It's more in the mode of a direct political and personal attack, its tone angry, even sneering, snarling, contemptuous, vindictive. Far from treasuring the lively intelligence and independence of Constance and Eva throughout their lives, the I of the poem laments, because of their later political involvements and commitments, what had become of their youthful innocence and beauty. The first stanza:

> The light of evening, Lissadell,
> Great windows open to the south,
> Two girls in silk kimonos, both
> Beautiful, one a gazelle.
> But a raving autumn shears
> Blossom from the summer's wreath;
> The older is condemned to death,

Pardoned, drags out lonely years
Conspiring among the ignorant.
I know not what the younger dreams –
Some vague Utopia – and she seems,
When withered old and skeleton-gaunt,
An image of such politics.
Many a time I think to seek
One or the other out and speak
Of that old Georgian mansion, mix
pictures of the mind, recall
That table and the talk of youth,
Two girls in silk kimonos, both
Beautiful, one a gazelle.

The poem creates the two sisters when young in aestheticised terms and images of a highly conventional kind. They are to be admired as 'girls in silk kimonos' as if, as in Orientalist discourse, their essence is to be sensuous; 'girls in silk kimonos' suggests both summer and that they would always be inside, even in summer; they are homebound, languorous, to be gazed at in still poses; they are treasured for their beauty, the property of the young, and Eva is referred to as a 'gazelle', recalling tired images from Elizabethan love poetry of the young woman as faun, the object of male attention, to be hunted. Yet these summer images were brutally sheared away by the women's self-chosen autumn of 'politics', of Constance's lonely life among 'the ignorant', Eva's dreams of a 'vague Utopia'. Eva's appearance, in particular, is, when old, withered and gaunt, the 'image of such politics', though the poet has already admitted he doesn't know what her politics and dreams are, except they are to be contemptuously dismissed as a vague utopianism. The complex maturity of their remarkable lives, lives of struggle, daring, courage, creativity and suffering, unconventional and cosmopolitan, are of no interest. Nor is there any interest in Eva and Constance's highly active upbringing of horse-riding and hunting in Sligo, when the two young women could ponder the significance of local legends of Lissadell House as near Knocknaree Mountain, where was reputedly buried Maeve, the High Queen of Connacht, the warrior queen, a powerful mythological presence for both Eva and Constance. Nor is there any intertextual referencing of Eva's Celtic Twilight plays exploring Celtic mythology featuring powerful female figures like Maeve.

What a contemptible construction this is! Ideally, women's youth and beauty are to be envisaged as being ravaged, as we see later in the poem, by their true enemy, time; women's ravaging by time would then become fit matter for elegiac pathos, for tragic reflection, by the male poet. Instead, to his disappointment and anger, the women in their maturity have deprived him of such reflections, choosing instead to be subjects in their own history.

In *The Life of W. B. Yeats: A Critical Biography* (1999), Terence Brown tells us that Yeats did not think ideological commitment was proper for women. Yeats valued in women the quality of sweetness, especially sweetness of voice, a quality that in Yeats' view Constance lost in her later life as a political agitator when she would become shrill in argument.[28] Yeats also conceived of women he admired in conventional nineteenth-century Romantic terms, figures of *la belle dame sans merci*. Brown suggests that Maud Gonne was his 'female ideal – erotic, death-haunted, noble in dangerous hauteur'.[29]

I can see no self-reflexivity in the poem, no questioning by the narrator of his own assumptions and the grounds of his anger: his thwarted longing as male poet to fix and possess Eva and Constance within his own androcentric imagery; his conventional view that women's appearance, mind, dreams and soul are damaged by political involvements while men's are not. For Yeats of course was not anti-political, far from it. Brown describes his political interventions when from 1922 he became a senator of the Irish Free State, appointed to advise on education, literature and the arts, and positioning himself as representative of a grand Anglo-Irish tradition reaching back to the eighteenth century in figures such as Swift, Grattan and Burke and forward to Parnell. In 1923 and 1924, Yeats, apart from speaking on cultural issues such as Irish manuscripts, the National Gallery and the School of Art, the National Museum and the role of Irish language in national life, addressed himself to 'such matters as the location of parliament, censorship of films, damage to property… national health insurance, inspection of prisons and Northern Ireland'. So, for Yeats, lots of political interests. Brown observes that in the senate Yeats 'swiftly identified' with a group of independent senators who 'made it their business to protect the interests of the former Unionist inhabitants of the new Free State'. Yeats also chose to join the 'Kildare Street Club, a bastion of privilege at the epicenter of Ascendancy society', practical men, whiskey distillers and the like, who set about defending the 'immediate economic interests of their caste and class'.[30] Reading this, one wonders why Yeats didn't harshly judge his fellow members of the Kildare Street Club and the Unionist senators he associated with for belonging to 'the ignorant'; ignorant of anything except practical business matters that advantaged the Anglo-Irish.

The poem scorns Eva for dreams of a 'vague Utopia'. Were aspects of Yeats' thinking and dreaming, however, immune from utopianism? After all, think of his famous interest in mysticism, in the occult and the Celtic Twilight, in experiments in spirit communication, in automatic writing, the paranormal, contact with mediums, pursuing altered states of consciousness in hashish (with Maud Gonne) and mescaline, politicking as it were in the theosophical Order of the Golden Dawn – weren't all these ways of seeking a utopia for humanity? As Brown phrases it Yeats believed in 'ritual magic' whereby the elect, 'agents of spiritual illumination', could 'raise mankind to the level of divinity'.[31] Don't we have here a utopian longing to overcome time and death in achieving contact with an eternal realm of the spirit?

Yeats's fury in the poem is that Eva and Constance didn't devote their lives – as in his view all women who interested him should – to *his* utopian project, on his terms, in his way.

At least in this poem, Yeats reveals an ugliness of soul.

Conclusion

Dear Reader, I've saved up a few reflections with which to close this chapter.

In most accounts, Eva and Constance are referred to as nationalists. Yet everything I read about them suggests to me that they were cosmopolitan internationalists. Believing in and working for freedom from a violent British Empire, whether for Ireland, Egypt or India, is in my view entirely compatible with anti-racism, anti-colonialism, internationalism and cosmopolitanism.

Another thought. In further reading, I did come across mention of a 'soviet' in an essay by the Irish historian Brian P Murphy on Ken Loach and Paul Laverty's controversial film *The Wind that Shakes the Barley*, which was shown in Ireland in 2006 soon after the ninetieth anniversary of the Easter Rising; the film encompasses the period of the Easter Rising, the War of Irish Independence (1919–21) and the Irish Civil War (1922–3). At one point Murphy refers to a soviet being declared in Limerick city in April 1919, then being suppressed by the British. Murphy admires Loach and Laverty's powerful film, as I do, and his essay is largely concerned with questioning its disparagement by the historian Roy Foster. Murphy's brilliant essay presents a devastating critique of Foster's historical commentary on the film.[32]

And a final flurry of thoughts. Foster, in his biography of Yeats, discussing 'In Memory of Eva Gore-Booth and Con Markiewicz', ventures crudely dismissive comments of his own on Eva and

Constance. With evident sympathy for the spirit of Yeats' poem, Foster takes its sentiments further, suggesting that the sisters had abandoned their father's Anglo-Irish Ascendancy house where they were brought up, with its 'great neoclassical beauty', in order to pursue 'abstract hatreds', which destroyed their lives and looks. Foster turns his animus particularly on Constance, writing loftily of her speech opposing the Treaty with Britain as 'histrionic', and brutally proposing that in his view Yeats 'may have been placing Markievicz among the phantoms of hatred, the innumerable harpies with their clanging wings'.[33]

What a curious comment from Foster, given the force of the hatred of the sisters revealed in Yeats's poem. And the force of Foster's own hatred for Constance that erupts in his prose, prose that attempts to be measured and magisterial. Constance Markievicz a harpy, with clanging wings: how subtle.

Foucault once said, in his essay 'Nietzsche, Genealogy, History' (1971), that we should openly admit our preferences in a controversy.[34] Irish historical writing, so often focused on key personalities, events, dates and commemorations, is passionate and intense.

Perhaps, in writing this chapter, I'm retrieving my own Irish ancestry.

Postscript: The Question of Genocide

In the Introduction to his 2008 book *The Irish Famine* Ruán O'Donnell reflects that the Great Famine of 1845–50 was one of modern history's most destructive episodes, its death toll, in terms of numbers and per capita impact, rivalling 'those endured in recent decades in Biafra, Ethiopia and Sudan'. He observes that while 'blight was natural', many survivors blamed the imperial power in London for its incompetent response. Furthermore, he points out, while the 'potato-dependent poor' of both Scotland and Ireland were simultaneously affected by the scourge of blight in 1845–6, many Irish, 'yet very few Scots, died'. In contrast to Ireland, the 'threatened populations of the Scottish Highlands received prompt and adequate government aid' to forestall the worst effects of the food shortages. Arguably, there was sufficient food in Ireland to feed those 'who died from starvation', and exports of 'livestock and cereals to Britain certainly continued throughout the crisis', Irish produce flowing 'unabated to the towns and cities of industrial Britain'. 'Outright starvation' in Ireland, as well as deadly diseases attacking the malnourished, 'killed huge numbers', and the disaster was aggravated by the mass evictions of the later years of the Famine, a brutal 'dispossession' consciously carried out by bailiffs, constables and landlords.[35]

As a genocide scholar, I was intrigued to read in O'Donnell's Introduction that 'the Irish Famine Genocide Committee and others' contend that 'London exploited a natural crisis in pursuance of strategic political objectives'; there is a 'suspicion that darker forces were at work'.[36] I must, I think, find out more. A little googling reveals that in the Irish diaspora, especially in the US, there is a conviction that the Great Famine of 1845–1850 was indeed genocide as legally defined by the 1948 UN Convention on the Prevention and Punishment of the Crime of Genocide. On the internet I come across an open letter, entitled 'Francis A. Boyle: The Irish Famine was Genocide', published on the website HNN, the George Mason University History News Network. Boyle addressed the letter to the New Jersey Commission on Holocaust Education. As he relates in the letter, the Commission was created by the New Jersey Legislature in 1991 to prepare curriculum materials on the Holocaust for use in the state's public schools; in 1994 the mandate was expanded to study and recommend curricular material on a wide range of genocides. Boyle explains that he has been asked by the Irish Famine Curriculum Committee, which had already submitted historical material to the New Jersey Commission, to give his opinion on the 'question whether the policies pursued by the British government from 1845 to 1850 in Ireland that resulted in the mass starvation of over one million Irish People constituted "genocide"'.

Boyle affirms that the British government policies did indeed constitute genocide, in terms of Article II of the 1948 UN Genocide Convention, which states, 'In the present Convention, genocide means any of the following acts committed with intent to destroy, in whole or in part, a national, ethnical, racial or religious group, as such'. He draws particular attention to Article II's clause (b), 'Causing serious bodily or mental harm to members of the group', and clause (c), 'Deliberately inflicting on the group conditions of life calculated to bring about its physical destruction in whole or in part'. Boyle's verdict:

> Clearly, during the years 1845 to 1850, the British government pursued a policy of mass starvation in Ireland with intent to destroy in substantial part the national, ethnical, and racial group commonly known as the Irish People, as such. In addition, this British policy of mass starvation in Ireland clearly caused serious bodily and mental harm to members of the Irish People within the meaning of Genocide Convention Article II (b). Furthermore, this British policy of mass starvation in Ireland deliberately inflicted on the Irish People conditions of life calculated to bring about their physical destruction in substantial part within the meaning of Article II (c) of the 1948 Genocide Convention. Therefore, during the years 1845 to 1850 the British government knowingly pursued a policy of mass starvation in Ireland that constituted acts of genocide against the Irish People within the meaning of Article II (b) and Article II (c) of the 1948 Genocide Convention.

Boyle urges that the 'British policy of genocide' against the Irish People 1845 to 1850 be included within the curriculum of any course dealing with the perpetration of genocides in the modern world, alongside study of genocides against the Jewish People, the Armenians, Native Americans and African Americans under slavery.

I'm not quite sure what Ruán O'Donnell thinks about the question of genocide, though it's clear he believes it should be raised and discussed. In his Conclusion, O'Donnell refers to the 'Irish Holocaust', and points out that as '1847 progressed, the persistent refusal of central government to finance, empower and organize its detached Irish relief organization doomed the first thousands of a million fatalities'. Such inactivity contrasted with the 'special treatment provided to blight threatened Scotland'. He also refers to the 'increasingly confused and contradictory attitude of the Executive towards Ireland'.[37]

Why, as O'Donnell darkly ponders, did Scotland during 1845–6, suffering also from potato blight, receive what looks like special treatment in the form of prompt and adequate government aid, so that only a few Scots died?[38]

Scottish historical writing is also haunted by the comparison of Ireland and Scotland in relation to the potato blight. The Scottish historian William Kenefick, in an essay 'Cruelty, Grievance, Denial' in the *Dublin Review of Books* in 2013, discusses the question while reviewing two books by well-known historians of Scotland, Eric Richards' *The Highland Clearances: The People, Landlords and Rural Turmoil*, and T M Devine's *Clearances and Improvement: Land, Power and People in Scotland 1700–1900*. Kenefick argues that Richards and Devine, through sustained scholarly investigation, have come to a kind of historical consensus, that the clearances in the Highlands were not unusual or unique to Scotland, but part of a broader European-wide context of rural change and transformation in the eighteenth and nineteenth centuries; the clearances were regional variations of a wider and longer pattern. Perceived from this European perspective, Irish as well as Scottish history have much in common in terms of going through more general processes of rural transformation.[39]

Devine in particular, Kenefick notes, provides a close analysis of why Ireland starved at the time of the Famine and the Highlands did not: the scale of potato dependence in Ireland was much greater than in Scotland; in Highland Scotland, the potential victims of the crop failure numbered in their thousands rather than millions as in Ireland, and so was more easily dealt with; while fishing off western Ireland was still a viable pursuit, commercial and subsistence fishing persisted longer in the Highlands, as did kelping, and the riches of the sea were more easily harvested by the majority of Highlanders; lines of communication were more open in the Highlands than in Ireland's far west; to the south and east of the Scottish Highlands there existed an industrialised society that provided work opportunities for migrants from the Highlands, a dimension missing from Ireland.[40]

One thing that struck me in these debates is that terrible events cause a kind of unresolved and volatile turmoil in historical consciousness, especially in the frequent gap between academic research and writing, and popular memory, intensified by interactions between the home societies and their worldwide diasporas. In the final sentence of *The Irish Famine*, Ruán O'Donnell contemplates the difficulty of historical understanding of such a disaster: 'The Great Famine dealt Ireland a profound physical and psychological shock, which altered the course of the nation's history to an extent that defies conventional narrative relation.'[41] In his review-essay William Kenefick reflects on the continuing tension in historical consciousness between the sober explanations of the Highland clearances by historians such as Richards and Devine in terms of long historical patterns, and the passionate anger that the clearances still inspire in the collective memory of Scotland and among Scots abroad (especially in Canada) on the worldwide web, often contending that the clearances constituted ethnic cleansing or genocide; an indignation that is increasing rather than diminishing in the passage of time. Devine writes, says Kenefick, that 40 years ago Canadians of Scots descent viewed themselves as pioneers and adventurers, while now they see themselves as victims of the Highland Clearances.[42]

This last observation by Devine in Kenefick's essay prompted me to a cynical thought. In recent years there has been critical inquiry into the role of Scots both as slave owners in the Caribbean, and as enthusiastic colonisers of Indigenous peoples and their lands, to the point of committing destruction of Indigenous nations including many massacres.[43] Such might explain why diasporic Scots, consciously or unconsciously, might be increasingly drawn to a view of the Scots in general as victims rather than victimisers.

Can similar thoughts be entertained of the diasporic Irish in settler colonial societies, in relation to Indigenous peoples? Haven't the Irish too been settler colonisers? Yet here nuanced stories must be told, given the centuries of suffering of the Irish at the hands of the British, and that historically Ireland itself has been a colony; as O'Donnell writes, the Famine revealed that 'Ireland's membership of the United Kingdom masked its true status as a problematic colony'.[44] In *The Famine Plot: England's Role in Ireland's Greatest Tragedy* (2012) Tim Pat Coogan, as had Francis A Boyle, unequivocally convicts the English authorities of genocide in terms of the 1948 UN Genocide Convention. Coogan concludes his book by arguing that the responsible Whig government and decision makers in England, supported by the influential civil servant Charles Trevelyan (who he regards as an 'architect' of Whig government policy and particularly despises as an eager and relentless genocidaire), pursued a genocidal plan: 'Whig policy was directed at getting the peasants off the land, and if it took mass death to achieve that objective, so be it... The underlying thrust of Whig policy had the aim of clearing man from the fields and replacing him with the bullock.' Whig decision makers, therefore, Coogan argues, perpetrated genocide during the years 1846–51 in terms of the clauses of Article II – causing seriously bodily or mental harm to the members of the group; deliberately inflicting on the group conditions calculated to bring about its destruction in whole or in part; imposing measures intended to prevent births within the group; and forcibly transferring children of the group to another group – as well as in terms of Article III, including here direct and public incitement to commit genocide and complicity in genocide.[45]

There are in Coogan's evocation of the Famine sad resonances with other genocidal practices in modernity, not least death marches such as the Trail of Tears in the US in the 1830s involving the Choctaw along with the Cherokee, Creek, Chicasaw and Seminole nations, and also anticipating later death marches, in the Armenian Genocide and the Zionist/Israeli genocide of the Palestinians in 1948.[46] Coogan tells us of the Doolough Lake incident, which took place on 30–31 March 1849, an event engraved in bitter popular memory. A large group of starving people, between 400 and 600, were instructed to make their way to Louisburgh in County Mayo on the west coast, but once there were told that the poor law commissioners were at Delphi Lodge, 16 kilometres away. The people then walked to Delphi Lodge, but when they got there learned that the commissioners were eating and could not be disturbed. Finally, the commissioners told the gathering that they did not qualify for tickets of relief and there was no food to give them. They then walked back through cold, hail and snowstorm to Louisburgh, many perishing on the way. Today, Coogan says, a monument stands next to the lake to commemorate those who died. The inscription, Coogan adds, 'also pays tribute to the Choctaw Indians who, having survived a horrific march from Mississippi to Oklahoma in 1841, identified with the Louisburgh marchers and somehow managed to collect $700 for them from their meagre resources'.[47]

In my essay 'Are Settler-Colonies Inherently Genocidal? Re-reading Lemkin', I note that Lemkin wrote that the Choctaw deportations involved great suffering, including a deportation insisted on by the authorities in winter, with Lemkin commenting: 'I do not understand why they were not made to leave in the spring or summer'. Many of the Choctaw deportees, poorly clad, died from exposure, demoralisation and cholera.[48]

1 My thanks to Mark Dorrian for telling me about this lovely Irish folk song.

2 My thanks to Mairéad Browne for telling me about Andy Irvine's song.

3 See Ruán O'Donnell, *The Irish Famine* (The O'Brien Press, Dublin, 2008).

4 See Sonja Tiernan, *Eva Gore-Booth: An image of such politics* (Manchester University Press, Manchester, 2012), pp.12-13.

5 Samuel Lewis, *Topographical Dictionary of Ireland*, with Historical and Statistical Descriptions (S. Lewis and Co., London, 1837), Vol.II, pp.204-205.

6 Sean Spellissy and John O'Brien, *Clare: County of Contrast* (privately published, Ireland, 1987), p.134.

7 Spellissy and O'Brien, *Clare: County of Contrast*, pp.135-36. In relation to Ireland as a whole, Roy Foster, *Modern Ireland* 1600-1972 (Penguin, London, 1989), writes in his chapter 'The Famine: Before and After' of 'the devastating extent of depopulation' and the 'horrific conditions in which lives were lost' (pp.323-325).

8 Spellissy and O'Brien, *Clare: County of Contrast*, p.136.

9 Spellissy and O'Brien, *Clare: County of Contrast*, p.136.

10 David Fitzpatrick, *Politics and Irish Life* 1913-1921 (Gill and Macmillan, Dublin, 1977), Prologue, pp.x-xii.

11 Fitzpatrick, *Politics and Irish Life* 1913-1921, pp.46-47.

12 Fitzpatrick, *Politics and Irish Life* 1913-1921, pp.48-50, 52-53, 55-56.

13 Fitzpatrick, *Politics and Irish Life* 1913-1921, pp.53-54.

14 Ann Curthoys and John Docker, *Is History Fiction?* (UNSW Press, Sydney, 2010), p.19.

15 Fitzpatrick, *Politics and Irish Life* 1913-1921, p.56.

16 Anne Haverty, *Constance Markievicz: An Independent Life* (Pandora, London, 1988), pp.81, 145, 165, 187–190, 206–210. I talk about Countess Markievicz in my essay 'Storm Troopers of Empire? Historical representation in *Breaker Morant*, Naguib Mahfouz's *Palace Walk* and other war histories', *History Australia*, Vol.8, no.1, 2011, pp.84–85.

17 Sonja Tiernan, 'Challenging Presumptions of Heterosexuality: Eva Gore-Booth, A Biographical Case Study', *Historical Reflections*, Vol.37, issue 2, 2011, pp.58-71, here at 58-62.

18 Sonja Tiernan, *Eva Gore-Booth: An image of such politics*, pp.16, 120, 120-125.

19 Sonja Tiernan, *Eva Gore-Booth: An image of such politics*, pp.16, 82, 85.

20 Sonja Tiernan, *Eva Gore-Booth: An image of such politics*, pp.82-86, 143.

21 Sonja Tiernan, *Eva Gore-Booth: An image of such politics*, pp.62-63, 224-225, 231-232, 250.

22 Sonja Tiernan, *Eva Gore-Booth: An image of such politics*, pp224-230.

23 Sonja Tiernan, *Eva Gore-Booth: An image of such politics*, pp.232-235.

24 Sonja Tiernan, *Eva Gore-Booth: An image of such politics*, p.249.

25 Sonja Tiernan, *Eva Gore-Booth: An image of such politics*, pp.211, 220.

26 Sonja Tiernan, *Eva Gore-Booth: An image of such politics*, p.258. It appears that Constance here is adapting lines from Shelley's *Adonais: An Elegy on the Death of John Keats*, XXXIX: 'Peace, peace! he is not dead, he doth not sleep,/He hath awaken'd from the dream of life'.

27 Sonja Tiernan, 'Challenging Presumptions of Heterosexuality: Eva Gore-Booth, a Biographical Case Study', pp.65-66.

28 Terence Brown, *The Life of W.B. Yeats: A Critical Biography* (Blackwell, Oxford, 1999), pp.230-231.

29 Brown, *The Life of W.B. Yeats*, p.229.

30 Brown, *The Life of W.B. Yeats*, pp.287, 293.

31 Brown, *The Life of W.B. Yeats*, pp.102, 114-117, 252, 379.

32 Brian P. Murphy, OSB, '*The Wind that Shakes the Barley*: Reflections on the Writing of Irish history in the Period of the Easter Rising and the Irish War of Independence', in Ruan O'Donnell (ed.), *The Impact of the 1916 Rising Among the Nations* (Irish Academic Press, Dublin and Portland, Oregon, 2008), pp.200–220; the reference to the Limerick soviet is on p.210.

33 R.F. Foster, *W.B. Yeats: A Life II: The Arch-Poet 1915-1939* (Oxford University Press, Oxford, 2003), pp.347-350.

34 See Ann Curthoys and John Docker, *Is History Fiction?* (UNSW Press, Sydney, 2010), p.184.

35 Ruán O'Donnell, *The Irish Famine* (The O'Brien Press, Dublin, 2008), pp.7-8.

36 O'Donnell, *The Irish Famine*, p.9.

37 O'Donnell, *The Irish Famine*, pp.132-34.

38 O'Donnell, *The Irish Famine*, pp.7, 133.

39 William Kenefick, 'Cruelty, Grievance, Denial', *Dublin Review of Books*, Issue 47, 16 December, 2013, pp.1-11.

40 Kenefick, 'Cruelty, Grievance, Denial', pp.4-5.

41 O'Donnell, *The Irish Famine*, p.134.

42 Kenefick, 'Cruelty, Grievance, Denial', pp.1-2, 6-10.

43 See Eric Graham, *Burns and the Sugar Plantocracy of Ayrshire* (MDPD, Edinburgh, 2014) and Ann Curthoys, 'Scottish settlers and Indigenous people in colonial Australia', in Alison Inglis and Patricia Tryon Macdonald (eds), *For Auld Lang Syne: Images of Scottish Australia from First Fleet to Federation* (Art Gallery of Ballarat, Ballarat, 2014, pp.83–100.

44 O'Donnell, *The Irish Famine*, p.133.

45 Coogan, *The Famine Plot*, pp.229-231.

46 John Docker, 'Instrumentalising the Holocaust: Israel, Settler-Colonialism, Genocide (Creating a Conversation between Raphaël Lemkin and Ilan Pappé)', *Holy Land Studies*, Vol.11, no.1, p.22.

47 Coogan, *The Famine Plot*, pp.91-92.

48 John Docker, 'Are Settler-Colonies Inherently Genocidal? Re-reading Lemkin', in A. Dirk Moses (ed.), *Empire, Colony, Genocide: Conquest, Occupation, and Subaltern Resistance in World History* (Berghahn, New York, 2008), p.95.

4

The Irish in Diaspora: my Father's Family in Sydney

How Irish, I wonder, did my father regard himself, especially when young and being part of the IWW and then helping launch the Communist Party in 1920? I think he did feel part of the Irish diaspora, both through his family and his political involvements; and by diaspora I mean, as I phrase it in the preface to my *1492: The Poetics of Diaspora*, a sense of belonging to more than one history, to more than one time and place, more than one past and future.[1] If, as he says in his reminiscences, his 'mother supported Home Rule for Ireland', then Ireland's recurring troubles must have been a subject of discussion in the family when he was growing up. In this chapter the IWW figures a great deal, and there will be a kind of dance back and forth between my father's reminiscences and Verity Burgmann's invaluable book on the Wobblies. I will also call on 'From Potato Famine to Gallipoli and Beyond', the genealogical research and reminiscences of Mrs Holmes, the daughter-in-law of Alice, Susan Nash's daughter.

The Easter Rising and the IWW

Yeats' 'In Memory of Eva Gore-Booth and Con Markiewicz' scorned Constance Markievicz's political radicalism. But such, if he knew of her, perhaps because of her role in the famous Easter Rising of 1916 which created intense int rest around the world, would I feel have appealed to Ted Docker. And he might well have known of her. In his reminiscences, my father says that the main speakers for the IWW in their meetings at the Domain in Sydney were Donald Grant, J B King, Tom Glynn, and 'Peter Larkin – I knew Peter well'. In her *Revolutionary Industrial Unionism*, Burgmann tells us that in the 'polyglot membership' of the Australian IWW, cosmopolitan home of so many nationalities and ethnicities, there were many Irish, including Peter Larkin and Tom Glynn; they were Roman Catholic, at least nominally, for the IWW was hostile to the churches. Arriving from Ireland in 1915 Peter Larkin, Verity notes, joined the Sydney Local of the IWW, and lectured to 'enormous meetings in Sydney and Melbourne in the wake of the Easter Rebellion', though Larkin, like the IWW in general, was critical of nationalist elements in the Rebellion.[2]

Verity writes that Larkin and Glynn were part of the Sydney Twelve, those framed for conspiracy to commit arson and seditious conspiracy; Larkin was found guilty and sentenced in December 1916. There immediately arose a sustained campaign to have the Sydney Twelve released, both in Australia and internationally. In July 1917 Peter Larkin's famous brother James Larkin was refused entry to Australia; nonetheless, their sister Delia Larkin organised a large gathering in Dublin, and there were protest wires sent to the NSW state government from the Norwegian and British Labour Parties. Peter Larkin was released in 1920.[3]

As a member of the IWW and from 1920 the Australian Communist Party, I'm sure my father would have been in sympathy with Constance Markievicz's anti-racism and internationalism revealed in her 1921 speech to the Dail where she denounces the Empire as 'treading down the people of Egypt and India'. I see Ted Docker as in his own way, in his own kind of diasporic consciousness, aware of his family's Irish ancestry and conscious of Ireland's political turmoil, as continuing the oppositional Irish Protestant tradition exemplified in Constance's denunciation of the British Empire.

Ted Docker's Atheism

Ted Docker's becoming at some stage of his life an atheist would have represented a sharp divergence from his family's inherited religious values, not least those of his mother; perhaps he was the first in the family to be so. He may have been influenced here by his joining the IWW or found them congenial because already he shared their characteristic atheism or agnosticism or non-religion; Burgmann points out that the IWW was hostile to religion in its institutional forms, often parodying religious music.[4] For my father, the issue of religion and his own atheism must have been a matter of sensitivity in his family context; his brothers Henry and Norman who had died in World War I had stated on joining the military that their religion was Church of England, and in his reminiscences Ted Docker recalls his church-going boyhood. He used to accompany his mother to the Church of England on Sunday nights; she would 'stand up when they sang hymns'. As a boy he also went to Sunday school; the teacher's name was Miss Chalcraft. The children went through stories from the New Testament: 'I won a prize for explaining a text.' His mother had the bible at home, she 'used to study it and explain what it meant on the Sunday'. My father suggested the family overall was quite religious: 'my nephew became a minister in the Church of England', 'my sister would take him to the church' when young.

Then came an interesting revelation. My father said that 'my mother stayed religious all her life – she never knew I was an atheist'. Later on, his mother knew 'I was a member of the Communist Party – she was getting on then, don't know whether she understood what it meant'.

When I was growing up in the Bondi flat my father would occasionally make disparaging remarks about priests and parsons as 'sky-pilots', and he said how appalling it was that the Catholic church in particular could build their churches on hills in Sydney; look at St Mary's Cathedral, the hills should belong to the people. Now I see a long continuity with the IWW's hostility to organised religion.

Australians All!

I would like now to contrast Ted Docker's radicalism with the attitudes, or at least implied attitudes, towards the Empire and the First World War of his uncle, George Nash, who, Ann and I feel pretty sure, had come as a teenager to Sydney on the *Clyde* on 23 June 1881 with his older sisters Susan and Harriet, and would earn a reputation as a songwriter and journalist. Family lore was wont to mention a brother of Susan's also in Sydney, but we didn't know from the genealogy sent by the Clare Heritage Centre which of her two brothers it might be, first-born William baptised in 1842 or last-born George baptised in 1863. Ann searched Ancestry.com and Trove for newspaper references for William, but nothing came up. When, however, Ann typed George in, there it was, a wealth of information suggesting that he had become quite prominent in early twentieth-century Sydney educational and musical circles.

I'll start my thinking about my great uncle George with information from his obituary in the *Sydney Morning Herald* of 22 June 1927, which related to its readers, in a considerably smaller society, that George Nash, born in 1863 in Kilrush, Ireland, was at the age of 19 employed by the NSW Department of Education, and worked there for 45 years; that is, by my calculation, he was first employed by the Department in 1882, a year after he arrived in Sydney with two of his older sisters. The obituary then says that George Nash edited the Department of Education's *Education*

Gazette for many years, and became a member of the Institute of Journalists.

My feeling, from newspaper references down the years, is that George Nash became something of a public figure with the success of his song 'Australians All' in 1909, a song that both celebrates the Federation of the different colonies into a nation some years before as the new century started, and anticipates the pro-war and pro-Empire patriotism of World War I. Encouraging such patriotism became part of what I would call official culture, a meshing of institutions like schools with government policies. 'Australians All' appears to have been a public success in advancing this official culture.

Reports in the *Sydney Morning Herald* of 9 and 12 February 1910 informed its readers that 'Australians All', written by George Nash and published by Paling and Co., was sung at Fort Street School by 200 children, boys and girls, in the presence of the minister for public instruction, and other executive officers of the Public Instruction department. I quickly googled and up came, with an exclamation mark, 'Australians All!', its frontispiece announcing that the song was 'Inscribed to THE NATIVE BORN', that the words of the song were by George Nash and the music by Theodore S Tearne, who was listed as State Superintendent of Music. The copyright date was 1909, and it would appear that already in 1910 it was in its 5th edition. (By *native born*, I presume George Nash meant white settlers born in Australia; I recall that the poet Bernard O'Dowd was in Melbourne a member of the Australian Natives Association which was influential in the late nineteenth century and early twentieth century.)[5] Of its eight verses, I'll quote the first four to give a sense of the strength of pro-British Empire sentiment leading up to the war, at a time when the British Empire must have appeared to itself as invincible, its glory and its extent surely to last for centuries if not for ever.

Australians all! – our mighty States
Are joined in union free,
We love our own Australia
With its blue encircling sea.

Britannia's fairest daughter,
With her locks of fleecy gold,
And starry eyes a-gazing down
The ages yet untold.

She sees her children's children
Amongst the Nations stand,
And honour, truth and justice
Are the watchwords of the land.

For we are sons of Britain,
Of sires who crossed the seas,
From Devon's sand and Galway's cliffs,
And distant Hebrides.

The reference to 'Galway's cliffs' suggests a confidence that the Irish, including the west coast Irish, are 'the sons of Britain' and that Ireland would always be part of the Empire.

'Australians All!' goes on to declare that the 'flowers of Empire [are] Built on justice to mankind', assuring audience and the school children singing that the Empire has a universal, even utopian mission to build a fair and just world for all and the new state of Australia is part of this mission. The song also presents a heart-warming portrait of Australia as a unified and harmonious nation, of all Britain's overseas progeny the 'fairest' – presumably meaning the whitest – with 'locks of fleecy gold', and as a new nation always to be guided by 'honour, truth and justice'. It ends watchfully, however, on a military note, aware that the Empire has enemies and reminding its listeners that being patriotic for Australia is the same as being patriotic for the Empire, for the 'sons of fair Australia' are 'ready when the Empire calls/To meet her foes once more'.

Dear Reader, I wonder if the Empire's 'foes' in a song first sung in 1909 might be not only external but also internal, such as Constance Markievicz, who in 1909 had given a lecture, entitled 'Women, ideals and the nation', where she asked the women of Ireland to 'discourage their boys from enlisting in the British army', which she referred to as a 'mercenary army', 'the most immoral army in the world'.[6] Did the Empire's internal 'foes' include the Wobblies? Burgmann in *Revolutionary Industrial Unionism* tells us that the IWW had been founded not long before, in Chicago in 1905, becoming established in Australia shortly after, in Sydney in 1907 and Melbourne in 1908, and steadily gaining influence in the labour movement.[7]

The *Education Gazette* and the First World War

In September 2013 on a visit to Canberra, I looked up in the National Library the *Education Gazette* for the war years, years when George Nash was editing the 'Official Gazette of the Education Department of New South Wales'. What stood out as I read it was that the *Education Gazette* was clearly enjoined as part of its brief to report on a range of educational activities that assisted Australia's participation in the First World War; activities that involved a pervasive militarising of schools primary and secondary. Turning over its pages, I could see no airing and discussion of different viewpoints on the war. The philosophy of education of the *Education Gazette*, 'Published under the Authority of the Minister for Education'; that is, was the reverse of Socratic.

I know there is a difficulty, in the following analysis of the *Education Gazette*, that George Nash was a public servant, employed by the department of education. I said before that I wished to compare the stances of Ted Docker and the Wobblies to the attitudes, or at least implied attitudes, towards the Empire and the First World War, of George Nash as revealed for example in the *Education Gazette*. But he may simply have been a public servant doing his job, rather than believing in whatever values were being exhibited in its pages which he was paid to edit and present. Nor do my father's reminiscences reveal the slightest hostility to his uncle George Nash, indeed his references to his uncle are unfailingly affectionate. At one point, my father says that his uncle George Nash 'voted for the Labor Party – he said his colleagues were surprised, given his position, that he voted for the Labor Party'. As we will see in the following chapter, my father when young, in a migrant family looking out for each other as migrant families do, owed a lot to George Nash in his becoming a carpenter.

Yet I think I will continue to assume that George Nash could not have edited the *Education Gazette* for so many years while being opposed to its imperial patriotism, which was after all the majority view and fervour of the population, and in any case had been so ringingly clear in 'Australians all!', whose words he wrote. Still, there's a nagging whisper of worry here for me. Am I being unfair to the history of the family?

I'll focus on a particular issue of the *Education Gazette* at the height of the war, 1 July 1916. I have to confess that I felt rather sympathetic, given my uncles Norman and Henry's overseas service before they died, towards an item 'Men's Knitted Sock Pattern' (p. 241), by Catherine Anderson of Auburn Public School: 'Knitted socks, as made by the following pattern, have found great favour with hundreds of our soldiers on active service, the men declaring that for comfort and wear they are unsurpassed.' On pp. 242 and 244, an article 'Drill and Physical Training', by a Major Reddish, tells us of the 'Senior Cadet Training' that must have become routine in schools: 'Girls' squads, as well as boys, perform... at our displays'. On p. 245, in 'Publications Received', we read of a publication, 'The Anzac Memorial', compiled by A G Stephens, ex-literary editor of the famous journal the *Bulletin*, currently 'editor of the *Bookfellow*'. The publication has a brief preface by Lieutenant-Colonel Owen, pointing out that its chief object is to record the 'names and deeds of soldiers and sailors of Australia and New Zealand... who have fought, are fighting, or will fight in the present "Liberation War of Humanity".'

A regular column provided a 'Supplementary List of Officers and Teachers Who Have Entered Camp to 7th June, 1916', giving a list of teachers, along with a separate list of 'Officers and Teachers of the Education Department Who Have Sons on Active Service' (on pp. 247–8). An article 'Junior Cadet Training' reported: 'A pupil becomes a junior cadet on the 1st July of the year in which he reaches the age of 12 years', remaining a junior cadet 'for two years, when he becomes a senior cadet'. Becoming a cadet at the age of 12, it is explained, is a legal requirement for all boys 'under the Defence Act and Commonwealth Military Regulations', and teachers 'must carry out this training' (pp. 249–50). There was also mention of the 'Department of Education Patriotic Fund' (p. 251). On display on the penultimate page of the issue was a war recruitment poster, referring to the alleged German atrocities in Belgium and northern France at the beginning of the war, which featured the spectacle of a bereft mother, her clothes torn, arms upraised, one breast exposed, her two dead children lying in a pool of blood at her feet. Below this scene was the exhortation 'AUSTRALIANS! ENLIST NOW!'

(I notice that Raymond Evans features this image in colour on the back cover of his 1987 book *Loyalty and Disloyalty: Social conflict on the Queensland homefront, 1914–18*).[8] Google Images tells me that a poster 'Women of Queensland! Send a man today to fight for you' and dated c.1914–18 had been created by a British-born Sydney-based artist John Samuel Watkins who conducted his own art school in Sydney for many years. The full text of the poster was: 'Women of Queensland! Remember how women and children of France and Belgium were treated. Do you realize that your treatment would be worse? Send a man today to fight for you!')

Cadet training by schools did not escape the critical gaze of the Wobblies, who, Burgmann points out, opposed the war from its beginning on 4 August 1914, and urged workers not to enlist. In Sydney, in the middle that momentous August, the IWW organised an anti-war demonstration in the Domain, drawing an 'exceptional crowd', and 800 copies of *Direct Action* were sold. In 1915 IWW meetings there attracted larger and larger crowds. During 1916 and 1917 the IWW became the leading force against the threat of conscription. The Wobblies expressed irritation and contempt for those in the society, including workers, who permitted their opinions to be formed for them by priests, parsons, politicians, newspapers and schools. They denounced the introduction of compulsory military training for boys, and, Verity notes, 'referred to the Compulsory Training Act as the Compulsory Traitor Act', forcing young and voteless working-class lads to 'betray their class', that is, the working class of all nations. The Wobblies, Verity argues, saw their anti-war meetings, demonstrations, speeches, songs and *Direct Action* writing and cartoons as alternative ways of educating the working class.[9]

The Wobblies were effectively destroyed as an organisation in the latter part of 1917 by state repression, especially the declaration of the Unlawful Associations Act introduced in federal parliament by prime minister William Morris Hughes; anyone perceived to be hindering the war effort by speech or action was to be arrested and jailed for six months. The Act was passed on 19 December 1916. Verity believes it was specifically aimed at the IWW. On the night of Sunday, 2 September 1917 'about 400 men and women marched through the city, singing Wobbly songs'.[10]

Perhaps Ted Docker was one of these on this particular night. In his reminiscences, Ted Docker told Ann and me that the Wobblies 'had a hall in the city' and 'held a lecture there every Sunday night'; they would have a 'street meeting in Bathurst Street between 7 and 8, then would sing songs walking along the street towards the hall', particularly, he recalled, 'Hallelujah I'm a Bum'.

In the *Education Gazette* No.1, 1 January 1917, in a regular section called 'Gleanings' there appeared a paragraph entitled 'The Great War' by the redoubtable William Morris Hughes, celebrating the war in exalted not to say exultant utopian terms; a utopia based on the superiority of the British race. It is true that the blood of the nation's sons saturates the earth, but, Hughes exclaims, these 'valiant dead' have 'died gladly' so that the country's 'liberties may be saved'. In this war, the 'British race has found its soul'. Hughes' language takes wings, soars: 'I rejoice that I am privileged to live in these days': it is 'a thrill' for all who have in their veins 'British blood' to see how the 'united people' of the nations of the Empire are revealing 'indomitable courage'; and by such unity and the 'spirit of self-sacrifice' in the young men who are dying to save our 'liberties', Australia will become a 'land more glorious than we have ever known, into which – if we prove ourselves worthy – we may enter.'

To the Wobblies, such talk by their chief persecutor of people being 'united' in a land of 'liberties' would have appeared fantastical. The federal Labor party, Burgmann tells us, was in 1916 split over the issue of conscription, with three quarters of the Caucus indicating they would refuse to pass a Conscription Act; after the defeat of the first referendum on conscription, Hughes broke away from the Labor Party and formed a pro-conscription minority National Labour government on 14 November 1916, governing with the support of the Liberal opposition.[11] Australia in general during 1916 and 1917 was a scene of schism and conflict, riven by nationalism as against internationalism, and pro – and anti-conscription opinion, conscription and the war being eagerly supported by the Protestant churches as well as the press.[12] There were people and groups vigorously opposing the war, including many Irish Catholics; the IWW, Verity notes, joined with Archbishop Mannix in the campaign to oppose conscription even while they were ruthlessly persecuted by the combined actions of the secret police of the various states and federal government intelligence services.[13]

In his reminiscences, Ted Docker saw 'Billy Hughes' as the main figure responsible for the smashing of the IWW.

William Morris Hughes Destroys Australia

In his excellent and much under-valued book *Enemy Aliens* (1989), on the implications for Australian history generally of the internment of people of German descent in World War I and the destruction of the pre-war German community, my friend Gerhard Fischer sees Hughes as a divisive figure, whose attitudes and actions had consequences for Australian society as a whole not only during the war but ever since. Pondering the Anzac legend, Fischer argues that whatever reputation for fierce independence the ANZACs were earning in Gallipoli and elsewhere was being systematically undermined on the home front by another kind of war, led by Hughes; a war on pre-World War I multiculturalism, plurality, cosmopolitanism and adventures of identity. Fischer points out that by the 1890s German-Australians, including the descendants of German-born migrants of the second and third generation who had become Australians by birth, constituted the largest group of non-British immigrants in Australia. Drawing on the traditions of 1948, the German-Australian community in the 1890s looked forward to Australia in the twentieth century becoming an independent, liberal society, with cultural autonomy assured for non-British groups.[14]

However, from the outbreak of war German-Australians

were classified as enemy aliens; German-language schools, clubs and newspapers were closed; Australians of German descent, although naturalised and often born in Australia, some with sons fighting with Australian forces overseas, were prevented from voting or standing for public office. Many lost their jobs, while others were interned for the duration of the war and beyond, then deported to a war-devastated Europe.[15] By federal government decree, German-Australians were transformed from citizens with full civil rights to outcasts who could be treated like criminals by the Department of Defence and military authorities, confident that they were beyond the scrutiny of the law. The defence minister could order internment without public trial and without disclosing the grounds on which the action was based.[16]

The long-term consequences for Australian society, politically and culturally, have, Fischer feels – and I very much agree – been profound. The home front experience during 1914–18 encouraged the idea of an interventionist state, not least in the vastly increased power and activity of the burgeoning intelligence departments who amassed secret information and practised surveillance not only on those now considered foreign like members of the long-standing German-Australian community, but also anyone who dared speak out against Hughes' and the federal government's total commitment to the war. These included not only the IWW but also Irish nationalists, pacifists, socialists, unionists, and political and church leaders. Such machinery of political surveillance, with its anonymous bureaucracy and institutionalised censorship, continued after the war and has become, Fischer reflects, a permanent feature of Australian government, a permanent threat to civil liberties.[17]

In Fischer's view hostility, deprivation of rights, internment of community and business leaders, and deportation destroyed the German-Australian community as an autonomous socio-cultural entity within Australian society, in turn destroying the presence and possibilities of multiculturalism that had existed before the war. Hughes and his government insisted on assimilation, ethnic homogeneity, and the primacy of a supposed British race. After the war there was insistent pressure on Australians to consider themselves as British only, while casting suspicion on all those who could not claim pure British stock, including not only Germans but migrants from Southern and Eastern Europe. Post-war Australia was shaped as a society of surveillance, persecution and Anglo-conformity.[18]

Perhaps, and here of course I'm speculating, what angered Hughes most of all about the IWW was their anti-racism and internationalism, their belief in a universal humanity. While talking about the *Education Gazette* of July 1916 before, I referred to a Lieutenant Colonel Owen in a preface to a publication 'The Anzac Memorial' suggesting that the world was at war was part of a Liberation War of Humanity. The last thing Hughes was interested in was the liberation of humanity.

At the Versailles conference in 1919, Hughes vociferously opposed a Japanese proposal for a racial equality clause to be included in the Covenant of the new League of Nations; the Japanese proposal was rejected by the major Western powers, a rejection that had far-reaching consequences in the decades to come.[19]

I have to confess to regarding Hughes as one of the most loathsome creatures ever to disgrace the Australian political stage.

Did George Nash influence my Father?

After the war and into the 1920s, George Nash continued to be a well-known public figure. The *Evening News* of 1 May 1922 noted in a character sketch that he had an excellent singing voice and an engagingly whimsical personality.

The obituary notice in the *Sydney Morning Herald* of 22 June 1927 reported that the funeral service for George Nash was held at South Head Cemetery, which is not far from Watsons Bay, near steep cliffs that look out on the Tasman Sea. The *Herald* mentions that, as well as representatives of Fort Street School, the mourners included Percy Humphries, George Humphries and Dr H G Humphries all of whom must have been related to Susan and Harriet's sister Mrs Jane Humphries of Watsons Bay; also present, said the *Herald*, were G and E Docker, his nephews George Docker and my father Ted. Curiously, all the mourners named by the *Sydney Morning Herald* are male, but female mourners must surely have been there, including his elder sisters Mrs Jane Humphries and Susan Nash, though not their sister Harriet. In her genealogical notes, Mrs Holmes tells us that Harriet married James John Hudson on 3 September 1888 at St Peters Church Sydney, and they went to live in Coogee; however, Harriet had died on 17 December 1895 from tuberculosis; she had been married for only seven years.

That George Nash was buried at South Head Cemetery looks at this distance a little surprising. While Susan and Mrs Jane Humphries and Harriet before she died had established themselves as part of eastern suburbs families, George Nash's death certificate adds to previous information that, at the age of 64, he was buried in the South Head 'Church of England Cemetery'; the certificate says that he had married Olive Byrnes, that there were two daughters living, Ruth and Alice, and he died in Rose Street, Chatswood. (Mrs Holmes writes that Ruth and Alice were very musical and became highly-qualified teachers of music.) Chatswood is on the north side of Sydney Harbour, and would then have only been accessible by ferry; it's a long way from South Head. On Ancestry.com, Ann found that George Nash had lived in Chatswood since 1920; previously, at least from 1890 onwards, he had lived in Glebe, at 4 Purves Street and then 35 Ferry Road, and was a parishioner of the large and imposing Anglican church St John's Bishopthorpe, on Glebe Point Road, where he had been married.

In *Grandeur and Grit: A History of Glebe* (2007), the local historian Max Solling writes that St John's Bishopgate, occupying an elevated site, attempted to reinforce the 'Church of England's pre-eminence as the original owner of the suburb'. At the 1891 census Anglicans comprised 49 per cent of Glebe's population, but the 'majority of Glebe's adult Protestants did not take up the churchgoing habit'; in particular, Glebe's working class turned their backs on St John's.[20] I'm going to presume that George Nash would have regarded himself as middle class. As a long serving public servant who rose through the ranks to become a songwriter and journalist he would have been considered middle class.

Ann and I were surprised and a trifle amused to think that George Nash had lived in Glebe for so long. As I write this, we are living there, and almost every day drive or walk past St John's Bishopgate, which always looks, in its sandstone grandeur, strangely isolated and remote. It stands across from Galluzzo's well-known fruit and vegetable shop. We are also familiar with Ferry Road, which we cross with on our morning walk to Blackwattle Bay. Perhaps, we thought, it was handy for George Nash to catch the ferry at the end of the street to Circular Quay, from where there would be a short walk up the hill to the Department of Education building in Bridge Street. However, the paddle steamer ferry service stopping at Ferry Road only ran from 1880 to 1903, the ferry finding it increasingly difficult to compete with the tram from Glebe to the city.[21]

While my father along with the IWW would have opposed the kind of attitudes on display in George Nash's 'Australians All!' and the *Education Gazette* he edited, I think he shared with his uncle a whimsicality and a certain journalistic ability and flair, as I learned when I read a couple of articles, entitled 'Carpenters and Job Committees' and 'Job Control Necessary' that he wrote in 1926 for the trade union magazine *Labor Monthly*, edited by Lyndall Ryan's father Jack Ryan.[22] I have written about these essays elsewhere, when thinking about the continuities in syndicalist thought in the 1920s between the Wobblies and the then nascent Communist Party.[23]

Phone call from a cousin I never met

I can't recall meeting any members of my father's family except as a child and teenager, visiting his brother George in South Coogee. I have a very vague awareness of my father referring to his sister Alice, and maybe I once visited her with my father; I'm not sure. My father never explained this lack of contact with Alice and her family. But more than once, I went with my father to visit George. I recall a cottage in a street not far from cliffs overlooking the sea; there was a kind of rowing boat in the garden, which my father said he had helped build when he was a young carpenter. I think we sat in the kitchen, George with his wife Eileen, and sipped tea. I also have a recollection that my father said George had been a drover, and that he would swim horses at Coogee beach for the Randwick racing stables.

In the A4 folder I've kept for many years, entitled John's Genealogy, I have two pages of notes of an interesting phone conversation I had with a family relative on my father's side, a cousin, who I have never met; I'm pretty sure that he said that he was Alice's son, the Church of England minister my father mentioned, and that his name was Jimmy Holmes. I think the call was prompted by news, that must have filtered through the family, that Ann and I had visited Kilrush in 1974, when Ann was pregnant: here working out, in a traditional way, dates from key bodily events. Cousin Jimmy Holmes said he had never visited Kilrush and nor had anyone else that he knew of in the family, which makes me wonder if Ann and I were the first to visit after Norman Docker visited when on leave in Britain. Unfortunately, I didn't write a date on my notes of the call, thus breaking one of Ann's golden rules as an historian about always dating everything.

My cousin said my father was always known in the family as Ed, or Edward. My cousin then talked of his grandmother Susan Nash, that she came from Kilrush at the mouth of the Shannon. He said that he knew the family well because he had spent a year living in Susan's house. He thought that Susan had a sister; also, that Susan had a brother high up in the Education Department, an education inspector, and that there was some kind of inscription to him above a doorway in the old Bridge Street Education building. He mentioned that two of Susan's sons had died in World War I. Susan Nash, he recalled, was a good singer, with a bright and engaging manner, the dominant personality in the household. Henry Docker, Susan's husband, said my cousin, was an Englishman, a skilled artisan and cabinet maker, with a beautiful set of carpenter's tools; my cousin found Henry Docker his grandfather a bit gruff, though concerned for his children's welfare, and worried about snakes; there were five acres around the rented weatherboard cottage behind a cemetery. Susan, he recalled, would say her husband was not a good provider because there was such a long time between jobs; Henry Docker the Englishman slept in different parts of the house. When Edward (Ted) Docker was in the Soviet Union, this was kept secret from Henry Docker, who rubbished his ideology. Edward once took a swing at his father, who ducked; my cousin said he was there when this happened and saw it.

My cousin said that my father was known in the family as a concocter of outrageous stories. Edward knew that the rest of his family were pro-British, and that, half-living in the bush in South Coogee, they were isolated. On one occasion, my father told them that a giant earthquake had occurred and half of Britain was under the sea. The family all lamented the loss of the motherland. When, my cousin said, they found out England was still there, they were going to skin him alive.

My cousin said that my father didn't allow his children to mix with Alice's children.

As we shall see, my mother hinted at a different perspective.

A People of the Sea

Thinking about my father's County Clare family as it made long journeys from Ireland to Australia, it strikes me that when they had settled in, they became eastern suburbs coastal families. They had migrated from Kilrush on the Shannon, not far from the Atlantic Ocean, to Sydney which faced the vast Pacific. Sydney's harbour may have felt reassuringly similar – as a grand gash in the coast, as it were – to the waters of the Shannon, a grand gash on the coast of Ireland. They left an island and a coast and came to an island and a coast. They left Kilrush a riverside port town, of ferries and ships, and came to Sydney, a port city of ferries and ships. It may be fanciful, but the more I think about the boat that Ted Docker lovingly crafted for his brother George and its presence beside George's South Coogee house, the more I think it signified for them a key part of the history of their family. (It reminds me now of well-known Klee paintings of boats, always freighted with symbolic meanings.) It kept alive consciousness of the voyages by sea that diasporas take; of closeness to the salt sea, the wine-dark sea that would connect to all the seas of the world, including the distant Atlantic beside County Clare and the Shannon.

I'll float some more speculative thoughts about diasporic consciousness. After her marriage in 1886 to Henry James Docker, Susan lived in inner parts of Sydney. But perhaps, coming from the relatively open spaces of Clare, Susan found inner Sydney too urban; she and her family were, after all, not urbanites from Dublin, and perhaps, like other Clare-ites, had never wished to be. (Here I will interpolate a conversation, early in 2014, with my Canberra friend Pat Tandy, an ex-Dubliner. When I proudly told her that I was descended from a County Clare family, Pat declared that I was a 'culchee'. I said, what's a *culchee*. Pat said that Dubliners regarded anyone from outside Dublin, including County Clare, as a culchee; however, Pat went on, non-Dubliners regard Dubliners as jackeens, that is, big city types who are untrustworthy and treacherous.)

On arriving in Sydney in 1881, Susan and her sister Harriet (and we think their brother George) had gone immediately to stay with their older sister Jane Humphries in Watsons Bay, near the Sydney Heads and the ocean swell at the entrance of Sydney Harbour. Now, in 1895, Susan took her family coastwards again, moving to South Coogee, which would then have still been semi-rural, to the degree that her husband Henry Docker feared snakes. Now they were not far from Chinese market gardens, while Ted's brother George swam horses at Coogee Beach. My cousin Einar Docker is sure the family attended the Anglican church in Coogee, perhaps the one my father refers to when he accompanied his mother. At Coogee, I'm thinking, on Sydney's coastal strip, they were in some ways returning in diasporic imagining to County Clare, the Church of England replacing the Church of Ireland.

Alice the swimmer

Einar Docker, the genealogical whiz, has unearthed some startling information about Ted and George's sister Alice, that when young she had been a very good competitive swimmer. According to her death certificate, which Einar forwarded to me as an attachment, Alice died on 30 November 1977 at the age of 85, and was buried in the Church of England Cemetery, Rookwood, the main Sydney cemetery. When she died she was living in Leichhardt, an inner-western suburb of Sydney. At the age of 30, she had married Richard William Holmes. In an email of September 2013 Einar says that according to Trove (Australia's invaluable digitalised research resource in finding old newspapers, maps and archives), Alice, born in 1892, won a number of swimming races at the Coogee Baths around 1908–09, which would have made her a contemporary of Mina Wylie and Fanny Durack, champion swimmers who also swam at Coogee Baths around this time.

According to Wikipedia, Wilhelmina 'Mina' Wylie (1891–1984), was one of Australia's first two female Olympic representatives, along with Fanny Durack (1889–1956). Mina Wylie grew up in Coogee, where her father Henry Wylie built Wylie Baths in 1907; the Wylie Baths are the oldest surviving communal sea baths in Australia.

Sarah Frances 'Fanny' Durack (1889–1956) learned to swim in Sydney's Coogee Baths and became close friends with Mina Wylie. Durack and Wylie attended the 1912 Summer Olympics in Stockholm, Sweden, when women's swimming events were being held for the first time. Durack won a gold and Wylie a silver medal. From 1910 until 1918, Durack was the world's greatest female swimmer at all distances from freestyle sprints to the mile marathon. Mina Wylie was inducted into the International Swimming Hall of Fame in 1975.

Einar also sent some black-and-white photos, portraits of Alice when she was young. In one photo we see a strong-minded young woman in an early twentieth-century swimming costume staring fearlessly at the camera. Alice is wearing a medallion which Einar has identified as similar to one in the Mina Wylie collection in the NSW State Library.

As Mrs Holmes reports in 'From Potato Famine to Gallipoli and Beyond', Henry Docker, who died in Belgium in October 1917, had written a letter dated 3 January 1917 from a military hospital in the UK to Alice, where he praises her swimming.prowess.

Watsons Bay and Vinegar Hill

There is also the Watsons Bay connection, where Jane Humphries *née* Nash had lived. Ann and I can find no record of the ship in which Jane Nash travelled to Sydney, a number of years before the *Clyde* arrived in 1881 – in any case, long enough for her to be married and reside at Watsons Bay. Mrs Holmes's information is that Jane, while on a migrant ship coming to Australia, met her future husband on board; his name was Patrick Humphries and his father owned a boat-building company in Watsons Bay; Jane Nash and Patrick Humphries were married on 29 January 1870 in the Scots Church, Sydney, and the minister was John Dunmore Lang, a leading figure in Australian colonial history, known for his fiery temper and radical ideas.

Mrs Holmes' notes here would appear to suggest that Jane Nash remained Protestant, though the Humphries family into which she married had started out in Australia as devoutly Catholic. Einar has relayed to me information about the Humphries family, whose journey to Watsons Bay begins in faraway Dublin in the 1790s. In 1791 – Patrick Humphries, born in Ireland in c1767, was found guilty of stealing lead sheeting, and sentenced to seven years transportation. He came to the colony of New South Wales on the convict transport *Boddingtons*, arriving on 7 August 1793, so only a short time after the establishment of the British colony in 1788. After serving his time as a convict, Patrick began a military career, in 1801 joining the NSW Corps, one of the 14 percent of the corps recruited locally; throughout his military service he remained a private. On 28 February 1802 Patrick married a young widow, Catherine McMahon *née* Mooney, from County Wicklow, Ireland. Catherine had arrived in Sydney Cove on 11 January 1800 on the *Minerva* with her husband, Pte Terence McMahon, a soldier in the NSW Corps who drowned in Sydney Harbour the following year. Patrick and Catherine, both Irish Catholics, were unable to marry in a Catholic church as there were none in Sydney in 1802, instead marrying in a Church of England church, St Phillip's; the ceremony was officiated by the Reverend Samuel Marsden, another influential parson of the time.

Patrick, like Terence McMahon, had been posted to Watsons Bay fishing village, which had been established in 1792 to provide food for the colony's hospital. Patrick and Catherine and her children by McMahon and their new children established themselves as a Watsons Bay family, though Patrick was often away soldiering and, later, farming. Patrick appears to have been involved in two notable events of the young colony.

The first was the Battle of Vinegar Hill near Castle Hill, to the west of Sydney. When a large number of Irish convicts attempted to revolt, troops of the NSW Corps, led by Major George Johnston, rushed from Sydney, and on 5 March 1804 promptly shot 15 rebels and later hanged another nine. The second was the notorious Rum Rebellion, when on 26 January 1808, soldiers of the NSW Corps led by Major Johnston deposed Governor Bligh.[24]

Discharged soldiers were entitled to land grants. In 1810 Patrick, having left the army, started a farm on the Central Coast with his eldest son Thomas, on land the British colonisers had stolen from the Guringai nation. Access to his property was probably via boat from Watsons Bay, sailing up the coast. In 1823 a land grant of 100 acres at Brisbane Waters and Kincumber was promised to Patrick, the land title being conferred in 1841; in the 1840s the Humphries family built at Kincumber the Holy Cross Catholic Church. A prosperous Irish Catholic family was now firmly settled, in the Central Coast and at Watsons Bay, where the family home was known as Wicklow.

In 2004 a lively re-enactment of the Battle of Vinegar Hill was staged. Stephen Gapps, who had done a public history course with Ann Curthoys at UTS and a subsequent PhD on 'Performing the Past: A Cultural History of Historical Re-enactment', explained in an essay how the re-enactment came about. In February 2003 Blacktown City Council placed an advertisement for an 'Authentic Re-enactment of the Battle of Vinegar Hill'. With another experienced 're-enactor' Brett Kenworthy, Gapps formed a history-performance company, Historica Pty Ltd., and then tendered for and won the contract. Gapps and his colleague worked hard to find '300 re-enactors'. They also searched for 'authentic' 1804 costumes, finding quite precise costuming details in an 1804 watercolour painting of the battle by an unknown artist, and acquiring costumes from Canada and the US 'where re-enactment is big business'. To find the re-enactors, calls went out to the Irish community in Australia, and then Gapps and Kenworthy 'scripted and cast an historical pageant with music, narration and amateur performers in costume'. The local Dharug people performed in the pageant, and there was also gender inversion, with a number of women portraying male convicts.[25]

Public interest in the Battle of Vinegar Hill, Gapps tells us, began in December 2003 when Blacktown City Council decided to devote its 2004 calendar, issued free to all residents, to the events of 1798 to 1804. Local newspapers picked up on the promised re-enactment, and then major newspapers, radio and television began to take an interest in an event that, Gapps thinks, had been relatively unnoticed in Australian history compared to the Eureka Stockade or Ned Kelly's last stand, even though Vinegar Hill was the first military conflict between Europeans in Australia, many of the mostly Irish convicts who took part being political prisoners from the 1798 Irish rebellion, their cry 'Death or Liberty'. In a concluding comment, Gapps writes:

> The unpredictability and magic of performance took hold and at the end of proceedings, as Koori women led a crowd of 1804 descendants over the hill and through the 'dead' and 'wounded' from the battle, many in the crowd of 10,000 were in tears.

The re-enactment, Gapps feels, was so dramatic and extraordinary that it garnered not only national but international media attention.[26]

I was interested to see if the 2004 re-enactment in Australia attracted attention in Ireland, and it looks like it did. I recalled that the Irish historian Ruán O'Donnell, whose book *The Irish Famine* I referred to in the previous chapter, had been working on a PhD thesis at ANU on Irish radicalism, both in Ireland and Australia, when Ann and I arrived there in 1995. From googling I saw that in 2004 he published an essay 'Castle Hill and Vinegar Hill: the Australian Rising of 1804'.[27] Ruán O'Donnell writes that counter-insurgency measures by the British in Ireland ensured that considerable numbers of 'Defenders and United Irishmen' were transported to Australia in the 1790s. By 1800 New South Wales was 'at least one-third Irish and home to at least 600 republican prisoners': 'The *Minerva* and *Friendship* transports, which arrived from Cobh in January/February 1800, carried such notorious figures as Wicklow "General" Joseph Holt, Dublin radical Richard Dry and Offaly rebel captain James Meehan.'[28]

What caught my eye here was a small detail that relates to the history of the Humphries family. O'Donnell notes that Irish political prisoners came out on the *Minerva* and *Friendship* in January/February 1800, while we know that Catherine McMahon, from County Wicklow, Ireland, had arrived in Sydney Cove on 11 January 1800 on the *Minerva* with her husband, Pte Terence McMahon, a soldier in the NSW Corps. Perhaps the Irish political prisoners on the *Minerva*, including Joseph Holt, were being guarded by Catherine's then husband Terence McMahon and other NSW Corps soldiers.[29]

O'Donnell goes on to speculate that there were 'clandestine negotiations in 1802 between French naval officers and United Irish leaders' in New South Wales and Van Diemen's Land, believing that the 'weakly defended and remote colony' might be vulnerable to a successful rebellion. It turned out not to be so, including for internal reasons among the rebels. Holt on 3 March 1804 learned that the secrecy he deemed essential had been compromised by 'loose talk', with the result that the 'famed Wicklow guerrilla fighter' severed his links with the plotters. In the event, in the next few days, up to '300 poorly equipped rebels' were no match for Major George Johnston's troops. O'Donnell wonders what the rebels intended to do if their revolt had succeeded. They may have tried to escape, by commandeering trading vessels, to Batavia in the Dutch East Indies, or to the United States; also, the French may have been tempted to use their Indian Ocean bases in Mauritius and Reunion to attempt to supplant the British in Australia, possibly with Irish assistance. But such attempts could not, he feels, have long withstood Royal Navy counter attack. In conclusion, O'Donnell is pleased that a major memorial to the Battle of Vinegar Hill was unveiled near the battle site during the Australian bicentennial commemorations in 1988, and that in March 2004 Blacktown City Council organised a week-long series of commemorations to mark the 200th anniversary of the battle.

Historical memory can slumber for long periods, and it is often a commemoration of an important but near-forgotten date that can quicken renewed interest in long-ago events. O'Donnell says that considerable numbers of Defenders and United Irishmen were key players in the failed 1798 rebellion, so I make a note to myself to find out more about them, especially Wolfe Tone of the United Irish, one of the leaders of that rising who, I gather, had been raised as a Church of Ireland Protestant and educated as a lawyer in Trinity College in Dublin; was attracted to the Enlightenment, and helped establish the Linen Hall Library in Belfast; influenced by Thomas Paine's ideas, he wished to expel the British from Ireland by insurrectionary force; and he hoped the United Irish could succeed in bringing together Catholics, Protestants and Dissenters in this republican endeavour. The United Irish, of which Tone was a founding member, were established almost simultaneously in Belfast and Dublin in 1791, two years after the French Revolution.[30]

Wolf Tone, I'm feeling, was another in a long dissident Protestant tradition that could have informed the rebelliousness of figures like Eva and Constance Gore-Smith, and which in turn could have influenced my father's life as a rebel in relation to the pro-British values and loyalties held by others in his Protestant family.

Conclusion

The Nash-Docker-Humphries family, Protestant and Catholic, variously from Clare through the Nashes and Wicklow and Dublin through the Humphries, were an eastern-suburbs family spread along the coast from Watsons Bay near the Heads to South Coogee near Maroubra. George Nash was not that far away by water, living in Glebe near Blackwattle Bay in Sydney Harbour. We know from the obituary that many of the Humphries family were present at the funeral of George Nash in 1927 in the Church of England part of the South Head cemetery. The family must have kept in contact.

In the eastern suburbs, between Watsons Bay and South Coogee, lived Jewish migrants, in Bondi in particular and spreading to North Bondi and Dover Heights and Rose Bay.

In the eastern suburbs, in the Communist Party, my father Ted Docker met my mother Elsie Levy, and they married in 1941, the same year, Mrs Holmes writes, that Ted Docker's mother Susan Nash died.

To say the least, this must have been an extraordinary happening for the Irish-descended family, one, perhaps, they couldn't easily accommodate. Perhaps this is what my father thought, that his new wife and his Jewish children, Jewish through their mother even if they were being brought up as atheists in a Communist home, would not have been accepted.

Jimmy Holmes, the cousin who rang but I never met, said on

the phone to me in the early 1970s that my father didn't allow his children to mix with his mother Alice's children. My mother, more than once, suggested that my father's family were not friendly to her, and she refused to see them.

I don't know if my mother was right or wrong in what she thought. Perhaps she was mistaken. But to my knowledge, when I was growing up, she never saw them. Perhaps this was a sadness in my father's life. Perhaps it was a sadness in my mother's life that she had no contact with her in-laws.

On the other hand, the Communist Party in its branches and friendship circles was a kind of alternative extended family – cosmopolitan, a house of many nationalities and ethnicities, as had been the Wobblies.

1 John Docker, 1492: *The Poetics of Diaspora* (Continuum, London and New York, 2001), p.vii.

2 Verity Burgmann, *Revolutionary Industrial Unionism: The Industrial Workers of the World in Australia* (Cambridge University Press, Cambridge, 1995), pp.71-72, 86.

3 Burgmann, *Revolutionary Industrial Unionism*, pp.71, 207, 214, 229-230, 242.

4 Burgmann, *Revolutionary Industrial Unionism*, pp.71-73.

5 Cf. John Docker, 'Politics and Poetics: Bernard O'Dowd's *Dawnward?* and Nineteenth-Century Chartist Poetry', *Southerly*, Vol.53, no.2, 1993, pp.13-33.

6 Cf. Docker, 'Storm Troopers of empire? Historical representation in *Breaker Morant*, Naguib Mahfouz's *Palace Walk* and other war histories', *History Australia*, vol.8, no.1, 2011, p.85.

7 Burgmann, *Revolutionary Industrial Unionism*, pp.11, 15, 16.

8 Raymond Evans, *Loyalty and Disloyalty: Social conflict on the Queensland homefront, 1914-18* (Allen and Unwin, Sydney, 1987).

9 Burgmann, *Revolutionary Industrial Unionism*, pp.181-186, 192-199.

10 Burgmann, *Revolutionary Industrial Unionism*, pp.221-225.

11 Burgmann, *Revolutionary Industrial Unionism*, pp.200-201.

12 Jeff Kildea, 'Australian Catholics and Conscription in the Great War', *The Journal of Religious History*, Vol.26, No.3, 2002, pp.298-299, points out that by contrast

to the Catholic church especially during the second referendum, the Protestant churches supported conscription.

13 Burgmann, *Revolutionary Industrial Unionism*, pp.5, 198; see ch.13, pp.203-228, for state persecution of the IWW, secret and overt. See also Patrick O'Farrell, *The Catholic Church and Community in Australia: A History* (Nelson, Melbourne, 1977), p.327.

14 Gerhard Fischer, *Enemy Aliens: Internment and the Homefront Experience in Australia 1914–1920* (University of Queensland Press, St. Lucia, 1989), pp.16–20, 24–26, 35. See also John Docker, *Dilemmas of Identity: The Desire for the Other in Colonial and Post Colonial Cultural History* (Working Papers in Australian Studies, Sir Robert Menzies Centre for Australian Studies, University of London, 1992), and Gerhard Fischer, 'Fighting the War at Home', in Nadine Helmi and Gerhard Fischer (eds), *The Enemy at Home: German Internees in World War I Australia* (UNSW Press, Sydney, 2011), pp.17–42.

15 Fischer, *Enemy Aliens*, pp.45, 47, 59-61, 94-95, 103, 122-9.

16 Fischer, *Enemy Aliens*, pp.43, 48-49, 62, 69, 70-71, 93, 122, 138-140, 146, 153, 174, 227, 241, 268.

17 Fischer, *Enemy Aliens*, pp.7, 44, 75-79, 96-97, 136-7, 296, 300, 304-307.

18 Fischer, *Enemy Aliens*, pp.7, 37, 45, 52, 99-100, 138, 151-2, 173, 305.

19 See John Docker, 'Storm Troopers of Empire?', p.83, and Marilyn Lake and Henry Reynolds, *Drawing the Global Colour Line: White Men's Countries and the Question of Racial Equality* (Melbourne University Press, Melbourne, 2008), pp.293, 303-306.

20 Max Solling, *Grandeur and Grit: A History of Glebe* (Halstead Press, Sydney, 2007), pp.127-128.

21 Solling, *Grandeur and Grit*, pp.84-85.

22 My thanks to Lyndall Ryan for sending me the articles and for information about *Labor Monthly*.

23 See John Docker, 'Troubled Reflections on my father', in Ann Curthoys and Joy Damousi (eds), *What did you do in the Cold War, Daddy? Personal stories from a troubled time* (NewSouth, Sydney, 2014), pp.87-113.

24 See Grace Karskens and Richard Waterhouse, 'too sacred to be taken away': Property, Liberty, Tyranny and the 'Rum Rebellion', *Journal of Australian Colonial History*, Vol.12, 2010, pp.1-22.

25 Stephen Gapps, 'Performing the Unknown: The Re-enactment of the 1804 Battle of Vinegar Hill', *History Australia*, Vol.I, no.2, 2004, pp.310-311.

26 Gapps, 'Performing the Unknown: The Re-enactment of the 1804 Battle of Vinegar Hill', pp.308-9, 311, 313. See also Tony Moore, *Death or Liberty: Rebels and Radicals Transported to Australia 1788-1868* (Pier 9, Sydney, 2010), pp.68-133.

27 Ruán O'Donnell, 'Castle Hill and Vinegar Hill: the Australian Rising of 1804', *The United Irishmen*, Volume 12.

28 See also Ruán O'Donnell, *The Rebellion in Wicklow* 1798 (Irish Academic Press, Dublin and Portland, Oregon, 1998).

29 Ruán O'Donnell, 'Liberty or Death': The United Irishmen in New South Wales, 1800-4', in Thomas Bartlett, David Dickson, Dáire Keogh, Kevin Whelan (eds), *1798: A Bicentenary Perspective* (Four Courts Press, Dublin and Portland, Oregon, 2003), pp.607-619, here at p.611, relates that there were at least two bids by the 1798 rebels to take over the *Minerva* by force.

30 My friend Mark Dorrian in an email sent me information about Wolf Tone. See also Kevin Whelan, 'The United Irishmen, the Enlightenment and Popular Culture', in David Dickson, Dáire Keogh, and Kevin Whelan (eds), *The United Irishmen: Republicanism, Radicalism and Rebellion* (The Lilliput Press, Dublin, 1993), pp. 269-296, and Marianne Elliott, 'The Defenders in Ulster', pp.222-233. See also Jim Smyth (ed.), *Revolution, Counter-Revolution and Union: Ireland in the 1790s* (Cambridge University Press, Cambridge, 2000).

5

A Revolutionary's Bookshelf

> I am unpacking my library. Yes, I am... share with me a bit of the mood – it is certainly not an elegiac mood but, rather, one of anticipation – which these books arouse in a genuine collector.
>
> Walter Benjamin, 'Unpacking my Library: A Talk about Book Collecting'[1]

Writing this chapter has not been easy. I don't know of any models or set genre that can help me. I did, however, recall the well-known essay of Walter Benjamin's on his being a book collector first published in 1929 and later became a chapter in *Illuminations*, which was edited and introduced by Hannah Arendt. 'Unpacking my Library: A Talk about Book Collecting' has helped me think about how to write this chapter on the cache of books and pamphlets that I inherited from my father when he died in 1983. As one would expect, Benjamin's essay, eccentric and playful, is replete with fascinating reflections and insights, reminding me of what I argued in the last chapter about his attraction to *Kunstchaos*. 'Every passion', Benjamin writes, 'borders on the chaotic, but the collector's passion borders on the chaos of memories.' A personal collection like his own, Benjamin stresses, constitutes a kind of 'confusion': 'For what else is this collection but a disorder to which habit has accommodated itself to such an extent that it can appear as order?' In the 'life of the collector', Benjamin feels, there is a precarious 'tension between the poles of disorder and order'. He hazards a thought that really interests me about my father's collection, that 'to a true collector the acquisition of an old book is its rebirth': 'This is the childlike element which in a collector mingles with the element of old age'. The collector's 'deepest desire' is to 'renew the old world', but from an 'angle' that is 'whimsical', for the collector's relationship to the objects he acquires does not emphasise their 'functional' and 'utilitarian value', their 'usefulness'. The collector 'studies and loves them as the scene, the stage, of their fate'. Benjamin says that his desire to acquire books influenced the way he travelled, how he explored cities, for he made his 'most memorable purchases on trips, as a transient': 'How many cities have revealed themselves to me in the marches I undertook in the pursuit of books!' Unpacking his collection that had been stored away for two years has stirred memories and images of Riga, Naples, Munich, Danzig, Moscow, Florence, Basel, Paris and Berlin.[2]

In this essay Benjamin also ventures an idea on the 'fate' of a collection that I find interesting for myself as someone who now possesses my father's collection. Benjamin reflects on being an 'heir' to a collection such as the 'two albums with stick-in pictures which my mother pasted in as a child', and that 'inheritance is the soundest way of acquiring a collection', for a 'collector's attitude toward his possessions stems from an owner's feeling of responsibility toward his property', and the 'most distinguished trait of a collection will always be its transmissibility'.[3]

While writing the paragraph above, curiously, on Anzac Day, 25 April 2012, that day of remembrance, I got a phone-call from my son Ned, and I told him how helpful it was to read Benjamin's essay (actually, re-read, I have markings all over it, though I can't recall why), including Benjamin's thought about the heir to a collection feeling a responsibility towards it and its transmissibility. Ned commented that this applies to Hannah Arendt also, reminding me that the last time Benjamin saw Arendt and her husband Heinrich Blücher, he entrusted to their care a collection of manuscripts, including 'Theses on the Philosophy of History', which had been written in the spring of 1940, and that while they waited for their ship in Lisbon, Arendt and Blücher read Benjamin's 'Theses' aloud to each other and to the refugees who gathered around them.[4] Later it was Arendt who did so much to bring *Illuminations* into existence, arranging as bookends that 'Unpacking my Library: A Talk about Book Collecting' be its opening chapter, 'Theses on the Philosophy of History' its last.

I might also record here that my old copy of *Illuminations* had become so fallen apart that I was trying to hold it together by an elastic band. A year or two ago, Ned bought me a new edition, with a dedication that reads: 'So that you may converse once again with Benjamin dad, for your memoir.'

I will interpret Benjamin on inheriting a collection to mean that as heir to my father's collection, I have a responsibility both to preserve it as a reflection of the past, and in my presentation of its contents, and through my occasional comments on items I find particularly interesting, to renew it in the present and for the future.

This is actually the first time I've looked at my father's books and pamphlets in any sustained way since I inherited them in 1983. I've stored them in the various houses we have lived in since that time, in Petersham in Sydney, O'Connor in Canberra, and once more in Sydney from late 2008 in North Bondi and then now where we live in Glebe. So even just listing them is a journey of discovery. I know, however, that I have to do more than simply tabulate a list. On Ann's sage advice, I've sorted the books and pamphlets into rough groupings, so that they form a rudimentary catalogue: Marx and Marxism, Engels, Lenin, the Communist

International, the Spanish Civil War, the USSR, Trotsky, Stalin, CPUSA (the Communist Party of USA), India, China, Australia, South-East Asia, New Left, Great Britain. Sometimes there is no author given, so within its group I include the title alphabetically.

I also try to list the items chronologically within each grouping, though here the pamphlets present a problem. In 'Unpacking My Library', Benjamin quotes Anatole France saying that the only exact knowledge we have is of the date of publication and the format of books.[5] But many pamphlets in my father's collection, written for the political moment, don't include a date of publication (neither do some of the books). In Benjamin's terms, pamphlets introduce the confusion of temporal uncertainty. I have to confess that it was usually the pamphlets I found most interesting. In what follows I indicate in square brackets when an item is a [pamphlet].

My father was self-educated; I remember him saying that he was allowed to stay in school until he was 14, which he said was quite late for a working-class boy. (In *A Proletarian Life*, Audrey Blake writes that in Victoria when a child turned 14, 'high school was no longer free; it cost two pounds a year which ... was beyond my mother's means').[6] Actually, to say simply that he was self-educated is not to say enough. I think, along with so many socialists and radicals in a society where university education was open to very few, my father was educated in what I would call an 'international proletarian public sphere'.[7] For my father, it was a sphere composed of radical groups differing and disputing, hearing speeches at the Domain on all sorts of topics more or less eccentric, usually more, and intense discussions of what socialism should and should not be; it was a sphere fuelled by books and pamphlets bought in leftwing bookshops and, in the Communist Party, inner-party classes. It was a sphere that was highly international, where what was happening elsewhere in the world, especially in the Soviet Union, was just as important and alive to my father as anything happening in Australia.

I think my father was also a collector to some degree in Walter Benjamin's sense. On the evidence of this collection, he didn't simply acquire and keep books and pamphlets he ideologically agreed with; his attitude to his collection was not simply utilitarian. There were a large number of books and pamphlets by and on Lenin, who he so much admired, and also, chillingly, by Stalin and Beria; but there was also a book on Rosa Luxemburg, a pamphlet by William Morris, and a reprinted lecture from 1892 by the early Australian trade unionist and socialist W G Spence. It was in coming across these three items in particular that I began to think this is a collection that my father was treasuring as a collection.

Also, like Benjamin exploring cities through collecting, perhaps when my father travelled as a high-up official of the Australian Communist Party, he may have explored leftwing bookshops in towns and cities for items to add to his collection.

Marx and Marxism

Lafargue, Paul, *The Right to be Lazy and Other Studies* (Charles H Kerr and Company, Chicago, 1907), a book which speaks to the utopian strand of socialist thought. In *Revolutionary Industrial Unionism*, Verity Burgmann writes that Lafargue's book was a left-wing classic frequently available in IWW libraries, and she quotes a passage where Lafargue exhorts the proletariat 'to accustom itself to working but three hours a day, reserving the rest of the day and night for leisure and feasting'.[8] In reminiscences I wrote down (dated 17 February 1979), my father recalls that *The Right to be Lazy* was for the IWW one of 'our key pamphlets to sell' down the Domain or in the IWW hall in Sussex Street in Sydney in the city.

Boudin, Louis B, *The Theoretical System of Karl Marx in the Light of Recent*

Criticism (Charles H Kerr and Company, Chicago, 1918).

Kautsky, Karl, *Ethics and the Materialist Conception of History* (Charles H Kerr and Company, Chicago, 1918).

Kautsky, Karl, *The Dictatorship of the Proletariat* (The National Labour Press Ltd, Manchester) (no date).

Marx, Karl, *Critique of the Gotha Programme*, with appendices by F Engels and V – .I Lenin (Martin Lawrence, London, 1933).

Marx, Karl, *Selected Works*, Vol.I, prepared by the Marx-Engels-Lenin Institute, Moscow (Co-Operative Publishing Society of Foreign Workers in the USSR, 1935).

Marx, Karl, *Selected Works*, Vol.II, prepared by the Marx-Engels-Lenin Institute, Moscow (Co-Operative Publishing Society of Foreign Workers in the USSR).

Verulam, Frank, *Production for the People* (Left Book Club Edition) (Victor Gollancz, London, 1940).

Frölich, Paul, *Rosa Luxemburg: Her Life and Work* (Victor Gollancz, London, 1940).

Marx and Engels on Reactionary Prussianism (Foreign Languages Publishing House, Moscow, 1943). [pamphlet]

Fundamentals of Marxism-Leninism (Foreign Languages Publishing House, Moscow, n.d.)

Marx, K and Engels, F, *Manifesto of the Communist Party* (Foreign Languages Publishing House, Moscow, 1952).

Marx, K and Engels, F, *Manifesto of the Communist Party* (Foreign Languages Publishing House, Moscow, 1959).

Cornforth, Maurice, *Philosophy for Socialists* (Lawrence and Wishart, London, 1961).

Leontiev, A, *Political Economy: A Beginner's Course* (Current Book Distributors, Sydney, n.d.)

Ablett, Noah, *Easy Outlines of Economics* (South Wales Miners' Federation) (published by the Plebs League, 176 Springvale Rd., Sheffield, n.d.) [pamphlet]

Rosental, Mark, *Contradictions and Motive Forces of the Present Epoch* (Novosti Press Agency Publishing House; no date, perhaps 1961 or 1962) [pamphlet]

Marx, Karl, *Critique of the Gotha Programme* (Progress Publishers, Moscow, 1971). [pamphlet]

Engels

Engels, Frederick, *Socialism: Utopian and Scientific*, Fourth Edition, August 1918) (Andrade's bookshop, 201 Bourke St., Melbourne, 32 Rawson Chambers, Sydney).

Engels, Frederick, *Herr Eugen Dühring's Revolution in Science [Anti-Dühring]* (Co-Operative Publishing Society of Foreign Workers in the USSR, Moscow and Leningrad, 1934).

Engels, F, *Articles from* The Labour Standard *(1881)* (Foreign Languages Publishing House, Moscow, n.d.). [pamphlet]

Engels, Frederick, *The Origin of the Family, Private Property and the*

State. In the Light of the Researches of Lewis H Morgan (Current Book Distributors, Sydney, 1942). [pamphlet]

Engels, Frederick, *Socialism: Utopian and Scientific* (Current Book Distributors, Sydney, 1944). [pamphlet]

Great Britain

Forsyth, P T, *Socialism, the Church and the Poor* (Hodder and Stoughton, London, 1908).

Morris, William, *Factory Work As It Is and Might Be*. A Series of Four Papers by William Morris (New York Labor News Co., New York, NY, 1922). [illustrated pamphlet, stamped inside: Socialist Labor Party, 107 Liverpool Street, Sydney] (I'm particularly delighted to see a pamphlet by William Morris, a favourite writer of mine of the late nineteenth century, whose libertarian socialist utopia *News from Nowhere* I wrote about in my PhD thesis, and then worked this analysis into a chapter of my *The Nervous Nineties*.)

Palme Dutt, *Fascism in Great Britain* (International Labor Defence Publication No.8, n.d), printed in Sydney). [pamphlet]

Lenin

My father and Lenin: inside Engels' pamphlet *The Origin of the Family, Private Property and the State. In the Light of the Researches of Lewis H Morgan* (1942), I see some folded paper with handwriting on it; I take it out and unfold it. I'm fairly sure it's in my father's hand, and the 10 small pages read like a speech in rough note form he must have given to an inner party group, entitled on the outside, 'Party Organisation'. Near the beginning my father says: 'Great revolutionary masters emphasized *importance* organization'. He refers then to Lenin saying that without organisation workers will be powerless, and that in this connection Lenin took to task Rosa Luxemburg and the Spartacists.

In contrast, the Party does not subscribe to the 'paralyzing theory of spontaneity': 'Our Party must be highly disciplined, be united, centralized and democratic'. The Party is of a 'new type', because it doesn't confine its activities to 'parliamentary struggle'; this is what is wrong with the Labor Party, and what was wrong with Kautsky: 'Kautsky leading theoretician 2nd International maintained that Socialism could be realised by capturing state.' The Party maintains that organisation in factories is also very important for the 'class struggle', my father calling attention to Lenin's slogan, 'Every factory must be a stronghold of the Communist Party'. The Party, he adds, has built a network of shop committees and job stewards. Also, says my father, 'Best branches in factory base during illegal period'. This last note suggests to me that my father was making this speech during the 1940–42 period of illegality. My father loved Lenin, and felt he could apply his insights to Australia. Lenin worked out that a revolutionary party to be successful could not simply, as Kautsky had maintained, confine itself to parliamentary struggle, which was also the limitation of the Australian Labor Party. Lenin saw that the mistake of Rosa Luxemburg and the Spartacists was their theory of spontaneity, leaving them powerless in situations of crisis. For a revolutionary party to survive through periods of persecution and perhaps illegality, it had to be highly organised, disciplined, united and 'centralized and democratic'.

In the Bondi flat when I was growing up, in voluble family discussions on almost any topic, my father would always begin with Lenin. Since he was only given five minutes to give his view – 'Dad, you've only got five minutes' – by the time he'd talked of the necessary relevance of Lenin, his five minutes would be up.

In a folder 'Ted Docker's Reminiscences' I came across a handwritten quotation often attributed to Lenin, though some googling suggests it is to be found in the Russian writer Nikolai Ostrovsky's *How the Steel Was Tempered* (1936). The quotation is headed 'Lenin said':

> 'Man's dearest possession is life, and since it is given to him to live but once, he must so live as not to be scared by the shame of a cowardly and trivial past; so live as to have no torturing regrets for years without purpose; so live that dying he can say – all my life and all my strength were given to the finest cause in the world – the liberation of humanity.'

Lenin on the Third International (Modern Publishers, Sydney, n.d.). [two copies of this pamphlet]

Lenin, N., *Bourgeois Democracy and Proletarian Dictatorship* (Andrade's Bookshop, 201 Bourke Street, Melbourne, 32 Rawson Chambers, Sydney, n.d.). [pamphlet]

Ulyanov-Lenin, *The Collapse of the Second International* (The Socialist Labour Press, Glasgow, n.d.). [pamphlet]

Lenin, N, *The Proletarian Revolution* (Communist Party, 21a Maiden Lane, Strand, London (on the title page, author given as V I Ulianov followed by N Lenin in parenthesis).

Lenin, N, *'Left' Communism: 'The Infantile Sickness of "Leftism" in Communism'* (on the title page, there is no date; publisher given as the Communist Party of Australia, based on the First Australian Edition, May 1921). [pamphlet]

Lenin, N, *Imperialism: The Latest Stage in the Development of Capitalism* (The Marxian Educational Society, Detroit, 1924). [pamphlet]

Bukharin, N, *Lenin as a Marxist* (Communist Party of Great Britain, Covent Garden, London, 1925). [pamphlet]

Gorky, Maxim, *Days With Lenin* (first published by Centrizdat, Moscow,

1931) (Current Book Distributors, Sydney, n.d., three copies). [pamphlet]

Lenin, V I, *Imperialism and Imperialist War (1914–1917)* (Selected Works, Vol. V) (Co-Operative Publishing Society of Foreign Workers in the USSR, Moscow and Leningrad, 1935).

Lenin, V I, *The Years of Reaction and of the New Revival (1908–1914)* (Selected Works, Vol. IV) (Co-Operative Publishing Society of Foreign Workers in the USSR., Moscow and Leningrad, 1935).

Lenin, V I, *From the Bourgeois Revolution to the Proletarian Revolution (1917)* (Selected Works, Vol. VI) (Co-Operative Publishing Society of Foreign Workers in the USSR., Moscow and Leningrad, 1935).

Lenin, V I, *After the Seizure of Power (1917–1918)* (Selected Works, Vol. VII) (Co-Operative Publishing Society of Foreign Workers in the USSR, Moscow and Leningrad) (can't see a date).

Lenin, V I, *The Period of War Communism (1918–1920)* (Selected Works, Vol. VIII) (Co-Operative Publishing Society of Foreign Workers in the USSR., Moscow and Leningrad, 1935).

Lenin, V I, *New Economic Policy and Socialist Reconstruction* (Selected Works, Vol. IX, Co-Operative Publishing Society of Foreign Workers in the USSR, Moscow and Leningrad) (no date).

Lenin, V I, *Will the Bolsheviks Maintain Power? Also: The Bolsheviks Will Maintain Power*, volume twelve of the Little Lenin Library (Martin Lawrence Ltd., London) (Gilmour's Bookshop, 165 Castlereagh Street, Sydney). (no date).

Lenin, V I, *Selected Works*, Volume X, *The Communist International* (The

Marx-Engels-Lenin Institute, 1938).

Lenin, Nikolai, *On the Road to Insurrection* (The Communist Party of Great Britain, London, n.d.).

Zinoviev, G. and Lenin, V I, *Socialism and War* (Martin Lawrence Ltd., London, n.d.) (Little Lenin Library).

Kovnator, Ray, *Lenin's Mother* (Foreign Languages Publishing House, Moscow, 1944) (opposite the title page is a photo of 'M A Ulyanova, Lenin's Mother'). [pamphlet]

Lenin, V. I., *What the 'Friends of the People' Are and How They Fight the Social-Democrats* (Foreign Languages Publishing House, Moscow, 1946).

Landa, N, *Lenin on Educating the Youth* (Novosti Press Agency Publishing House, n.d.) [pamphlet]

Lenin, V I, *What Is To Be Done?* (Foreign Languages Publishing House, Moscow, 1947). [pamphlet]

Lenin, V I, *The State and Revolution* (Foreign Languages Publishing House, Moscow, 1949). [pamphlet]

Lenin, V I, *Socialism and War* (Foreign Languages Publishing House, Moscow, 1950). [pamphlet]

Lenin, V I, *Critical Remarks on the National Question* (Foreign Languages Publishing House, Moscow, 1951). [pamphlet]

Lenin, V I, *Karl Marx* (Foreign Languages Publishing House, Moscow, 1951). [pamphlet]

Lenin on the Third International (Modern Publishers, 191 Hay St., Sydney, n.d.). [pamphlet]

Lenin, V I, *Preliminary Draft of Theses on the Agrarian Question* (Current Book Distributors, Sydney, 1951). (three copies) [pamphlet]

Zinovieff, G, *Nicolai Lenin: His Life and Work* (Andrade's Bookshops, Melbourne and Sydney, n.d.). [pamphlet] (In a preface, Zinovieff notes that the booklet is 'the shorthand report of a speech delivered by me on the 6th of September, 1918, at a meeting of the Petrograd Soviet'.)

Kuusinen, Otto, *Triumphant March of Lenin's Ideas* (speech at the Lenin Anniversary Meeting, April 22, 1960). [pamphlet]

Lenin through Australian Eyes: An Australian Contribution to the Lenin Centenary 1870–1970 (articles by Tom Payne, Arthur Calwell, Katharine Susannah Prichard, Pat Clancy, Ralph Gibson). [pamphlet]

Lenin, V I, *What Is To Be Done?* (Foreign Languages Press, Peking, 1973).

The Communist International

The Communist International was extremely important to Communist Parties around the world; membership conferred on a Party an official status within the worldwide Communist movement.

Fourth Congress of the Communist International (Abridged Report of Meetings held at Petrograd and Moscow, Nov. 7-Dec. 3, 1922) (published for The Communist International by the Communist Party of Great Britain).

Bolshevising the Communist International. Report of the Enlarged Executive of the Communist International, March 21st to April 14th, 1925 (published for The Communist International by the Communist Party of Great Britain, Covent Garden, London). [pamphlet]

Theses and Resolutions: XII Plenum E.C.C.I. (Modern Books Ltd, London, n.d, 1931 or 1932) (first sentence refers to the meeting of the Executive Committee of the Communist International in Moscow). [pamphlet]

J Lenz, *The Rise and Fall of the Second International* (International Publishers, New York, 1932).

Palme Dutt, R, *For a United Front Against Fascism* (International Labor Defence, 537 George Street, Sydney, n.d., maybe 1933) [pamphlet]

Programme of the Communist International. Draft Adopted at the Fifth Congress of the Communist International (Published for The Communist International by the Communist Party of Great Britain, Covent Garden, London, n.d.) [pamphlet]

Dimitrov, *The Working Class Against Fascism*. Speech in Reply to Discussion, Seventh World Congress of the Communist International (Modern Books Limited, London, n.d). (Inside, there are two pages of densely handwritten notes, quotations, it would appear, from Dimitrov) (My father, along with Lance Sharkey, attended the Seventh Congress in Moscow in 1935, and according to David Lovell and Kevin Windle in their book *Our Unswerving Loyalty*, brought back the new Comintern policy of the popular front against fascism, which was adopted by the Australian Communist Party later in that year.)[9] At the beginning, Dimitrov says he is summing up 'the eight-day discussion' (p.3). [pamphlet]

Communist International, Vol. XIV, No. 7–8 (can't see a date, maybe

1936–7; the first essay, 'Two Years of Struggle for the Anti-Fascism Front', refers in its opening sentence to 'our World Congress, two years ago' which decided that the 'struggle for the formation of a united proletarian and anti-Fascist people's front was the central task of the policy of the Comintern'; this sounds like the conference that my father attended in 1935 with its new popular front policy).

Communist International, Vol. XVII, No. 2, February, 1939 (the front cover featured: 'Against Munich'; P Vidal, 'The Special Congress of the Socialist Party of France'; A. Claire, 'Socialism Demands Labour Discipline'; W Molotov, '"The Third Five-Year Plan": Theses for Report to the 18th Congress of the C.P.S.U.'). [pamphlet]

Dimitrov Accuses the Nazis at the Reichstag Fire Trial (Current Book Distributors, Sydney, 1942) [pamphlet] (A brief note entitled 'Dimitrov's Life Story' at the end of this pamphlet says that George Dimitrov was born in a town near Sofia, the capital of Bulgaria in 1882; he became a revolutionary in turbulent times, and in 1923, when a military dictatorship came to power and put down an armed revolt of workers and peasants, went underground. While living as an exile in Germany, he was arrested by the Gestapo and charged with setting fire to the Reichstag; the stand Dimitrov made in court compelled the Nazis to admit his innocence and to release him; he went to Moscow, where the Soviet Government gave him citizenship, and he became Secretary of the Communist International. The pamphlet consists mainly of a transcript of Dimitrov's final remarks to the court, including sharp exchanges with the presiding judge. In a foreword, 'This Was Hitler's First Defeat', Harry Pollitt, General Secretary, Communist Party of Great Britain, writes that on the night of 27 February 1933, Hitler and his accomplices burned down the Reichstag, the German Parliament, which became, in Pollitt's words, the 'pretext for the wholesale butchery and torture of German Communists in the first place, and then of Socialists,

Liberals, Church people, Jews, musicians, writers, scientists and progressives of every kind'; Hitler accused the Communists of the burning of the Reichstag, and Dimitrov and other Communists were arrested and charged. In Pollitt's view, Dimitrov's final speech in the courtroom in Leipzig where the trial was being held in September 1933 'inflicted the first great political defeat on the Nazis': 'The Nazis were compelled to release him.')

Dimitrov, George, *The War and the Working Class* (published by the Central Committee of the Communist Party of Australia, Hay Street, Sydney, n.d.) (Dimitrov here is explaining that World War Two is an 'imperialist war' between the 'biggest capitalist states', Britain and France on the one hand, and Germany on the other. My father has marked out in a penciled line in the margin a passage where Dimitrov says that the 'essence of the present war' is a battle for 'hegemony in Europe, for colonial possessions in Africa and other parts of the globe, for oil, coal, iron, rubber, and not at all in defence of "democracy", "liberty", "international law" and the guarantee of the independence of small countries and peoples, as the bourgeois press and the Social-Democratic deceivers of the working class are howling'. Dimitrov says the bourgeoisie of England and France wish to continue to 'hold undivided sway over hundreds of millions of colonial slaves'. In the margin, my father has written, I think, 'Read', it's a bit faded, so he may have read out this and other passages at some kind of Communist Party class held perhaps during the time of the Hitler-Stalin pact when the Party was illegal, before the Soviet Union, having been attacked by Hitler's Germany, came into the war on the side of Britain and France.)

Spanish Civil War

I'm especially interested in this section because of a general sense of the immensity of the betrayal of Spanish democracy in the 1930s by the Western powers, who in effect colluded with

Mussolini's Italy and Hitler's Germany; we have intimate knowledge of that betrayal, including British upper class admiration of Hitler throughout the 1930s, in Jessica Mitford's evocations, as devastating as they are witty, of her upper-class family in her autobiographies, *Hons and Rebels* and *A Fine Old Conflict*.

In *Communist International*, Vol. XIV, No. 7–8 (I think 1936–37) there is a section, 'In the Far West and the Far East (letters by Comrades Mao Tse-Tung and Chu De', pp. 1131–4. These are letters addressed to the Spanish people, Mao writing: 'The cause for which you are fighting is also our cause... Many comrades in the ranks of the Chinese Red Army... would also like to go to Spain, there to participate in your struggle... Were we not now occupied with the Japanese invaders, we should certainly have joined you and taken our places in the ranks of your foremost fighters.')

International Press Correspondence, Vol. 16, No. 26, 4th June, 1936, English Edition (a newspaper, with articles on Spain and also an article on Hitler, 'Hitler Fascism is Driving Towards War'). [pamphlet]

Ibarruri, Dolores, *Implacable War Against Fascism!* (Foreign Languages Publishing House, Moscow, 1941). [pamphlet] (I'm embarrassed to admit I didn't immediately recognise this name, though something in the pamphlet sent bells faintly tinkling, when Ibarruri, in a section addressed to 'Wives and mothers, you who read these pages', suggests that Hitler's invasions of European countries in World War II were assisted by the indifference of outside powers to the Spanish Civil War: 'When the women of Spain proclaimed aloud to the world the horrors of the roads from Malaga that were strewn with the corpses of thousands of women and children, a compassionate smile or a gesture of incredulity was the only reply elicited from most of the future victims of fascism... Thus, the anguish and torment that had its inception in Spain has spread everywhere.' Intrigued, I googled, various sites came up for her name, and I chose the Marxist Internet Archive, which tells me that Dolores Ibarruri (1895–1989) was always known as *La Pasionara* (The Passion Flower). She was born in the Basque country, grew up in an impoverished mining family, and was elected to the Provincial Committee of the Basque Communist Party in 1920. In 1931 she mounted a campaign for the improvement of conditions for Spanish women. In 1934 she helped organise the World Conference of Women Against War and Fascism. In 1936 she was elected to the Cortes (national legislative assembly). Throughout the Spanish Civil War, she served as one of the main spokespeople for the Republicans. She is best known for uttering the famous words '*No Pasaran!*', 'They [the fascists] shall not pass!', during a radio address made at the height of the Battle of Madrid. Following the fall of Madrid to Franco's forces in 1939, Ibarruri went into exile in the USSR. She returned to Spain following the death of Franco, and was once more elected to the Cortes at the age of 81. In terms of birth and death dates, she is almost an exact contemporary of my father.

In a reminiscence of his early life that I included in my *1492: The Poetics of Diaspora* (2001), my uncle Lew Levy, growing up in Bondi, talks of meeting Bella Weiner, who 'had fled Poland because of its anti-semitism. There she had been a member of the Bund, a Jewish Social Democratic Party, but when I met her she was a Communist'. Lew writes that Bella was an extraordinarily dynamic figure, 'our Rosa Luxemburg and La Pasionara'.[10]

In *Interesting Times: A Twentieth-Century Life* (2002), Eric Hobsbawm tells us he can still remember hearing La Pasionara speak in the first months of the Spanish Civil War in Paris.[11]

In August of 2012, in Russia, two young women, Nadezhda (Nadya) Tolokonnikova and Maria (Masha) Alyokhina, of the feminist punk-rock band Pussy Riot, which had been founded in August 2011, were put on trial on charges of hooliganism and inciting religious hatred, after performing a 'punk prayer' entitled 'Mother of God, Chase Putin Away', on 21 February 2012 in the Cathedral of Christ the Saviour in Moscow. In the courtroom, in a glass cage, Nadya could be clearly seen wearing a blue t-shirt reading NO PASAREN . Nadya has also written in a letter to supporters of their protest against President Putin's attacks on freedom and democracy: 'I'm grateful to everyone who has said: Freedom for Pussy Riot! We are witnessing a big and important political event, and the Putinist system is having a harder time controlling it… Whatever the verdict for Pussy Riot, we and you have already won. Because we have learnt to be angry and speak politically' (*Sydney Morning Herald*, 18–19 August 2012, based on a report in *Guardian News and Media*). Nadya and Masha were jailed for two years, amid protests in Moscow and worldwide. Struck by the reference to La Pasionara's no pasaran, I wondered if Nadya was, in paying homage to La Pasionara who had been in the Spanish Communist Party, also alluding to the powerful traditions of anarchism in Spanish history that had been evident in the Spanish Civil War,[12] as well as, clearly, to powerful female figures in revolutionary history.

Nadya and Masha served 21 months of their sentence. They were released on 23 December 2013, on the basis of an amnesty, not long before the Sochin Winter Olympics hosted by Russia which began in early February 2014, the general suspicion being that Putin wanted to create a measure of favour with the West in order to make sure the games would be a success. Outside the Winter Olympics, Nadya and Masha demonstrated with other Pussy Riot members against what they refer to as the Putinist system. They were attacked with whips by the Cossack militia that had been employed as security; the police did not intervene.

In 2014, the Russian-American writer Masha Gessen, a friend of the Pussy Riot women who held meetings in Gessen's flat in Moscow, published *Words Will Break Cement: The Passion of Pussy Riot*, a fast-moving account of the formation of Pussy Riot as a feminist punk band and the trial and jailing of its two key members Nadya and Masha in 2012. The title is adapted from something Solznenitsyn once wrote that Nadya quotes in her trial speech. 'So', Nadya refers to Solznenitsyn saying, 'the word is more sincere than concrete? So the word is not a trifle? Then may noble people begin to grow, and their word will break cement.' While making her closing statement on day eight of the trial, Nadya, Gessen tells us, 'was wearing a blue T-shirt emblazoned with a yellow fist and the words NO PASARAN'. Gessen also reports that when Pussy Riot had publicly performed at an earlier demonstration, they 'had waved a purple NO PASARAN flag with a fist in it'.[13]

Gessen, alluding to Marx's famous aphorism in the *Eighteenth Brumaire*, refers to the blatantly pro-state proceedings as 'a Soviet political trial repeated as farce'. At one point, Gessen notes, the 'judge directed the court marshals to remove anyone who laughed', and indeed a 'journalist was removed from the courtroom for smiling'. Invited to make statements by the judge, Nadya and Masha, inheritors of a venerable revolutionary tradition, denied the legitimacy of the court, and then set out at length before the court, and in effect the world's media, the aesthetic and philosophical basis of their actions, including the influence on them of philosophers of the ancient world such as Socrates, and an array of modern philosophers like Heidegger and Sartre. Pussy Riot, Nadya explains, were seeking in the cathedral 'true sincerity and simplicity… in the holy-fool aesthetic of punk performance'. Their ideal 'philosopher is a person who loves wisdom and strives for it, but can never possess it'.[14]

Gessen points out that Pussy Riot's intellectual interests reprise historical features of Russian dissident history, in particular, feminism, anarchism and avant-garde art movements. Pussy Riot, Gessen reflects, also wished to associate art with a 'spirit of fun and mischief'.[15]

The Pussy Riot young women were students who were very dissatisfied with Russian schooling and higher education institutions for the narrowness of their humanities teaching, for example, a lack of gender studies departments that could introduce students to contemporary feminist and queer theory. Consequently, in the spirit of self-education, they read widely in radical social theory. Feminism, Gessen notes, had once been a vibrant presence in Soviet Russia. It had been part of Bolshevik ideology in the 1920s, when bourgeois morality was to be replaced with a revolutionary morality that would abolish marriage and monogamy, and introduce free love, communal children, and full gender equality; the world's first laws against sexual harassment in the work place were developed. From the 1930s on, however, bourgeois morality was increasingly restored. Pussy Riot, Gessen feels, see themselves as reintroducing feminism to Russia.[16]

Nadya, Gessen says, immersed herself in Western feminist theory, carrying around with her, and reading on the Metro, Julia Kristeva's *Revolt, She Said*. In September of 2011, at a conference of Russian opposition groups, Nadya presented a slide show suggesting that Russia's lack of a feminist movement had to be addressed; she drew to the attention of the mostly male audience Shulamith Firestone's *The Dialectic of Sex: The Case for Feminist Revolution*, and also the issue of 'race in feminist art', talking about the 1980s New York art group Guerrilla Girls and the writings of bell hooks. Pussy Riot considered, however, that the time was right for a performance art that didn't merely repeat what other dissident artists around the world had done. Positioning themselves as self-conscious outcasts and outsiders, they called on the memory of Russian avant-garde artists such as the Constructionists of the 1920s, the Union of Real Art who were a collective of futurist artists, writers and musicians of the 1920s and 30s (purged in 1937), and the Conceptualists of the 1970s through to the 1990s, and also dissident intellectuals and writers like Joseph Brodsky. In November 2011 Pussy Riot produced a video song called 'Kropotkin-Vodka' invoking the name of the iconic Russian anarchist. At their trial, Nadya made it clear that Pussy Riot were against institutional religion such as that embodied in the Orthodox Church, in their view, as Gessen caustically comments, 'a reliable ally of Russian dictators through the centuries'. However, Pussy Riot admire the Christ of the New Testament, which, Nadya told the court, 'supports the search for truth and the constant overcoming of one's self, of what you once were'.[17]

Pussy Riot's intense years of wide reading in philosophy, discussion of dissident ideas, and performing daring anarchist actions in public places, which they always videotaped, culminated in their instantly famous punk prayer in the Cathedral of Christ the Saviour, a song and associated rock music, dance and visual display, which Gessen believes will one day be recognised for what it was and is, 'great art'.[18] Its opening lines:

Virgin Mary, Mother of God, chase Putin out,
Chase Putin out, chase Putin out.

Its central section:

Shit, shit, holy shit!
Shit, shit, holy shit!

Virgin Mary, Mother of God, become a feminist
Become a feminist, become a feminist
The Church sings the praises of rotten dictators
Black limousines form the procession of the Cross

This remarkable prayer established Pussy Riot as world figures of dissidence.[19]

Since their release, Nadya and Masha have toured the world, feted wherever they go. According to an article in *The Sydney Morning Herald*, not long before they visited Sydney they posed with Hillary Clinton in the US, Nadya saying, 'It's quite obvious why Hillary Clinton posed with us – it's an echo of the Cold War'. Asked if she regretted it, Nadya replied: 'Of course no. We have to communicate with all people.' While in New York, Nadya and Masha visited Occupy Wall

Street activist Cecily McMillan at Rikers Island prison, in order to stress that injustices against which they campaign are not limited to Russia (*The Sydney Morning Herald*, 22 August 2014).

In late August 2014 Pussy Riot came to Sydney to participate in the annual Festival of Dangerous Ideas at the Sydney Opera House. In the Australian edition of the online *Guardian*, Monica Tan in an article 'Pussy Riot members liken Australian asylum detention to Russian justice' on Saturday 30 August, reports Nadya and Masha's comment on Australian government mistreatment of refugees: 'We were surprised by the problems here, such as detention camps, which are similar to what is happening in Russia'. They said what was happening in Russia should stand as a warning to all countries.

Fans of Pussy Riot, Ann and I booked seats at the Sydney Opera House to see them the following day, on Sunday, 31 August 2014. They appeared in the very large concert hall, which seats thousands, and there were indeed thousands there to hear them, including the presence of many young women, we were interested to see. When they came on stage, Nadya and Masha were accompanied by Masha Gessen as interviewer, and Nadya's husband Petya as translator, Nadya and Masha speaking mostly in Russian. I can't recall in detail what was said that night, except that at the beginning Nadya and Masha made a statement to the effect that 'Pussy Riot' was not only to be understood in terms of their specific actions in Russia, but was now an idea for the world; they hoped people everywhere would share in its spirit of questioning and dissent in relation to their own societies, however small were the acts and activities they created and participated in. The audience were extremely attentive and we all laughed a lot. Thinking about it later, what struck me was how different Nadya and Masha were from Soviet-era Russian dissidents, most of whom, despising the Soviet Union, would then oleaginously admire the US and the West: dissidents in the Soviet Union or Communist eastern Europe, once they reached the West their dissidence towards whatever the West did in the world, however brutal, stupid and destructive, such as in the Iraq War, suddenly vanished.

Nadya and Masha reminded me of the anarchist New Left in the 1960s and 1970s, extremely critical of both the Soviet Union and the US, interested in creating a new historical consciousness, a third way, that history should start again. Masha, Gessen records her saying at the trial in Moscow, admired the stance of the students in Paris in May 1968. 'My cause', Masha said, 'may be hopeless, but I find my freedom in the responsibility I take on, and to retreat for me would be to die a little, to use the words of the students protesting at the Sorbonne in 1968'.[20] Perhaps the independence of their thinking is why the Pussy Riot young women are attracting extreme interest around the world.

I was interested to read in Gessen's book that Pussy Riot were opposed to high or institutional art, that they agreed that 'art should be concealed by a spirit of fun and mischief'.[21] There is perhaps a context for Pussy Riot's wild dance involving masking and grotesquerie, comic yet riven by passion and anger, in the cultural history of World Upside Down which flourished in early modern Europe, especially in the importance of gender inversions. The American cultural historian Natalie Zemon Davis, in an essay entitled 'Women on Top', argues that the female sex was thought the disorderly one *par excellence* in early modern Europe; in pictorial representation and at festival time, the disorderly woman appeared as full of life and energy, clever, powerful, resourceful, witty, Amazonian, rebellious, prompting new ways of thinking and acting, licensing widespread criticism and mockery of unjust rule and rules.[22]

Pussy Riot performances are also perhaps part of the cultural history of fools and tricksters which flourished in early modern Europe in story, legend and performance, a history, I think, that illuminates Pussy Riot's anarchic aesthetic of the grotesque body. In my book *Postmodernism and Popular Culture: A Cultural History*, I evoke the great Russian cultural theorist Mikhail Bakhtin's thoughts on the importance to humanity since ancient times of the fool and especially in early modern Europe. In Bakhtin's view, fools are the representatives of the carnival spirit in everyday life outside of set carnival times. Fools for Bakhtin are life's maskers; they possess the time-honoured privilege to be other in this world, the right not to make common cause with any of life's available categories; they have the right to confuse, to tease, to hyperbolise; they have the right to blunt language and to anger, to rage at others with a primeval, almost cultic rage. Furthermore, they don't exempt themselves from parody and mockery.[23]

Bakhtin's writings suggest that the grotesque body of carnival in early modern Europe, revelled in by fools and tricksters, created a kind of chaos of values, a thought I very much like. And then I think of Nietszche's *Thus Spake Zarathustra*, where Zarathustra the holy fool exhorts the value of chaos: 'I tell you', says Zarathustra, 'one must have chaos in one to give birth to a dancing star.'[24]

Pussy Riot, I think, are bringing these long cultural histories to life in new forms, in the perilous political context of Putin's Russia.

Palmer, Nettie, and Fox, Len, with the help of Jim McNeill and Ron Hurd, *Australians in Spain* (Current Book Distributors, Sydney, May 1948). [pamphlet]

The USSR

My father's admiration for the Soviet Union never wavered. When I was still living at home in our Bondi flat, he continued to read with great thoroughness and attention the *New Times* magazine which came from Moscow.

Price, M Philips, *My Reminiscences of the Russian Revolution* (George Allen and Unwin, London, 1921) (cover page says Price is Former Correspondent of the *Manchester Guardian* in Russia).

Zinoviev, G, *Russia's Path to Communism* (Communist Party of Great Britain, London, 1925). [pamphlet]

The Programme and Rules of the Communist Party of the Soviet Union (Bolsheviks) (Co-Operative Publishing Society of Foreign Workers in the USSR, Moscow, 1932). [pamphlet]

Kuubyshev, V V, *From the Sixth to the Seventh Congresses of Soviets* (Co-Operative Publishing Society of Foreign Workers in the USSR – Moscow-Leningrad, 1935). [pamphlet]

The Soviet Union and the Path to Peace (A collection of statements and documents 1917–36 by Lenin, Stalin, Molotov, Voroshilov, Litvinov, Tukhachevsky) (Lawrence and Wishart, London, 1936).

History of the Communist Party of the Soviet Union /Bolsheviks Edited by A Commission of the Central Committee of the Communist Party of the Soviet Union (Bolsheviks.) (Foreign Languages Publishing House, Moscow, 1939).

Vyshinsky, A Y, *Against Preparations for a New War – For a Five-Power Peace Pact* ('Soviet News' Booklet, London, 1949) (Speech at United Nations Political Committee on 16 November 1949). [pamphlet] (Bob Boughton, describing the Pilbara strike from 1942 to 1949 in his excellent essay on the Communist Party of Australia's involvement, from its formation in 1920, in the struggle for Aboriginal and Torres Strait people's rights, tells us that in 'October 1949, the Soviet Foreign Minister, Andrei Vishinksky', referring to the treatment of Aboriginal workers in the Pilbara pastoral industry, 'accused Australia in the United Nations of openly violating fundamental freedoms and human rights'.)[25]

Kalinin, M I, *On Communist Education* (Foreign Languages Publishing House, Moscow, 1950).

Ilyin, M., *The Earth and Man* (Current Book Distributors, Sydney, August 1950). (On an inside page there is an acknowledgement: 'This pamphlet is a reprint of two articles which appeared in Nos. 22 and 23 (1950) of the Soviet weekly magazine, *New Times*').

Titarenko, S, *Patriotism and Internationalism.* A Soviet News Booklet (published in UK at 3 Rosary Gardens, London, SW7, n.d.) [pamphlet]

Anashkin, G and Babin, N, *Freedom of the Individual in the USSR* (Foreign Languages Publishing House, Moscow, n.d.) [pamphlet]

Decisions of the Central Committee, Commission of the Central Committee of the Communist Party of the Soviet Union (Bolsheviks) *on Literature and Art (1946–1948)* (Foreign Languages Publishing House, Moscow, 1951). [pamphlet]

Beria, L, *Speech at the Nineteenth Congress of the Commission of the Central Committee of the Communist Party of the Soviet Union (Bolsheviks)* (Foreign Languages Publishing House, Moscow, 1952). [pamphlet] (Beria! The very name is chilling, signifying Stalin's most sinister henchman, in charge of purges and assassinations; after Stalin's death in 1953 Beria himself was purged and executed.)

The Soviet Union and the Socialist Theory of the State (not dated, published for the Labour Research Association by Auckland Service Printery, New Zealand). [pamphlet]

Leonidov, F, *Racism – An Ideological Weapon of Imperialism* (Progress Publishers, Moscow). (n.d., it appears to have been published in the 1960s, perhaps 1963 as Kennedy's assassination is mentioned as recent.) [pamphlet]

Here's a surprise for a genocide scholar, which I have been since the early 2000s. One of the chapters is entitled 'Genocide – The Grave Crime Against Mankind'. So my father owned a pamphlet which talked about genocide, though I'm pretty sure he never mentioned the term when I was growing up. However, another connection: my memory is that my parents revered Paul Robeson. In the chapter on genocide the pamphlet refers to *We Charge Genocide*, a 'well-grounded petition to the United Nations charging the American government with genocide'; it was signed, says the pamphlet, by progressive figures in the US, including Paul Robeson, and highlighted 'nearly 3,000 instances of criminal acts carried out by racial terrorist organisations against the Negro population of the United States with the connivance of the authorities' (pp. 36–37).

When Ann and I were invited to write an essay, 'Defining Genocide', for *The Historiography of Genocide* (2010) edited by Dan Stone and began researchfor it, we luckily came across a mention of *We Charge Genocide* in an endnote to a book by the American sociologist Irving Louis Horowitz, *Taking Lives: Genocide and State Power* (1982 edition). (There's another connection here; I recall that when in my undergraduate days, I was keenly reading C Wright Mills, I noticed that Horowitz was an associate of Mills, and I became interested in his writings as well.) In *Taking Lives*, Horowitz considers the question whether or not the violence directed against African Americans, for example by the Ku Klux Klan between 1865 and 1920, was genocide. Horowitz decides it's not genocide (defined as systematic extermination that is politically directed) but vigilantism (defined as the maintenance of some kind of social order without legal or state support), though he concedes that the Ku Klux Klan was indeed assisted by legislative assemblies and courts in southern states. Ann and I discuss Horowitz's uneasiness in making this distinction in our essay. We also followed up on Horowitz's reference to the 1951 *We Charge Genocide* petition and made a sustained analysis of it. The petition was presented to the UN in New York by Paul Robeson on behalf of the Civil Rights Congress (CRC), a Communist-led organisation. The petition charged that the lynching and other forms of assault on the lives and livelihood of African Americans from 1945 to 1951, especially the frenzied attacks on returning Black American veterans, amounted to genocide according to the 1948 UN Convention. The CRC, we note, believed that a focus on Jim Crow laws and deprivation of Blacks' rights would be an embarrassment for the US abroad and might hasten overdue reform; a strategy that, as Mary Dudziak observes in her book *Cold War Civil Rights: Race and the Image of American Democracy* (2000), was successfully adopted by the American Civil Rights movement a decade later.[26]

It's not difficult to see that Leonidov's pamphlet, which refers to the 1948 UN Convention and was an attack on the West in general and the US in particular, for racism, colonialism, imperialism and genocide, was part of Soviet strategy in the Cold War to undermine the West's claim to moral superiority based on pointing out the political terror amounting to genocide practised by the Soviet Union. Yet Leonidov's pamphlet does conduct a powerful argument. It defines 'genocide as a form of racism'. It suggests genocide is a wide ranging process, involving physical extermination; the suppression of national languages and culture as a way of 'removing a nation from the ethnographic map and destroying national identity and unity'; biological genocide in depriving a persecuted people of the possibility of reproduction by deliberately separating men from their womenfolk for long periods of time; biological genocide also in involving compulsory mass operations and experiments to prevent childbirth; and genocide as land eviction, leaving 'the population in a given colony to die of starvation, while the greater part of the best land becomes concentrated in the hands of an insignificant minority of white settlers, who enslave the indigenous population' (pp. 35–6).

Leonidov writes that in the US, 'Indians were the first victims of genocide. They were followed by the Negroes. Placed in incredible conditions they are being systematically persecuted' (p. 36). Despite the 1948 UN Convention, Leonidov says, such genocide continues in the US (pp. 38–9), as it does under Apartheid in South Africa (pp. 47–53). Nor does Leonidov spare the British: 'The British imperialists do not lag behind the Americans.' The history of the British Empire is 'full of facts about the brutal exploitation and annihilation' of 'coloured peoples'. The British massacred the 'whole aboriginal population of Tasmania and most of that of Australia.' (p. 38)

As we can see in other pamphlets in my father's collection, Australian Communist authors also made powerful critiques of racism, colonialism and imperial exploitation in relation to indigenous peoples; but their arguments were always shadowed by the knowledge that the Soviet Union, especially under Stalin for decades, had also been committing terrible crimes against humanity.

Grant, Nigel, *Soviet Education* (Penguin, Harmondsworth, 1964).

Trotsky – or, rather, anti-Trotsky

Olgin, M J, *Trotskyism: Counter-Revolution in Disguise* (Workers Library Publishers, New York, 1935). [pamphlet]

Defence of the Party and The Fight Against Provocation. A Communist Publication, 1949 this pamphlet, printed in Newtown in Sydney, appears mainly to be polemical attacks on Trotskyists; the pamphlet is composed of two reprints from Soviet sources.

First reprint: 'Revolutionary Vigilance and Progress in Party Work', *Pravda*, 4 January 1937; on p. 2 we read: 'The last years have been characterized by the fact that the bourgeoisie acquired the service of faithful dogs in the shape of the Trotskyite-Zinoviev scoundrels'.

Second reprint: 'Our Tasks in the Struggle Against Trotskyist and Other Wreckers, Diversionists and Spies' – 'Extracts from Articles by V M Molotov, published in 'International Press Correspondence', 1937. I could have put this 1949 Australian Communist Party pamphlet in the USSR group of works, but the reprinting of the 1937 Soviet material might indicate that in 1949 the Australian party was no longer in an inclusive popular front mood, rather it felt surrounded by those they recurrently deemed social fascists. On the first page of the reprint from *Pravda*, a quotation from Lenin is marked in the margin in pencil, I presume by my father: 'Lenin said: "We are encircled by the world bourgeoisie, who is eager to seize upon every minute of vacillation in order to bring back to power those belonging to its class, in order to restore the rule of the big landowners and of the bourgeoisie"'. Did the Australian Communist Party feel encircled by hostile forces in 1949, including Trotskyists?

Stalin

I confess to being pleasurably surprised that my father's Stalin material is relatively small, certainly compared to the number of items by and on Lenin. I can't recall him ever quoting Stalin in family contexts, whereas Lenin for him was his enduring touchstone of wisdom.

Stalin, Molotov, Litvinov, *Our Foreign Policy* (Modern Publishers, Sydney, n.d.) opens with 'Stalin's Interview with Walter Duranty, Correspondent of the "New York Times", December 25, 1933'). [pamphlet]

Stalin, Joseph, *Leninism*, Volume II (Co-Operative Publishing Society of Foreign Workers in the USSR, Moscow, 1933).

Stalin, J, *Lenin* (Co-Operative Publishing Society of Foreign Workers in the USSR – Moscow-Leningrad, 1934) [pamphlet]

Stalin, Joseph, *Marxism and the National Colonial Question*. A Collection of Articles and Speeches (Co-operative Publishing Society of Foreign Workers in the USSR, Moscow and Leningrad, 1935).

Stalin, J, *On the Great Patriotic War of the Soviet Union* (Foreign Languages Publishing House, Moscow 1942). [pamphlet]

Joseph Stalin: The Short Official Biography, prepared by The Marx-Engels-Lenin Institute, Moscow, First Australian Edition (Current Book Distributors, Rawson Chambers, Sydney), introduced by L L Sharkey, June 1942. [pamphlet]

Stalin, J, *Anarchism or Socialism* (Foreign Languages Publishing House, Moscow, 1950).

H G Wells' Interview with J V Stalin (Current Book Distributors, Sydney, April 1950). [pamphlet] A note on an inside page tell us: 'H G Wells visited the Soviet Union in 1934 and on July 23 he interviewed Joseph Stalin.'

India

Palme-Dutt, R., *India Today*. Summarised by Jack Lindsay, Research Officer, Trades and Labor Council (no date, Current Book Distributors, Sydney). [pamphlet]

CPUSA (Communist Party of USA)

Browder, Earl, *An American Foreign Policy for Peace* (speech of 10 October, 1940) (published by Workers Library Publishers, New York). [pamphlet]

Mandell, William, *On Socialist Man: A Reply to Isaac Deutscher* (A Boomerang Publication for a Return to Marxism-Leninism, a Political Affairs Reprint) On the back is the information that *Political*

Affairs is a 'theoretical magazine analyzing the crucial issues of our day from the viewpoint of the Communist Party, USA) From a footnote the pamphlet appears to be a reply to an address by Isaac Deutscher to a Socialist Scholars Conference of September 1966). [pamphlet]

China

Liu Shao-Chi, *On Inner-Party Struggle* A Lecture Delivered on 2 July 1941 at the Party School for Central China (Foreign Languages Press, Peking, China). [pamphlet]

Mao Tse-Tung, *On People's Democratic Dictatorship* (Foreign Languages Press, Peking, 1950). [pamphlet]

Burchett, Wilfred G, *China's Feet Unbound* (World Unity Publications, Melbourne, 1952).

Mao Tse-Tung, *A Single Spark Can Start a Prairie Fire* (Foreign Languages Press, Peking, 1953). [pamphlet] This appears to be a reprint of a Mao essay of 5 January 1930.

A Proposal Concerning the General Line of the International Communist Movement: The Letter of the Central Committee of the Communist Party of China in Reply to the Letter of the Central Committee of the Communist Party of the Soviet Union of March 30, 1963 (Foreign Languages Press, Peking, 1963). [pamphlet]

Certain Aspects of Party Life in the Communist Party of China. Reprinted from *Pravda*, 28–29 April 1964, printed at 21 Ross Street, Forest Lodge, Sydney. [pamphlet]

The Australian Communist. A Journal of Marxism-Leninism (Melbourne, March 1964) [pamphlet] This appears to be a journal published by those members of the Australian Communist Party who chose to follow China after the split between China and the Soviet Union, and considered that they represented true Marxism-Leninism, its key figure E F Hill. Hill has an essay, 'Another Article (Written 1960) L. Aarons thought "Sectarian"'. There is also an essay entitled 'More Light on L L Sharkey's Betrayal of Marxism-Leninism'. I know my father, who continued always to believe in the Soviet Union, was very upset by the split, mentioning the names of people in the new pro-Chinese party who had once been 'fine comrades' and colleagues of his in the Party over a long time.

Nonetheless he became very hostile to China. I was reminded of just how hostile when I was re-reading in the Mitchell Library my parents' letters to me while Ann and I were in London in 1973–4. Looking at my notes of the letters, I see that in a folder of London Letters 1973, my mother mentioned in a letter of 27 December that 'your father is reading neville maxwell's book and will write to you'. I must have been reading, for reasons I can't remember, Neville Maxwell's account of the 1962 border war between India and China, *India's China War: How the Chinese Saw the Conflict* (1972), and must have mentioned to my father that I liked Maxwell's pro-China analysis. I see from my notes that I had already received a letter dated 14 October 1973, from 'E J Docker', addressed to 'Dr Ann Curthoys, John Docker, 130 Chatsworth Rd., Willesden Green, NW2', a long jeremiad against Mao, Maoists and China, with sympathetic comments on India. My father concludes: 'John I believe you have dangerous views regarding the Chinese leaders. As for that Mao stooge and liar [Maxwell], I'm really surprised that you should be influence[d] by his trick journalism. He like the late Edgar Snow is accepted by the Maoists because he distorts and twists the facts: Snow wrote some fine articles in a different period. I have more to say about Mao and Maxwell but another time.' Ann and I must have suggested in a previous letter that we were intending to visit Ireland to see where his mother came from; my father concludes his letter hoping Ann and I would visit Ireland; the handwriting is a little unclear, but my father talks about both his brothers going to Ireland during World War I: 'About Ireland England's first colony. Could you make the journey? both my brothers while on leave. Could pay a visit to County Clare... by ferry?' I'm very touched by this.

In a folder 'Letters Answered 1974' in my Mitchell notes, I record that I received two letters from my father very critical of Maxwell's book. In another folder, 'Letters Answered 1976', I note that my mother includes inside a mauve letter a cutting of a letter on Mao published in *Tribune*, the Communist Party newspaper of 13 October, by Ted Docker, Bondi, NSW, Mao having died a month or so earlier. Under the title 'Mao held back China's progress', my father wrote:

The passing of Mao Tse-tung should enable progressive changes to develop in China. Under Mao, China was rapidly moving into the camp of imperialist reaction.

Even Malcom Fraser was greatly impressed with Chinese developments and the possibilities to serve the interests of the big employers.

Has China moved forward during Mao's period in office?

Apart from increases in the population, nothing notable has happened. On the contrary, owing to incorrect policies, China has almost ceased to move ahead.

One way to determine progress is to find out the rate and extent of industrial growth. China, a backward country, made considerable progress in co-operation with the Soviet Union.

This was a development that Lenin had in mind. Had this friendship and unity continued China would have rapidly developed into an advanced industrial country.

Soviet plans and machinery were rejected in an abrupt and insulting manner. It was made clear by the Maoists that China would place their own plans for industrial growth into operation, and Soviet advice and friendship were not required.

What were these plans? One was called China's Big Leap Forward and consisted of a great number of Back Yard foundries. These proved a dismal failure. This childish plan had previously been rejected by Soviet experts and consequently the result was no surprise.

Another mistake was the 'cultural revolution' which left the Chinese people more backward educationally and culturally.

The Maoists never lose an opportunity to slander and viciously attack the Soviet Union and other socialist countries. The attitude of China towards the Angola War in supporting the USA and other reactionaries must never be forgotten.

Australia

Spence, W G, *New Unionism*. Lecture by Mr W G Spence, delivered in Leigh House, Sydney, on Sunday Night, June 12th 1892, under the auspices of the Australian Socialist League (1892).

Wright, T, *Russia To-Day: An Australian Trade Union Delegate's Report* (Sheet Metal Workers' Union, Trades Hall, Sydney, May 1928). [pamphlet]

Rodd, L C, *Australian Imperialism* (Modern Publishers and Importers, Sydney) (no date is given, but from the listing of sources consulted it could be the mid-1930s; there is a reference, for example, to 'Mrs M M Bennett, authoress of "The Australian Aboriginal", writing to "The West Australian", January 15, 1934'. [pamphlet]

Much of the pamphlet is an eloquent denunciation of imperial domination and exploitation practised by Australian governments in New Guinea, while supposedly observing Australia's obligations under its Mandate for the New Guinea Territory, the pamphlet quoting from Article 2 of the League of Nations Mandate: 'The mandatory shall promote to the utmost the material and moral well-being and social progress of the inhabitants of the territories subject to the present mandate.' The pamphlet mordantly notes: 'To advance the interests, not of the native inhabitants of New Guinea who, according to the League of Nations Mandate, should be Australia's first care, but the interests of Australian capitalists, some fifty gold mining companies have been formed to exploit the gold mines of New Guinea.' The pamphlet also denounces the racist exploitation of the Indigenous people of Australia: 'In the Northern Territory and Western Australia the natives have been dispossessed of their lands to make way for pastoral and mining interests. Where the aborigines serve upon the white man's stations, they are permitted to exist; but where they endeavour to preserve a tribal unity and independence and consequently threaten the white man's property, they become the subject of a debate as to the humanitarian advantages of chains or handcuffs.' In more general terms, the pamphlet observes, 'the Australian people have permitted an exploitation of native lands and peoples by capitalists who show little regard for native rights and who totally ignore the question of national self-determination'. The pamphlet also denounces Australian imperial exploitation in the Malay States, Siam, Burma, Borneo, Fiji and Nauru. (pp. 7, 9, 18–20, 24)

I was reminded of this pamphlet's section on Australian gold mines in New Guinea when on 21 March 2012 Ann and I went along to the NSW State Library for the launch of Michael Waterhouse's fine book, *Not a Poor Man's Field: The New Guinea Goldfields to 1942 – An Australian Colonial History*, which with great sensitivity deploys a kind of 'world history' approach, evoking both the experiences and perspectives of the Australian miners and of the New Guinean villagers who lived near the goldfields. In his speech, Waterhouse referred to massacres of New Guinea men, women and children by the Australians; there was a slight gasp in the audience. As a genocide – and massacre-studies person, I was so intrigued that I read the relevant section of the book, which draws on Australian documents as well as interviews with New Guinean survivors, as soon as I could. In chapter 13, 'Early Encounters: The European Perspective', Waterhouse writes that it didn't take long after the gold rush began in 1926 for problems to develop. The New Guinea carriers the mining companies employed, drawn from elsewhere, were interfering with local villagers' gardens, while Europeans were shooting their pigs. Early in 1927 the villagers killed some carriers, which angered the Edie Creek miners who depended on them.[27]

Here, very interestingly for those of us who skeptically ponder the Anzac Legend, Waterhouse tells with some irony and scorn of J D McLean, the Mining Warden, who had arrived from Australia less than a fortnight before at the Edie Creek gold field. As Waterhouse phrases it, McLean didn't 'let his lack of local experience discourage him from direct action'. Waterhouse notes that in his report McLean claimed that 'official action was required as *the miners were going to organize a force to deal with the natives under Anzac rules*'.[28] The italics are in Waterhouse's text. Anzac rules? We have to wonder, from this cryptic reference, what they are, especially as the Anzacs are so heroized in Australian popular and official historical memory and commemoration as the creators of settler Australia's national spirit, to be admired by the world.

McLean organised a punitive expedition of eight Europeans and 20 New Guinean police, all issued, Waterhouse believes, with rifles or shotguns. In his report, McLean mentioned burning down Lambaura village and destroying its gardens, shooting some local Biangai people, and then burning another village, Kaisinik. In chaper 14,'Pacification of the Kukukuku', Waterhouse refers to massacres that he considers occurred in 1931 and 1932 as relations between the European miners and the local Kukukuku people worsened, especially after the murder of a German prospector, Hellmuth Baum. In the collective punishment of villagers by police patrols that followed, there occurred the massacres of men, women and children that Waterhouse referred to in his State Library talk. The ensuing patrol reports, Waterhouse observes, were careful to underplay what had happened and to conceal the extent and details of the killings. Waterhouse notes silences in the reports that may indicate other massacres than those already known to have occurred. One young boy, Mokera, was not killed, but rather brought back to be taught pidgin in order to be used as an interpreter. Waterhouse concludes this chapter with the reflection that the 'reprisals' enacted on 'whole communities' carried out by patrol officers and sanctioned by the Australian Administration were 'morally indefensible', especially when we consider, he points out – just as Rodd's pamphlet *Australian Imperialism* pointed out in the mid-1930s – Australia's 'responsibility under the League of Nations Mandate to promote the material and moral well-being and social progress of the inhabitants of New Guinea'.[29]

Vagueness and silences in official reports of killings by patrol officers that Waterhouse evokes in New Guinea in the late 1920s, early 1930s will readily remind us of Ray Evans bringing to light similar practices of concealment, denial and circumlocution by those who carried out massacres of Indigenous people in Queensland in the nineteenth century.[30]

As for *Anzac rules* in dealing with non-European peoples, we know something of their parameters in the Surafend massacre in Palestine in December 1918 after the war was over, a massacre in which the Australian Light Horse were conspicuous.[31] In my earlier chapter on my father, the IWW and World War I, I referred to Suzanne Brugger's illuminating study of the behaviour of Australian troops in Egypt during the war, suggesting that the Australian troops assumed that 'as white men, as Britons', they were 'imperial overlords', at all times insisting on their 'personal superiority', and that nothing was beyond them in terms of physical violence or insult and abuse.[32] I also referred to Peter Stanley in his *Bad Characters* (2010) arguing that many Australians in the AIF in Cairo 'behaved with the disdain "white men" felt for what they saw as inferior races', freely thrashing Egyptians with whips and knocking them out if they perceived any impudence towards them as superior beings.[33]

In *Not a Poor Man's Field*, Michael Waterhouse tells us that Brigadier-General Evan Wisdom, the Administrator, aired his general 'philosophy', writing in February 1927 that the local people had to be disabused of the 'idea that they could treat the white man with contempt', for example, by resisting 'the arrest of murderers'.[34]

We can now, perhaps, define Anzac rules: any non-Europeans, in any country the Anzacs happened to be, who did not immediately recognize the Anzacs' racial superiority as white men and Britons were to be reminded of such superiority by a well-tried repertoire of violence ranging from verbal abuse to massacre.

Mason and McShane, *What Is This Labor Party?* [pamphlet] This vigorous attack on the Australian Labor Party, was printed for the Communist Party of Australia; it is not dated, nor are initials given for Mason and McShane. In a preliminary authors' note, Mason and McShane inform their readers: 'Our starting point is Marxism-Leninism, more especially Lenin's well-known analysis of the Australian Labor Party, made in 1913. Then the great revolutionary leader declared that the A.L.P. was not a Socialist Party, 'even in words'; that it was a Liberal (a capitalist) party in essence, that its aim was not Socialism, but an independent Australian capitalism... One day, Lenin continued, the party of Labor-Capitalism would have to make way for a genuine "Socialist, workers' party"'. The authors' note concludes that 'a new, Socialist workers' party, pledged to Marxist-Leninist principles... must replace the moribund, dying, treacherous Labor Party'. (The pamphlet appears to have been written during World War II, at the time of the illegality of the Communist Party, 1940–42.)

Sharkey, L L-, *A Reply to Father Ryan by L L – Sharkey, President, Australian Communist Party* (published by Communist Party of Australia, Sydney), n.d., perhaps 1943.

Wright, T, *New Deal for the Aborigines*. Foreword by Katharine Susannah Prichard, second edition (Current Book Distributors, July, 1944). The first edition of this well-known pamphlet came out in 1939. Tom

Wright was Federal President of the Sheet Metal Workers' Union and the pamphlet was endorsed by the Labor Council of NSW. So interesting did I find this pamphlet that, as the reader will see, I spend some considerable time writing about it.[35]

In her foreword, dated July 1944, Prichard suggests that Australia's 'prestige in the eyes of the world has suffered considerably by our treatment of the aborigines': 'Stories of atrocities committed by pioneering settlers against the native race have aroused horror and condemnation.' She quotes from Marx: 'As Marx said – "The native races know us chiefly by our crimes"'. She writes of the 'shame' that she feels most Australians are conscious of 'in connection with our treatment of the aborigines'. Prichard particularly draws attention to the perfidy of the Western Australian settler government in the late nineteenth century after the state was granted self-government by Britain with a proviso that the Aboriginal people would receive assured financial support: 'The Constitution Act for Western Australia of 1899 provided that after the gross revenue of the Colony exceeded five hundred thousand pounds in any financial year, an amount equal to one per cent. of such gross revenue should be devoted to provision for the aborigines. But when finances of the Colony began to flourish and exceeded the specified amount, the Forest Government moved to have this section of the Act repealed.' Prichard points out that in Western Australia, Government revenue for the year ending in June 1939 was estimated at nearly £11,000,000: 'had the conditions on which this State was granted self-government been adhered to', there would have been funds available to make adequate provision 'for the dispossessed native race'.[36] Now, Prichard warns, Aboriginal people across the continent are facing 'extermination'; what is urgently needed is scrutiny of the methods by which Australia provides so-called protection, and new practical measures at a national level 'based on a scientific and realistic approach'.

There are aspects of Prichard's attitudes in this foreword that are certainly unfortunate, based on a kind of nineteenth-century evolutionism that descends from Marx and Engels. Prichard writes that it is 'true that the progress of humanity demanded the development of this country' rather than it continue to be the 'vast hunting ground of scattered tribes of primitive people', but some way should have been found to maintain the rights of this 'primitive race', in the spirit of the British Government instructing Captain Cook and Sir Arthur Phillip to 'treat the natives well and to refrain from arousing their hostility'. For Prichard, then, it was right to dispossess the Aboriginal peoples in order that the continent be productively developed; but the settler atrocities against them that occurred during this dispossession have created a shameful historical and ethical crisis. In this desperate situation, 'a remnant of the aborigines' can be saved from 'extinction' by the measures suggested by Tom Wright, in the necessity of 'reserves for full-blooded aborigines' and a new deal for 'peopled of mixed blood'.[37]

Powerfully written, Tom Wright's pamphlet is scathing of religious missions and state and federal governments. On the cover is a photo of a young smiling Aboriginal man; in an introductory note for the 1944 edition, Wright tells us that the 'young aborigine of 1939, whose photograph is again used on the cover of this pamphlet, went to work for a white exploiter, and has since died from tuberculosis'. Like Prichard, Wright makes a sharp distinction between 'the half-castes and others of mixed blood', and 'the Aborigines proper, the full-blooded natives, thousands of whom still live under tribal or semi-tribal conditions'. Wright says he will focus on the problem of these, 'the real aborigines'. The pamphlet denounces white settlement, for while we can be proud of its 'great development' to the 'advanced community of today', it has been accompanied by 'tragedy' for 'our aboriginal population': 'pride will be linked with feelings of the deepest shame'. Wright quotes the anatomist, naturalist and anthropologist Professor F Wood Jones, author of the 1934 book *Australia's Vanishing Race*, concerning the complexity of traditional

Aboriginal society. A 'happy and vigorous race' when the 'whites first settled in Australia', the 'normal form of contact with Europeans brought and still brings ruin and death to the aborigines'. While many of the Australian tribes have been made extinct, in Arnhem Land and in parts of North and Central Australia, and in Northern Queensland and Cape York, and parts of West Australia, the tribes are sufficiently intact to be able to survive if proper actions are taken. (pp. 7–9)

Wright refers to Dr Donald Thomson being commissioned by the Commonwealth Government to conduct a 'scientific survey of the natives of Arnhem Land in 1935–36–37'. Wright approvingly records Thompson's recommendations to the Commonwealth Government, that the 'native tribes in Federal Territory not yet disorganised or detribalized' should be 'absolutely segregated' in order to 'preserve intact their social organization, their social and political institutions, and their culture in its entirety'; that the 'native reserve Arnhem Land' be made 'inviolable'; and that similar steps be taken to render inviolable 'any other reserves in which the native population remain undetribalized'. Thompson, says Wright, made it clear that the proposed segregation should last 'only until a sound policy has been tested and proved, preserving the natives and their culture in the meantime'. Wright expresses his disgust, however, at the Honorable J McEwen, the Minister for the Interior, who in a statement in February 1939 ignored Donald Thomson's recommendations, instead affirming that the federal government will concentrate on 'immediate physical needs' and on training Aboriginal people to perform 'useful service', for example, a useful occupation, in order to turn them away from their traditional 'nomadic' inclinations towards a 'settled life'.[38] McEwen, says Wright, is actually recommending that Aboriginal people become workers 'generally without wages' for the very station owners, miners and mission stations that have helped destroy the Aboriginal population, treating both male and female Aborigines as 'chattel slaves'. (pp. 10–12)

Wright is critical of McEwen's view that Aboriginal peoples are nomadic, for while Aboriginal Australians are invariably described as such, 'they would normally have left their tribal territory only for short periods, returning always to the same home-locality, the clan's estates, on which their tribal organization and culture are based, and from which they cannot be divorced without irreparable harm.' (p. 12) Wright's critique here resonates with later thinking by Indigenous and non-Indigenous thinkers.

In the opening chapter of my *The Origins of Violence*, I recall that in the latter 1990s Ann and I attended a speech given by the central Australian Aboriginal leader, Galarrwuy Yunupingu, to the National Press Club in Canberra (13 February 1997). It is the European colonists, Yunupingu pointed out, who were and are the wanderers on the face of the earth, they are the ones who travel to distant places and once arriving in a place such as Australia continue to roam within the continent. Yet, Yunupingu noted with some scorn, it is the Aboriginal peoples, who stay on their own lands as far as they are permitted by the colonisers to do so, to look after their country and because they belong to it, who are always labelled nomads. Ann and I often talked about Yunupingu's speech and how it changed our thinking about colonisation, migration and world history, for it highlighted the reverse narratives and mythologies that colonisers construct. We concluded that it is through such narratives and mythologies that the supposedly settled and urbanised peoples attempt to conceal from themselves that they are the nomads of world history.[39] A few years later we were pleased to find that the anthropologist Hugh Brody, in his book *The Other Side of Eden: Hunter-Gatherers, Farmers, and the Shaping of the World* (2000), based on research with the hunter-gatherer peoples of the Canadian Arctic, had come to a very similar conclusion as had Galarrwuy Yunupingu. 'It is agricultural societies', Brody reflects, 'that tend to be on the move; hunting peoples are far more firmly settled. This fact is evident when we look at these two ways of being in the world over a long time span.'[40]

J McEwen also, Wright tells us, ignores key features of traditional

Aboriginal society and history, for example, 'the fact that the aborigines have their own land property rights and laws'. Wright is also alarmed that McEwen wishes to keep encouraging the 'religious missions' that in Wright's view have 'long and unsuccessfully' worked for the 'conversion of the aborigines' in condemning and forbidding 'all the aborigines' own social standards, moral codes and spiritual beliefs'. (p.13) Here Wright is anticipating Raphaël Lemkin. In an essay 'Are Settler-Colonies Inherently Genocidal?', I point out that Lemkin, in an unpublished essay 'Spanish Treatment of South American Indians Essay, n.d.', refers to the entwined cultural and religious genocide committed by the Spanish missions that abounded in Mexico, California, Louisiana and elsewhere. In Lemkin's view the Spanish missions attempted to destroy pre-Columbian spiritual and cultural life through conversion, force and cruelty; corporal punishment was inflicted on Indians of both sexes who failed in their religious duties; if an Indian escaped from the mission village, he was brought back by soldiers and lashed.[41]

Wright devotes several pages to his condemnation of religious missions. (pp. 14–19) He tells us that Dr R.M. Crookston, who accompanied Dr Thomson on the Queensland part of his expedition, told a Sydney audience on 30 April 1939 that 'he knew of a missionary in Queensland who chained young native women to posts, whipped them and turned them into the bush'. Dr Crookson referred to the employment of Aborigines as a slave trade. Elsewhere in Australia, Wright continues, sacred stone objects, stolen from their rightful inheritors, have been purchased by missions for an insignificant sum, the missions then reaping a big profit from their sale to museums and collectors in Australia and abroad. A 1930 report of the Finke River Mission Station (Lutheran) by its Pastor Superintendent revealed that many Aborigines died on the mission from illnesses such as scurvy and complications brought on by measles, chiefly pneumonia and dysentery. A chief reason the missions were able to survive is that the converted Aborigines work, usually without wages, for various white enterprises outside the mission. Wright argues that the missions of all denominations in all parts of Australia reveal a similar story, of making converts to their particular denomination in the name of saving their souls, while preparing those converted for exploitation by whites as a way of training them to be useful citizens. (pp. 14–19) Yet such destruction of their Aboriginal religious concepts is 'facilitating their demoralization and final extinction'. Wright writes that much of the 'literature of the missions is nauseating for its sanctimonious hypocrisy and the general glossing over of the indignities suffered by the natives physically, stressing instead the alleged "spiritual" uplifting'. (p. 27) Again I'm reminded of Lemkin, who wrote in another unpublished essay 'Revised Outline of Genocide Cases' that demoralisation, together with forceful conversion and prohibition of cultural activities, are techniques of cultural genocide.[42]

I'll close these comments by quickly mentioning some of the reforms which the pamphlet concludes are urgently necessary. These include that each tribe should possess its own separate reserve, whose absolute legal ownership of the land, together with all mineral and other resources to be found there, is to be recognised; no mission stations are to be allowed in the vicinity; all economic activities are under Aboriginal control; and contact with the reserves is to be confined to medical services and non-missionary advisers. (pp.30–32)

Wright's pamphlet endures as a remarkable challenge to 1930s conventional governmental and missionary thinking, though the distinction between 'full-blooded' Aboriginal people and 'half-castes' looks very dated now (a penultimate section suggests that people of 'mixed blood' should be treated with equality 'in all respects with other citizens, full civil rights, equal education and opportunities for employment and the rights that all other citizens have in regards to unemployed benefits and pensions and social services generally').[43] Rather dated, too, is Wright's belief in anthropology as a science.

However, Wright also evinces a robust distrust of anthropologists of the time who in his view are merely helping governments to institute measures that will destroy Aboriginal societies. He writes that it is a disgrace that 'the anthropological and clerical advisers' to governments share a belief in the conception that Aborigines are a vanishing race, while knowing 'quite well that it is whites who have deliberately caused their destruction'. (pp. 22, 30)

Fitzpatrick, Brian, *The Rich Get Richer. Facts of the Growth of Monopoly in the Economic Structure of Australia Before and During the War* (Rawson's Book Shop, Melbourne, May 1944).

Fitzpatrick, Brian, *Public Enterprise Does Pay* (Rawson's Book Shop, Exhibition St. Melbourne, n.d.). [pamphlet]

Calwell, Arthur A, *How Many Australians Tomorrow?* (1945) (On cover: Arthur A Calwell, Minister for Information and Immigration). [pamphlet]

Ward, E J, *Shall the People or the Banks Rule*. Speech delivered by the Hon. E J Ward, Minister for Transport and External Affairs, in support of the Commonwealth Government's Banking Legislation. [pamphlet – 1945]

Campbell, E W, *People Versus the Banks*. Printed at the Newsletter Printery, 21 Ross Street, Forest Lodge, Sydney, n.d. [pamphlet]

Campbell, E W *Political Economy – A Simple Outline* (Current Book Distributors, Sydney, n.d.) [pamphlet]

Dark, E P, *Who Are the Reds* (Sydney, 1946) (an opening page refers to E P Dark as the Author-Publisher, Katoomba, NSW). [pamphlet]

Sharkey, LL., *For Australia Prosperous and Independent*. The Report of L.L. Sharkey to the 15th Congress of the Australian Communist Party, May 1948 (Current Book Distributors, Sydney).

Ross, Edgar, *The Coal Front: an Account of the 1949 Coal Strike and the Issues It Raised*, by Edgar Ross, Associate Editor 'Common Cause', Official organ of the Miners' Federation. [pamphlet]

Blake, J D, *The Great Coal Strike of 1949* (Australian Communist Party, August 1949). [pamphlet]

Dixon, R, *The Trial of L. L. Sharkey: speech by R. Dixon to Sharkey Protest Meeting held in Sydney October 21, 1949* (Current Book Distributors, 1949). [pamphlet]

'Jagara', *Frederick Engels, Lewis Morgan and the Australian Aborigine* (Current Book Distributors, Sydney) (n.d., perhaps 1946 or 1947). [pamphlet]

What a remarkable jeremiad this is. It defends the tradition of evolutionary anthropology as articulated in the nineteenth century by Lewis Morgan in his *Ancient Society* and the deployment of Morgan by Engels in his *The Origin of the Family*, books in the view of the pamphlet that are of great benefit to the working class, especially its 'class-conscious workers'. (p. 7) At the same time the pamphlet repudiates what it sees as conventional 'bourgeois' academic anthropology dominating universities in Britain, the US and Australia. The Preface refers to the 'bitter antagonism of contemporary anthropologists towards Lewis Morgan', and hopes the pamphlet will be a kind of alternative guide for the anthropological student faced with the 'outpourings of the anti-Morgan, anti-evolutionist Schools'. For while Morgan's work does reveal 'theoretical and practical shortcomings', which the pamphlet readily concedes, his basic evolutionary approach remains true.

Present features of many societies such as the Australian Aboriginal – for example, the 'classificatory system' or 'system of consanguinity' – are relics of previous stages of evolution, as in Group Marriage which worked as a way of avoiding incest. Such relics of Group Marriage can be found across the world, among the Hawaiians as well amongst the 'desert aborigines to the north of the Nullabor Plain'. (pp. 6–7,16)

The pamphlet believes that what is at stake are not merely different conceptions of anthropology. For Jagara there is a deeper issue, and it is related to why in the capitalist world anthropologists wish to dismiss Morgan, whereas, because of the Russian Revolution, Morgan is appreciated by Soviet anthropologists. The pamphlet points out that the objects of the science of anthropology are for the most part the 'oppressed colonial peoples'. The course which 'orthodox anthropology' is adopting is 'retrograde', reflecting the 'last stage of decaying capitalism' (in Lenin's phrase quoted in the pamphlet's Glossary), and putting science at the service of those who control wealth and power in the world. (pp. 5–6, 62)

The pamphlet refers to the assault on Morgan by the American school of diffusionists 'influenced by Boas', such as R H . Lowie in his *The History of Ethnological Theory*. Here Lowie wrongly argues, says Jagara, that the diffusion of cultures disproves Morgan's positing of a universal law of sequence in human cultures. The other main academic school, that of the functionalists, especially evident in the writings of Malinowski, has also joined in the 'chorus against Morgan'. The pamphlet quotes from Malinowski's posthumously published *A Scientific Theory of Culture and Other Essays* where Malinowski contends that Morgan's evolutionary schemes were fantastical and misled anthropological research for generations by regarding phenomena, such as the classificatory system of kinship, as survivals of what had been, rather than exploring a functional analysis of present cultural practices. At Sydney University, says Jagara, we also find an assault on Morgan from the neo-functionalists (defined in the Glossary as those who see Malinowski's functionalism as too rigid) such as Dr A Capell. (I recall hearing Capell lecture on linguistics when I did anthropology as an undergraduate, starting in 1963!) Another contribution to the 'anti-Morgan barrage' came from Professor A Radcliffe-Brown, the first professor of anthropology at Sydney University (later Chair of Social Anthropology at Oxford), who wrote in *The Social Organisation of the Australian Tribes* that, as against Morgan, what we should study is the functional relation between the kinship terminology of a tribe and the social organisation of that tribe as it presently exists; and then there is Dr Kaberry, trained in what the pamphlet refers to as the Sydney School, who in her book *Aboriginal Woman* says that Malinowski had exorcised once and for all the phantom of primitive promiscuity or group marriage from Australian anthropology. (pp. 7, 10–11, 17, 63)

I won't rehearse the remainder of the pamphlet, which offers a detailed description of cultural survivals of classificatory systems among 'primitive people', as in the survival of 'sexual group marriage' among Australian Aborigines in a tribal state. The pamphlet, it becomes clear, wishes to defend evolutionary anthropology as part of an overall acceptance of 'social evolution or, in Marxist terminology, *Historical Materialism*'. Jagara compares the neo-functionalists to 'their political counterpart, the Social Democrats'. Both neo-functionalists and Social Democrats, however, will be cast aside like the 'skin of a snake' by the 'victorious advance of the working class'. Jagara does, nonetheless, praise A C Haddon, the last member of the 'famous liberal Cambridge school' of anthropologists, who in his *History of Anthropology* wrote that for all the criticisms that have been made of Morgan's work it remains of lasting value. Jagara concludes his historiographical discussion of Morgan's critics by noting that when Professor Haddon retired in 1934 from the Cambridge Chair of Anthropology, he was followed by 'Professors Hodson and Hutton, both retired members of the Indian Civil Service, that stronghold of Imperialism'. (pp. 13, 17–18)

In terms of my father's collection, Jagara's interest in Western anthropology's possible imbrications with colonialism and imperial power relates to his other pamphlets in the immediate post-war world, drawing attention to the plight of Aboriginal people in Australia and the scandal of the attempted re-assertion of control by European powers in South-East Asia after the defeat of Nazi Germany and Imperial Japan. These pamphlets protesting against racism and colonialism in the 1940s and 1950s form a kind of family in the collection.

Who was Jagara? Ann hazarded Jagara could have been Frederick Rose, a Marxist anthropologist close to or in the Communist Party who did a lot of work in Australia on kinship classification, before going to live in East Germany; Ann has a memory that, encouraged by her father, who was an admirer of Fred Rose as were many others in the Communist Party, she was introduced to him when he re-visited Australia on one occasion, perhaps in Melbourne; a memory too that perhaps her parents Barbara and Geoff Curthoys visited Fred Rose in East Germany. There is a reference in the pamphlet which supports Ann's hunch that Jagara might be Fred Rose. On p. 33, the pamphlet says its description of social evolution in Australia, for example in relation to avoidance of incest, will draw on 'an article in "The Annals of Eugenics" London of July 1943 by Jolly and Rose, "The Place of the Australian Aboriginal in the Evolution of Society"'. Fred Rose's co-author was the medical practitioner, Dr Alec Jolly. In an essay in *Aboriginal History* in 1994, 'Black and Red: The Pilbara Pastoral Workers' Strike 1946', Michael Hess relates that in Perth in 1946 Alec Jolly was chair of the Committee for the Defence of Native Rights, and that Katharine Susannah Prichard spoke at its inaugural meeting.

On 1 May 2012 I emailed Nic Peterson of the Anthropology department at ANU, and he confirmed by email that in conversation Fred Rose had told him that he was Jagara.

On 30 May 2012 I emailed Peter Monteath of the History

Department at Flinders University. Some googling had indicated he and Valerie Munt were writing a biography of Fred Rose. Peter emailed back saying that Fred Rose was Jagara, and that the pamphlet was published in 1946.

Fred Rose is not a forgotten figure in academic anthropology, which in the 1960s and 1970s, inspired by the New Left, would confront questions of anthropology's relation to colonialism and imperial power. Ken Maddock, in an obituary essay 'Frederick Rose, 1915–1991: An Appreciation', in *Oceania* in 1991, tells us that Rose studied under A C Haddon in Cambridge, his research in Australia beginning in 1937 when he arrived in Darwin; in 1956 Rose left Australia to take up a position at Humboldt University in East Germany; from there he continued to engage in argument and controversy, and his detailed studies of classification systems remain highly valued.

There are also glimpses of Fred Rose in the British anthropologist and sociologist Peter Worsley's memoir *An Academic Skating on Thin Ice* (2008). Worsley was part of a mid-twentieth century generation of young scholars, including also E P Thompson and John Saville, who were attracted to the British Communist Party and would then be shattered by the revelations of Stalin's crimes by Krushchev in 1955, leaving the Party to help inaugurate the New Left. Worsley would later become well-known for popularising the term 'Third World'.

In 1942 Worsley became a student at Cambridge University, principally studying English Literature (as did E P Thompson also at Cambridge, and Stuart Hall at Oxford). He attended lectures given by F R Leavis, a critic who would figure in my education. At Cambridge he joined the Communist Party. During the war he was called up to serve in an artillery unit, which was sent to Africa, by which he became fascinated. Back at Cambridge after the war, Worsley switched from English to Social Anthropology, and after graduating took up a research post at the University of Manchester with the renowned social anthropologist Max Gluckman, spending a number of years studying various African societies under British colonial control. When, however, he was appointed to a research institute in Africa, his appointment was blocked by MI5. Worsley abandoned any hope of doing research in Africa and instead travelled to Australia to do a PhD at a new department of anthropology being established at the Australian National University. His ship arrived in Australia just as the result of Menzies' referendum to ban the Australian Communist Party was announced. For his doctoral research he was to conduct fieldwork in the Central Highlands of New Guinea. When he went to collect an entry permit for New Guinea, which he thought was a formality, he was told by an Australian government official that he was banned from going there: 'MI5 had struck again.'[44]

At a loss what to do next, Worsley was advised by his friend Frederick Rose to go to Groote Eyland in the Gulf of Carpentaria, where Rose had studied the kinship system of the Umbakumba people. Rose told Worsley that 'they couldn't stop [you] doing field research within Australia'. Worsley spent many months collecting kinship data and was struck by its inconsistencies. Kinship, he began to theorise, was not constituted as an algebraic 'perfectly fitting system of kinship terminology, as the functionalist school had argued'. Rather, kinship always got out of kilter, if only because, in a gerontocratic society, 'men took women who did not belong to the right "marriageable" category' and then 'started calling them and their immediate relatives new terms for "mother-in-law" or "sister-in-law"'. The result, he thought, was that in the 'midst of this disorder, there were only what I called "islands of order"'.[45]

Worsley feels that after World War II the kind of functionalist theory which, in practitioners like Malinowski and Radcliffe-Brown, had dominated anthropology, was being increasingly questioned, especially the assumption that societies were formed as coherent systems: 'For many of us, this was far too systematic.' In the post-war world, Worsley observes, 'new theoretical schools began to take the place of functionalism', especially in the US, influenced by the pragmatism of John Dewey, or the sociology of C Wright Mills which was influenced by pragmatism; a prominent new school was symbolic interactionism.[46]

Worsley's formulations concerning the inconsistencies of Groote Eyland kinship patterns anticipate, I think, the kind of postmodern theory we would come to associate with Chaos Theory, where order breaks down into disorder; order and disorder exist in an unresolvable tension (a theory that Ann Curthoys would come to apply to feminism and what she memorably called its 'three-body problem').[47]

There is something else, startling and shocking, to be recorded about Fred Rose. I finished writing this chapter in October 2014. Peter Monteath and Valerie Munt's excellent biography *Red Professor: the Cold War Life of Fred Rose* was published the following year. I read it with great interest, and have just looked at it again now. I see I've highlighted it all over. The Prologue dramatically features the revelation that Fred Rose spied for the Stasi for decades until the fall of East Germany in 1989, including spying on his own family, his wife Edith, who also worked for the Stasi, and his son Kim. Monteath and Munt write that 'for many years [Rose] reported on family, friends, colleagues and strangers with no sign of compunction or regret'. In their Epilogue, they conclude that 'when the Stasi arrived at his doorstop, it was Fred Rose who signed for that most Faustian of bargains – and kept it'.[48]

Monteath and Munt tell us that from modest beginnings in the 1950s the Stasi became a 'behemoth', which by the end of the GDR had 'swollen to the size of 91 000 full-time employees', developing an 'insatiable appetite for the gathering of information about the GDR's own citizens'; by the time the 'Berlin Wall fell, the Stasi had created 111 kilometres of documents, including some 39 million file cards, 1.4 million photographs and 34 000 sound recordings'; in both its 'longevity (40 years) and its level of penetration (there were some 55 Stasi full-time personnel for every 10 000 GDR citizens) the Stasi were unique in the twentieth century'.[49]

We can say that Fred Rose participated in a regime that must rank as one of the most grotesque societies in history – participated willingly, assiduously, eagerly.

Marxism and Youth (reprint of articles prepared by the Australian Communist Party, not dated, though most recent date of the articles is 1949; the articles are by Lenin, Stalin, Dimitrov, Togliatti, Kuuisinen, Mikhailov, Jen Pi-Shim, and Feng Wen-Ping). [pamphlet]

Mical, Wolf, *A New Type of Youth Organisation: From the concluding speech of Wolf Mical at a Congress of Youth Leagues* (Central Committee, Australian Communist Party, 695 George Street [Sydney]), no date; stamped on the front is: Riverina District Committee, Australian Communist Party, 90 Baylis Street, Wagga). [pamphlet]

Dark, E P, *The Press Against the People* (1949?) (Printed by The Pinnacle Press, Hume Highway, Bankstown) (the inside cover tells us that the same author has published: *Medicine and the Social Order*, *Who Are the Reds*, *The World Against Russia?*). [pamphlet]

Walshe, R D, *1854*, *The Eureka Stockade* (Current Book Distributors, Sydney, 1954). [pamphlet]

Mortier, Paul, *Art: Its Origins and Social Function* (Current Book Distributors, Sydney, October 1955).

Buckley, K, *The Facts About Cyprus*. Foreword by Clive R Evatt, President, Committee for Cyprian Self-Determination, Sydney, NSW, Australia (October 1956) (K Buckley, Lecturer in Economic History, University of Sydney, NSW). [pamphlet] (In his Foreward, Clive Evatt tells that 'Mr Buckley, who is an esteemed Vice-President of the Committee for Cyprian Self-Determination, has obviously made a close study of the issues involved'.)

Sharkey, L L, General Secretary of the Communist Party of Australia, *Report* [of 18th Congress, April 1958] and *Resolution: A Land of Plenty Free from War* (Current Book Distributors, Sydney, 1958). [pamphlet]

Theory of the State: Selections from Marxist-Leninist writings on the State (Current Book Distributors, Sydney, 1960). The selections and extracts are from: 'Lecture on the State', by V I Lenin; 'State and Revolution', by V I Lenin; 'The Proletarian Revolution and the Renegade Kautsky', by V I Lenin; 'Declaration of Meeting of Communist and Workers' Parties in Socialist Countries'; 'Programme of the Communist Party of Australia'; 'Socialism in Australia', by L L L Sharkey; 'The Changing Role of the State', by E F Hill; 'The Trade Unions', by L L Sharkey. [pamphlet]

McPhillips, Jock, *Penal Powers Cost Unionists $1,000,000!* (Current Book Distributors, Sydney, September 1963). [pamphlet]

South-East Asia

Peel, Gerald, *Indonesian Introduction. What You Want to Know About the Dutch East Indies* (Current Book Distributors, Sydney, April 1945).[50] [pamphlet]

This is a denunciation of Dutch colonial rule in Indonesia and of the Dutch desire to return as the colonial masters when the Japanese, who had conquered Indonesia during World War II, were defeated, as was looking increasingly likely. Peel vigorously condemns the attempts of the Dutch to suppress the communist-led Indonesian movement for national independence, attempts which during the war, he recounts, took a bizarre form. In the pamphlet's Chapter 5 'Indonesia Awakes', Peel tells of the harsh repression of the national independence movement, including sending well over a thousand

Indonesian communists to a concentration camp, Tanah Merah, about 500 miles up the Digoel River in Dutch New Guinea (though, in a comment odd for someone concerned by Dutch racism towards Indonesians, Peel adds here that the concentration camp was located in 'jungle-country inhabited by head-hunting savages'). In 1943, as the Japanese were advancing, the Dutch brought the inmates of this camp to Australia, 'where they were again interned. It was only after Australian democratic bodies campaigned for their release that those of them who wished to play a part to win the war were released. Since when they have given of their best for the defeat of Japan, and the liberation of the Indonesian people... Many other Indonesians man the ships which play a big role in Pacific campaigns, and many *have given their lives in the war*' (Peel's italics).

On our morning walk of 9 March 2012 round Blackwattle Bay in Glebe, I told Ann of this pamphlet and this particular passage. Ann suddenly launched into a passionate speech about the bitter ironies of history. Ann said that because the trade unions and subsequently the Australian Labor Party so much supported the Indonesians against the Dutch, the Labor Party has been forever blindly loyal to whatever Indonesian government has been in power, with the eventual result that the Labor Party, including leaders like Whitlam and Keating, couldn't care less about the East Timorese when they were being brutalised by the Indonesians. Nor, thinking about Ann's comments later in the day, does the Labor Party now, including the present federal Labor Government in 2012, take the slightest interest in the plight of the ex-Dutch New Guineans, the West Papua that is being genocidally colonised by the Indonesians.

More recently, from reading Australian security reports, I realised that my father knew Peel, a 1942 report noting that Ted Docker would be visiting 'Muswellbrook with Gerald PEEL'.

Peel, Gerald, *Hands Off Indonesia* (Current Book Distributors, Sydney, 3 October, 1945) [pamphlet]

70 Million Indonesians Claim Independence! (Authorised by Committee of Indonesian Political Exiles in Australia) [pamphlet] (n.d.)

Blaschke, Walter, *Freedom for Malaya*. With a Foreword by L L Sharkey (Current Book Distributors, Sydney, n.d.). [pamphlet]

Lockwood, Rupert, *Malaya Must Cost No More Australian Blood* (the front page of this pamphlet notes that Rupert Lockwood is a 'Former news correspondent in Malaya') (Current Book Distributors, Sydney, February, 1951).

Campbell, E W, *The Truth About Indo China* (the front cover of this pamphlet has a drawing of Ho Chi Minh) (Current Book Distributors, Sydney, n.d.) (looking through this pamphlet, the date could be 1954).

New Left

Marcuse (A Communist Party Publication, not dated, could be 1968) (includes Herbert Marcuse, 'The Obsolescence of Marxism', whose first two sentences by Marcuse are: 'I feel that I have to begin by objecting to the title given to my paper. A most important thing was omitted – the question mark'; an interview with Marcuse entitled 'The Question of Revolution'; and a critique by Franze Marek, 'Prospects for "Modern Industrial Society" – The Political World Scene according to Herbert Marcuse', translated from a Communist theoretical journal, '*Weg und Ziel*', no. 10, 1967, Vienna.) [pamphlet]

I will conclude with Walter Benjamin that like any collector my father was pleased by his collection, that he treasured its diversity, the wide variety of people, places and issues addressed in the books and pamphlets he brought together, and which he preserved as much as he could as a collection. I think again of Benjamin saying that 'to a true collector the acquisition of an old book is its rebirth', for the collector's 'deepest desire' is to 'renew the old world', but from an 'angle' that is 'whimsical'. That, I think, is what I found myself doing in this chapter when an item led me to talk, for example, about *La Pasionara* and Pussy Riot, or my father's love of Lenin, or his interest in colonialism and imperialism and racism including a reference to genocide, or his possessing Tom Wright's *New Deal for the Aborigines* with its foreword by Katharine Susannah Prichard, or the mystery of the identity of 'Jagara'.

Perhaps also my father knew, in Benjamin's terms, that the 'fate' of his collection would be that I would inherit it and write about it.

1 Walter Benjamin, *Illuminations*, edited and introduced by Hannah Arendt (1968; Schocken Books, New York, 2007), p.59.

2 Benjamin, 'Unpacking My Library', pp.60–63, 67.

3 Benjamin, 'Unpacking My Library', p.66.

4 See Elisabeth Young-Bruehl's great biography, *Hannah Arendt: For Love of the World* (Yale University Press, New Haven, 1982), pp.162, 166–7; see also my essay reflecting on the Iraq war, '*Après la guerre*: dark thoughts, some whimsy', *Arena Journal*, New Series, No.20, 2002/2003, p.14.

5 Benjamin, 'Unpacking My Library', p.60.

6 Audrey Blake, *A Proletarian Life* (Kibble, Melbourne, 1984), p.15.

7 See my essay, 'Politics and Poetics: Bernard O'Dowd's *Dawnward?* and Nineteenth-Century Chartist Poetry', *Southerly*, Vol.53, no.2, 1993, pp.13–39.

8 Verity Burgmann, *Revolutionary Industrial Unionism: The Industrial Workers of the World in Australia* (Cambridge University Press, Cambridge, 1995), pp.73, 131–132.

9 David W. Lovell and Kevin Windle (eds), Our Unswerving Loyalty: *A documentary survey of relations between the Communist Party of Australia and Moscow, 1920–1940* (ANU E-Press, Canberra, 2008), p.277.

10 'Lew Levy: his story', in John Docker, *1492: The Poetics of Diaspora* (Continuum, London, 2001), p.165.

11 Eric Hobsbawm, *Interesting Times: A Twentieth-Century Life* (2002; Abacus, London, 2012), p.133.

12 Cf. Vanessa Castejon, 'Identity and identification: Aboriginality from the Spanish Civil War to the French Ghettos', in Frances Peters-Little, Ann Curthoys and John Docker (eds), *Passionate Histories: Myth, Memory and Indigenous Australia* (ANU E-Press, Canberra, 2010), pp.219–228.

13 Masha Gessen, *Words Will Break Cement: The Passion of Pussy Riot* (Granta, London, 2014), pp.106, 195, 204.

14 Gessen, *Words Will Break Cement*, pp.196, 200.

15 Gessen, *Words Will Break Cement*, pp.60, 168–69, 188, 190, 205–206, 220.

16 Gessen, *Words Will Break Cement*, pp.60, 64.

17 Gessen, *Words Will Break Cement*, pp.15, 39, 51, 59–69, 74, 108, 204–5, 215, 288.

18 Gessen, *Words Will Break Cement*, p.291.

19 Gessen, *Words Will Break Cement*, pp.117–118.

20 Gessen, *Words Will Break Cement*, pp.82–83.

21 Gessen, *Words Will Break Cement*, p.60.

22 Natalie Zemon Davis, *Society and Culture in Early Modern France* (Stanford University Press, Stanford, 1975), ch.5, 'Women on Top'.

23 John Docker, *Postmodernism and Popular Culture: A Cultural History* (Cambridge University Press, Cambridge, 1994), p.199.

24 Keith Ansell Pearson and Duncan Large (eds), *The Nietszche Reader* (Blackwell, Oxford UK and Mass., US, 2006), 'Thus Spake Zarathustra: A Book for Everyone and No One' (188–5), Prologue, pp.258–259.

25 Bob Boughton, 'The Communist Party of Australia's Involvement in the Struggle for Aboriginal and Torres Strait Islander Peoples' Rights, 1920–1970', in Raymond Markey (ed.), *Labour and Community: Historical Essays* (University of Wollongong Press, Wollongong, 2001), p.274.

26 Ann Curthoys and John Docker, 'Defining Genocide', in Dan Stone (ed.), *The Historiography of Genocide* (Palgrave Macmillan, London, 2010), pp.15–21, 27–28.

27 Michael Waterhouse, *Not a Poor Man's Field: The New Guinea Goldfields to 1942 – An Australian Colonial History* (Halstead Press, Canberra, 2010), pp.129–131.

28 Michael Waterhouse, *Not a Poor Man's Field*, p.131.

29 Michael Waterhouse, *Not a Poor Man's Field*, pp.131–138, 145.

30 See Ray Evans, 'The country has another past: Queensland and the History Wars', in Frances Peters-Little, Ann Curthoys and John Docker (eds), *Passionate Histories: Myth, Memory and Indigenous Australia* (ANU e-Press, Canberra, 2010), pp.13–32.

31 See Paul Daley, *Beersheba: A Journey through Australia's Forgotten War* (Melbourne University Press, Melbourne, 2009), pp.1–8, 252, 267, 270, 274–276; see also my essay, 'Epistemological vertigo and allegory: thoughts on massacres, actual, surrogate, and averted – *Beersheba, Wake in Fright, Australia*', in Frances

Peters-Little, Ann Curthoys, John Docker (eds), *Passionate Histories: Myth, Memory and Indigenous Australia* (ANU E-Press, Canberra, 2010), pp.55–62.

32 Suzanne Brugger, *Australians and Egypt 1914–1919* (Melbourne University Press, Melbourne, 1980), pp.36, 42–43, 59, 75–77, 96. See my essay, 'Storm Troopers of empire? Historical representation in Breaker Morant, Naguib Mahfouz's *Palace Walk* and other war histories', *History Australia*, Vol.8, no.1, 2011), pp.80–83.

33 Peter Stanley, *Bad Characters: Sex, Crime, Mutiny, Murder and the Australian Imperial Force* (Pier 9, Sydney, 2010), 33–34.

34 Michael Waterhouse, *Not a Poor Man's Field*, p.133.

35 Concerning Tom Wright, see Bob Boughton, 'The Communist Party of Australia's Involvement in the Struggle ...', pp.267–270. See also Douglas Jordon, Conflict in the Unions: The Communist Party of Australia, Politics and the Trade Union Movement, 1945–1960, PhD thesis, School of Social Sciences and Psychology, Victoria University, 2011, ch.7, '"They have lit a fire that will – and should – blaze ...': The CPA and the Aboriginal Rights Movement', pp. 246–306.

36 This crude coloniser anti-Indigenous action by the West Australian government is discussed Ann Curthoys and Jessie Mitchell, *Taking Liberty: Indigenous Rights and Settler Self-Government in Colonial Australia, 1830–1890* (Cambridge University Press, Cambridge, 2018), ch.16, '"A Slur upon the Colony": Making Western Australia's Unusual Constitution, 1885–1890', pp.385–404, esp.403. See also Ann Curthoys, 'The Impossibility of Section 70: Aboriginal rights and the contradictions of settler colonialism', *Studies in Western Australian History*, Vol.30, 2016, pp.13–28.

37 Prichard's foreword to Wright's pamphlet is reprinted in Delys Bird (ed.), *Katharine Susannah Prichard: Stories, Journalism and Essays* (University of Queensland Press, St. Lucia, 2000), pp.57–58.

38 Cf. Ann Curthoys, 'Good Christians and Useful Workers: Aborigines, church and state in NSW 1870–1883', in Sydney Labour History Group, *What Rough Beast: The State and Social Order in Australian History* (George Allen and Unwin, Sydney, 1982), pp.31–56.

39 See my *The Origins of Violence*, pp.34–35; Ann Curthoys, 'Whose Home? Expulsion, Exodus, and Exile in White Australian Historical Mythology', *Journal of Australian Studies*, No.61, 1999, pp.1–18; see also Ann Curthoys and John Docker, *Is History Fiction?* (2010 edition), pp.27–28.

40 Hugh Brody, *The Other Side of Eden: Hunter-Gatherers, Farmers, and the Shaping of the World* (2000; Faber and Faber, London, 2006), p.7; *The Origins of Violence*, pp.35–37; *Is History Fiction?* (2010), pp.238, 256–7.

41 See my essay 'Are Settler-Colonies Inherently Genocidal?' in A. Dirk Moses (ed.), *Empire, Colony, Genocide: Conquest, Occupation, and Subaltern Resistance in World History* (Berghahn, New York, 2008), pp.90–91.

42 See my 'Are Settler-Colonies Inherently Genocidal?', p.89.

43 Bob Boughton, 'The Communist Party of Australia's Involvement ...', pp.275–277, discusses how the distinction between 'full bloods' and 'half-castes' was dropped in the early 1950s.

44 Peter Worsley, *An Academic Skating on Thin Ice* (Berghahn, New York, 2008), pp.20–26, 33, 53, 69, 77–79, 82–83.

45 Worsley, *An Academic Skating on Thin Ice*, pp.83–84.

46 Worsley, *An Academic Skating on Thin Ice*, pp.174–75.

47 Ann Curthoys, 'The Three Body Problem: Feminism and Chaos Theory', *Hecate*, Vol.17, no.1, 1991, pp.14–21.

48 See *Red Professor: the Cold War Life of Fred Rose* (Wakefield Press, Adelaide, 2015), pp.4,199, 201, 202, 203, 204–205, 206, 207, 248, 283–4, 304.

49 *Red Professor: the Cold War Life of Fred Rose*, p.200.

50 Concerning Gerald Peel, see Bob Boughton, 'The Communist Party of Australia's Involvement ...', pp.270–272.

6

The Intellectual and the Revolutionary: Walter Benjamin and Ted Docker in Moscow

My memory is that family lore said that my father was in Moscow in 1934. But I'm sure now it was during both 1934 and 1935, given information in declassified documents of the Commonwealth Investigative Bureau, forerunner of ASIO, which suggests that Ted Docker was being followed by the security service at least from 1930. One of these documents is a copy of Ted Docker's application for a passport to travel overseas in April 1934, only a few months after his visit in January 1934 to Kalgoorlie in Western Australia when anti-Yugoslav and anti-Italian riots were breaking out there.

The security police's interest in Ted Docker was particularly piqued by his visit by ship to London in 1934, on his way to Moscow via Leningrad. There is a letter, dated 16 April 1934 and marked secre, by J Adams, Acting Inspector, Investigation Branch, informing the Director of the Commonwealth Investigation Branch, based in Canberra, that he has attached a copy of Ted Docker's application for a 'passport covering travel to England and France'. Ted Docker, Adams informs his superior, is an 'organizer for the Carpenters Union', a 'member of the executive of the

Minority Movement', was one of the 'prominent leaders in the 1929 Timber Strike', and was a Communist candidate for Phillip Electorate at the NSW State Elections in June 1932.[1] The copy of Ted Docker's application for a passport, dated 5 April 1934, which I now have before me, tells its various readers that his father was born in Birmingham, England. (As we saw in Chapter 3, he was born in Dallington, but grew up in Birmingham.) My father puts down 'seeing my relatives' as the purpose of his visit, that he would also be travelling to France, and that he expected to be absent from Australia for 'two years'. He would be leaving the port of Sydney on the ss *Orama* on 24 April 1934. In answer to categories on the form requesting particulars of one's appearance, my father said his height in ordinary boots was 5 feet 6 inches, his eyes were 'blue', and the colour of his hair was 'fair'.

In his letter of 16 April, Mr J Adams the Acting Inspector relates his suspicion that while 'stating that he desires to see relatives, it seems more feasible, in view of his Communist associations, that he is proceeding abroad on business connected with the Movement'. Mr Adams' suspicions were borne out. In another letter, dated 18th June 1934, a British security official responds to a telegram of 8 May 1934 sent by Lt Colonel H E Jones, of 'Secretariat No.1, Canberra',[2] that Docker arrived at Tilbury Dock on the ss *Orama* on 7 June 1934. 'To comply with the regulations of the Board of Trade', said the letter, Docker had given his intended address as 209 Prospect Road, Scarborough, 260 miles north of Tilbury Docks, but in fact he 'spent two nights' at a hotel 'near the station' and on '9th June embarked on a Soviet ship for Leningrad.' The letter then noted that Docker had 'attracted attention on board the boat owing to his extreme views', and that his luggage had been searched, revealing that there was 'literature' therein, including a printed booklet 'containing extracts from speeches of various Australian communists', and a 'rough note book' with 'statistics relevant to Australia (mineral wealth, population, exports and imports, etc.)'. The letter concluded with a description of Docker 'provided by the police officer at Tilbury Dock', revealing that my father was quite a smart dresser:

> Born at Sydney on 26.11.94; height 5'6'; slim build; clean shaven; eyes blue; hair fair; sharp features; dressed in dark grey mixture suit with black stripes, light brown trilby hat with dark brown band, cream coloured shirt and collar, light blue tie, black shoes, carrying light grey overcoat.

Reading this now, I wonder if my father knew he was under surveillance, even perhaps on board the boat in the long journey from Sydney to London, that continued as soon as he arrived in Tilbury Dock, and that his luggage had been searched. Surely he did. Surely he was aware that for many years he and other prominent Communists were being tracked and shadowed.

However, I don't only have to rely on the observations and speculations of the intelligence services in Australia and Britain for his time in London. In the folder 'Ted Docker's Reminiscences' there is in handwriting a couple of pages entitled 'Ted Docker: Chief Dates', which I must have asked him about in the 1970s. Here my father offers his own, very specific, memories of arriving in London in 1934. He says that he was 'selected by the Political Committee to go to Moscow and be the representative of the Central Committee in the Comintern'. A 'year or two prior to the Seventh Congress' he got a ship to London, which 'pulled up opposite near London Bridge'; he was by himself; he 'went to see the British CP – went to a bookshop – luckily there was a meeting on, and they found out who I was and my credentials and they allowed me to sit down – Palme Dutt was there, a chap called Campbell, and Harry Pollitt'. (In an aside, my father said Harry Pollitt was a wonderful speaker, he heard him at the Seventh Congress, where he spoke for three quarters of an hour and never had a note; most of the others did.) He didn't see any women there. It was, my father said, not a meeting of the Central Committee, it was a meeting to determine what articles should go in the next issue of their paper. 'After the meeting', he adds, 'I stayed at the Salvation Army in Petticoat Lane', in Middlesex Street he thought.

(Ann and my friend Fiona Paisley, in her 2012 book *The Lone Protestor: A M Fernando in Australia and Europe*, evokes the remarkable life of an Aboriginal man who in Europe and England publicly condemned the British for their treatment of Aboriginal people; Paisley includes a photograph of the Salvation Army Hostel in Middlesex Street where Fernando lived in London in 1929 and 1930.)[3]

It's strange to think that my father stayed in the East End not that far from where my mother and her family lived in London before they left for Australia in 1926. In the 'Concluding Mosaic' to my 2001 book *1492: The Poetics of Diaspora*, I observed my mother's delight when Ann and I visited Petticoat Lane market with her. While looking at a stall selling smoked salmon, she exclaimed that one of her aunts used to say of the salmon: 'Eyes of diamonds and sides of silver! Eyes of diamonds and sides of silver!' My mother then insisted we buy some, which we took home to our Stoke Newington flat in north-east London and ate it, instructed by my mother, with lemon juice and black pepper, which is still how I like to eat smoked salmon.[4]

From London, my father journeyed to Moscow via Leningrad. David Lovell and Kevin Windle write in *Our Unswerving Loyalty* that Lance Sharkey and Ted Docker were present at the Comintern's Seventh Congress in 1935, the congress where the new policy of the Popular Front was worked out, aiming as Lovell and Windle put it, to 'fight fascism by creating strategic, cross-class alliances and supporting the (formerly demonized) social democratic parties'.[5] In *The Reds*, Stuart Macintyre notes that from the late 1920s Australian Communists had been going to the Lenin School in Moscow, run by the Communist International, and that Ted Docker, along with Stan Moran, was at the Lenin School in 1935.[6] According to an online essay by John Halstead and Barry McLoughlin, the International Lenin School opened its doors in the summer of 1926 at Vorovsky Street 25A in central Moscow; in 1933 a separate sector was founded for British, Irish, Australian and New Zealand cadres; by the end of 1936 the International Lenin School had come to a close.[7]

My father has left his own account of the Comintern's Seventh Congress of 1935. In 'Ted Docker's Reminiscences', there is a hand-written page entitled 'The 7th Congress of the C-I', where he writes:

> The most important event in my life was attendance at the 7th Congress of the Communist International held in Moscow in 1935. It was attended by leading communists throughout the world. It was made more impressive by the presence of Dimitrov, who had narrowly escaped death at the hands of Hitler. I had worked in the headquarters of the Comintern situated a couple of hundred yards from the Moscow river. I was later joined by Lance Sharkey. Although Dimitrov spoke in Russian not one word was missed by those present, due to the presence of numerous interpreters who translated his speech into a dozen languages, or more, which was relayed by earphones to various language groups. I spoke for about twenty minutes after Sharkey had spoken. We had nominated Sharkey to be our representative on the executive of the Communist International which showed unanimous support.

I don't know how long my father stayed in Moscow during 1934 and 1935. If, however, he attended both the Comintern's Seventh Congress, which was held in July-August 1935[8] and the International Lenin School, his stay was not negligible. In a note that I scribbled down and attached to the reminiscence 'Ted Docker: Chief Dates', my father says he was in Moscow 'for at least a year' and also that he 'learnt Russian'. (I hesitate over this memory of my father, after reading of doubts over Katharine Susannah Prichard's claims that she had learnt Russian while in Moscow in 1933.)[9] I do recall him saying that by the end he felt homesick for Australia.

Looking through my father's reminiscences I cannot detect any doubts arising from his stay in Moscow concerning the Soviet Union. It was clearly for my father a wholly positive experience, as is evident in his reminiscences when he talks of his return with his Australian comrades from Moscow to London. Later in this chapter I will contrast my father's wholly positive experience with the reminiscences of Audrey Blake, a Comintern visitor to Moscow in 1937, in her 1984 memoir *A Proletarian Life*. Audrey Blake was a family friend.

In 'Ted Docker: Chief Dates', my father relates that with Lance Sharkey and Stan Moran who had also been in Moscow with him, they travelled by ship from Moscow to London 'second or third class'. They had a 'talk to the Captain, told him who we were and we were Communists and had been at the Seventh Congress... he shifted our luggage to the best first-class cabins, it was a Russian ship and he was a Russian, he would speak English, save us the best of food'. Back in London, 'we went to Highgate Cemetery where Marx was buried there, and his wife, and housekeeper', though my father was not sure of this.

In the second part of 'The 7th Congress of the C-I', my father also talks of his return to London:

> On our return we visited Highgate cemetery and Marx's grave and placed flowers in the vase. The headstone was low with a marble slab about 3/4' thick fused to its surface and had a low

> stone kerb. Around this grave [had] stood some of the leading revolutionaries including Frederick Engels who delivered the funeral oration. Marx and Engels were life long friends. They had worked together for 49 years during which time they exchanged views on numerous political and economic questions.

For my father, then, the stay in Moscow culminated in the visit to Marx's grave in London, paying homage to Marx and his great collaborator Engels for creating the theory and vision of a new world which the Soviet Union was now establishing for humanity's future. The circle was complete.

Also, perhaps in memory of his first work as a 16-year-old as a stone mason for cemeteries, of which more in the chapter on my father and the loaded revolver, my father recalls technical details of Marx's gravestone.

Moscow

What was it like for my father being in Moscow in a daily sense?[10]

I remember my father once saying that whenever he visited a place, the first thing he did was to send a postcard of it back home. (He once mentioned visiting Napier, the town in New Zealand that had been destroyed by an earthquake in 1931 and rebuilt as an art deco city, and how he had sent home a postcard of it.) Once Ted Docker had arrived in Moscow in the Russian summer of June 1934, did he immediately send a postcard of Moscow to his mother Susan Nash in South Coogee in Sydney? Sadly, I don't possess any postcards or letters from that period of his life, nor a diary, though I don't know if he kept one. I do, however, have more reminiscences to call on from my folder 'Ted Docker's Reminiscences', which I will do in the latter part of this chapter.

What I'd like to do now is try to get a possible sense of my father in Moscow indirectly.

I want to bring in a mischievous comparison of my father with

Walter Benjamin, an idea I've tucked away in the back of my mind since I began thinking about this ego histoire, given that both had visited Moscow, if almost a decade apart. They were of the same generation. Benjamin was born in 1892, my father in 1894. One of the first things I did in preparing to write this chapter was to read carefully a book I'd meant to look at for a long time, Benjamin's diary of his two months in Moscow from 6 December 1926 to the end of January 1927.

I'm hoping that by giving a detailed sense of Benjamin in Moscow less than a decade before – a sense of the grain of his daily life, of snow, ice, streets, shops, cafés, markets, museums – there might be clues to how my father might have lived there in 1934 and 1935. Both Benjamin and Ted Docker were experienced travellers; they would have brought to their travelling and arriving in a new city a certain confidence.

At the same time as I try to envisage my father in Moscow somehow through Benjamin's diary, I will also in effect be exploring my relation to both of them. I keep trying to understand them: Benjamin the intellectual I feel close in spirit to; Ted Docker the revolutionary who was not an intellectual and indeed distrusted and despised intellectuals. And I became an intellectual.

Yet, importantly for my story in this chapter, Walter Benjamin and Ted Docker in the 1920s did share a common interest, in syndicalism, with its close relationship to anarchist thinking, including opposition to the state.

Walter Benjamin and Ted Docker as Syndicalists

In *Walter Benjamin: A Biography*, Momme Brodersen refers to Benjamin's thoughts, most remarkably in his essay 'Critique of Violence' (first published in 1920/21), on the morality of revolutionary violence in the light of Georges Sorel's *Reflections on Violence*.[11] In his introduction to Benjamin's *Reflections* Peter Demetz writes of Benjamin's 'intense interest in anarchist theory

(Sorel)' in the early years of the Weimar Republic.[12] In 'Critique of Violence', Benjamin bases his comments on Sorel on the 1919 French edition of *Reflections on Violence*. Sorel, Benjamin says, can take the credit for distinguishing between two different kinds of general strike, the political and the proletarian. Sorel dislikes the political general strike because its practitioners, for example, the moderate socialists, aim by it to strengthen state power, transferring power 'from the privileged to the privileged'; for the mass of producers, the only difference will be a change of their masters. By contrast, Sorel suggests, the proletarian general strike, indifferent towards material gain, sets out by non-violent means to destroy state power, to abolish the state; it desires a whole transformation of work itself; it is anarchism in action.[13] Clearly, Benjamin here is sympathetic to Sorel's attitudes and preferences.

In 1926 Ted Docker wrote two articles for the *Labor Monthly* entitled 'Carpenters and Job Committees' and 'Job Control Necessary'. The *Labor Monthly* was published by the Labor Research and Information Bureau, Sydney, for the NSW Trades and Labor Council, and was edited by Jack Ryan, Lyndall Ryan's father, from its inception in July 1926 to its demise in July 1930.[14] In 'Carpenters and Job Committees', Ted Docker issues a plea to carpenters to give up their 'old craft form of organization', which has made them vulnerable, he feels, in the new age of arbitration as an instrument of the state. The carpenters surrender initiative, energy and struggle to a 'set of union officials' who plead their case 'for better conditions before a parasitical judge'. Carpenters and others in the building industry should follow the 'bricklayers', who devote their energies to organising where they work. The essay's final sentence reprises classic IWW syndicalism, hoping that by direct action 'on the job', with a militant 'job committee', the 'present apathetic rank and file will see the futility of craft unionism, and the necessity for One Union in the Building Industry'.[15]

In 'Job Control Necessary', published in December 1926, Ted Docker again explains why he believes the bricklayers and their union are showing the way towards the necessity of 'one union in the industry': 'The bricklayers in N.S.W. have for a number of years kept away from the Arbitration Court, and have relied upon their organizational strength on the jobs to improve their conditions.' The bricklayers 'refuse to be bound by any Arbitration Awards', and instead 'fight their battles on the jobs'. By contrast, the 'rank and file' of other building trades unions are 'apathetic because nothing is expected, or asked of them'. Arbitration is a 'gigantic fraud', where unions 'without a militant leadership' are treated contemptuously by the judges 'who delay their cases, and finally give a very poor award'; a situation sanctioned by the 'union officials, who have developed into very capable lawyers'. In this situation, the workers become 'servile'.[16]

What my father was advocating was a kind of egalitarian plurality of localised, diffused, militant actions in specific workplaces, rejecting the authority of union officials perceived to be complicit with the state and its arbitration system, which made the rank and file feel excluded, apathetic, and 'servile'. My father's use of 'servile' surprised me, making me think of Sorel. I recall that the term appears in 'The Servile State' (1943), a key essay in the Sydney freethought tradition, by John Anderson, professor of philosophy at the University of Sydney in the middle decades of last century, from 1927 to 1958, whose essays I'd written about in my first book, *Australian Cultural Elites* (1974). There I discuss John Anderson talking about the importance he placed on Sorel in thinking through his own theories of a pluralist society.[17]

How John Anderson valued Sorel in the early 1930s, especially Sorel's distinction in *Reflections on Violence* between producers and consumers, is surprisingly close to how my father deployed syndicalist thought in 'Job Control Necessary' to distinguish between bricklayers and carpenters.[18] What is also clear is that syndicalism attracted the interest in the 1920s and 1930s of many intellectuals and radicals across the world. (Jeff Sparrow notes that on board ship in 1933 on their journey to Russia, Betty Roland and Guido Baracchi read together from Georges Sorel's *Reflections on Violence*, disguised from other passengers by a cover emblazoned with the romantic title *Thoughts on Violets*.)[19]

Ted Docker's 1920s syndicalism, however, with its opposition to the state, was not to last; and herein lies a key difference from Walter Benjamin in relation to the Communist Party, the Soviet Union and questions of consciousness, interiority and self-fashioning. I'll begin exploring these questions by looking in detail at Benjamin's diary of his mid-twenties visit to Moscow, a quite remarkable creation.

Walter Benjamin and Asja Lacis, Moscow, Winter 1926–7

Life on the page, even in a diary, will, we know, arrange itself into genre, into patterns of narrative. So I will regard *Moscow Diary* as a literary text, with many generic elements tumbling about in any one daily entry: a sad attempt at romance; an autobiographical revealing of various obsessions and fetishes, which pique me personally as someone also given to obsessions and fetishes; a traveller's reflections comparing particular cities, Moscow, Naples and Berlin; a fascination with toys and dolls that breaks down the distinction between the adult and the childlike; pondering about what joining a Communist Party would mean for one's personality and sensibility; thoughts on academic failure; thoughts on his own mode of writing; and a strain of absurdity and farce.

Let's begin with the romance, remembering that romance as a genre features two characters whose relationship can only come to fruition when various conflicts, differences, difficulties and obstacles are explored and resolved, often by transformation or metamorphosis in the key characters – think of Elizabeth Bennet and Mr Darcy teasing, taunting, upsetting, infuriating, disturbing, challenging each other.[20] The drama and suspense of romance focusses on what divides the key characters; if differences and conflicts are not resolved, if insuperable obstacles remain, we speak of tragic or sad or failed romance.

In the romance narrative of *Moscow Diary*, then, Walter Benjamin the German freelance intellectual, daring not to say highly eccentric and idiosyncratic cultural theorist, book collector, translator of Proust, travel writer, Francophile, Italophile, goes to Moscow to see and hopefully seal his love for Asja Lacis (1891–1979), a Russian Communist from Riga who is an actor and experimental children's theatre director, but who is currently ill in a Moscow sanatorium.[21] In the two months he is there, Benjamin visits Lacis in the sanatorium or she visits Benjamin where he is staying, though he rarely sees her alone because of the presence of Bernhard Reich (1894–1972), a theatre director and associate of Brecht, as was Lacis. In *Zarathustra's Sisters: Women's Autobiography and the Shaping of Cultural History* (2003) Susan Ingram tells us that in 1922, Lacis, interested in expressionist theatre, had travelled to Berlin, where she met Reich and his colleague Bertolt Brecht; when Reich and Brecht were appointed to a theatre in Munich, Lacis moved with them and was hired as an assistant director. Reich is a rival suitor of Lacis, is already in Moscow, and would later become her second husband.[22] The presence of Reich is an obstacle and difficulty indeed for Benjamin, who at one point in *Moscow Diary* exclaims that with Reich so often present he was 'facing an almost impregnable fortress'. He continues: 'Nonetheless I tell myself that my mere appearance before this fortress, Moscow, already constitutes an initial triumph. But any further, decisive victory seems almost insurmountably difficult. Reich's position is strong…'[23] Also, another suitor, a Russian general, makes an appearance near the end of his stay, creating an element of absurdity and farce in the narrative.

Benjamin and Lacis had first met on the island of Capri in 1924, a part of Italy, from Naples southwards along the Malfi coast, that seems to have been peculiarly favoured by European intellectuals in the early twentieth century; Benjamin spent six months there during 1924. Along with Bernhard Reich as her companion, Lacis and her daughter Daga by her first marriage were staying there. Also nearby was Brecht, at this time known only to Benjamin by name. Benjamin spent many hours in conversation with his fellow German intellectuals on Capri or in Naples, including sitting for nights on end with Ernst Bloch in a bar by a Capri beach, arguing over cultural matters.[24]

A distant memory recalled for me that Capri was also favoured by Russian intellectuals and exiles. I have just googled Wikipedia, which yields the information – which I hope is right! – that from 1906 to 1913 Gorky lived on Capri; in 1909 he invited Lunacharsky to visit him there, and along with other Russian intellectuals Bogdanov and Bazarov, they developed the idea of an *Encyclopedia of Russian History* as a socialist version of Diderot's Encyclopedia. On Gorky's invitation, Lenin visited Capri.

In their biography, Eiland and Jennings write that Benjamin was well aware that Gorky had founded a 'revolutionary academy' on Capri and that Lenin had spent time there.[25]

As we shall see, Lunacharsky, later the Soviet Union's first People's Commissioner for Public Education, from the 1917 October Revolution to 1929, figures in a key moment in Benjamin's *Moscow Diary*. Unfortunately for Benjamin, their paths, at least indirectly, were to cross.

At the very beginning of his surrealist *One-Way Street*, written in 1925 and 1926, Benjamin confides to the reader: 'This street is named Asja Lacis Street after her who as an engineer cut it through to the author', declaring in this dedication how much she almost immediately influenced him.[26] In romance terms, for Benjamin meeting Lacis leads to challenge, transformation and metamorphosis. Yet the intensity, duration and intellectual productivity of their friendship, that lasted for many years, has puzzled later commentators. Benjamin's old friend Gershom Scholem, for example, remarks with some annoyance in his Preface to *Moscow Diary* that, for all its personal frankness, the diary 'leaves us without insight into or understanding of precisely this intellectual dimension of the woman he loved'; there is in the diary, Scholem complains, an 'absence of any convincing evocation of her intellectual profile' that would make his passion for her comprehensible.[27]

I disagree. I think a detailed reading of *Moscow Diary* yields many clues to interests and conceptions Benjamin shared with Asja Lacis. I also agree with the feminist critique by Susan Ingram of decades of Benjamin scholarship that wishes to downplay Lacis's influence and interest as an historical figure; Ingram is particularly, and rightly, irritated at what she regards as Scholem's demeaning of Lacis in his Preface to *Moscow Diary*. Yet as Ingram points out, not only does Benjamin dedicate *One Way Street* to Lacis, but she was also the co-author of the essay 'Naples', first published in 1925, and later included in the 1978 selection of Benjamin's essays, *Reflections*.[28]

An interest in Naples threads through *Moscow Diary*, so I think it's worth while to look at 'Naples', an entrancing essay I've written about before.[29] 'Naples' challenges a long tradition that in the nineteenth century, in figures like Madame de Staël and Ruskin, unfavourably compared an alleged southern European indolence and sterility, especially in Italy, with northern European creativity, as in Gothic architecture.[30] It is precisely this assumption of northern European superiority that the essay overturns. 'Naples' asks what does it mean to be European, how do we conceive Europe; terms like civilised and barbarism are questioned, the essay referring to Naples' 'rich barbarism'. As the essay continues, it is northern Europe which more and more comes off badly in the comparison. In northern Europe, Benjamin and Lacis say, the 'Nordic sense' of architecture assumes that 'the house' is the cell of a city's architecture, signifying the 'civilized, private, and ordered'; they refer to the 'gloomy box of the Nordic house'. By contrast, they observe, everything in Naples, including its architecture, is 'porous', a repeated term: 'Porosity is the inexhaustible law of the life of this city, reappearing everywhere'; the 'stamp of the definitive is avoided'; the 'scope to become a theater of new, unforeseen constellations' is everywhere preserved. Porosity results 'above all' from a passion for improvisation. In the 'great panorama' that is Naples, buildings are used as a 'popular stage', divided into 'innumerable, simultaneously animated theaters', where balcony, courtyard, window, gateway, staircase, and roof are at the same time 'stages and boxes'. The city's storehouses are like 'bazaars'. Benjamin and Lacis notice a 'toyshop' that reminds them of 'fairy-tale galleries'; and the main street of Naples, the Toledo, is also like a 'gallery'. They admire the liveliness of the 'small traders' stalls'.[31]

For Benjamin and Lacis then, what characterises Naples is a kind of energy for improvisation which permeates all spheres and breaks down the rigid distinctions between the private and the public that bring gloom to northern Europe. Naples lives in its porosity, intermingling and theatricality, and its theatricality is touched with fairytale-like fantasia and fantasticality. Here Benjamin and Lacis' essay reminds me of Goethe's observations of carnival in Rome in 1788 in his *Italian Journey*, observations that fascinated my other favourite cultural theorist, Mikhail Bakhtin, which I write about in my *Postmodernism and Popular Culture*.[32] In Naples, everything is turned inside out and upside down. Benjamin and Lacis note that Neapolitans participate in the many festivals and feasts associated with Catholicism: from July to September, there are firework displays over the sea, seen along the coast from Naples to Salerno; each parish has to outdo the festival of its neighbour with 'new lighting effects'. Whereas for the Northern European to exist is the 'most private of affairs', Naples has much in common with the 'African kraal': 'each private attitude or act is permeated by streams of communal life'. The house is 'far less the refuge into which people retreat than the inexhaustible reservoir from which they flood out', so that the living room reappears on the street, 'with chairs, hearth, and altar'. From the windows of the top floors of the tenement blocks 'come baskets on ropes for mail, fruit, and cabbage'. On the fourth or fifth storeys 'cows are kept'. Unlike in the 'protected Northern sleep', men, women, and children snatch sleep anywhere during the day and night. The worlds of adults and children are not kept separate; interesting toys and dolls are everpresent for all ages. And in Naples the 'language of gestures' goes further than anywhere else in Italy; ears, nose, eyes, breast, and shoulders are 'signaling stations activated by the fingers'.[33] (I love that carnivalesque image of cows on the fourth or fifth storeys of the tenement blocks.)

Benjamin and Lacis talk about cafés in a way that interests me personally in my obsessive devotion to coffee shops, fretting if I can't get to my favourite one in the morning; if for some reason a day goes by that I haven't had an expresso-machine coffee of some kind, I start to get headaches; I lack a sense of wellbeing by which to face the day. The Neapolitan café, Benjamin and Lacis point out, is the 'opposite of everything Viennese, of the confined, bourgeois, literary world'. By contrast, Neapolitan cafés are 'laboratories' of the 'great process of intermingling' that happens everywhere in the city: 'Life is unable to sit down and stagnate in them', for a 'prolonged stay is scarcely possible' and only a few people briefly sit. People order a 'cup of excessively hot *caffé expresso*' – 'in hot drinks this city is as unrivaled as in sherbets, spumoni, and ice cream' – and then leave.[34] On our morning walk I told Ann about this passage and we agreed that contemporary

Australian cities such as Sydney and Melbourne have been Mediterraneanised for decades now in a southern Italian way as Benjamin and Lacis describe it in the Naples essay, with a vastly increased street life including outdoor eating and coffee drinking. Coffee shops, however, which we haunt in the Bohemian inner parts of Sydney, partake, we think, of both the Viennese and southern Italian modes: in a Viennese way, encompassing people reading books or newspapers, trying to do crosswords and the sudoku, staring intently at their laptops, supervising anxious doctoral students; in a Neapolitan way, engaged in lively conversations, excitedly discussing ideas and projects, eating and subject to invasion by armadas of mothers with new babies in gigantic prams. Sometimes, you feel, there is tension in them between Viennese quietness and Neapolitan noisiness.

In *Moscow Diary* Benjamin applies and extends the insights into different Europes he and Lacis work out in 'Naples', not as we might expect aligning icy snow-filled Moscow with cold Northern Europe but with sunny southern Italy, with Naples rather than Berlin. For Benjamin, Moscow offers the traveller new perspectives on the northern Europe to which he reluctantly returns. Back in Berlin, after his visit, Benjamin wrote in his diary:

> *January 30.* I am adding certain things about Moscow that have only occurred to me here in Berlin... For someone who has arrived from Moscow, Berlin is a dead city. The people on the street seem desperately isolated, each one at a great distance from the next, all alone in the midst of a broad stretch of street. Furthermore: as I was traveling from the Zoo railway station toward the Grunewald, the neighbourhood I had to cross struck me as scrubbed and polished, excessively clean, excessively comfortable. What is true of the image of the city and its inhabitants is also applicable to its mentality: the new perspective one gains on this is the most indisputable consequence of a stay in Russia. However little one

> might still know of Russia, one learns to observe and judge Europe with a conscious awareness of what is taking place in Russia.[35]

Benjamin explores and evokes Moscow much as he and Lacis explored and evoked Naples, drawn to its theatricality and fantasticality revealed in its street life, market stalls, coffee and pastry shops, toy shops, the toy museum, shops to buy clothing materials, places to buy dolls. 'Everything', he says, 'shoe polish, picture books, stationery, pastries and breads, even towels, is sold out in the open on the street, as if the minus twenty-five degree Moscow winter were in fact a Neapolitan summer'. (20 December, p. 36) The 'inventory of the streets is inexhaustible'; there is an abundance of 'paper flowers', with peddlers proudly brandishing throughout the city huge hollyhocks on lampshades; there are cakes shaped like lyres; he sees a man selling small skates for dolls. Only in Moscow, he feels, 'can you find pictures created out of nothing more than spun sugar, sweet icicles on which the tongue takes its revenge against the bitter cold'. (1 January, p. 58) By early January, he observes that what characterises a 'good portion of Moscow's streets' is a 'configuration of market and fairground'. (5 January, p. 68) Visiting the Kremlin, he is struck not only by its 'extraordinary topography and architecture' but a feature, or absence, that is a basic condition of its beauty: 'none of its broad expanses contains a monument'. By contrast, Benjamin reflects, there is hardly a square in Europe 'whose secret structure was not profaned and impaired over the course of the nineteenth century by the introduction of a monument'. (4 January, p. 65) What interests him when he strolls through the Sukhaevsky market is the reverse of the monumental, the imposing intimidating presence of the official in public spaces. I'm reminded of Rimbaud saying how much he prefers 'idiotic pictures, decorative lintels, theatre sets, fairground backdrops, shop-signs, popular prints' to institutional art galleryor museum art; a huge aspect of twentieth-century modernism, as in Dada.[36]

For Benjamin in Moscow, the reverse of the monumental is to be found in toys and dolls, magical objects, paper art, startling sights and, not least, similarities with southern Italy. Benjamin records that in the Moscow market, 'for the first time since Naples', he comes across someone selling 'magic items', a man with a 'small bottle in front of him in which a large cloth monkey was sitting'; Benjamin recalls that a 'Neapolitan used to sell bunches of flowers of the same sort'. (5 January p. 68) The entry for 26 January records that Moscow is experiencing some 'wonderful warm weather'; he sees peddlers selling 'colored baskets that look somewhat like the ones you can buy everywhere in Capri'. (p. 106) In the entry for 29 January, Benjamin, after failing to meet up with Asja Lacis as he thought they had arranged, takes a solitary streetcar ride to the last stop on a far side of Moscow, a part of the city with which he was completely unfamiliar: 'For the first time I noticed the absolute similarity between certain parts of the outskirts and the harbor streets of Naples'. (p. 112)

How do you explore a city you're visiting? In *Moscow Diary* Benjamin refers to his 'fanatic urge to travel', though he feels it has 'diminished in me over the past two years'. (20 December, p. 35)[37] In his 1931 essay 'Unpacking My Library: A Talk about Book Collecting' reprinted in *Illuminations*, which I talk about in the following chapter on my father's books and pamphlets, Benjamin reflected that searching for books is invaluable for the traveler in a new place. But I don't think he did this in Moscow; in the diary he remarks that he went to the Ironworkers' Bridge to look at bookstores in a street where Moscow's largest bookstore is located, but realised books are too expensive to buy: 'I even saw foreign literature in the windows, but at outlandish prices'. (28 December, p. 48) The main way, I think, Benjamin explores Moscow is through his interest in toys and dolls, an interest he shares with Asja Lacis and which he enjoys doing almost as soon as he arrives. Nearly every entry mentions toys and dolls. (Later he would write a short essay, 'Russian Toys', which is included in *Moscow Diary* by the editor Gary Smith as an appendix.) We also learn that he and Lacis buy toys for each other. On one occasion Lacis, Benjamin and Reich look at the 'shop windows along Petrovka', and Benjamin admires a 'splendid store featuring articles made out of wood'. He adds: 'At my request, Asja bought me a tiny little pipe.' Benjamin also notices in this store 'those Russian eggs, each one encased in another, and animals carved out of lovely soft wood', and makes a note to himself to come back later to 'buy toys for Stefan and Daga', Stefan, his son with his wife Dora Pollak (they were married from 1917 to 1930), and Daga, Lacis's daughter. (11 December, p. 18)

(A brief excursus here. Reading Eiland and Jennings' biography of Benjamin enables me to see that Benjamin's interest in toys and books for children and childhood more generally was longstanding in his life, pre-dating his visit to Moscow, indeed it was an interest he shared with Dora Pollak from early in their marriage. In exile in Switzerland in 1917, Benjamin indulged his passion for book collecting, especially in the area of old and rare children's books; Dora, now pregnant, also took pleasure in building up their library of illustrated children's books. On 11 April 1918, their only child Stefan was born, and over the coming years Benjamin took great delight in observing Stefan's behavior and development, especially the development of speech. Benjamin began keeping a notebook devoted to Stefan's 'opinions and *pensées*'. His interest in the perceptual and imaginative world of childhood led to his creating a minutely observed archive of his son's childish sayings. After their return to Berlin in March 1920, and while often in very straitened circumstances, Benjamin and Dora continued to add to their collection of children's books, mostly from the nineteenth century, which would finally comprise more than 200 volumes.[38]

His attempts to become an academic having failed, Benjamin turned toward a career as a journalist and wide-ranging cultural critic. In the years 1924 to 1931, stimulated by conversations with his friend Siegfried Kracauer, he wrote on popular culture and the media, including writing essays on children's literature and children's theatre. Whenever he could, he added to his collection of children's books and wrote essays on collecting them. He took great interest in children's games and toys. He pondered the role of children's books in the history of pedagogy in Germany. In August 1925, Benjamin published his first contribution, 'Collection of Frankfurt Children's Rhymes', for the *Frankfurter Zeitung*, the oldest and most widely read of the left-liberal dailies in Germany. In December 1925, settling back into family life after many travels, Benjamin spent more time with Stefan, now 7½, reading to him several hours a week from his and Dora's collection of stories for children. For Hanukkah, Benjamin retrieved a puppet theatre from his own childhood and staged with some friends a play for Stefan.)[39]

In Moscow Benjamin likes to buy toys and dolls for himself as well as for others. Benjamin and Lacis take 'a sleigh into town' and visit stores on Petrovka, and Lacis helps him buy a small doll for her daughter, though, Benjamin confesses, 'I primarily want to take advantage of the opportunity to get one for myself as well'. (16 December, pp. 27–28) In his 'wanderings' he procures, on one of the main streets of the left bank of the Moska, 'three little houses made out of colored paper'. (19 December, p. 32) On 21 December, on an 'extremely cold' day, Benjamin walked 'the entire length of the Arbat and reached the market on Smolensk Boulevard'; the path is crowded with 'baskets of delicacies, tree decorations, and toys'; he buys a 'kitsch postcard' and a 'balalaika and little paper house'. With all his purchases, he has a difficult time reaching the 'toy museum'. (pp. 36–37)

In the diary Benjamin reveals his keen interest in the toy

museum. On 24 December, Benjamin takes Lacis to her dressmaker 'before going on to the toy museum' by sleigh. Benjamin's guide in the museum, Nikolai D Bartram, presents him 'with a copy of his study, *From Toy to Children's Theater*, which would become my Christmas present to Asja'. (pp. 41–2) On 13 January he records that he wanted to take the number nine bus to the toy museum, but it broke down on the Arbat. (p. 80) On 21 January he visits the toy museum and discusses with them the 'photographs I wanted to have made up'; the museum people show him 'some photos for which there were negatives available', and he orders 'about twenty of them'. (p. 98) On 27 January Benjamin is pleased by a visit to the toy museum; it looks like something can be worked out with the photographs. (p. 106) The entry for 1 February, the day he leaves Moscow, records that Benjamin goes to the toy museum to pick up photographs he ordered (though some are not ready). (p. 120)

More non-monumental toys, dolls, small objects, icons: searching for them takes up much of Benjamin's time and desires. On a street he buys a 'Chinese paper fish'. (24 December p. 43) At the 'famous Sukharev Park' markets, he finds 'among the toy stalls ... my Christmas tree decoration in the shape of a samovar'. (5 January, p. 68) He has a 'short, passionate infatuation' with lacquer boxes, hoping to buy three of them. One day he purchases a 'quite beautiful' box with 'two girls sitting by a samovar', though it 'has none of that pure black which is often the most beautiful thing about lacquerwork'. (11 January, p. 75) The next day, at the Kustarny Museum, he buys a 'lacquer box on whose cover a female cigarette vendor is painted against the ground of black'. (12 January, p. 75) He remembers a lacquer box he once saw at the home of Ernst Bloch and Else Bloch von Stritzki in Switzerland, and though he can't recall the motif that decorated it, he can 'imagine just how unforgettably these images on a ground of black lacquer must impress themselves on children'. (p. 76) Also on this day he discovers some 'fabulous postcards, the kind I had long been looking for, old white elephants from the czarist days'. (p. 76) On 14 January, as the weather gets colder and colder, the average temperature below 20 degrees, he 'hunted up some new toys', wooden toys, though he is not very happy with what he buys, a 'rather silly wooden model of a sewing machine' and a 'paper-mâché rocking puppet on a music box'. (p. 83) On 17 January at the upper levels of the state store GUM he purchases 'the dolls and riders I had been eyeing'. (p. 91)

On 18 January Benjamin goes to the Historical Museum to view its 'extraordinarily rich icon collection'. That evening Lacis visits where he is staying and Benjamin is pleased to show her his various purchases: 'I bought her caviar, tangerines, candy, and cakes. On the windowsill on which I keep my toys I had also set up two clay dolls, one of which she was to choose for herself.' Benjamin later sees the doll she has chosen 'sitting across from her bed in the sanatorium'. (pp. 92–94) On 21 January, 'the anniversary of Lenin's death', Benjamin arranges to visit Muskin the director of the children's books division of the State Publishing House on the following Saturday, 'to look at his collection of children's books'. (p. 98) In the entry for 22 January Benjamin notes that the 'visit with Muskin was well worth it', although he saw only 'one truly important children's book, a Swiss children's calendar of 1837, a thin little volume with three very beautiful color plates'; he is disappointed to see that the great majority of the Russian children's books he is shown are copies of German models; Muskin notes down Benjamin's comments; Benjamin explains to Muskin his documentary project on Fantasy (never carried out). (pp. 100–101) On 26 January he sees a peddler with a 'bundle of children's pistols hanging from his shoulders', while other peddlers sell baskets that look like 'the ones you can buy everywhere in Capri'. (p. 106)

When you stay for a while in a new city, how can you make

it as if your home? How do you make it homely, even if only for the while?

Reading *Moscow Diary*, I'm very interested to see that Benjamin does what Ann Curthoys and I like doing when we travel. Soon after arriving in Moscow, Benjamin begins to notice pastry shops, serving coffee as well as cakes.[40] For the entry of 8 December he records seeing pastry shops in the street where the Hotel Liverpool is (p. 12); that day he buys Lacis 'some halvah in a pastry shop'. (p. 14) On 11 December, Lacis and Benjamin visit a pastry shop: 'They serve cups of whipped cream there. Asja had a cup with meringue, I had coffee.' (p. 18) By 6 January, when Benjamin has been in Moscow for a month, he is referring to a favourite coffee shop that he visits with Reich: 'we were having coffee in the friendly little pastry shop, which I will probably often think back on'. (p. 69) On 8 January Benjamin notes that around seven in the evening he had coffee with Reich 'at our usual pastry shop'. (p. 72) The entry for 17 January records his morning coffee: 'I had had some coffee and cake in my regular cake shop.' (p. 90) On 22 January he is disappointed to find that 'my usual cafe' is closed. (p. 100) His final entry for the diary, 1 February, begins: 'I once again went to my pastry shop that morning, ordered coffee and ate a sweet roll'. (p. 120)

Let's return to the romance of Walter Benjamin and Asja Lacis, so suffused on both sides by ambivalence and uncertainty. Their relationship, or friendship, or love, was undoubtedly stormy, turbulent, almost harshly conflicted. In the entry for 18 January (p. 94) Benjamin notes that even in the wake of their 'violent quarrels' he had sensed that for some days 'she had been feeling more strongly drawn to me'. Lacis visits in the evening, and Benjamin is surprised by her warmth: 'Tendernesses that had nearly been forgotten resurfaced.' Benjamin had put on his bed some letters he'd just received from Europe with good news about publication of his essays: 'Asja had me remove the letters and she lay down on the bed. We kissed at length.' (p. 94) But what excites him 'most deeply' is the touch of her hands; he recalls that Lacis herself had once told him that 'everybody who was attached to her felt the extremely powerful forces that emanated from her hands'. Benjamin places his right palm directly against her left palm and they remain in this position for a long time. An image of southern Italy recurs, this time for Lacis: 'Asja recalled the beautiful tiny letter that I had presented to her one night in the via Depretis in Naples as we were sitting at a table in a small cafe on a nearly deserted street'. (p. 94) (Several days before, in the entry for 12 January, p. 77, while in an art museum, the Tretiakov Gallery, Benjamin, looking at a couple of paintings of Sorrento and surrounds, recalled the 'indescribable silhouette of Capri, something that will always be linked in my mind to Asja'.) Then Benjamin reads to her the 'lesbian scene from Proust' and 'Asja grasped its savage nihilism'. Benjamin explains to her how 'within every fracture evil explicitly shows its true substance – "humanity", or even "kindness"'. As he explains his theory, it becomes clear to him how closely it coincides with 'the thrust of my baroque book', and this gets him thinking about how, reading alone the night before, another passage from Proust develops a conception 'that corresponds at every point to what I myself have tried to subsume under the concept of allegory'. (p. 95) In this scene, erotic embrace, intellectual passion, a meeting of hands in stillness, Italophilia centred in Naples, reading Proust aloud, and the excitement of making new theoretical connections weave in and out of each other as in an arabesque.

Yet this is a rare moment in the diary. Mostly in the entries we see that their conflicts and ambivalence are never resolved. The final sentence for 30 January reads: 'Animosity and love were shifting within me like winds…' (p. 116)

Nonetheless, in the diary, there are many clues I think to why Benjamin was so deeply drawn to Lacis. One I think is clear: he associates his love and desire for her – as she did for him – with memories of southern Italy, with Naples and Capri, which he links with Moscow in winter. Another reason is something I want to hazard. I keep thinking about their birth dates, that Lacis was born in 1891 and so was a year older than Benjamin. Could it be that he regarded her as a mentor, someone who gives him sage advice? Was Lacis one of those gifted with a kind of wisdom about life? In any case, we remember that soon after their meeting in Capri Benjamin had dedicated *One-Way Street* to her as an engineer of his soul. Several days after reaching Moscow, in the entry for 11 December, while they are in a pastry shop, 'facing each other over a small table' (an image that brings to mind for me a famous Cézanne painting), we read: 'Asja reminded me of my intention to write something critical of psychology, and I once again realized just to what extent the possibility of tackling these subjects depends on my contact with her'. (p. 18)

Christmas Eve is eventful for Benjamin. In the entry for 24 December, he tells of coming across a museum which he had not intended to visit; once inside he sees that it has a very good collection of modern Western art, and to his delight finds himself in one of its two Cézanne rooms looking at an 'extraordinarily beautiful Cézanne' of a road running through a wood, with a group of houses to one side. Benjamin then records one of those intriguing insights that make him so enduringly interesting a cultural theorist.[41] It suddenly occurs to him that 'it is even linguistically fallacious to speak of "empathy". It seemed to me that to the extent that one grasps a painting, one does not in any way enter into its space; rather, this space thrusts itself forward, especially in various very specific spots. It opens up to us in corners and angles in which we believe we can localize crucial experiences of the past; there is something inexplicably familiar about these spots.' (p. 42) That night, both Reich and Lacis are in his room, and looking at her Benjamin 'experienced something I had not felt in years, a sense of security on Christmas Eve'. The conversation turns to a 'job that Asja was to have taken', then to Benjamin's book on the baroque mourning play the *Trauerspiel*, to be published in 1928 as *Ursprung des deutschen Trauerspiels* and later in the century translated into English as *The Origin of German Tragic Drama* – a book I treasure and Ann and I have written about.[42] Benjamin reads aloud an angry note he was thinking of including in the book 'directed against the University of Frankfurt'; he felt sure that the university would reject his book as a habilitation thesis, and so had withdrawn it. Then he gives Lacis's response: 'Asja's opinion may take on importance for me; she thought that despite everything I should simply write: rejected by the University of Frankfurt-on-Main.' (p. 43)

It very much appears that Benjamin agreed to what I will call Lacis's mentoring suggestion. A footnote by the editor to *Moscow Diary* tells us that Benjamin eliminated from the published version of the *Trauerspiel* book the 'preliminary note – a bitter fairy tale about Benjamin's prickly relation to academia'. (p. 43, footnote 69)

More Lacis mentoring. Benjamin and Lacis vehemently disagree about gas warfare; Reich intervenes, and after calm is restored Lacis 'said I should put my points down in writing and I promised myself to compose an article on the subject' for publication. (19 January, p. 95) (Arguments don't only occur between Benjamin and Lacis; in the entry for 10 December, p. 16, Benjamin notes that when he visits Lacis at the sanatorium, she is in no mood to see him, she 'had had an argument with Reich about living arrangements'; a couple of days later when the three were 'sitting in a cafe, Asja and Reich got into a big argument, during which Reich made it clear that he was planning to cut all his ties with Germany and concentrate on Russian matters' – 12 December, p. 19.) In the entry for 21 January Benjamin mentions that instead of working on his ongoing translation of Proust, he is crafting a reply to an 'ugly, insolent obituary' that a critic called Franz Blei had composed on Rilke. 'Later', says Benjamin, 'I read what I had written to Asja and her comments encouraged me to rework it that very evening and the following day.' (p. 99)

Benjamin and Reich ponder the possible source of her mentoring wisdom and intellectual insights. Is it because of her contact with Western Europe? Benjamin writes:

> It is obvious, even now, she is still attracted to Western Europe. It is not merely the attraction of travel, foreign cities, the amenities of cosmopolitan bohemianism, but also the liberating influence her thinking underwent in Western Europe, especially through her contacts with Reich and me. Indeed, as Reich was lately saying, it's fairly mysterious how, being here in Russia, Asja managed to develop the acuity of insight which she was already displaying in Western Europe. (20 December, p. 34)

The two Western European intellectuals, slightly patronisingly, wish to believe that it was her contact with them and the Europe they represent that liberates her thinking; yet they also uncomfortably realise that Lacis already possessed an 'acuity of insight', that she brought it with her to Europe.

There are more clues in *Moscow Diary* to interests Benjamin shared with Asja Lacis. One clearly is children, an abiding interest of Benjamin's: recall that in the *Illuminations* essay 'Unpacking My Library', Benjamin tells us of his collection of children's books that began with scrap books from his mother; and Benjamin also from 1927 to 1933 gave radio talks for children, including, we learn from Jeffrey Mehlman's *Walter Benjamin for Children*, a talk on Naples that was recast from the essay he wrote with Lacis.[43] Benjamin admires Lacis's work with children and children's theatre. Benjamin notes that she speaks with 'great animation' of how, at the children's centre she works at, she keeps the 'normal children' separate from the 'wildest' children, those she regards as the 'most gifted ones': 'it is very evident that Asja, as she says herself, is most successful with the wildest children'. (14 December, p. 21) Lacis tells Benjamin and Reich, who are visiting her in the sanatorium, that there is a possibility that she may become an assistant director in a theatre which puts on shows for proletarian children. (19 January, p. 95)

I think that Benjamin is profoundly attracted to Lacis not only for her knowledge of theatre but more broadly for her sense of theatricality as a quality of life. Recall that in *Illuminations* Benjamin admires writers such as Kafka and Brecht who perceive life as a *theatrum mundi*; in his essay 'Franz Kafka: On the Tenth Anniversary of His Death', Benjamin reflects that 'Kafka's world is a world theater. For him, man is on the stage from the very beginning.' In 'What is Epic Theater?' Benjamin praises the 'philosophic sophistication' of Brecht who, 'in writing his plays, always remembers that in the end the world may turn out to be a theater'.[44]

Benjamin is sometimes discussed as if his ruling mood were melancholy, and that, philosophically, melancholy was the ground of the way he thought.[45] In a more mundane sense, *Moscow Diary* reveals Benjamin in many moods, from anger, animosity, sadness, to pleasure and joy. His references to southern Italy, to Naples and Capri, with whom he associates Lacis and Moscow, are certainly not dominated by melancholy, nor was the 'Naples' essay they had previously written together, nor is their shared interest in theatricality, nor in toys and dolls, nor in sweets and cakes like halvah and marzipan. They laugh and joke: Benjamin writes in the entry for Christmas Eve that they were 'very close that evening' and that 'Asja got a lot of laughs out of some of the things I was saying to her' (24 December, p. 43). Visiting Benjamin, with Reich there as well, on 12 January, Lacis stays for half an hour, doing 'impressions of actors' and imitating the cabaret song *San*

Francisco: 'I knew the song from Capri, she occasionally used to sing it there'. (p. 76)

They share an interest in dress materials and clothes. When she and Reich drop in on Benjamin on 12 December, Lacis helps unpack his suitcases and picks out 'two ties for herself that she liked'. (p. 19) They like shopping together, taking a sleigh into town and visiting a number of stores on Petrovka in order to buy 'fabric for her dress', which he jokingly calls her 'uniform', since Lacis insists that 'her new dress be exactly of the same cut as the old one from Paris'. (16 December, p. 27)

In relation to clothes and dress materials, Benjamin, we might say, reveals in *Moscow Diary* a kind of feminised consciousness, an intense and minute interest bordering on (male) fetishism. The entry for 9 December (p. 15), three days after he arrived, records that Lacis dropped round to his place, where he 'gave her presents: blouse, hose', and reads out to her the remarkable paragraph from *One-Way Street* about adoring wrinkles in the beloved: 'as birds seek refuge in the leafy recesses of a tree, feelings escape into the shaded wrinkles, the awkward movements and inconspicuous blemishes of the body we love…'.[46] In mid-December Benjamin expresses his dismay that the sanatorium is making it difficult for Lacis to leave it for visits outside, especially as they were 'planning to buy material for her dress'; he also confesses that often he barely hears what she is saying because 'I am examining her so intently'. (14 December, p. 21) Walking through the passageway that leads from Revolution Square to Red Square, he notices the street vendors selling 'women's lingerie (corsets)', 'neckties' and 'shawls'. (14 January, p. 84)

I was struck by the diary's images of scarves, shawls and wraps. Going to the theatre, Lacis and Benjamin view a staging by Stanislavsky of Rimsky-Korsakov's opera *The Czar's Bride*, and in one of the intervals conversation turns to the 'ochre-yellow Italian scarf she is wearing'. (10 December, p. 16) On 31 December he notices that she 'was again wearing her yellow shawl'. (p. 57) On another occasion, Lacis sits near Benjamin, and he sees that she had 'wrapped my silk Parisian scarf around her'. (25 January, p. 105) He also refers to an evening when 'Asja was wearing the new dress for which I had provided the fabric. Around her shoulders she was wearing the yellow wrap that I had brought from Rome to Riga for her'. (30 January, p. 116)

Reading these references uncomfortably reminds me of a time, around the writing especially of my *1492: The Poetics of Diaspora* (2001), when I took a fetishistic interest in women's scarves and veils, including, rather too uncannily, a yellow scarf, I have to confess. I've just drawn it out of a wardrobe drawer and am looking at it now. In my chapter in that book on Sir Walter Scott's early nineteenth-century medieval fantasia *Ivanhoe*, I note that its female characters, both Saxon and Norman, wear veils, as do its major figures Rebecca and Rowena, while in my concluding mosaic I confess that 'I'm a voyeur of veils. I envy female decoration.' I also note that Molly Bloom in her soliloquy at the end of James Joyce's *Ulysses* makes caustic comments on men's 'derisory fetishes they think are so interesting and give them the illusion of substance' (these are my words, not Molly's).[47]

In questioning melancholy as the dominating mood of Benjamin's writing,[48] I don't wish to diminish the sadness of his final days in Moscow as disappointment looms for his hopes of a relationship with Lacis. Yet even these final days reveal that Benjamin, perhaps under the influence of Lacis, has become a kind of connoisseur of theatricality, including absurdity and farce, even when occurring in life in its most intense moments. In late January, when Lacis leaves the sanatorium, a new suitor makes a bizarre appearance: 'There was an ever-present Red Army general who had only been married two months but who was courting Asja in every conceivable fashion and who had asked her to run off with him to Vladivostok, where he was being transferred. He said he wanted to leave his wife behind in Moscow.' (23 January, pp. 101–102; also 27 January, p. 108) I think even in the final scene that closes the drama of the diary and his visit, Benjamin reflects on the manner of his own sadness. As he says good-bye to her in his room, he weeps: 'Finally, since there were only a few minutes left, my voice began to falter and Asja noticed that I was crying... We held each other tight.' Outside in the street, Lacis hails a sleigh.

> ... I invited her to ride to the corner of Tverskaia with me. I dropped her off there, and as the sleigh was already pulling away, I once again drew her hand to my lips, right in the middle of the street. She stood there a long time, waving. I waved back from the sleigh. At first she seemed to turn around as she walked away, then I lost sight of her. Holding my large suitcase on my knees, I rode through the twilit streets to the station in tears. (1 February, p. 121)

Remember Benjamin talking about Kafka and Brecht perceiving the world as a *theatrum mundi*. Benjamin is here suggesting, I think, that Moscow, like Naples and southern Italy but unlike Berlin and northern Europe, permits a kind of public performance of emotion and passion, as Benjamin draws Asja's hand to his lips, 'right in the middle of the street'.

Benjamin had written in the diary a few days before, on 27 January, that he realised that life in Russia was 'too difficult for me within the Party' and there were few prospects outside it, while in contrast Lacis had 'put down a number of roots here in Russia'. Yet he still hoped that one day she might live with him in Europe. Benjamin thinks of her 'nostalgia for Europe, which is closely connected to what she might find attractive about me', and that living with her in Europe 'could one day become the most important, the most tangible thing for me, if only she could be won over to it'. (p. 109)

Benjamin and Lacis did see each other again in Europe. According to Gary Smith in his Afterword, they lived together in Europe for two months during 1928–30,[49] but lost sight of each other after her return to Moscow in 1930, though it appears he continued to write to her. (Afterword, p. 142)

To Join or Not to Join the Communist Party

Leaving aside the egregious Red Army general, almost a stage figure, the triangular relationship of Benjamin, Lacis and Reich is pervaded by the anxiety of three intellectuals of how to survive in exceedingly fraught worlds.

Lacis and Reich chose to remain in the Soviet Union, yet even at the time of Benjamin's mid-twenties visit it was clear that political, intellectual, and cultural life was becoming increasingly restricted, especially because of Stalin. Benjamin arrived on 6 December 1926, and in his first entry written a few days later he recalled how on the morning of 7 December he listened to Reich's 'sharp and amusing' stories of the follies of life in the Soviet Union, as well as more ominous tidings: 'then the political news: members of the opposition removed from important positions. And in identical fashion: countless Jews removed from middle-level posts. Anti-Semitism in the Ukraine.' Reich confides his 'reservations about joining the Party', focusing on the 'Party's reactionary bent in cultural matters' and that 'measures' were being taken against the 'cultural front of the left'; also, the 'leftist movements which had proved useful during the period of wartime communism' were now being discarded. (9 December, pp. 10–12) According to Gary Smith, Reich during the 1930s and beyond suffered repeated banishment and imprisonment. (Afterword, p. 142)

In *Zarathusta's Sisters*, Susan Ingram tells us that after leaving the sanatorium and recovering her health, Lacis worked with Lenin's widow Nadezhda Krupskaya, to establish a children's cinema; in 1928 she was appointed cultural attaché to the Soviet trade commission in Berlin, where she met up again with her friends Benjamin and Brecht and was active in furthering the cause of Soviet film, including experimental filmmakers like Vertov; in 1930 she returned to the Soviet Union, working in film and pursuing doctoral studies in theatre in Moscow; in 1937 she was arrested, and spent 10 years in a gulag in Khazakhstan.[50]

In *Moscow Diary* Benjamin ponders his future. He wonders whether he should remain a 'left-wing outsider', which could be economically productive for him, or should he become part of the German Communist Party. (8 January, p. 72) Benjamin inscribes in the diary a passage debating with himself whether to 'join the Party'.

> Clear advantages: a solid position, a mandate, even if only by implication. Organized, guaranteed contact with other people. On the other hand: to be a Communist in a state where the proletariat rules means completely giving up your private independence. You leave the responsibility for organizing your own life up to the Party, as it were. (9 January, p. 73)

Perhaps loss of 'private independence', in Benjamin's view,[51] is what could happen to Asja Lacis, or was happening, at least occasionally.

In the diary, Benjamin relates that he had written an essay on Goethe for the *Soviet Encyclopedia*, and Reich had dropped it off at their office. However, the essay was looked at there by a leading party official, Karl Radek, who was scornful of it. Reich reports the incident to Benjamin. Benjamin now feels that the chances of it being published are 'extremely slim', for the 'wretched directors of this project are far too insecure to permit themselves any possibility of a personal opinion'. Later in the day, Benjamin and Lacis engage in a furious exchange, when he discusses with her Reich's gloomy prediction about the Goethe article. Lacis 'immediately started off by saying that there must have been some justification for what Radek had said. I certainly must have gone wrong somewhere, I didn't know how one had to go about things here, and other comments of the sort. Then I told her straight to her face that her words merely expressed her cowardice and her need to bend, at whatever cost, wherever the wind was blowing.' (13 January, p. 81)

Gary Smith says that the Goethe article was indeed rejected for the *Soviet Encyclopedia*, a decision in which Lunacharsky was influential. Smith reproduces, in an appendix to *Moscow Diary*, Lunacharsky's letter to the editors of the *Encyclopedia* of 29 March 1929, criticising Benjamin's Goethe essay: 'All in all, I again recommend that Benjamin's article not be printed.' (pp. 130–32) In her Introduction to *Illuminations*, Arendt refers to the importance of this rejection for Benjamin given that 'in the middle twenties he came very close to joining the Communist Party'.[52]

The *Moscow Diary* itself, I think, is evidence that by not joining the Party and remaining a left-wing outsider, Benjamin had the outsider's freedom and independence to make critical observations of Russian society under the impact of an oppressive state. Benjamin is dismayed at the way Russia is moving anti-left and by the increasing censorship and self-censorship. He dislikes 'how careful one has to be here', which he sees as 'one of the most conspicuous symptoms of the thoroughgoing politicization of life'. In his Introduction to *Reflections* Peter Demetz writes that in correspondence, when the question came up why he did not join the Communist Party, Benjamin cryptically alluded to his 'old anarchism'.[53] By his old anarchism I think Benjamin is referring to his sympathy for Sorel's syndicalism with its denunciation of the state. Let's recall the key passage from 'Critique of Violence', where Benjamin quotes Sorel's dislike of those who call for a political general strike:

> ... he [Sorel] says: 'The strengthening of state power is the basis of their conceptions; in their present organizations the politicians (viz. the moderate socialists) are already preparing the ground for a strong centralized and disciplined power that will be impervious to criticism from the opposition, capable of imposing silence, and of issuing mendacious decrees.'[54]

Arendt observes in her Introduction to *Illuminations* that Benjamin during the 1920s and 1930s was never going to commit himself, however tempted, either to joining the Communist Party or to political Zionism.[55] One powerful reason may be that joining either would commit Benjamin to belief in the power of the state (if we recall that in the pre-1948 decades in Palestine political Zionism was continually striving to become a state within a state).

Kunstchaos

It is Benjamin's individuality of perception, and the eccentricity and idiosyncrasy of his ideas and the way he writes, which he preserved by not joining the Communist Party nor the political Zionist project in Palestine, that intrigued postwar cultural theorists and my New Left generation. It's why I like him so much.

In *Moscow Diary* there is an illuminating discussion between Reich and Benjamin about Benjamin's distinctive mode of writing. On the evening of 26 December, 'Reich and I had a long conversation about my work as a writer and about the future direction it should take'. Reich made the 'very pertinent observation that in great writing the proportion between the total number of sentences and those sentences whose formulation was especially striking or pregnant was about one to thirty – whereas it was more like one to two in my case. All this is correct.' Benjamin takes Reich's critical comment as true, suggesting in a parenthesis that perhaps his way of writing was influenced by early contact with expressionism. Benjamin is here, then, accepting that his way of writing could, as Reich was implying, never be 'great writing'. Yet, now, we surely might think that Reich had put his finger on the very note that makes Benjamin's writing so remarkable and memorable, a frequent abbreviation where 'especially striking or pregnant' formulations stand out; a distilling, a winnowing, concentrated moments of constellation, where Benjamin's writing tends towards the fragment or parable or epigram or aphorism, the suddenly surprising, which perhaps comes to its searing culmination in 1940 in 'Theses on the Philosophy of History'.

There is an anarchistic quality to Benjamin's interests and writings, a kind of *Kunstchaos*. I'm thinking of the discussion of fragment literature in the Enlightenment in Lacoue-Labarthe and Nancy's *The Literary Absolute*, which they argue is a kind of '*Kunstchaos*, in other words, chaos produced by art or philosophical technique'.[56] Here's an example from *Moscow Diary*. In the packed entry for 19 December, Benjamin notes, a trifle unfeelingly, that because Reich was ill, having suffered some kind of heart attack, he went to the Meyerhold Theater alone in order to see Meyerhold's production of Gogol's *The Inspector General*. Benjamin is astonished by the 'extravagance' of its visual effects, especially in its stage sets. (Here I'm reminded again of Rimbaud). The audience response, however, Benjamin notices, is quite 'restrained', which he puts down to the Party having come out against the production, with 'even the moderate review by Pravda's theater critic' being rejected by its editors, making Benjamin think of the 'general atmosphere of cautiousness here when it comes to openly revealing one's opinions'. Benjamin admires the 'guiding principle' of the production, the 'concentration' of the action into an 'extremely restricted area', creating an 'extraordinarily luxurious density of dramatic values'. On the whole, Benjamin feels, the effect is like the 'architecture of a cake', which he considers a 'very Muscovite simile – only the cakes here could explain the comparison'. (pp. 32–4)[57]

I love this, Benjamin comparing the staging of a play to the 'architecture of a cake'. I wonder if one day I could do this, compare a text I'm interested in to the 'architecture of a cake', or even produce a text like the 'architecture of a cake'. However, as Benjamin suggests, one would have to know what a Moscow cake *circa* 1927 looked like.[58]

Moscow for Visiting Communists

Perhaps my father knew what a Moscow cake looked and tasted like *circa* 1934.

I'm still not sure how to compare Benjamin's two-month stay in Moscow in the mid-1920s to my father's much longer stay in Moscow in the mid-1930s. But I'll try to do so now.

If my father was in Moscow during 1934 and 1935, he experienced winter. I wonder, coming from Sydney, had he ever seen snow before? (I did not see snow falling until Ann and I lived in Washington DC for nine months in 2003–4.) Benjamin writes that during his first few days in Moscow he is 'above all struck by the difficulty of getting used to walking on the sheet ice of the streets', though the situation improved for him when 'Asja bought me a pair of galoshes'. (11 December, p. 17) I have to picture my father possibly walking on sheet ice; were the delegates to the Comintern's Seventh Congress and International Lenin School in 1934–35 provided with galoshes? Benjamin explored Moscow in searching for toys and dolls. I wonder if my father, if and when he had time off from the Congress and the International Lenin School, explored Moscow in some particular way, perhaps in searching for English-language bookshops for Marxist books and pamphlets. I wonder if he was like Benjamin who sought homeliness in a favourite cake shop. Benjamin drank coffee. I can't recall my father ever making or drinking coffee, but, a chocoholic as people interested in 'health foods' so often are, he might have enjoyed a cup of tea and some kind of chocolate; given how austere my father was about food and diet, I doubt that he would eat cakes. Perhaps, as Benjamin had, he made repeat visits to a pastry shop where after the second or third time they recognised and were friendly to him, and, like Benjamin, he felt a certain sadness knowing when he left he would never see the pastry shop people again.

Did Ted Docker, a man of 41or so in 1935, unmarried, a single man who lived at home in Sydney in his mother's house when he wasn't travelling on behalf of the Party, a smart dresser, fall in love in Moscow? It would, after all, be some years before he married. While working on this chapter, Ann and I were talking to some young female colleagues of ours in the history world. The conversation turned on what we were all writing at the moment, and I said for my memoir I'm working on a chapter on Walter Benjamin visiting Asja Lacis in Moscow and the tearful ending of the visit as recorded in his diary; then, perhaps unwisely, I added that I was thinking of constructing a fantasy for my father that he fell in love with a woman while there. With the cruel irreverence of the young, they immediately joked that I should speculate that Ted Docker and Asja Lacis had an affair in 1935.

Perhaps my father did have a romantic relationship in Moscow, and the relationship failed, or given distances could not be sustained, and, like Benjamin, he wept on the way to the train station; wept because he was sad, and wept because in Moscow you could publicly weep. For, perhaps, like Benjamin, he appreciated the expressiveness and theatricality of street life in Moscow.

Audrey Blake in Moscow in 1937

Nonetheless, I now realise that it would have been very difficult for Ted Docker as a visiting Communist delegate to the Comintern to meet ordinary Russians and wander freely about Moscow like Benjamin had done in the mid-1920s. Ted Docker's life like the lives of the other foreign Communists at the Comintern, was probably highly regulated and watched in the 1930s, as Stalin's Terror deepened, a terror often directed at Communists themselves. We can catch possible glimpses of his time in Moscow and where he might have stayed from Audrey Blake's memoir *A Proletarian Life*, published in 1984, though I kept it on my shelves and didn't read it until during the writing of this chapter. We also can register in her account the deepening terror. Audrey Blake, born in 1916, joining the Communist Party in Melbourne, was prominent in the 1930s in its youth wing the Young Communist League (later the Eureka Youth League), but moved to Sydney in 1949 with her husband Jack Blake; she was on the Central Committee.[59]

When my father died in 1983, I asked Audrey to help organise the Red Funeral that was held in a funeral parlour in Bondi Junction for him, giving her material on his youthful attraction to the IWW and his involvement in the early years of the Communist Party. Audrey had belonged to the same Party branch as my father and mother, the Bondi branch, until she resigned her membership of the Party in a passionate letter to the branch in 1966. Included in *A Proletarian Life*, Audrey charged that the Party leadership had never yet come to terms with the revelations of the Twentieth CPSU Congress of 1956, which revealed the chief characteristic of Stalinism – a term I never heard my father use – as the 'use of authority to stifle thought, opinions and discussion', the end result of which in the Soviet Union were 'the camps and the executions'. Audrey closes her letter of resignation by expressing her 'deep appreciation and thanks' to the Bondi branch, which 'has always, even in the most difficult years, shown a warm regard for me and despite the occasional sharp exchanges, a tolerance'.[60] Ann Curthoys and I had got to know Audrey as part of the loose penumbra of radical intellectuals in Sydney who related to the Melbourne journal *Arena*, its key figure Geoff Sharp, in which Ann and I published from the late 1960s onwards. I was aware that Audrey had known my family.

In the story that particularly interests me, 'Moscow Days', a story of danger and menace, Audrey tells of her time in Moscow in 1937.[61] Audrey and Jack and their baby stay in London while waiting for their Soviet visas, and then travel by Soviet ship to Leningrad and by train to Moscow. Dedicated Communists, Audrey has come as 'the Australian representative in the KIM – the Young Communist International', while Jack is representing the Australian Party at the Comintern; in the early 1930s Jack had spent two years at the Lenin School, returning to Australia in 1933. Audrey says that for her and Jack their inspiration came from the Russian Revolution and they completely believed in the Soviet Union: 'the Communist Party of the Soviet Union and the Comintern were our infallible authorities'. In 1937 home for both the Comintern and the KIM community was 'the Lux, a rambling, pleasant old hotel on Gorky Street'; they would travel to and from the Comintern offices 'in special Comintern buses'. They do, however, have one free day and night a week, and would see a film or go to the theatre or ballet.[62] Which makes me think: perhaps my father also stayed in the Lux in 1934–5 and went to and from work in special buses with other Comintern delegates, largely cut off from the society around them except for one day and night off.[63]

Almost immediately for Audrey and Jack there are shadows and unease. While Jack goes to work immediately, Audrey spends time arranging for Anissa, a peasant girl, to come and live with them to look after the baby. Impatient at this delay, Audrey asks Jack to help hurry things up for her, and he goes to see his immediate chief, Georgi Dimitrov, 'of the Reichstag fire trial and the Seventh Congress of the Comintern, 1935' (as we've seen, the highlight of my father's life) who was the General Secretary of the Communist International. The next day a Russian Comintern official named Brigadirov comes to see Audrey; he impresses on her that she should keep to her own circle and not mix with any Russians, for they might be spies and saboteurs. Another week passes without Audrey receiving her notification that she could start work. Jack seeks out Brigadirov to ask why, and on his return tells Audrey in a 'strained, uncertain voice' that 'Brigadirov's been taken. His room is sealed. It seems he's an agent'. The 'sealed doors' on the first floor of the Lux where they reside 'became more frequent'. Their corridor became 'strangely deserted and the lead seal would appear outside another apartment'. Audrey and Jack have dinner with an American there who was representing the Communist Party of USA, who remarks: 'The Australians and Americans will soon be the only ones left on this floor.'[64] Reading this I think of Gothic literature, images from German Expressionist film, a phantasmagoria.

When Audrey finally starts work, she shares an office with Lewis, a representative of the Young Communist League of Great Britain; the head of their section is Alex, another Englishman. She learns that most of the central committee of the Komsomol, the Young Communist League of the Soviet Union, had been arrested for being spies and counter-revolutionaries. A disturbing episode occurs some months later that relates to her personally. A serious-looking Alex informs her that an article on Australia she wrote risked being rejected by the KIM's editorial committee because it revealed certain nationalist illusions, in particular, because it admired Australia's democratic ethos and achievements like the eight-hour day; the committee, Alex said, wanted changes in order to strengthen the article's 'class viewpoint'. Audrey reflects that in London and now here in Moscow she had indeed been feeling 'a bit homesick', missing 'the democratic feel of my own country'. Audrey refuses to change the article, pointing out that Lenin in 1914 had written an essay entitled 'On the National Pride of the Great Russians' arguing that pride in the Russian motherland was consistent with an internationalist striving for revolution on behalf of humanity. As it turned out, Audrey won this particular tussle; she refused to be censored or engage in self-censorship.[65]

Travelling back to their hotel on the Comintern bus, Audrey gets to know Molly, a Jewish woman from South Africa who lived with her mother in the Lux. They invite Audrey and Jack and others in their English-speaking group to dinner in their room, Molly's mother making gefilte fish. Audrey and Jack and the others enjoy the night, telling stories and singing revolutionary songs, while 'Molly's mother sang us an old, sad, Yiddish song'.[66]

In 1937, we recall, Asja Lacis was arrested, and spent ten years in a gulag in Khazakhstan.

I cannot say that for my father what Audrey Blake experienced in Moscow in 1937 was identical with what my father experienced in 1934–5, yet nor can I think it was entirely different, that such surveillance and segregation from the society and an atmosphere of threat and menace were absent.

However, in his reminiscences 'Ted Docker: Chief Dates' and 'Ted Docker's Reminiscences' there are no such shadows and, in jubilant spirit, my father obviously enjoyed his long journey home on leaving Moscow, expressing no regrets or misgivings about his stay there in 1934–5.

Conclusion

By way of concluding this chapter, I come back to the passage in *Moscow Diary* where Benjamin felt that 'to be a Communist in a state where the proletariat rules means completely giving up your private independence. You leave the responsibility for organizing your own life up to the Party, as it were.' (9 January, p. 73)

I'm very struck by Benjamin's phrasing here, because I think that is what happened to Ted Docker in the Communist Party of Australia. In Benjamin's terms, my father gave up his 'private independence'; he left the responsibility for organising his life 'up to the Party'. Yet it did not need to happen. At the end of the 1920s, my father had a choice. He could continue to practise as he had in his syndicalist mid-1920s essays a fluid and insouciant kind of writing and thinking that continued IWW traditions; or he could accept the new Comintern line, conveyed by visiting Comintern agent Harry Wicks (also known as Herbert Moore) sent by the Comintern to Australia in 1930–31, that condemned such fluid thinking, and its corollary an inclusive radical politics, as 'social fascism'. The moment of choice was 1930 and 1931, when Ted Docker could either join with 1920s Party leaders Jack Ryan and his colleague Jack Kavanah in sustaining an open and inclusive Communist culture emphasising discussion and the right to disagree, or those in the Party who, following Harry Wicks' harsh Comintern lead, were moving to expel Ryan and Kavanah. My father chose to join with those who expelled Ryan and Kavanah, thereby revealing and exercising a new sensibility, stern, unyielding and authoritarian. Ann's mother Barbara Curthoys, in a 1993 essay entitled 'The Comintern, the CPA, and the Impact of Harry Wicks', is, quite rightly, sharply critical of Ted Docker for welcoming the new Comintern culture of harshness towards dissent. Barbara mourns the loss of the 1920s culture of relative openness and hospitality to different viewpoints.[67]

Early in 1934, Ted Docker was in Kalgoorlie; in mid-1934 and in 1935 in Moscow; and in 1936 he was in New Zealand.

We know this because Lovell and Windle's *Our Unswerving Loyalty* includes a document, Document 84, where Sid Scott, a New Zealand Communist, provides information to the Comintern on his Australian comrades, including Ted Docker, mentioning that my father had come to New Zealand 'as a fraternal delegate in 1936 (to a Plenum) and took part in a controversy with a sectarian group'. Sid Scott says that he personally found Ted Docker to be a 'very good comrade', but he gained

> a reputation in Wellington for being somewhat tactless and inclined to browbeat offenders. The charge certainly had some truth in it, but I think it was because of his strong sense of Party discipline and the fact that he did not sufficiently allow for the weaker development (particularly then) of the NZ Party compared with Australia.[68]

Somewhat tactless, inclined to browbeat, with a strong sense of Party discipline: this is how Ted Docker is remembered in the histories of the Australian Communist Party.

Yet, I still wonder, or still wish to wonder. In Benjamin's terms, I wonder if my father gave up all his independence and individuality in his commitment to life in the Party.

I suppose, in these chapters on my father, that is what I'm trying to find out.

1 Barbara Curthoys, 'The Comintern, the CPA, and Impact of Harry Wicks', *Australian Journal of Politics and History*, vol. 39, 1993, p.26, writes that the 'Militant Minority Movement ... held its first major conference in February 1929, its aim being to strengthen militant activity in the NSW Trades and Labour council and trade union movement generally'. Phillip, an eastern suburbs electorate in Sydney, includes Bondi.

2 Stuart Macintyre refers to Colonel H.E. Jones in *The Reds: The Communist Party of Australia from Origins to Illegality* (Allen and Unwin, Sydney, 1998), p.394.

3 See Fiona Paisley, *The Lone Protestor: A M Fernando in Australia and Europe* (Aboriginal Studies Press, Canberra, 2012), Figure 15 and pp.145-8.

4 John Docker, 1492: *The Poetics of Diaspora* (Continuum, London, 2001), p.250.

5 David W. Lovell and Kevin Windle (eds), *Our Unswerving Loyalty: A documentary survey of relations between the Communist Party of Australia and Moscow, 1920-1940* (ANU Press, Canberra, 2008), p.277.

6 Stuart Macintyre, *The Reds*, pp.133, 285.

7 John Halstead and Barry McLoughlin, 'British Students at the International Lenin School' http://geocities.com/IrelandSCW/ibvol-ILSchool.htm

8 John Mahon, *Harry Pollitt: A Biography* (Lawrence and Wishart, London, 1976), p.195.

9 See John McNair, '"Comrade Katya": Katharine Susannah Prichard and the Soviet Union', in Sheila Fitzpatrick and Carolyn Rasmussen (eds), *Political Tourists: Travellers from Australia to the Soviet Union in the 1920s-1940s* (Melbourne University Press, Melbourne, 2008), p.148.

10 There is of course a considerable literature concerning 'political tourists' to Russia in the interwar period, as in Sheila Fitzpatrick and Carolyn Rasmussen (eds), *Political Tourists: Travellers from Australia to the Soviet Union in the 1920s-1940s*, its introductory essay by Sheila Fitzpatrick, 'Australian visitors to the Soviet Union: The view from the Soviet side', pp.1–39. See also John McNair, 'Mary Poppins and the Soviet Pilgrimage: P.L. Travers's *Moscow Excursion* (1934)', *PORTAL Journal of Multidisciplinary International Studies*, vol.10, no.1, 2013, pp.1–12, analysing P.L. Travers's entertainingly sceptical reflections on her 1932 visit with a political tourist group to Leningrad and Moscow in her *Moscow Excursion* (Reynal and Hitchcock, New York, 1934); the narrator positions herself throughout, in relation to the rest of her party of political tourists, as 'the outcast, the irreverent one' (p.70). Sheila Fitzpatrick in her Preface to *Political Tourists* says that Travers's account of her visit is 'hilarious': see p. ix, also her essay 'Australian visitors to the Soviet Union: The View from the Soviet side', p.21. A tiny little caveat here: just because Travers's *Moscow Excursion* is enjoyably sceptical concerning political tourism to the Soviet Union, should not mean that the book is beyond critical scrutiny as a text. What also might be worth reflecting on is what I read as a smug anti-semitic joke concerning 'Jewish financiers' in *Moscow Excursion*, p.101, presumably confident her intended readers would share her whimsy here; it did occur to me that in 1932, back in England, Oswald Mosley visited Mussolini and launched the BUF, the British Union of Fascists. On p.107 there is another smug joke that relies on the Western legend of Hottentots' limited intelligence; and in the final few pages, pp.117–119, the narrator relates how her giving of lemons to ordinary Russians led to the 'breaking of the Communist mould' (p.118) and a release of the repressed, of fun and hilarity 'like children at a party' (p.119). I thought of Oblomovism.

11 Momme Brodersen, *Walter Benjamin: A Biography*, translated by Malcom R. Green and Ingrida Ligers (Verso, London and New York, 1997,), p.118.

12 Walter Benjamin, *Reflections: Essays, Aphorisms, Autobiographical Writings*, edited with an Introduction by Peter Demetz (Schocken Books, New York, 1978), pp.xii, also xxiv, xli. See also Eiland and Jennings, *Walter Benjamin: A Critical Life*, pp.131-3.

13 Benjamin, *Reflections*, pp.291-2.

14 I thank Lyndall Ryan for sending me the articles and for information about *Labor Monthly*.

15 Ted Docker, 'Carpenters and Job Committees', *Labor Monthly*, August 1, 1926, pp.11-12.

16 Ted Docker, 'Job Control Necessary', *Labor Monthly*, December 1, 1926, p.19.

17 John Docker, *Australian Cultural Elites: Intellectual Traditions in Sydney and Melbourne* (Angus and Robertson, Sydney, 1974), ch.8, 'John Anderson and the Sydney Freethought Tradition', pp.131-44.

18 Docker, *Australian Cultural Elites*, p.139.

19 Jeff Sparrow, 'Guido Barachi, Betty Roland and the Soviet Union', in Sheila Fitzpatrick and Carolyn Rasmussen (eds), *Political Tourists: Travellers from Australia to the Soviet Union in the 1920s-1940s*, p.123.

20 See Ann Curthoys and John Docker, 'Popular Romance in the Postmodern Age', *Continuum*, Vol.4, no.1, 1990, pp.22-36.

21 Cf. Eiland and Jennings, *Walter Benjamin: A Critical Life*, pp.267-79.

22 Susan Ingram, *Zarathustra's Sisters: Women's Autobiography and the Shaping of Cultural History* (University of Toronto Press, Toronto, 2003), ch.4, 'Asja Lacis', pp.78, 80.

23 Walter Benjamin, *Moscow Diary*, edited by Gary Smith (Harvard University Press, Cambridge, Mass., 1986), 20 December 1926, p.34.

24 See Momme Brodersen, *Walter Benjamin: A Biography*, pp.135-37.

25 Eiland and Jennings, *Walter Benjamin: A Critical Life*, p.207.

26 Walter Benjamin, *One Way Street and Other Writings*, introduced by Susan Sontag (Verso, London, 1992), Publisher's Note, p.32, and Benjamin, 'One-Way Street', p.45.

27 Walter Benjamin, *Moscow Diary*, Scholem's Preface, pp.5-8. In *Walter Benjamin: A Critical Life*, p.84, Eiland and Jennings tell us that Scholem wrote critically of his friendship with Benjamin that he, Scholem, 'would sometimes find himself playing the role of the spurned lover and later, vis-à-vis Benjamin's wife [Dora Pollak], of the rival held at arm's length'. Can we think similar thoughts of Scholem in relation to Benjamin's later liking for Lacis? Eiland and Jennings suggest, p.83, that Scholem's feelings towards Benjamin were always ambiguous, mixing admiration with resentment that Benjamin would not conform to what Scholem wanted of him. Benjamin, in his turn, resisted Scholem. On p.86 Eiland and Jennings observe that while Scholem continually pressed Benjamin to identify himself as a Zionist, 'Benjamin criticized the "agricultural Zionism" championed by Scholem'. On p.84, Eiland and Jenning write that Scholem's diaries for these years 'record his persistent longing to see Benjamin share his Zionist beliefs, something that he pretty much knew from the start could never happen'. In my view, Scholem wished to possess Benjamin's soul, to remake Benjamin in his own Zionist image, and if that could not happen, to always claim that he was Benjamin's truest friend.

28 See Susan Ingram, 'The Writing of Asja Lacis', *New German Critique*, no.86, 2002, pp.159-177; her critique of Scholem is on pp.166-168.

29 See my 'A "Hermaphroditic Position": Benjamin, Postmodernism and the Frenzy of Gender', in Gerhard Fischer (ed.), *'With the Sharpened Axe of Reason': Approaches to Walter Benjamin* (Berg, Oxford and Washington D.C., 1996), pp.75-6.

30 See my *The Nervous Nineties* (Oxford, Melbourne, 1991), pp.88, 102.

31 Walter Benjamin, *Reflections*, 'Naples', pp.163, 166-168, 170-171.

32 See my *Postmodernism and Popular Culture: A Cultural History* (Cambridge University Press, Melbourne, 1994), pp.175-180.

33 Benjamin and Lacis, 'Naples', pp.169, 171-2

34 Benjamin and Lacis, 'Naples', pp.172-3.

35 Walter Benjamin, *Moscow Diary*, pp.113-14.

36 In his essay 'Surrealism' (1929) in *Reflections*, pp.178-79, 187-188, Benjamin discusses Surrealists like Breton in relation to Rimbaud; on p.178, Benjamin writes that Rimbaud's *Saison en enfer* 'no longer had any secrets' for the Surrealists, who strove to push the poetic life to the 'utmost limits of possibility'.

37 In 'A Berlin Chronicle' (1932), Benjamin attributes his love of travel to a kindly grandmother, who was herself a great traveller. See 'A Berlin Chronicle' in Walter Benjamin, *One Way Street and Other Writings*, introduction by Susan Sontag (Verso, London, 1992), p.327, where Benjamin talks of his collection of picture postcards: 'The main contributor to this collection was my maternal grandmother, a decidedly enterprising lady, from whom I believe I have inherited two things: my delight in giving presents and my love of travel'. Benjamin adds that it is 'certain that none of my boys' adventure books kindled my love of travel as did the postcards with which she supplied me in abundance from her far-flung travels'. See also John Docker and Subhash Jaireth, 'Introduction: Benjamin and Bakhtin – Vision and Visuality', introduction to special series of essays for *JNT: Journal of Narrative Theory*, Vol.33, no.1, 2003, p.7.

38 Eiland and Jennings, *Walter Benjamin: A Critical Life*, pp.98, 100-103, 145, 120, 124.

39 Eiland and Jennings, *Walter Benjamin: A Critical Life*, pp.205-6, 213, 217-18, 236, 243.

40 Cf. Eiland and Jennings, *Walter Benjamin: A Critical Life*, p.274.

41 Cf. Eiland and Jennings, *Walter Benjamin: A Critical Life*, p.275.

42 See our 'Time, eternity, truth, and death; history as allegory', *Humanities Research*, no.1, 1999, pp.5–26; *1492: The Poetics of Diaspora*, Concluding Mosaic, pp.247–248; *Is History Fiction?* Pp.93–95.

43 Jeffrey Mehlman, *Walter Benjamin for Children: An Essay on His Radio Years* (University of Chicago Press, Chicago, 1993), pp.37-38. See also Walter Benjamin, *Radio Benjamin*, edited by Lecia Rosenthal (Verso, London and New York, 2014), talk on 'Naples', pp.145-51.

44 Benjamin, *Illuminations*, pp.124, 153.

45 See Max Pensky, *Melancholy Dialectics: Walter Benjamin and the Play of Mourning* (The University of Massachusetts Press, Amherst, 1993).

46 Benjamin, *One Way Street and Other Writings*, p.52.

47 See my *1492: The Poetics of Diaspora*, pp.60, 260.

48 Cf. Eiland and Jennings, *Walter Benjamin: A Critical Life*, p.5.

49 See also Brodersen, *Walter Benjamin: A Biography*, p.175.

50 Susan Ingram, *Zarathustra's Sisters*, p.78.

51 Cf. Eiland and Jennings, *Walter Benjamin: A Critical Life*, p.273.

52 Arendt, Introduction to *Illuminations*, p.10.

53 Walter Benjamin, *Reflections: Essays, Aphorisms, Autobiographical Writings*, Introduction (pp.xii-xiii).

54 Benjamin, 'Critique of Violence', p.291.

55 Arendt, Introduction to *Illuminations*, p.36. My thanks to Ned Curthoys for suggesting to me that Benjamin would always draw back from either from Communism's or Zionism's assumption of the centrality of the state (in relation to Zionism, despite Scholem's entreaties that Benjamin learn Hebrew and emigrate to Palestine).

56 See P. Lacoue-Labarthe and J-L. Nancy, *The Literary Absolute: The Theory of Literature in German Romanticism*, trans. Philip Barnard and Cheryl Lester (State University of New York Press, Albany, 1988), pp.50-52, 135 note 24. See also Docker, 'Sheer Folly and Derangement: How the Crusades Disoriented Enlightenment Historiography', in Alexander Cook, Ned Curthoys and Shino Konishi (eds), *Representing Humanity in the Age of Enlightenment* (Pickering and Chatto, London, 2013), pp.41-52.

57 Cf. Eiland and Jennings, *Walter Benjamin: A Critical Life*, p.274.

58 The narrator in P.L. Travers's *Moscow Excursion* at one point refers to Moscow cakes (p.94).

59 Audrey Blake, *A Proletarian Life* (Kibble Books, Melbourne, 1984), pp.43, 51.

60 Blake, *A Proletarian Life*, pp.97-101.

61 Blake, *A Proletarian Life*, pp.21-35.

62 Blake, *A Proletarian Life*, pp.22, 24, 31. See also Stuart Macintyre, *The Reds*, p.376.

63 Various essays in Fitzpatrick and Rasmussen's collection *Political Tourists* mention Australians staying at the Hotel Lux. Terry Irving, 'Esmonde Higgins in the Soviet Union', mentions that on his 1920 visit to Russia, Esmonde Higgins stayed at the Lux (p.45). Jeff Sparrow, 'Guido Baracchi, Betty Roland and the Soviet Union', p.143 note 32, observes that many 'left-wing foreign visitors stayed at the Hotel Lux in Moscow'. Sparrow refers the reader to Betty Roland's memoir *Caviar for Breakfast*, which records that Katharine Susannah Prichard stayed at the Lux in 1933 (p.131). Roland, in the 1989 edition, *Caviar for Breakfast* (Collins, Sydney), writes in a diary entry that Prichard 'had just arrived in Moscow and is staying at the Lux Hotel, a place reserved for party members, trade union officials and delegates from abroad. It is crowded and expensive, and she does not like the atmosphere, which strikes her as rather depressing. We had heard about the Lux from Freda [Utley], who said it was full of political go-getters, so have suggested to Katharine that she move in with us, in true Moscow fashion' (p.65). John McNair, '"Comrade Katya": Katharine

Susannah Prichard and the Soviet Union', also notes that Prichard stayed at the Hotel Lux (p.148).

64 Blake, *A Proletarian Life*, pp. 21-4.

65 Blake, *A Proletarian Life*, pp. 23, 26-8, 30, 35.

66 Blake, *A Proletarian Life*, p.32.

67 Barbara Curthoys, 'The Comintern, the CPA, and the Impact of Harry Wicks', pp. 23-36.

68 Lovell and Windle, *Our Unswerving Loyalty*, p. 360.

7

'I was supplied with a fully-loaded six-chamber revolver': My father in his own words, and thoughts on his legacy

In this chapter I present my father talking about his life in his own voice. In a syncopated way, I'd like his voice to cut across my voice. In the first section I explore his reminiscences that I've been quoting in earlier chapters for what he says about his early life, up to and including the formation of the Communist Party in 1920. From memory, recording these particular reminiscences of my father took up one visit by Ann and me; we discussed it with my father, and we all agreed that from now on he himself should write about episodes, events and personalities of the past he felt important, which he would give to us on subsequent visits. As I now realise from the folders I have, he wrote reminiscences throughout the 1970s, shaped into vignettes. Most were written in the small Bondi flat my mother and father had lived in since during World War II, though sometime in the 1970s they left the Edward Street block of flats – they must have paid rent to the landlord upstairs there for decades – for a small unit in an old people's home (part of a larger church complex) in Wellington Street, Bondi, opposite the primary school where I used to go to school. I present these vignettes roughly chronologically. I've kept the rhythm of my father's writing, though sometimes I've silently corrected spelling, punctuation and occasionally a date. In the final part of the chapter, I note what material possessions my father left me when he died, and reflect on what a revolutionary's lasting legacy to his son might be, both negatively and positively.

Some Memories of Early Life in Sydney 1894–1920

Born in Sydney in 1894, a child of the *fin de siècle* in all its turbulence and uncertainty, Ted Docker would have begun his schooling in the late 1890s. In notes which I jotted down while he talked, to which I gave the title 'Edward Docker's Reminiscences', he says that even at school he 'had radical views'. He recalls taking part in a debate at the school he went to in inner Sydney, Albion Street Public School: 'I supported the Labor Party'. He also recalls that he was 'captain of the football team'. (By football I think he meant rugby union; rugby league began in NSW in 1908 when a group of players split away from the amateur game in order to become professionals, forming a different, more working-class, competition). 'I didn't distinguish myself academically at school', my father says, though he left at 16, which was, he felt, a long time then to stay at school. My father recalls that his mother 'had a belief in education' – 'she got her eldest son to become a schoolteacher' – so this may explain why she insisted that he stay at school until 16. My father also says: 'I was the youngest child'. This statement, though, is a bit puzzling, since public records indicate that the youngest child was Robert; there's some mystery here.[1] Nonetheless, it would appear that my father grew up as if he were the youngest child.

At 16 my father entered the workforce with a couple of false starts. His first job was with a monumental mason firm, Ross and Bowman, in Coogee. My father tells this story in greater detail in the next section, 'My first job and my first strike'.

After working at the monumental masons 'for a few weeks', my father read an ad 'in the paper, [Sydney Morning] *Herald* I think, where Bacchus Marsh milk company wanted boys – 15 shillings a week – putting rubber bands around the top and bottom of the tins of condensed milk – I was the quickest there – it was a very good machine, very mechanis-zed, but a noisy place'.

Ted Docker left the milk company 'because my uncle' George Nash, who 'had an office in Bridge Street, was in charge of Inspectors', secured him employment working for the Education Department, in a place in Ryde where desks and so on, 'portable classrooms', were made. He 'didn't become an apprentice', he 'went to various schools and helped erect classrooms – did this for a couple of years – learnt to be a carpenter'. He also recalls working in 'Gloucester Street, down in the Rocks area of the Quay… built 17 cottages in Gloucester Street', at the 'corner of Essex Street and Gloucester Street', just near 'the old cottage' (Cadman's Cottage?), also 'near Argyll Cut'. However, he was only getting 'small wages, so eventually I threw it up – I thought I knew enough to get out'. 'I went to tech. college, in Mary Ann Street, near Harris Street' [this is a beautiful building, in Ultimo, still standing, just down the street from the ABC headquarters]. There, 'I learned carpentry and joinery'. The Mary Ann Street college, says my father, also 'taught drawing, but stupidly I didn't do this… I should have, because it was a weakness that I could never read plans and understand them… made it extremely difficult for me to become a foreman'.

My father says that he 'didn't stop work till five' in the afternoon, so he didn't have time to go home to Coogee before attending college classes. His usual practice was, after five, to 'go to a picture show', the 'Lyric (for 3d.) in George Street'; he would eat some sandwiches, then leave the cinema at about 'ten to seven' and 'go to Mary Ann Street'. The reason he didn't take the course on drawing was because it would have meant 'another night out' away from his home in Coogee, so 'I concentrated on the practical work' at the tech.

[In a note in my handwriting appended to his reminiscence 'Ted Docker: Chief Dates', my father says he was a member of the Carpenter and Joiners Union (the 'Amalgamated Society of Carpenters and Joiners') and became secretary of the Bondi Junction Carpenters and Joiners, in a 'stormy period of its history'. This must refer to when he was older and had become established as a carpenter. I'm not sure what my father meant by his brief reference to the carpenters and joiners' union experiencing a stormy period in its history, but it could relate to the devaluation of craft skills that carpenters and joiners were experiencing in the 1920s. In the article 'Carpenters and Job Committees' that Ted Docker wrote in the mid-1920s for the *Labor Monthly*, he refers to how proud carpenters and joiners traditionally were of their trade, but that they were increasingly suffering poor wages because most of the 'big jobs in the city to-day are being built of steel and concrete', requiring only a 'small amount of skill': 'there are no box frames, sashes, joists, and rafters, and wooden stairs (the pride of every joiner) are a thing of the past', for in 'concrete constructional work' almost the only skill required is to 'erect the boxing for the laborers to insert the concrete'.][2]

My father reminisced about World War I on the home front. 'I was about 20 when the war started'. There was 'compulsory military training', and something he enigmatically called 'boy transcription'. At least, that's what I wrote down, but I'm sure he meant 'boy conscription', which must have been quite a prominent aspect of the newly federated Australian nation, from early in the twentieth century, perhaps indicating that the new nation was being militarised almost from its birth. In John Barrett's study of boy conscription *Falling In* (1979), we learn that between 1905 and 1909, the government of prime minister Alfred Deakin and other non-Labor governments introduced a form of conscription for boys from 12 to 14 years of age. An Australian Labor Party government instituted a system of compulsory military training for all males aged between 12 and 26 from 1 January 1911.[3]

A key event associated with compulsory military training appears to be the defeat of Russia by Japan in 1905, stimulating long-held racial fears of Asia and encouraging military training of the population, beginning, we can see, at an early age. Greg Lockhart, in an essay entitled 'Race fear dangerous denial', in *Griffith Review* in 2011, challenges how conventional military historians have constructed a fantastical view of pre-1914 military preparedness. Lockhart argues that the post-1905 perceived danger from Japan sprang from colonial insecurities about Asia. British imperial officials, Lockhart suggests, encouraged Australian government officials to believe that Japan was such a threat to the new nation that it should develop an expeditionary force for military service outside Australia, which would then become available, through secret undertakings unknown to the population, to support Britain in its wars. Thus developed what Lockhart calls an expeditionary strategy that continues to this day, associated with a historical culture that nurtures the autocratic war-making powers of a few ministers each time they decide to send off a military expedition. Lockhart concludes: 'The expeditionary strategy and related culture has saved us from nothing, caused great grief and could cause more.'[4]

'My mother', Ted Docker continues, reflecting on why he didn't enlist to fight overseas like his brothers Norman and Henry, 'thought with my two brothers killed, and I was helping round South Head guarding etc (I was in the Citizens Military Forces) ...' My father says that during this time he 'didn't have a knowledge of imperialism' concerning the war. 'I was against conscription and compulsory military training, like large sections of the working classes, though I think it was a Labor government which brought in the compulsory training'. My father adds: 'After a couple of years I threw away my uniform.' (I wonder now if the compulsory military training included weapon training, given the story I later transcribe, which gives this chapter its title.)

Always interested in questions of food and cafés, I notice that my father says that in the 1920s there was 'a big Chinese restaurant near the Hotel Sydney, known as the "Dirty Kitchen", though it wasn't dirty and the food was scrupulously clean'. It had 'chop suey' and 'long soup', my father particularly liking the long soup.

My First Job and First Strike

We lived [said my father] near the Randwick cemetery. Ross and Bowman, Monumental Masons, with headquarters at Waverley cemetery [on a headland at Clovelly, looking over the sea], opened a branch near the cemetery gates. My mother came to know Mr Doughty the mason in charge. He offered me a job. I was about 16 at the time. Should I prove suitable I would be indentured and become a monumental mason. My mother considered it an unhealthy trade due to the dust that was inhaled. I received a weekly wage of six shillings. My job was to smash the marble into little pieces using a small long-handed hammer. These small pieces were placed in the tomb. With each blow of the hammer a considerable amount of dust would arise that would envelop me. I liked the trade which required considerable skill. [My father told me he used to 'make little monuments at home' as well, he had got some chisels to work with.] But I didn't like its unhealthy character. I watched Mr Doughty making a marble cross. Every now and again he would press one side of his nose at a time and blow out streams of marble dust. He didn't last long after I left, [his] death being due to the dust he inhaled.

The small wage troubled me. I asked for an increase, and on refusal left the job. After a few days my mother was informed that on return my wages would be increased. The increase was only 1/– but I found a better job in the paper.

Bobby Pearce

Bobby Pearce was the world's fastest sculler. His performances at the Olympic Games proved this. He was a carpenter and boat-builder by occupation. This was also my trade and we worked for the Public Works Department at La Parouse at the Prince Henry Hospital.

Although a champion sculler he was not a very fast runner. He challenged me to a race, over a distance of 150 yards. It created great interest, and all the workers lined both sides of the track. Bobby had his supporters. The opinion was expressed that the world's fastest sculler must also be a very fast runner. I was an unknown quantity without reputation. I had no backers. There was one exception, the foreman, who said 'I back the little fellow, he might be a dark horse.' We started off and were neck and neck until the last 4 yards, when by a supreme effort, I won by about 2 feet.

Bobby realising that there were few prospects in Australia left for Canada, where he is now living with his wife and family.

[I had never heard of Bobby Pearce until I read my father's story about him. A littledigging reveals that Bobby Pearce, 1905–76, was famous not only for his Olympic victories in sculling but also for his action in the quarter-final against a French sculler, Victor Saurin, at the 1928 Amsterdam Olympics. Pearce was leading, but heard shouts from the shore and saw a duck and her ducklings crossing the race course just ahead of him. Pearce stopped his boat and waited for the ducks to cross. Saurin had taken the lead, but Pearce soon after caught up and passed him; he later took the gold medal. The story of stopping for the ducks became legendary. In the early 1930s he moved to Canada. In 1932, although living in Canada, he competed for Australia at the Los Angeles Olympics and again won gold.]

Socialists in the Domain in Sydney

My father talked to Ann and me of his early involvement in

politics, though I'm not sure of the precise dates. They appear to be from around 1910 to 1920. For young working-class people interested in radical or unorthodox ideas, the Domain was a space for political and religious speakers and eccentrics of all kinds, very important for self-education and formation of identity and sensibility away from the family and ordinary schooling. It was and remains a kind of open field behind, on one side, Macquarie Street where the NSW parliament stands next to the State Library; on the opposite side is the NSW Art Gallery; at one end are the Botanic Gardens leading down to the Harbour, and at the other end is St Mary's Cathedral, massive symbol of Catholic power in Sydney. I recall going to the Domain myself as a teenager on Sundays, the eccentrics on their soap boxes especially being very entertaining, fulminating and denouncing.

My father said that in the aftermath of the destruction of the IWW in late 1917 by William Morris Hughes and the Unlawful Associations Act, the banned IWW then 'formed and built the Industrial Labor Party'.

[I think my father here is referring to the Industrial Socialist Labor Party, which was founded in 1919 and lasted till 1921. There is an interesting portrait by Bob Gollan and Moira Scollay in the *Australian Dictionary of Biography*, vol. 7, 1979, of Percival Stanley Brookfield (1875–1921), an historical figure who was associated with the radical culture of socialist organisations, during and immediately after the war, that included the Industrial Socialist Labor Party. During World War I, Gollan and Scollay write, Brookfield was an anti-conscriptionist and advocated peace in Europe. In September 1916 he was fined for cursing the British Empire and calling W M Hughes a 'traitor, viper and skunk'; he was gaoled for refusing to pay the subsequent fine. In February 1917 he won a Legislative Assembly by-election for the seat of Sturt in NSW. Brookfield defended the Russian Revolution, supported direct action rather than arbitration, and campaigned with the journalist H E Boote for the release of Donald Grant and the other 11 gaoled IWW members. In July 191, he resigned from the Parliamentary Labor Party and in 1920 won Sturt as a member of the Industrial Socialist Labor Party. Holding the balance of power in parliament, he persuaded J Storey's government to appoint a second royal commission into the sentence of the IWW Twelve, with Mr Justice N K Ewing substantially accepting the claim that they had been convicted on perjured evidence.[5] He played a vital role in settling the 1919–20 miners' strike, helping to obtain a 35-hour week and maximum compensation for tubercular and fibrotic miners in the Workers' Compensation (Broken Hill) Act. On 22 March 1921 Brookfield was shot on Riverton railway station, South Australia, while trying to disarm Koorman Tomayoff, a deranged Russian who had already wounded two people. Mary Gilmore commemorated his death in verse in the *Australian Worker*.]

My father recalls other socialist parties at the Domain competing for attention as the only true radical or socialist party. 'All these organisations put out plenty of pamphlets.' Also, 'all the different organisations had differences – if you asked a question, they would attack the other parties and expose them'. He refers to a socialist party led by a 'Luke Jones', though only mentions his name. [Some digging reveals that Luke Jones was a prominent figure in the Australian Socialist Party and a renowned orator at the Domain, though he died young. The obituary, 'The Death of Luke Jones', recorded in *Labor News* of Saturday 7 June 1919, laments the death of the 'fresh-faced, handsome, black-haired' young man who at the Domain would, with 'tremendous intensity', tell his audience of 'a day of deliverance from the thraldom of Capital'. The funeral was in the tradition of the Red Funeral. Comrades in the socialist movement gathered at his home and then proceeded to the cemetery, the 'long procession' headed by a 'group of ladies of the Peace Army', the hearse behind with 'its red flag draping'. At the grave, orations were delivered including by the 'well-known Socialist clergyman Rev. A. Rivett', and Vance Marshall, the coffin being lowered 'to the singing of "The Red Flag"'. Among the mourners was P J Brookfield.]

There was also the Social Democratic Labor Party, which had a hall in Wentworth Avenue [off Oxford Street where it meets Hyde Park, in the city, on the western side of Surry Hills]. Then there was the Socialist Labor Party, 'Ernie Judd's party', Judd being its founder and leading member. My father recalls that 'Jock Garden and members of the CPA' called Judd the undertaker because Judd wore a hard hat and a black suit: 'we all reckoned the material of his suit was the same as undertakers wore'.

[Judd was an important figure in socialist circles of the time. In 1918 he played a key part, as Verity Burgmann notes, in helping expose, by amateur sleuthing in relation to the Crown witnesses, that the IWW Twelve had been set up by the police.[6] Judd also featured in a confrontation in 1921 at the Domain between socialists and violent Empire loyalists, evoked in Terry Irving and Rowan Cahill's *Radical Sydney: Places, Portraits and Unruly Episodes* (2010). In a chapter colourfully entitled 'The Trades Hall Reds versus the Domain Fascists', Irving and Cahill include a striking photo of Judd in 1921 on a platform, in a black suit, surrounded by police who were there to maintain public order; they describe how Judd, seeing that the loyalists surrounding him were becoming increasingly menacing, drew a pistol out his pocket. In the ensuring mayhem, Judd and a police superintendent were among a dozen people later treated at nearby Sydney Hospital.][7]

My father talks of the birth of the Communist Party in Australia. 'The ASP [Australian Socialist Party] received literature from Moscow and they sent out a call for the formation of a Communist Party'. The call was 'sent to Jock Garden, secretary of the Trades and Labour council' and Jack Howie, its president; 'also to Judd's party, but Judd ignored it, though some others in his party didn't'. When, my father says, the Communist Party was formed in 1920, 'at first I was a rank-and-file' member. He tells the story of the formation of the CPA in the next vignette.

The Formation of the Communist Party of Australia

[The story of the formation of the Communist Party of Australia is told in the chapter 'Foundation' in Stuart Macintyre's *The Reds*, pp. 12–27.]

The Communist International (Third International), known later as the Comintern, was established [my father said] on the advice of Lenin.

The Russian Revolution in 1917 was led by the Bolsheviks. Trotsky, who had not long arrived from the US, and realising that his opposition to Lenin and the Bolsheviks had failed and that the Mensheviks were discredited, decided to join the Bolsheviks. Lenin knew that communist parties were being formed in various countries, the leaders of which in a number of instances had theoretical weaknesses. He issued the call for the formation of a centralised political organisation, which could give guidance to its various sections.

The Communist Party of Australia was formed in Sydney in 1919. This arose out of a conference comprising in the main of members of the Australian Socialist Party, the Socialist Labor Party, the Industrial Workers of the World, and the Sydney Trades and Labor Council. Conference elected its officials, including a secretary and editor.

The ASP strongly objected to Billy Earsman and also Tom Glynn being appointed to what they considered the two leading positions – editor and secretary. This was in my opinion a legitimate complaint, as the ASP was a long-established Marxist party which had published two of Lenin's classics, 'The State and Revolution' and 'Left Wing Communism', both printed on their own press. Although I consider that the ASP section should have received either the secretary's or editor's position, they were not warranted in splitting the Party.

One of the important conditions for membership of the Comintern was that there must be only one Party in each country. By breaking away the ASP section had violated this condition. Both Parties (the ACP and the ASP) appealed to the Comintern for recognition, but both were refused, and informed that they should unite to form one Party and the application to join would be reconsidered.

In fact the Comintern had sent to each Party a long document outlining the position, and calling for the formation of a united Party. The Sussex Street Party (ACP), so called because its headquarters were in Sussex Street, had distributed copies of the document. The ASP Party, situated in Goulburn Street, refused to do so. Many members of its Sydney Branch, however, were indignant at this refusal. Jock Garden discussed the matter with Stetler, Secretary of the ASP Sydney Branch. They decided upon a course of action, which involved seizing the furniture in the [ASP's Goulburn Street] hall, and shifting it to the Sussex Street hall. This required extreme secrecy, particularly as the Goulburn Street headquarters were alongside the Central Police Court.[8] Stetler handed over the key of the front door and the key to the door at the top of the stairs leading to the large dance hall. The plan was to make the raid at the conclusion of the Saturday night dance.

The raid was carried out at midnight.

The Sussex Street raiders comprised Jock Garden, Secretary of the Labour Council; Jack Howie, President of the Council; Oliver Griffin; Fatty Bourne, Secretary of the Undertakers Union; and Ted Docker, Political Committee. It was hard work. All furniture, comprising chairs, forms, pictures, the stage and the piano, was taken. The place was left completely bare, even the floor was swept. It took several trips to the lorry to shift it to Sussex Street.

There was only one incident of a very slight character. While loading the lorry a young policeman arrived and asked why the furniture was being removed at the early hour. Fatty Bourne answered that 'the tenants upstairs did not pay their rent, so we are removing our furniture'. Apart from a hard look, the policeman moved on.

When the speakers arrived on Sunday to procure the platform to hold the Sunday meeting, they were astounded to find an empty hall. No meeting was held. In fact the ASP never recovered from the blow.

I was given the job of guarding the furniture. I was supplied with a fully-loaded six-chamber revolver, which I kept under my pillow. I slept on a hammock strung between two posts. I slept alone for a few days, until joined by Judah Waten and George Lansbury, a son of Lansbury of the British Labour Party. Both comrades slept on the floor beside me.

Although there were a number of threats about issuing a summons, nothing transpired. They wanted to compromise, and receive some of the furniture, particularly the piano.

But we were firm. We told them that they had betrayed the working class in opposing the building of a united Party.

A unity conference was held comprising representatives of the Sydney Branch of the ASP and the CPA. Stetler was elected Secretary. The Comintern were informed that there existed one Communist Party and asked for recognition. This was granted.

So ended the struggle for a united Party in Australia.

(A slightly shortened version of this vignette, entitled 'The struggle for a united party', along with a brief article by my father entitled 'The IWW and the CPA', both drawing on his reminiscences, are reprinted in the Communist Party's newspaper *Tribune*, 15 October 1980, p. 11, as a contribution to its commemoration of

60 years of existence. I don't know how this was arranged, if I were involved or not, I can't remember.)

'Lang is greater than Lenin'

It is interesting to know [said my father] why J S Garden, Secretary of the Trades and Labor Council and a well-known communist, who had travelled overseas to Moscow and met Lenin, had uttered such a slogan. Garden's statement shocked Party members. Not only were Party members astounded but also friends and non-Party members were surprised. Garden's statement gave rise to all kinds of speculations and conjectures: Had Garden left the Party and joined Labor? His statement really implied that he had deserted communism.

Garden explained his position to me by saying that Lang had passed some magnificent reforms such as motherhood endowment, workers' compensation etc which had been of considerable benefit to the working class. I consider that there were other reasons why Garden had left the Party. Sometime previously Garden had stood in the parliamentary elections... and received about 300 votes. This was a great shock from which he never recovered. There is no doubt that Garden was well known in trade-union circles and the small vote was quite unexpected.

It is true that he was well known to the militant section of the trade union movement but was not known in the localities, to the housewives and other women, and the youth and pensioners. It was quite apparent that very little work had been carried out among the people in his electorate. Nothing had been done to bring these issues before the people. There was no Party branch and day-by-day agitation. Garden had not been seen and was unknown. It is not sufficient to hold several meetings on the eve of the election. It is necessary to make a close study of local conditions and to conduct a consistent campaign around these issues.

Garden's knowledge of Marxism was very scanty. True, he was

carried away by the Russian revolution, but he did not understand its inner forces. This explains why Garden lost his enthusiasm when the revolutionary forces diminished with the change in the political and economic situation.

[Stuart Macintyre in *The Reds*, pp. 82–3 and 109–113, provides context here. Macintyre tells us that Jock Garden, a founder of the Communist Party in 1920 who had in 1922 attended in Moscow the Fourth Congress of the Communist International, was expelled from the Party in 1926. He was secretary of the Labor Council, and he went on to become Lang's lieutenant, promoting Lang's 1930 election campaign with the slogan, 'Lang is Greater than Lenin'. Garden was subsequently elected to federal parliament, fell out with Lang, lost his preselection, was found guilty and then acquitted of corrupt business dealings, ran racehorses as well as an astrology publication, and remained, Macintyre comments, a 'plausible rogue to the last'. Macintyre also notes that in the 1920s the then tiny Communist Party kept in touch with Garden after his expulsion, Garden being allowed to debate his expulsion with Jack Kavanah who was then high up in the Party, and continuing to publish in Party newspapers such as the *Workers' Weekly*, where in 1927 he declared that 'Australian communists had lapsed into a "pure infantile sickness"'. Macintyre concludes his reflections on Garden and the Communist Party in the 1920s: 'it says much for the freedom of discussion at this time that he enjoyed such license – that the Communist Party was "suspended in the air" and "absolutely isolated from the masses"'.]

The Lockout of 1929 – the Timberworkers

[Stuart Macintyre discusses the timberworkers' dispute of 1929, and the involvement of Communist officials, in *The Reds* pp. 155–56.]

The timberworkers' strike [my father says] and the following northern miners coal lockout were very clear indicators of the world economic crisis, or as it is commonly called, the great depression. The strike was mostly confined to Sydney and Newcastle where most of the large timber yards were situated. The basic causes of the two were the same: the attempt of the employers to reduce the wages and worsen the conditions of the workers.

In Sydney the mass meetings of the timberworkers, when not held in the Trades Hall, were held in the streets close to the timber yards. When convenient I attended these meetings, which comprised a single file along one side of the street. Usually they were addressed by their top officials and members of the Labor Council including Jock Garden. On one occasion Chief Inspector McKay attended. I saw him punch one worker who he considered to be out of line. McKay had a very commanding personality which he used to full advantage.

(The following is a short reminiscence, perhaps written at a different time in the 1970s, that also talks about Inspector McKay.)

The depression or economic crisis commenced towards the end of 1929 and continued into the middle of 1930. This depression was preceded by the timberworkers' strike... The timber strike was assisted by the Labor Council, although the picket line was strongly supported by many unionists. Many timber yards were close to the Trades Hall and convenient for unionists to attend. This was the first time I saw Chief Inspector McKay. He used a straight-arm punch against those who were out of line in the picket. I heard that J T Lang while in England had invited McKay to visit Australia. Soon after arrival, he was placed in charge of the NSW police force.

Chief Inspector Mackay[9]

I was walking along Vincent Street, Cessnock, from Letts Corner when I was confronted by two uniformed policemen who asked me to accompany them to the police station near the end of the street, where I took a seat. I was soon to find out why I was arrested. From the adjoining room the chief inspector of the NSW police Mr Mackay sat opposite me. 'Docker,' he said, 'I want to raise some matters with you. You are not a coal miner and are not locked out, and do not live in Cessnock or Kurri Kurri. You came from Sydney, and you should return and leave the miners alone. They can manage their own affairs without your help.' I replied that I was a leading communist and had been sent to the coalfields to assist the miners to win their struggle. They are pleased to have the Sydney speakers here which is shown by the applause they receive. He then gave me some advice. 'You are a capable person, but you are wasting your time. Why don't you leave the communists? You should look after yourself and family. Look at Donald Grant, where did he get to?'

Grant was sentenced on the charge of attempting to burn down Sydney and had served a long term in prison. After serving several years, he was released. Donald, to the disgust of IWW members, was later elected a member of the NSW parliament. This along with other interests enabled Grant to become fairly wealthy.

Realising he was making no impression, Mackay warned me to leave the coalfields. Needless to say this threat or advice was not accepted.

I Was Told to Leave

[This appears to be another and similar anecdote about my father's time in Cessnock.]

It was the practice of the Party to hold a Sunday evening meeting in Cessnock. At the first meeting after my arrival I very foolishly attacked [verbally] one of their prominent union leaders. This was resented by one member of the audience who advised me to get back to Sydney. I obviously should have waited until I was better known. One Sunday evening when a large crowd had assembled, I had no sooner left the box when a policeman, rather tall with very long whiskers protruding straight out from his mouth, approached the platform and said: 'Docker I'm the sergeant of this town, I give you seven days to leave and return to Sydney.' I again mounted the platform when the speaker had stepped down and addressed the crowd. 'I've been given seven days to leave Cessnock… I feel very resentful, as no charge was laid against me. I want to make my position clear: the crowd do not resent me being here (the crowd said *hear hear*). I've not broken any laws and regulations. Under these circumstances I will be unable to carry out the sergeant's order. I not only intend to be in Cessnock seven days, but will be here 70 days should the lockout continue.' This brought claps from some of the crowd.

Joe Shelley and the Jam-Tin Bomb

[This story relates to the killing of a miner, Norman Brown, shot by the police during protests against a mine-owner lockout in the last months of 1929 on the northern NSW coal fields. On pp. 156–57 of *The Reds*, Stuart Macintyre tells us that armed NSW police were particularly savage on the miners protesting the lockout, including ambushing a march to a coal pit in Rothbury by 10 000 protesters. 'Forty men', Macintyre writes, 'were wounded; Norman Brown died of a shot in the stomach'. The police then conducted a reign of terror, in which baton charges, violent assault and arbitrary arrest became habitual; leading communists journeyed repeatedly from Sydney into the Hunter Valley to stand on the platform with local comrades and endure bashings, fines and imprisonment.

The following reminiscence is in my handwriting, so my father must have talked while I scribbled.]

Joe was a German, had been in Australia a number of years, a member of the Party, and a well-known member of the Seaman's Union. He was in charge of the Party's 'choir'; he had a good strong voice, would tell the choir when to soften down, or go louder. The 'choir' was at public meetings or gatherings, singing revolutionary songs, the 'Red Flag', the 'Communist International', and so on.

Joe came up to Cessnock after Norman Brown's death.

We held meetings every Sunday afternoon in Vincent Street; I generally chaired these meetings; I'd call on this one or that one to speak, and we had someone selling *Tribune*. Quite unexpectedly, Joe came up from Sydney. He introduced himself to me, said he was sent up from Sydney by the Central Committee. (Joe never had a great deal of money – I wasn't sure where he got the money to come up and stay.) I asked him to speak. After some preliminary remarks about the lockout (it was still going on at the time of these meetings), the attempt by the employers to lower wages, he then made the main part of his speech the death of Norman Brown. He dealt with the question of how profits came before men's lives, he said the miners if they were to win this struggle they've got to take action to prevent the police from knocking them about and even shooting them. 'There will be many more Norman Browns unless we take appropriate action,' he said. 'I consider' (he went on) 'we've got to make a number of jam-tin bombs.'

Joe explained: you get the jam-tin and he showed with his hands how to do it and what to put [in], and you get the gun-powder and put it in, put some pieces of stone and gravel, then put the wick in. (I didn't get how to block it up at the end, where the lid was – perhaps soldered and a hole left for the wick.) Joe said: 'Now this is a purely defensive weapon; if the police attack us or are out to shoot us, we're to use these jam-tin bombs in defence.'

Joe got a rousing reception, 'hear hear' etc, when he finished. I was looking around and calling to people for the next speaker, so didn't take it all in.

The crowd were astounded, they didn't know where they were. After the speech he became very popular with the miners; they thought he had the remedy or solution to stop the police knocking the miners around.

He spoke at two meetings, the first outlining the jam-tin bombs – he wasn't arrested then. After the second meeting (he must have stayed in Cessnock, someone put him up, he was a hero) when he talked of jam-tin bombs he was arrested. I knew nothing about it, didn't know anyone else who knew, they must have arrested him and tried him, and he went to Maitland jail. If I'd known he was there I would have gone to see him.

I've seen Joe at May Day marches since, but I've never got around to asking him what he was sentenced for and how long he was in jail.

[In her book on the Wobblies, Verity Burgmann tells us that the novelist Judah Waten was 'greatly impressed by a former Wobbly, Joe Shelley, upon whom he based the character of the IWW member, George Feathers, in *The Unbending*', Waten's 1954 novel.[10] In *The Reds*, p. 113, Stuart Macintyre refers to Joe Shelley as a 'German firebrand' who came to Sydney from West Australia in the mid-1920s.

In his reminiscences about radical figures like Joe Shelley, who came from Germany, and the Scotland-derived Jock Garden, my father, I think, was casting his mind back to the 1920s as a kind of theatrical scene replete with strong, not to say eccentric personalities and mavericks, an international cast of 'characters' in Australia in the 1920s in or near or expelled from the Communist Party. As I note in my chapter 'My father Ted Docker, the Communist

Party, and Intellectuals', Ann's mother Barbara Curthoys argued, much as does Stuart Macintyre in *The Reds*, that in the 1920s the political culture in the Communist Party was open to debate and discussion; an openness that was severely curtailed in 1930 and for many years afterwards by a Comintern-supervised uniformity of ideas and of personality and sensibility as well.

Some of these 1920s 'characters' had been in the IWW, as Verity Burgmann stresses, their Wobbly anti-authoritarian effervescence never completely disappearing in the Party's subsequent history, always there as a kind of subterranean alternative or haunting memory.][11]

Long Bay Jail

[This reminiscence, in a different coloured biro, may have been written by my father at a different time in the 1970s. It appears to be referring to events in 1930 and 1931 involving a group of gaoled communists known as the Clovelly Boys.]

My most unique experience involving Long Bay Jail arose out of the jailing of several communists. Unemployed and living on the dole they had taken over an empty house in order to have shelter and cook their meals. All were arrested and convicted of trespassing and damaging property and sentenced to a month in jail. The comrades were indignant at this unjust and harsh treatment and decided to go on a hunger strike, a decision endorsed by the State Party Committee. At the conclusion of about 10 days it was considered advisable to make a medical examination. I rang the jail Governor who granted permission to visit the jail and make an inspection. Our car was allowed to enter the jail and the prisoners were brought before us in a room. The doctor who accompanied me and drove the car made an individual examination. He reported that they were a little weak, but all were determined to continue with the strike. However, despite their determination to continue, we were of the opinion to end the strike. I addressed them, stating that they had made a splendid stand and that the State Committee were very pleased with their performance.

On their release a social and dance was held in their honour.

[A little digging reveals that my father is referring to a hunger strike in December 1930 by the Clovelly Boys, as the Communist Party members became known at the time. In an *Australian Dictionary of Biography* entry for Pat Devanny, the daughter of the writer Jean Devanny and also in the Communist Party, written by Jack Stevens (ADB, Vol. 13, MUP, 1993), we learn that Patricia Devanny (also known by her subsequent married name of Pat Hurd) was arrested in Sydney in November 1930 for participating in an unauthorised street demonstration and sentenced to 14 days imprisonment. While she was in Long Bay gaol, a hunger strike was mounted by the Communist Party to support the Clovelly Boys, who had been imprisoned for burning the house of a landlord who had evicted an unemployed family. Patricia joined a number of other young women in this protest until her sentence ended eight days later.

There's an indirect connection here with Patricia Devanny and my father, the devoted follower of the new Comintern line brought to the Australian Party in April 1930 by Herbert Moore, that insisted on a more disciplined, univocal and hierarchical Party, perhaps also dedicated now to a kind of unWobblyesque public humourlessness. Carole Ferrier, in her biography *Jean Devanny: Romantic Revolutionary* (1999), writes that one of the other communist women in gaol with Patricia Devanny was Joy Barrington. A little earlier in her biography, Carole Ferrier tells us that Joy Barrington was temporarily expelled in April 1930 for 'flippantly comparing Ted Docker to Mussolini', but was reinstated in May after recanting, an example, Carole wryly suggests, of the practice of self-criticism introduced by Moore.[12]

From further digging, it would appear that the Clovelly Boys, alleged to have set fire to a landlord's house, may have been framed for arson by the NSW police as the IWW Twelve had been framed in 1917, until largely cleared in 1920 by the Ewing Royal Commission.[13] In December 1930 newspapers became very interested in the progress of the Clovelly Boys' hunger strike. A front page story in Broken Hill's *Barrier Miner*, 5 December 1930, reported that the 'Communist hunger strike at the Long Bay Gaol has reached a serious state', with the men involved, some 18 or 19, and five women, showing 'undoubted effects', with one man on the verge of lapsing into a coma. A follow-up report on the front page of the *Barrier Miner* of 8 December 1930 reported, however, that most of the 'Communist hunger strikers in the Long Bay Gaol are eating now, according to prison department officials'. A little over a month later, the *Sydney Morning Herald*, 14 January 1931, reported that approval had been given by the Executive Council to release two of the Communists who had been convicted of 'maliciously damaging property at Clovelly': 'This action followed the perusal by the Minister for Justice (Mr Lamaro) of the depositions taken at the recent inquiry conducted by Mr Gates, retired C.S.M.' The implication, I feel, is that the charge of arson had been found to have been concocted by the police.

The Free Speech Fight 1934 and Time in Jail

[In *The Reds*, Stuart Macintyre comments on the attempted state repression in the early 1930s of political meetings in Melbourne and Sydney, and resistance to such repression by the Free Speech League, a campaign that involved both Communists and Labor Party members. On pp. 216–17 Macintyre refers to police attempts to close down public meetings traditionally held by the Communist Party in Sydney at the Domain; in Sydney in 1934 the battle between the police and radicals lasted for nearly a year.

Here my father reminiscences about the battle for Bathurst Street in Sydney, Bathurst Street meetings having been important for the Wobblies as well during World War I.]

Although [my father says] it had been the practice of the Party to hold Sunday evening meetings in Bathurst Street for several years, the NSW Gov. decided to prohibit these meetings on the ground that they interfered with the flow of traffic.

The Party considered that this prohibition was a blow to freedom of speech, one of the vital freedoms of the people. It was decided to fight the Gov. on this issue.

It was considered advisable to make a test case, by placing influential speakers on the platform. With this object in view, Jock Garden and Jack Howie the Sec and Pres NSW Labour Council were selected to speak first. Despite their standing in the Trade Union movement, both were arrested and sentenced to a fortnight in Long Bay Jail.

Next Sunday evening Tom Payne[14] and Ted Docker were selected to speak, and were subsequently arrested and received a similar jail sentence, then followed Digger Dunn MP.

The food was OK for anybody who wanted to reduce. For breakfast it consisted of a plate of thin gruel without sugar and milk. Lunch was a plate of thin soup with 1 piece of [can't decipher word] and 1 piece of meat along with 2 slices of stale bread. The bread would have to do for your evening meal.

Why we were given stale bread was not clear because very good bread was baked inside the jail.

The hard labour was not heavy. Digger Dunn and Tom Payne were gardeners, which allowed them to walk about the jail grounds inspecting the plants. Jock and Jack looked like a pair of baboons, as their black beards were rather long as there were no shaving facilities. On the last day the jail barber shaved you with a blunt razor, 'open cut'.

My hard labor job was to polish the garbage bins with a piece [of] pumice stone on the outside. It was said my job was the hardest of all of us.

I was given the condemned prisoner's cell. I was informed that those [who] were to be hanged were granted the concession of being supplied with the best food and drink prior to being hanged. There was a long pole projected outwards from the cell from which the prisoner was hanged.

I was given this information by a warder who was an ex-Black and Tan.

I did not attend church on the 1st Sunday. I soon realised that this was a mistake, as the warders gave you a lot of exercise.

Next Sunday I stepped forward, and was marched with others to church.

This consisted of a fairly large room, containing a number of long seats. The front 3 or 4 rows of seats were taken by women.

The men sat at the back. I believe concerts were held here now and again.

The minister who came from the outside spoke about Jesus and his disciples.

[My father's reference to the warder being an ex-Black and Tan is of interest, connecting to the Black and Tans in Ireland and the story of Constance Markievicz. In *Eva Gore-Booth: an image of such politics*, Sonja Tiernan reminds us of the viciousness of the Black and Tans as Britain's auxiliary force, established by Lloyd George in February 1920: 'they inflicted untold horrors on the Irish population at large', shooting people and burning villages and houses. In this situation, Eva Gore-Booth feared for her sister's safety. In June 1919 Constance had been imprisoned in Cork Jail by the British for making a supposedly seditious speech in County Limerick. Sonja Tiernan comments: 'Markievicz was released from Cork Jail in October 1919 and spent most of the next year on the run. She was in danger of arrest or attack by the Black and Tans'. Eva became 'extremely anxious about the situation in Ireland and feared for her sister's safety'.)[15]

The 1934 Race Riots in Kalgoorlie, Western Australia

[Of the vignettes that my father wrote for Ann and me, this one, his evocation of the infamous race riots in 1934 in Kalgoorlie and the nearby town of Boulder, intrigued us as particularly striking for its immediacy, drama and historical interest. I've kept the handwritten vignette as well as other material in an A4 folder entitled 'Reminiscences: Kalgoorlie Riots, 1934 etc'.]

I was sent to Perth where the Party headquarters were situated, by the Political Committee of which I was a member, to investigate the position of the Party in WA.

On arrival in Perth I interviewed the Secretary, Bill Mountjoy. He said he was concerned about the position of the Party branch at Kalgoorlie. It was comprised of Yugoslavs, it was a Yugoslav branch, but there were two factions.

My job was to liquidate the factional differences and restore unity to the Party branch.

I arrived at Kalgoorlie the day after my arrival in Perth, Jan 27 1934.

I did not contact the Branch nor hold a branch meeting as the riots started straight away, on the same day.

The death of this young Australian Jordan precipitated the explosion. I attended one meeting of the miners, which was held in a hall in Kalgoorlie.

Their main complaint appeared to be, that the foreigners received employment while sons of Australians could not get a job.

This complaint was repeatedly made.

It was an amazing scene in the evening. The only tall building, 4 storeys high and made of wood I believe, was ablaze from top to bottom, the Home from Home.

The main street of the shopping block was on fire too and one or two other buildings were alight.

The Police had vanished leaving the workers completely in charge.

The foreign shopkeepers had left for the bush with their families. The Salvation Army supplied them with food and other requirements.

The foreign shopkeepers locked their shops and departed to the bush leaving their shops intact.

I walked up the street with the rioters, who smashed up all the shops, then set alight to the premises including the till.

After the burning and ransacking, the workers or rioters gave attention to Boulder.

I never saw trams so stacked with people. They were hanging on sides, roofs, each end and top of everywhere, you could not see the trams with the exception of the wheels, it was completely obscured.

It was a remarkable sight. The crowd journeyed to the top of the hill. The flat down below was sprinkled with miners with one-room shacks. These very small buildings which appeared to be windowless were made of sheets of iron and whitewashed.

They were in the main inhabited by foreigners. The flat was grassless, cold and clammy in the winter, or after rain I was told. The mining company demanded a small rental.

On top of the hill a lorry was used, and from here they addressed the crowd. The union officials were in charge. It was chaired by the union officials. Many miners, Australians, also got up and addressed the crowd which consisted of a number of thousands (no women).

The speakers attacked the mining companies for employing so many foreigners, while Australians were unemployed.

My two comrades, who were young miners, helped me to get

roneoed a leaflet, which I had written, the main content of which was directed against the mine owners. It was decided that the best place to give the leaflets out was halfway up the hill when the workers, the miners, were walking up the hill to the meeting place. I was the only one giving the leaflet out.

The tone of the speakers was very racist. We decided that one of us should mount the lorry and strive to change the direction of the discussion to the following. Opposition should be directed against the mine owners over wages and conditions. A log of claims had been presented to the owners, who had not given their consent. This should be our main attack, and to achieve these demands, the unity of all workers irrespective of race is needed.

I mounted the lorry but it was considered unwise for me to attempt to speak, because I was not a miner and I was unknown to the gathering.

I jumped up on top of the lorry and stood there, the eldest of the two comrades jumped up and addressed the crowd. He put forward the correct position. He was well received.

In the late afternoon towards the end of the meeting several shots from the vicinity of the flat were heard. It was rumoured that someone had been shot. We three left the hill, and went to the flat to find out what happened. Those huts without a notice on the door indicating that they were Australians were smashed, and set alight.

We subsequently heard that the person shot was a Yugoslav and that he had left a will indicating that there should be no religious ceremony at his funeral, as he was an atheist, Joseph Katich. The funeral was held on the outskirts of Kalgoorlie – on Jan 29 or 30? – in the cemetery. There was a good roll up of Yugoslavs. I marched with them and spoke at the funeral.

I was the only Australian there.

The Salvation Army assembled some 100 yards away, but made no attempt to attend the funeral service.

I left the graveside and spoke to the Salvation Army people

informing them that in Joseph Katich's will he wanted to be buried an atheist.

I had discussions with both factions [of the Yugoslav branch], and they decided to sink their differences. They agreed on a common policy. I then left Kalgoorlie for Perth where I delivered a report to the Party.

[This vignette occasioned some family drama, and the version here, which I think was the first version my father wrote for Ann and me, was later to be augmented when I helped prepare it for publication in *Labour History* in November 1976. Indeed, in the folder there are a number of versions with added details. Initially, when Ann and I had talked with my father about this story, he was concerned that he didn't know the exact dates of the Kalgoorlie and Boulder events. Ann the young historian said she would do some research to see what she could find out to try and help my father, which she did with remarkable thoroughness. Ann produced for my father a kind of fact-sheet, which I still have in the folder, in yellow paper. (Ann says she remembers the yellow paper fact sheet – don't historians forget anything?!) Here it is:

Kalgoorlie Riots 1934

Jan 29–30 1934.

Causes: racial antipathy between British, Italian, Jugoslav, Greek workers.

Precipitated by death of man after fracas in Italian-born owned hotel in Kalgoorlie and wild rumours about death.

First day: hotel attacked and burned, other Italian and Greek business places wrecked, some hotels and shops wrecked in Boulder.

> Second day: Jugoslav camp at Boulder attacked (slum area); resistance; two killed and a number wounded.
>
> Police reinforcements arrived next day and no further disturbances.
>
> Damage: 92 places burned; 78 shacks, 1 club and 2 hotels at Boulder; 3 hotels at Kalgoorlie.
>
> Total damage estimated at $74,000. (possibly exaggerated)

Ann also listed for my father some references from the *Workers Weekly*:

> 2 February 1934.
> p. 1 Article 'Riots in West Australia. CP Calls – Smash Racial Divisions'.
>
> Gives Communist views on racism. No details at all.
>
> 16 February 1934 Further report. Re Premier Collier trying to blame race conflict on CP.

As well Ann prepared a list of references to books that might be relevant, including books with Australian National Library catalogue numbers or page numbers, for example, Geoffrey Blainey, *The Rush That Never Ended*, p. 311, and R Gerritsen, 'The 1934 Kalgoorlie Riots: A Western Australian Crowd' in *University Studies in History* (published in WA) 1969.

I've just talked this over with Ann, who says it's likely that she did this research in Canberra, after we returned from London in late June 1974, though my father seems to think she was still in London. (Ann says we left London while the Wimbledon tennis was on. I said, how do you remember that; she said, she just does.).

These notes by Ann were attached to a letter to me from my father, which he signed, with curious formality, Edward Docker (I wish he had given a date for the letter!). The address given at the top of the letter, '15/30 Wellington St Bondi 2026', is that of the little flat in the old people's home they had moved into from the Edward Street block of flats, I'm not sure of the year.

> Dear John,
>
> The girl showed me your book [*Australian Cultural Elites*, published late 1974] at the Waverley Library. I left with her the notes that Anne sent from London re dates of Kalgoorlie riots.
>
> The librarian could not find any information, but later rang to say that there was [were] some papers written in Newcastle on the subject, she would send them to us.
>
> I have written up the events that took place to the best of my memory.
>
> Elsie went to Dixon St [CPA headquarters I think] and has to do research on 1974 Tribunes in which an article was written.
>
> Those notes of dates [by Ann] will be returned.
>
> Yours,
> Edward Docker

It appears that the family, from Ann to my mother, were busy searching far and wide for information for my father, who was anxious that, relying only on memory, he might have got something wrong.

A minor family disturbance occurred over the publication of the reminiscences in *Labour History*. Ann and I and our then baby son Ned, born in Sydney in November 1974, moved to Canberra in early 1975. I had received a scholarship to begin a PhD in the English department at ANU. Ann already had her PhD from Macquarie University, and during 1975 she did research and part-time teaching before becoming ANU's first lecturer in Women's Studies early in 1976. When we first came to Canberra, we stayed for a week or two with Lyndall Ryan before moving into a house in a residential complex for ANU postgraduates (for those who know Canberra, in Hughes in the Woden valley). We got to know John Merritt, the editor of *Labour History*, and I told him of my father's reminiscence of the Kalgoorlie riots. He liked the idea (he came from Western Australia himself) of publishing it in *Labour History*, saying that we could add a commentary by Rolf Gerritsen because of his 1969 essay on the riots, which was based on oral evidence among people who had been in the Communist Party in Kalgoorlie at the time. John Merritt also suggested certain points in my father's reminiscence could be amplified or clarified. In particular, I was to ask my father for more information concerning who suggested to him he should visit the Kalgoorlie branch, and was it usual to have a kind of ethnic branch, like the Yugoslav branch, in the Communist Party?

I did ask my father for more information on these points, which was included in the published version. The second paragraph now reads: 'Dixon, Sharkey, or Miles – probably Miles – said reports from WA indicated that there were differences in the Party in Kalgoorlie. They wanted me to go to Kalgoorlie to make an investigation, decide which side was right. We didn't know what the differences were.' In the third paragraph a parenthesis was added as a kind of gloss on there being a Yugoslav branch in Kalgoorlie: 'It's not considered good practice by the Party to build a branch like that. Generally, we have everyone in the same branch. There were Jewish branches in Sydney and Melbourne – but they were a departure from what we considered was the best form of Party organisation.' In conversations with my father about John Merritt's queries, he must have added more memories, which were included in the final printed version, including a nice detail concerning the Salvation Army attending from a distance the atheist funeral of Joseph Katich: 'When we left the graveside, when we were about a hundred yards away, I looked back and saw the Salvation Army forming a circle around the grave.'

Ann and I must also have showed my father the published essay by Rolf Gerritsen, because in one of the versions he prepared for me he has a footnote where he writes: 'In an article [Gerritsen's] on the Kalgoorlie riots it says that several hundred Australian miners were present at Katich's funeral. This was not so.' In his commentary in *Labour History* Rolf Gerritsen is very gracious towards the reminiscence, but wonders about my father's memory that he was the only Australian at Katich's funeral, whereas from his research he thought there would be mourners from the Kalgoorlie Communist Party branch also in attendance. My father insisted, however, that he was indeed the only Australian present. There were other details as well added to the final version, that I feel came from the conversations with my father talking about various points.

I thought, when it was published, the family would be pleased, but it turned out not to be so. As often occurs in these family dramas, infused with misunderstandings or different interpretations, a minor storm blew up, not helped by us being in different cities. Accusing letters went back and forth between Canberra and Sydney. It appears my father and mother were very concerned that I had added material that was not in the original reminiscence, especially concerning John Merritt's queries, suggesting it was done without their knowledge, that I had not asked their permission, and particularly that the *Labour History* article misrepresented their position concerning ethnic branches, which was that ethnic branches were quite standard within the Party, an approved practice. In the folder is a long, typed letter from me, which I'm now rather ruefully reading. The address is 25 Groom Street, Hughes, ACT, the date Friday 26 November 1976, and in this long letter, with 12 numbered points, I insist that my mother and father had agreed that I could incorporate the new information into the *Labour History* essay. I end my letter (on yellow paper) on a particularly petulant and sarcastic note, which is perhaps not unknown in these kinds of family disputes:

> I admire your way of saying thank you, John, for helping in having Dad's article published. You might have noticed that I gave many hours of hard work into getting Dad's reminiscences put *accurately* into print so that other people could read them, enjoy them, and learn from them. Already people in Canberra have told me that they have read and liked Dad's article.
>
> Thank you
> John

I look at this now and think, John, this isn't a letter to be proud of, so hectoring and insensitive, especially considering how old my parents were at this stage of their life, my father 82 or 83, my mother though younger than my father suffering from middle-age diabetes (which came upon her while she was staying with us in London in Stoke Newington for two or three weeks in 1974). Also, I now murmur to myself, I should have been more sympathetic to my parents, who, not having had the opportunity to be tertiary educated, did not know that it was standard academic practice for an editor of a scholarly journal to ask for more information or clarifications; I should have explained about this more.[16]

I can conclude these reflections on my father's reminiscences of the 1934 riots on a happier note, by reporting other documents in the folder, which I had completely forgotten about. I see in the folder that an edited version of the *Labour History* article was reprinted, with *Labour History*'s and 'Ted's kind permission', in the Communist Party's newspaper *Tribune* on 14 May 1980, p. 11, entitled 'The 1934 Kalgoorlie Riots', as part of what must have been a year-long commemoration of 60 years of the CPA. The sentences in the *Labour History* version near the beginning that had particularly troubled the family were edited out, and it reads very well.

My father had been anxious to find out if the leaflet that he remembers writing in Kalgoorlie, to be handed out to the Australian miners as they walked up the hill in Boulder, still existed. During 1975 he must have written a letter to old comrades he once knew in West Australia to see if anyone in the Party there possessed a copy. In the folder there is a typed letter addressed 'Dear Ted' to my father and signed 'Yours fraternally, Annette Aarons'. I gather that Annette Aarons (1920–2008) was a West Australian feminist and political activist, had been radicalised by the Spanish Civil War, joined the Communist Party in 1941, and spent some time in Sydney working for the Party; she was jailed for a short period after her arrest during a campaign supporting Indonesian independence from Dutch colonialism; she returned to Perth, and was a lifelong friend of Katharine Susannah Prichard. In her letter, dated 28 October 1975, Annette Aarons says that my father's query had been passed on to her to see if she could help; she had contacted Jack Coleman, one of the comrades who in 1934 had assisted in the production of the leaflet, and learned that he had made a tape of his memories, but didn't have a copy of the leaflet. Annette Aarons also reported that the West Australian Chamber of Mines had been contacted, whose Secretary, she writes, 'said this morning that he knows of the leaflet in question', understands that there is a copy in their Kalgoorlie office, and is 'now going to send to Kalgoorlie straight away and get them to Photostat the leaflet if it is there'. The Secretary adds, a little enigmatically, that 'he has also had an enquiry from Sydney'.

I don't know about the enquiry from Sydney, whether it was

from my parents, but in the folder is a draft of a letter I must have written to the Chamber of Mines of Western Australia saying that I would be very grateful if they could send me a copy of the leaflet my father had written in 1934, and that I understood from Rolf Gerritsen's article in *University Studies in History* 1969 that it was located at file no. R 1391; I signed the letter, John Docker, PhD student, English, ANU. What pleasure to see in the folder a letter from G. Deas, General Secretary of the Chamber of Mines addressed to Mr J. Docker, Department of English, ANU, dated – perhaps astonishingly – 11 November 1975, informing me that they were sending two leaflets, though the originals are not on file, only typewritten copies; also they were sending a news item from the Kalgoorlie *Miner* of 3 February.

If I didn't immediately write back to the WA Chamber of Mines thanking them I should have, what they sent was ego historian's gold. I'm delighted.

So, there in the folder is the leaflet. Here it is:

A CALL FOR UNITY!
The foreign born worker is not our enemy.

For a United front of all workers for struggle against our real enemy – the MINEOWNERS.

FELLOW WORKER
At a Mass Meeting this morning it was decided by majority vote to refuse to work with foreigners who are employed in the mines.

Let us examine the precise meaning of this resolution. In the first place can it be said that if such a stand is taken against the foreign workers that this step will be in our interests – in the interests of the working class?

Certainly not.

This is the only correct way we, as workers, can analyse this resolution. If we place all passion and prejudice aside and calmly reason the question from this basis we can only arrive at one conclusion – and that is, THAT BY STRIKING AGAINST THE FOREIGN WORKERS WE ARE CREATING A DIVISION IN OUR OWN RANKS.

We have to remember that despite the death of Ted Jordan, the blame for this unfortunate occurrence cannot be placed on all the foreign workers, who deplore his death just as much as we do.

Regardless of our nationality or where we were born we are all miners exploited by the mineowners who are making huge profits at our expense.

The foreign worker is not our enemy; is not the one who is robbing us, paying small wages, speeding us up and compelling us to work long hours. Our enemy, our class enemy is the mineowner, and it is in his interests for the miners to be divided into rival sections, fighting each other.

As we have presented a log of claims to the mineowners demanding improved wages, conditions and shorter hours we must do all we can to preserve unity in our ranks, to build a United Front of all workers including Australians and foreign born in order to win our demands.

WE HAVE TO ORGANISE TO STRIKE – NOT AGAINST A SECTION OF OUR OWN WORKERS, BUT AGAINST THE GREED OF THE MINEOWNERS WHO ARE OUR REAL ENEMIES.

MINEWORKERS! Let us at all costs preserve unity in our ranks – by struggling amongst ourselves we create dis-unity and will be unable to conduct a successful struggle against the mineowners thereby assisting them to defeat us.

DIVIDE AND CONQUER IS THE BOSSES' MOTTO

OUR MOTTO must be – THE UNITY of all workers, of all nationalities regardless of our religious or political beliefs, for struggle against the mineowners for £1 per shift and a 35 hour week.

Issued by the Kalgoorlie Unit of the
Communist Party of Australia.
30th January, 1934

The letter kindly sent to me by the WA Chamber of Mines also enclosed a long leaflet issued soon after by the Communist Party of Australia, dated 1 February 1934, presumably from the Kalgoorlie Unit, angrily replying to accusations apparently made by the WA Premier of the day, Mr Collier, a Labor premier no less. This second leaflet makes immediate reference to the leaflet prepared during the riots by my father and the two local comrades in order to refute what premier Collier had said, blaming the Communist Party for the race riots. Here is the second leaflet:

OUR ANSWER TO COLLIER

The following is an answer to the deliberate lying statement of Collier in yesterday's 'Miner'. He blames 'a few disgruntled communists from Perth' for the recent serious disturbances.

The Communist Policy was clearly outlined in a leaflet issued 12 hours before the appearance of Collier's lies.

The Communists stand four-square for UNITY AMONGST ALL WORKERS irrespective of racial, political or any other differences.

They stand for UNITED FRONT OF THE WHOLE WORKING CLASS AGAINST THE CAUSE OF ALL UNEMPLOYMENT, MISERY AND POVERTY – THE CAPITALIST SYSTEM.

Had this policy been adopted no bloodshed or burning of workers' homes would have occurred.

Now what lead was given by Collier's supporters, Williams, Kenneally and Co. Their reactionary proposals were: That we workers go back to work and refuse to work if foreigners are on the job. WHAT IS THIS BUT DELIBERATE VICTIMISATION OF HUNDREDS OF WORKERS. What is this but incitement to burn, smash and beat up the foreign workers. If they were working class representatives (which they are not) their advice should have been – that they were strictly opposed to one section of workers attacking another. That the British and foreign workers were class brothers who slave together in the bowels of the earth and their enemies were not to be found amongst workers but the wealthy mine-owners who exploit all workers.

It is because of these misleaders – the Politicians both Labor and Conservative, the Capitalists and their Press that 50,000 Australians laid down their lives in the last world war of 1914.

For What? For their country? No. The workers have no country. All for them is the dust they take into their lungs.

They fought not in their own interests but in the interests of the wealthy Capitalists who own everything including these mines, and although thousands of miles from here rake in the huge profits the workers are producing.

It is because of the threatening war danger that the Communist party emphasize the absolute necessity of Unity amongst workers.

We strive our utmost to break down this national and patriotic feeling shown by many workers in the last few days.

We say again – The working class have no fatherland but one – The Soviet Union.

Just imagine a war against the Soviet Union, which the capitalists are preparing!

How easy for the Capitalists to recruit some of the goldfields workers who have been misled into a bitter hatred for the foreign born workers to a fight against the Soviet Union – the only country owned by the workers and where unemployment is abolished.

The Communist Party calls upon all workers to demand from the Government that all workers homes and furniture destroyed, both Australian and Foreign, be adequately compensated for.

That ample relief and housing accommodation be provided for those made destitute and hungry.

That employment be given not to one section of workers but all on the fields.

OUR SLOGAN IS NOT AUSTRALIAN AGAINST FOREIGN WORKERS BUT CLASS AGAINST CLASS. THE MINEWORKERS AGAINST MINE OWNERS FOR IMPROVED WAGES, SHORTER HOURS AND BETTER CONDITIONS.

Issued by the Communist Party of Australia
1st February 1934

The WA Chamber of Mines also sent to me a third item, a statement two days later by the 'Kalgoorlie Miner', 3 February 1934:

> We [says the *Miner*] have been requested to publish a leaflet entitled 'Our Answer to Collier'. The paragraph in the leaflet relating to the recent riots reads: 'The Communists stand four-square for unity amongst all workers irrespective of racial, political or any other differences. They stand for a united front of the whole working class against the cause of all unemployment, misery and poverty – the capitalist system.
>
> Had this policy been adopted no bloodshed or burning of workers' homes would have occurred.'

Coda: when, in September 2014, a collection edited by Ann Curthoys and Joy Damousi, *What Did You Do in the Cold War, Daddy? Personal stories from a troubled time*, was published, containing an essay of mine entitled 'Troubled reflections on my father' that mentioned his involvement in the 1934 Kalgoorlie riots, I received an email, dated 30 September 2014, from the Sydney feminist political scientist Sue Wills, telling me of an article by Herbert V Evatt: 'The international responsibility of states in the case of riots and mob violence: A study of the Kalgoorlie riots case, 1934', published in the *Australian Law Journal* Vol. 9, Supplement 9, 1935, considering issues of international law raised by the riots. Evatt, born in 1894 and trained in law at the University of Sydney, was in 1930 appointed a justice of the High Court of Australia. Later he would go into politics. From 1941 to 1949 he was both attorney-general and minister for external affairs in the wartime Australian Labor government and prominent in the formative early years of the United Nations in 1945 and afterwards.

I had not known of Evatt's 1935 essay, and read it with great interest. It adds valuable new information on the immediate aftermath of the riots, especially concerning the death of Jordan, who had died in the fracas with the Italian barman at the hotel where Jordan was attempting to obtain alcohol. Evatt writes that the barman was committed for trial on a charge of manslaughter shortly after the riots. In order to 'avoid local prejudice' the trial was held in Perth and resulted in an acquittal of the barman, medical evidence disclosing that Jordan's skull was unusually thin. In addition, criminal proceedings were launched against a large number of those who had participated in the riots.

After the trial, Evatt tells us, claims for indemnity under international law were made upon the Commonwealth government, by Consuls 'on behalf of Italy, Jugo-Slavia, and Greece'. Evatt argues that it was longstanding international law, reaffirmed at the 1930 League of Nations Conference at the Hague for the Codification of International Law, that international responsibility for such indemnity lay with the federal state, in Australia's case, the Commonwealth, rather than a local political unit such as Western Australia. The Australian government, Evatt tells us, accepted such international obligations, and directed the Western Australian government to address the claims made by the Consuls on behalf of their nationals: 'The Premier, Mr Collier,' Evatt writes, 'raised no dispute with the Commonwealth authorities on the question of international responsibility and handled the claims until a satisfactory solution was reached.' Accordingly, money was set aside to build and furnish new cottages, the settlement of their claims for indemnity being 'received with great satisfaction by the Yugo-Slav community'. The Western Australian government also provided financial assistance to help businesses in Kalgoorlie affected by the riots to start afresh.

Evatt offers some general reflections on the history of riots going back to the mid-nineteenth century, in particular, that it is difficult to separate out motives, for 'the onslaughts of the mob against foreigners are directed by racial, economic, social or religious motives rather than mere motives of nationality'. A riot, he feels, may begin as non-racial in motive, but soon transforms 'into something of a racial or national pogrom'. He gives international examples that provide context for the 1934 Kalgoorlie riots. There was Don Pacifico's Case 1847, where a mob attacked the house of Don Pacifico, a 'British subject of Jewish race and a resident of Athens', who was held to have persuaded the Greek government to prevent a popular custom, 'their annual ceremony of the burning of Judas Iscariot', the attack on his house being made with the encouragement if not the aid of local soldiers and police. In 1851 in the case of the New Orleans Riots, a serious riot took place directed against the Spaniards resident in the city. In 1880 there was the case of Attacks on Chinese at Denver, Colorado, the Chinese residents being made the special object of the mob's 'hatred and violence'. In 1885 in the case of The Rock Springs massacre, the Chinese being accused of not joining in a widespread demand for higher wages, there were 'scenes of dread and horror, 28 Chinese being killed and a large amount of property destroyed and stolen'. Throughout the 1890s in the US, there was killing and lynching of Italians as well as 'frequent lynchings of negroes in the Southern States'. In 1895 in the case of Claims by Mexicans, a mob in California broke into a prison and lynched two prisoners, one of whom was Mexican (the prisoners had been arrested on a charge of murdering two people). Evatt's final contextual example occurred in 1909, concerning 'serious riots against Greeks in South Omaha' in an attempt to 'rid the city' of Greeks.

Evatt's interest is in the international law accepted by most nations that compensation has to be paid to states whose nationals have met with death or injury in another society.

In *Labour History* November 1976, Rolf Gerritsen comments

on Ted Docker's reminiscence: 'As a stranger to Kalgoorlie, Docker was not in a position to view the riots in their local historical context. Had he knowledge of the riot of 1919 he may have seen some of the events of 1934 within the context of a pattern of goldfields riot behaviour.' This is a helpful observation, the Kalgoorlie goldfields riots of 1919 apparently being directed against southern Europeans. The observation could be extended far beyond the Kalgoorlie goldfields into Anglo-Celtic-Australian history more broadly, both in Australia and outside of it, if we think of the mid-nineteenth-century riots in NSW against Chinese miners; the behaviour of Australian troops in Cairo during World War I; the significant Australian contribution to the assault on Surafend, a Palestinian village, in 1918; and the actions of the Australian Light Horse while helping the British to suppress a revolt for national independence in Egypt in 1919.[17] There were also the attacks on villagers in mandated New Guinea in the late 1920s and early 1930s (as told in Michael Waterhouse's 2012 book, *Not a Poor Man's Field: The New Guinea Goldfields to 1942 – an Australian Colonial History*), which I talk about in my chapter on 'A Revolutionary's Bookshelf'.

Talking with our friend Ann Genovese about the Kalgoorlie events, she suggested there were long continuities in terms of xenophobia and race riots from, at least, Kalgoorlie in 1934 to the 2008 anti-Lebanese riots in Cronulla in Sydney. She also mentioned that her family on its Italian side had been affected by hostility and discrimination in Ingham in North Queensland, and she had once made a visit with her father to North Queensland where he told her of his memories.

Pig Iron Bob

[For this vignette my father placed a date, 'Nov 18th 1939', just underneath the title 'Pig Iron Bob'; in *The Reds*, pp. 308–9, Stuart Macintyre refers to this incident, dating it at 1938. My father also refers to Robert Menzies as Prime Minister, when at the time of the incident he was Federal Attorney General and Joseph Lyons was Prime Minister.]

It is interesting to learn how Mr Menzies when Prime Minister (Aus) won the title of 'Pig Iron Bob'. I was in charge of Industrial Activities being appointed by the Political Com.

While in my office which was situated in George St Sydney I received a ring from the Party in Melbourne.

They informed me that a ship named the *Dalfram* was on its way from Melbourne to Port Kembla, where it was to be loaded with Pig Iron to Japan. Without delay I phoned Ted Roach, Sec Waterside Workers Branch at Wollongong and informed him that preparations must be made immediately to inform his members, and the Trades and Labour Council.

That ship I said must not be loaded and permitted to leave Port. [My father adds here as a 'foot note': 'I left that afternoon for Wollongong and stayed with Ted Roach and wife and daughter, I stood in line and did my share of hooting.']

Ted did a good job. Every man ashore, along with the officials of the TLC, were notified.

When the ship arrived it became the centre of very curious sightseers.

The Port Authorities were informed that as the ship was to be loaded with Pig Iron to Japan the men decided that it would not be allowed to sail. At that time Japan [was] an aggressor, was in bad odour with all progressive people in Australia.

The decision of the men received warm support among the workers in Australia. Opposition came mainly from the Liberals, particularly from the PM Mr Menzies, who was disgusted at the action of the men. However, the men knew they were right. Many resolutions were carried throughout Australia in support and condemning the Gov.

Mr Menzies decided he would discuss the question with the men, he felt certain he could change their decision and load the ship. He arrived at Port Kembla on Nov 18th 1939 [1938]. He was without escort or police. It was decided that the discussions be held in a large room on board the *Dalfram*, which was moored close to the wharf.

Menzies walked between 2 lines of men about 3 ft apart stretching from the embankment to the ships entrance, the noise was almost deafening. He was called a traitor a scab and hissed and jeered. But Menzies a big man never looked right or left. He listened to their insults and boos and passed into the ship.

Needless to say Menzies did not accomplish his mission. The crowd hooted when he walked from the ship and walked across the wharf to his car.

Ted told me afterwards that, from Menzies' standpoint, he put up a good case. This shows that eloquence won't carry the day, if it is not supported by logic and common sense backed by sound working class principles.

From then onwards that is how Menzies earned the title of Pig Iron Bob.

[The *Sydney Morning Herald* of 18–19 November 1938 p. 11 reported an interesting argument, between the Liberal government and Ted Roach as leader of the Port Kembla waterside workers, concerning international law. On Friday 18 November the *Herald* noted that Prime Minister Lyons regarded the waterside workers' refusal to load the *Dalfram* as usurping the functions of the government, which, said Mr Lyons, 'has the responsibility of determining what attitude it shall adopt towards the Sino-Japanese dispute'. Mr Lyons hoped that the 'Government's decision on the export of pig iron will make it clear to the waterside workers at Port Kembla that the action they have taken is in conflict with the recognised principles of orderly government and international trading'. The next day, readers of the *Herald*, Saturday 19 November 1938, p. 11, could consider Ted Roach's very different opinion of the Sino-Japanese war, which Lyons had strangely referred to as a 'dispute' between China and Japan, implying that it was not particularly important and that the government certainly didn't regard Japan as in any way the aggressor in a war. Roach said in response, putting forward his own understanding of international affairs: 'We are putting in operation article 16 of the League of Nations which declares sanctions on belligerent nations'; he reminded the 'Australian Government [that it is] a party to the League of Nations'. Lyons' notion of international relations, in contrast to Roach, clearly did not take account of international law as in the League of Nations, but included only 'international trading'.)

Some sense of the times is provided in Christopher Waters' *Australia and Appeasement* (2012), which is mostly concerned with how from 1933 when Hitler came to power and almost to the very last moment when war was declared in September 1939, conservative politicians such as Lyons and Menzies urged appeasement. When war broke out in July 1937 between China and Japan and China appealed to the League of Nations, the Australian position, Waters tells us, was to 'avoid any notion that the League of Nations might employ economic or military sanctions or even moral censure against Japan'. The Lyons government, despite a 'chorus of public protest from the Australian people against Japan's savage aggression, consistently adopted a policy of neutrality to the Sino-Japanese war'.[18]

The notorious Nanjing massacre, it might be noted, had occurred between December 1937 and March 1938.)[19]

Objects I Inherited from My Father

My parents owned neither a house nor a car. The flat they lived in in Edward Street, Bondi was rented.

When my father died in 1983, I inherited from him not only his collection of leftwing books and pamphlets but also the following objects: books on carpentry and joinery and bookbinding; carpentry tools; a three-piece suit, a heavy winter overcoat, a scarf and a cloth cap; three drawings of birds he did as a 16 year old; and three photos. I'll talk about these now, in the spirit of E P Thompson suggesting in his famous preface to *The Making of the English Working Class*, that the historian seeks to 'rescue the poor stockinger, the Luddite cropper, the "obsolete" handloom weaver, the "utopian" artisan, and even the deluded follower of Joanna Southcott, from the enormous condescension of posterity.'[20]

Practical books: For much of his life my father was a fully paid functionary of the Communist Party, until his fall from grace in the late 1940s, when he went back to work as a carpenter, though I recall him saying the carpentry work on construction sites he was employed on was very rough. All these years he kept two books of practical instruction that I am looking at now. One of them is a slim green volume published by Cassell in Britain entitled *Bookbinding: with numerous engravings and diagrams*, part of a series of Work Handbooks edited by a Paul N Hasluck, first published in 1902 and reprinted in 1903 and 1907. On the inside cover there is a sticker pasted in, indicating that my father probably purchased the book at Gilmour's Bookshop, 6 Victoria Arcade, opposite Hotel Australia, Sydney. There is a Preface by P N Hasluck, who gives his address as, in italics, *La Belle Sauvage, London*. A little digging tells me that John Cassell (1817–65), with expanding interests in publishing and a grocery business, chose to rent part of La Belle Sauvage, a London inn which had been a playhouse in Elizabeth times; it was destroyed in 1941 during bombing. I don't know why my father chose to keep this book through the decades. I can't remember him ever talking about bookbinding, nor do I know if he ever learned bookbinding (but never mentioned it).

The other volume is a large and heavy book entitled *Carpentry and Joinery*, with a lengthy subtitle: *Comprising Notes on Materials, Processes, Principles, and Practice, Including about 1,800 Engravings and Twelve Plates*. It was published by Cassell in London in 1912, and was also edited by Paul N Hasluck, the company's address still being *La Belle Sauvage*. It is 567 pages long. Inside the cover are lots of technical notes and diagrams in my father's hand, and yellowing newspaper cuttings, one dated 1958, the other 1963. On another inside page is a newspaper cutting dated 1956, with instructions on how to make an ironing board. I had thought the book was used by my father as a textbook when he was young and was attending carpentry and joinery classes at the technical college in Mary Ann Street, Ultimo, but perhaps he returned to using it after he became an ordinary party member again in the late 1940s, and did carpentry work for the family, including, I think, for my mother's brothers. When in 1969 Ann and I started living together in a tiny stone cottage in a cul de sac off Evans Street in Rozelle in inner west Sydney, my father caught buses over to our place from Bondi. We then drove to a timber yard he knew about in Glebe, maybe called Hudsons, and then made for us a lovely coffee table and also bookshelves for Ann's growing range of history books.

Tools: I inherited my father's carpentry tools, which had descended to him from his father, beautiful tools of wood and metal. I think they came to me after my parents left their flat in Edward Street, Bondi, to move into the much smaller flat or unit in nearby Wellington Street. Disgracefully, I didn't look after the tools properly. When Ann and I and Ned moved back from Canberra in the late 1970s, we rented a house in Rozelle, in Rosebery Street, off the serpentine Mullins Street that wended its way from White Bay to the Balmain Town Hall; it was not too far from the little stone cottage we lived in for a year or two from 1969. I stored my father's tools underneath the house, but exposed to the air. They began to rust badly. Once, when the historian Bob

Gollan's son Klim, an archaeologist, was visiting, I told him about the tools under the house and he was frankly disgusted; he took them away and some months later returned them to us, restored to their former elegance. Not trusting myself to look after them as I should, and being near useless with my hands – I, son of a carpenter, had after all failed woodwork at high school – I donated some of the tools to the National Museum of Australia in Canberra.

Suit and scarf: I inherited Ted Docker's three-piece suit, which he wore in the 1930s, along with a scarf; he had worn it to Ann and my wedding in July 1971. I recall him once saying that in earlier times everyone wore their best clothes, there was no casual attire like there is today. I donated suit and scarf to the Powerhouse, where it was looked after, coincidentally, by a relative, Einar Docker, then a curator there, who surprised me one day by emailing and asking if we are related. We checked relatives and became confident that we are, through my father's brother George. In an email of 13 January 2012, Einar Docker wrote that he had photographed the suit on a mannequin and had also received the go-ahead to enter suit and scarf onto the Australian Dress Register.[21]

In the same email, Einar sent me a scanned photo of my father in his three-piece suit, which he tells me is part of a group of photos handed down by Eileen Docker (*née* Wheatley), his grandmother, wife of George Docker. Einar also asked me to comment on a draft entry about the suit he was crafting for the Australian Dress Register. In an email of 19 July 2012 Einar enclosed the draft entry, which notes that I donated the suit to the Powerhouse Museum in 1991. The suit was 'made by the Communist Party of Australia's own tailor, Tim Stillman, a suggestion supported by the fact that the suit is professionally made, yet has no label'. Einar adds that given Ted Docker never owned a house or car (information I had supplied him), the 'individually crafted suit' was 'probably his most valuable possession'. 'The significance of this suit', records the entry, 'lies in its completeness and excellent provenance as an example of menswear from the 1930s', and also as a 'direct link' with the 'ferment' of Australian politics at the time, 'which was caught up with global political developments culminating in the outbreak of the Second World War'.

My cousin Einar Docker turns out to be a keen family genealogist. We have never met, but we maintain interesting sporadic email conversations swapping information, and he and Ann have emailed about genealogical discoveries they share on Ancestry.com.

Photos: I inherited an old group photo of three rows of carpenters, with my father sitting cross-legged in the front row, all the carpenters including my father wearing hats or caps and what look like old suits; my father appears to be the youngest there; the photo was perhaps taken outside of or near the building site they were working on, I'm not sure.

There is also a larger photo, perhaps taken during a march, perhaps the annual May Day march. Two rows of workers, in what appear to be their best suits, are kneeling and standing in front of one of those remarkable old trade-union banners, featuring three young women in flowing robes under a heading of Amalgamated Society of Carpenters and Joiners of Australia; underneath the women I can make out the words 'Justice' and 'Perseverance'. My father, again looking young, is in the back row, to the side. Some banners are being held up, including '8 Hours for 5 Days – 40 Hour Week', 'Building Workers Unite!! One Big Union for the Building Industry', '40 Hours for All Building Trade Workers', and 'Building Workers! Organise!!! On Job!!! Form Job Committee[s]'. These banners surely reveal the influence of the IWW's anarcho-syndicalist ideals and demands, especially those referring to One Union for the Building Industry and Organise on the Job.

Another photo is of my father. It looks like a studio portrait, a head shot as it were. Smiling for the camera and looking very handsome, with a shock of brown hair, my father, perhaps then in his mid-thirties, is wearing a suit along with a striped bow tie and a neatly turned old-fashioned shirt collar.

These three photos are part of an assemblage of photos and books on shelves on our dining area wall where we now live in Glebe. The photo of my father, and the photo with the quite beautiful union banner, are also on the Powerhouse Museum website. For the Powerhouse Museum's History Week 2012, the photos along with reflections on my father's suit and a biographical sketch are included under the heading 'Ted Docker – Enemy of the State?' Overcoat: I also inherited my father's heavy winter overcoat, which he said he wore in Moscow in 1934–5. My memory, that I gave the overcoat as well as some tools to the National Museum of Australia, has been confirmed by an email correspondence with Anthea Gunn in late 2013, Dr Gunn being then the National Museum's Curator, Australian Society and History. In an email dated 1 October 2013 Anthea Gunn writes that I donated 'both the overcoat and some tools which now form the "John Docker collection."'[22]

Another scarf: I also inherited a maroon-coloured scarf of my father that I kept for my own use, and still occasionally wear it now; it doesn't have the name of the maker, and has some holes in it, but it did help keep me warm in Canberra's long cold winters in the 14 years Ann and I spent at the Australian National University there, from 1995 to 2008. I like scarves anyway; I'm a sort of scarves tragic, reaching for a scarf at the merest puff of cool breeze. I'm looking at this scarf now.

Cloth cap: I also inherited my father's rough woollen cloth cap that I'm fairly sure he said he wore in Moscow. I perched it on my head in Canberra's winters with such enthusiasm that it finally began to fall apart, so that when I ordered a coffee at Tilleys, a vaguely bohemian café and bar not too far from where Ann and I lived in O'Connor and where we spent many hours, the people serving would look at it and try to conceal a smile. What was your order again, they'd say. I even tried to get my father's now forlorn cap repaired at the expert Vietnamese tailors in Canberra, in the city, not far from the university. But it was tilting so alarmingly, that I reluctantly decided to stop wearing it. I'm fondly looking at it now.

When my father entered the workforce when he was 16, it was as a kind of artisan, with craft or artistic leanings. As he records in his reminiscences, he liked his initial trade of stone mason, only objecting to the lethal dust; he used to 'make little monuments at home', he had got some little chisels to work with. At 16, while living at home, he skilfully drew some pictures of birds in crayon, which I inherited, and Ann and I had them framed; they hang now in our house in Glebe, and I'm pleased whenever I look at them. There are three pictures, one of a sparrow, one of a magpie, and the third of a dove; the sparrow is perched on a native plant that appears to be a grevillea, with red flowers.

In terms of skill, whatever my father thought of his son at high school failing carpentry, he was very impressed with Ann on one occasion. We had bought quite cheaply, as young people do when they start living together, a dining room table from the Salvation Army, which, however, had a kind of raised ridge running down the middle of the table top. We borrowed a large and long wooden plane from my father, and he was very impressed when he saw how well Ann had planed flat the ridge with great *attaque*.

How did My Father Influence Me, I Ponder

Family lore has it that it was at Sydney's outdoor political theatre the Domain that my father was convinced by a speaker to become a devotee of health foods. He had great belief in wheat germ. He was suspicious of ordinary milk, putting water only on his breakfast cereal: from memory, weetbix with honey on top, then hot water to melt the honey, and then adding wheat germ. My father liked honey and prized certain kinds such as yellow box (actually, not sure about this), and he warned against sugar, especially white sugar, saying that people should be able to get all the sugar they need naturally, from the fruit they eat. The Bondi flat was always replete with fresh fruit, and as a parent I was always plying our son with fresh fruit. The secret of presenting fruit, I think, is always to cut it up, something I learnt in Singapore when Ann and I spent some days there in 1973; visiting the markets at night, there were stalls with fruit, pears from Australia for example, cut up into enticing segments, with the seeds cut out. I'm still obsessed with fruit. As for sugar, even now I feel chary of ever using white sugar; I don't have sugar in my tea or coffee, nor do Ann and I have white sugar in the house; we have brown sugar, that we use when needed in cooking, especially Asian cooking. My father also warned against ordinary salt, saying we should eat only celery salt, and indeed I still have a reluctance when cooking or eating to use salt with any liberality, so much so that when a recipe lists a teaspoon or two teaspoons of salt I feel myself jibbing, I can't do it, I only put in a little salt; I also notice that when my son and I cooked together when he would visit from Canberra (before he and his family moved to Perth early in 2014), he gently insisted on putting in more salt than I had just done, saying, quite rightly, that the salt brings out the flavours in the food. However, I'm always a little astonished to note how much cookbook writers and TV chefs recommend, a teaspoon or two teaspoons of salt.

My father loved dried fruits, and would go from Bondi into the city to Blooms health food store to acquire dried apricots and prunes and also, because he clearly had a sweet tooth, dark chocolate (Smalls, I think). Whenever we couldn't think of a birthday or Christmas present for my father, we would go to Blooms. An affection for dried fruits and dark chocolate has stayed with me. When I obtained in 1998 Claudia Roden's *The Book of Jewish Food: An Odyssey from Samarkand and Vilna to the Present Day*, which had been published in the UK the year before, I was delighted to find in it a recipe for *pruneax aux noix*, prunes stuffed with walnuts, which she includes as a festive side dish to serve with couscous, though I haphazardly serve it with a variety of dishes.[23]

In terms of attitudes and sensibility, I try to think how my father influenced me but I'm not sure how. For his part, my father must have been profoundly disappointed by how I turned out in my late teens and into my twenties.

My father must have wanted his son to follow ideals he had cherished and that shaped his life from a young age as an activist and a revolutionary. I know he wished me to become a revolutionary; I recall his saying that he was pleased I was being educated at university, so that one day I could prove superior to the ruling class in arguments and knowledge. I'm sure too that he would have liked me to have become a public speaker, like he had been at the Domain, addressing large public meetings. (At high school, however, I recall a particularly humiliating episode, when I tried to participate in a debate, held in the school library, on a topic I can't remember; I stood up to speak, quickly realised I couldn't think and talk on my feet, then lapsed into a silence that must have been agonizing, or pleasing, for my fellow students to observe; I began to blush furiously, and then rushed out of the library in the middle of the debate.)

My father must have wanted me to admire the Soviet Union as humanity's future, yet I've already referred to the awful arguments in my late teens where I expressed to him my abhorrence of Stalin and the murderous Soviet state. He must have wanted me to become part of the Australian Communist Party, yet I left the Party, which I had grown up with, in my student years and could never find in myself the slightest interest in it afterwards.

He must have wished me to become a Marxist, but my interest in Marx was intermittent and wayward. I simply couldn't understand the 'economic Marx', and I don't think I ever tried to read *Capital.* I did, however, like the 'early' or 'metaphysical' Marx as in Marx's interest, from memory, in the notion of human 'species being' in his 1844 *Economic and Philosophic Manuscripts*; and I very much enjoyed *The Eighteenth Brumaire* featuring his scintillating portrait of Louis Napoleon, which Ann Curthoys and I would later write about in our *Is History Fiction?*[24] My father detested Trotsky, but I recall reading with great interest Isaac Deutscher's huge biography, and when I learned about it recoiled at the brutality of Stalin's long-range assassination of Trotsky.

My father must have hoped I would devote myself to economics as necessary intellectual training for a revolutionary, but it became clear in the final year or two of high school that I was no good at economics (I think my parents arranged some tutoring in the subject for me) and was fortunate to gain a pass in it at the final high school exams. At Sydney University I certainly didn't do economics and also wasn't interested in doing political science, instead devoting myself to literary studies – yet my father built shelves in the Bondi flat for me to place novels and poets I loved reading.

From my father I developed certain dislikes in terms of terminology. My father would judge that some position or idea was 'correct' or 'incorrect', and to this day I cannot say those words. I also still hesitate over the term 'imperialism'. I heard the word imperialism, as in American imperialism, used so much by my father that I have a lifelong aversion to using it in my writing. I would still rather deploy a term like imperium or an adjective like imperial.

My differences from my father were, I believe, not simply personal, but constitute an allegory of different generations in conflict. In my essay in *Island Magazine* in 1984, entitled 'Father and Son: From Old Left to New', I suggest in its opening paragraph that I would try, a year after he died in 1983, to reflect on 'certain features of a strand in Australian left history highlighted by the differences between the "old left" of his and subsequent generations and the New Left which came of age in the 1960s'.[25]

Certain features of my upbringing, nonetheless, cut across this narrative of different and sharply contrasting political generations, of my father and his son as allegorical characters in any clear cut sense of Old Left as opposed to New Left. I think of Walter Benjamin's remarkable theory of allegory in his *The Origin of German Tragic Drama* (1928), that studies the *Trauerspiel*, the seventeenth-century German baroque mourning play. (Here I draw on Ann Curthoys and my interpretation of Benjamin's notion of allegory in our *Is History Fiction?*)[26] Benjamin proposes that baroque theatre and art offer to modernity a mode of allegory which stresses uncertainty and even contradictoriness rather that clear distinctions and oppositions. There is in such allegory, Benjamin suggests, a tension, that is never resolved, between the initial clarity of the idea, in this case my father and his son as representing the Old Left and New Left, and the multitude of accompanying comments, stories, representations, which multiply meanings so that they become increasingly ambivalent.

Perhaps, looking back, the most enduringly valuable legacy of my upbringing was growing up in a household without racism, and what I most particularly admire about my father was his anti-racism and internationalism. I've just checked with Ann who said that she too was brought up in a household without racism, and there, perhaps, in the mystery of things, may be a reason why we were attracted to each other.

I think I also inherited from my father a certain fierceness in argument and debate, which perhaps made becoming a Leavisite literary critic in my later undergraduate years a congenial activity, Leavisites being known for their disputatiousness, something I will discuss later.

I will end these chapters on my father now by mentioning that when he died in 1983 Ted Docker was given a Red Funeral, which I helped organise. I contacted Audrey Blake as an old family friend, and she asked me to bring along material about my father's history, and from memory on a visit I showed her material concerning his being in the IWW and a foundation member of the Communist Party in 1920 (perhaps I showed her the *Tribune* stories of 15 October 1980). On the day of the funeral, which was held at a funeral parlour at Bondi Junction near the bus depot in Oxford Street, not too far from Centennial Park, my mind was in something of a haze, and I can't clearly recall the event at all. I've asked Ann and she fortunately recalls that our son Ned, then eight or nine, came with us, that my uncle Jock Levy presided with his clear and sonorous voice, addressing everyone there as 'comrades', and that a member of the Holmes family, I think Allan Holmes, spoke, saying that Ted was always known as 'Ed' in the family and that when in the 1930s he travelled for his work for the Communist Party, his room, which was full of books, at his mother's house in South Coogee, was always kept shut; no one was allowed to go into it. Ann also remembers that 'Joe Hill' was played from a Paul Robeson record.

At my father's funeral the casket was left open. I kissed my father's cold cold forehead.

O my father

O my father

1 Relatives have suggested the youngest child was perhaps severely impaired and placed in a home, but I've been unable to confirm this.

2 Ted Docker, 'Carpenters and Job Committees', *Labor Monthly*, 1 August, 1926, pp.11-12.

3 John Barrett, *Falling In: Australians and 'boy conscription'*, 1911-1915 (Hale and Iremonger, Sydney, 1979).

4 Greg Lockhart, 'Race fear, dangerous denial', *Griffith Review*, Edition 32, 2011.

5 Cf. Verity Burgmann, *Revolutionary Industrial Unionism: The Industrial Workers of the World in Australia* (Cambridge University Press, Cambridge, 1995), p.242.

6 Burgmann, *Revolutionary Industrial Unionism*, p.240.

7 Terry Irving and Rowan Cahill, *Radical Sydney: Places, Portraits and Unruly Episodes* (UNSW Press, Sydney, 2010), pp.156-9.

8 Stuart Macintye, *The Reds: The Communist Party of Australia* (Allen and Unwin, Sydney, 1998) , p.55, writes that the ASP had its press and meeting hall in Liverpool Street, while its office was in Goulburn Street.

9 I typed up this vignette from a handwritten story in one of my folders containing my father's stories, but I soon realized that I had already quoted it before, in the concluding section of my essay 'Father and Son : From Old Left to New', in *Island Magazine*, vol.18-19, 1984. There I note that my father remembered the incident as occurring in about 1929 or 1930, during the time of major conflicts on the coalfields.

10 Verity Burgmann, *Revolutionary Industrial Unionism*, p.5.

11 Burgmann, *Revolutionary Industrial Unionism*, p.6.

12 Carole Ferrier, *Jean Devanny: Romantic Revolutionary* (Melbourne University Press, Melbourne, 1999), pp.66, 71; see also Stuart Macintyre, *The Reds*, pp.170-71.

13 Burgmann, *Revolutionary Industrial Unionism*, pp.242-3.

14 There are many references to Tom Payne in Macintyre's *The Reds*, e.g. p.199.

15 Sonja Tiernan, *Eva Gore-Booth: An image of such politics* (Manchester University Press, Manchester, 2012), pp.218-19.

16 Concerning ethnic branches in the Communist Party, I notice in *The Reds*, p.113, Stuart Macintyre recording that in 1925 there were 'groups of Russian and Greek Communists'.

17 See John Docker, 'Storm Troopers of Empire? Historical representation in *Breaker Morant*, Naguib Mahfouz's *Palace Walk* and other war histories', *History Australia*, Vol.8, no.1, 2011, pp.67-88.

18 Christopher Waters, *Australia and Appeasement: Imperial Foreign Policy and the Origins of World War II* (I.B. Taurus, London, 2012), pp.26-27.

19 For the historiographical controversy between Chinese and Japanese historians over the Nanjing massacre, see Ann Curthoys and John Docker, *Is History Fiction?* (UNSW Press, Sydney, 2010), pp.224-9.

20 Ann Curthoys and I quote the passage in *Is History Fiction?* (UNSW Press, Sydney, 2010), p.140.

21 The link to Ted Docker on the ADR and PHM blog is http://www.australiandressregister.org/garment/388/ & http://www.powerhousemuseum.com/insidethecollection/2012/09/history-week-2012-threads-ted-docker-enemy-of-the-state/

22 http://www.nma.gov.au/collections-search/x.p?p=results&QueryTerms=john+docker+collection&Limitpp=30&search=basic&Startrec=30.

23 Claudia Roden, *The Book of Jewish Food: An Odyssey from Samarkand and Vilna to the Present Day* (Viking, London, 1997), p.422.

24 Ann Curthoys and John Docker, *Is History Fiction?* pp.124-5.

25 John Docker, 'Father and Son: From Old Left to New', *Island Magazine*, Vol.18-19, 1984, p.77.

26 Curthoys and Docker, *Is History Fiction?* p.95.

8

A Week in the West Coast of Ireland

> ... in these parts... people... allow for oddities.
>
> Niall Williams, *History of the Rain*, 2014[1]

> Clare people don't like to be too blunt.
>
> Niall Williams, *History of the Rain*, 2014[2]

In the middle of 2014, Ann and I ventured to Europe and the UK for a visit bookended by two conferences. The time between, we thought, would give us an opportunity to revisit after many decades County Clare on the west coast of Ireland; perhaps my last chance to see Kilrush again, where my father's Irish grandparents married and started a family in the early 1840s. On the advice by email of a distant relative who we have never met, also part of the Nash family descendants, we had booked the Merchant House, near the square that lies at the centre of the town, for a week-long stay, and we looked forward to being there; according to the relative's email, the Nash family in the nineteenth century had lived near the square, though the exact address is not known.

When we made our travel arrangements to go to Ireland during the week of 14–21 June, I had forgotten all about 16 June being commemorated around the world every year as Bloomsday, the day Leopold Bloom walks around Dublin in James Joyce's *Ulysses*. This was all the more shameful given that while writing my

1492: The Poetics of Diaspora I had found Bloom, the most famous Jewish character in modern literature, so interesting that I had written four chapters about him, reflecting on his Jewishness and questions of Jewish identity in history. Also, after Ann and I had attended a conference 27–30 June 2007 at the University of Ireland, Galway, on the theme of Ireland and colonialism, we hired a car and drove north to Connemara, with its extraordinary flat-top mist-laden hills. I'd noticed in the Lonely Planet Ireland that the Joyce family history had started in Connemara, indeed that its mountainous region was regarded as Joyce Country. From then on, I had associated Joyce not only with Dublin and then exile from Ireland in Europe, but also Ireland's west.

During the week in Kilrush in 2014, I would have occasion to think about Bloomsday in a new light. Any travel through Ireland is also a kind of literary journey, and increasingly perhaps also a filmic journey; it excites you as a writer to be there, it provokes you, unsettles you, it shakes your being.

In London, early on the Saturday morning of 14 June, we made our way to Finsbury Park tube station and thence to Stanstead airport and caught a Ryanair flight to Shannon airport, picked up a car we had booked online, went down some one-way streets the wrong way while still in the airport to the frustration of the NatSav. With blind luck we burst onto an exit road and thenceforth made a slow way westwards into County Clare, NatSav finally having calmed itself. We did not drive directly to Kilrush because it was too early to book in, but to the seaside town of Kilkee where we had stayed in a guesthouse called Stella Maris for a few days in the early 1970s. It was now approaching lunchtime. The weather was warm, we were enjoying wearing short sleeves. We parked and wandered along O'Curry Street, a kind of café and bar street parallel to the beach, coming across a homely and evidently popular eating place, The Pantry Deli-Café-Bakery, where we chose a sort of seafood cottage pie followed by a large wedge of apple tart accompanied by local cream, or cream we hoped was local, which we liberally poured over it.

We stayed there for quite a while, at a table next to the front window, reading. Then we walked through a lane next to the café, where The Pantry ran a deli, and onto the beach. We picked our way across the grey sand and smooth pebbles, the tide a long way out. A few people were bathing, laughing and splashing. We walked along the beach and made our way to a seat on one of the headlands, looking over a scene where we had not been for so long. Curiously, given that Kilkee is part of Ireland's west coast Wild Atlantic Way as the tourist brochures say, the vast Atlantic nestled into the well-formed bay, reminding us of how beautifully shaped Bondi is as a bay. It seemed to be completely still. It was as if we were looking at an etching.

We sat there for a long time. We had come back to the west coast of Ireland, a week of adventure before us, an adventure of reflection.

You never travel to any place without some preliminary thoughts already playing at the edges of your mind. My delight in being again in Kilkee, and later that day in Kilrush, was mixed with a kind of melancholia concerning Ireland itself. For this memoir I'd been thinking and writing for months on how my father's Irish ancestry intersected with Ireland's histories, so often beset by disaster. While reading Sonja Tiernan's excellent biography of Eva Gore-Booth, I had come across an epigraph for one of her chapters where she quotes a line, 'Buried the broken dreams of Ireland lie', from an Eva Gore-Booth poem 'Heroic Death, 1916'.[3] I was immediately very struck by it. In my head, however, the line always comes out as *Broken are the dreams of Ireland*. This misremembered line not infrequently occurs to me, especially in the last year or so when I've been looking at films about Ireland, films

I eagerly see, films set in Ireland's west. In Sydney before we left, we'd seen *Philomena* with Steve Coogan and Judy Dench, in part set in County Tipperary, adjacent to Clare. In London during this visit, before we went to Ireland, we saw Ken Loach's *Jimmy's Hall*, set in County Leitrim, adjacent to County Sligo. When we returned to Sydney, we saw *Calvary*, set in County Sligo. These intense disturbing films evoke the domination of Ireland since independence in the 1920s by the omnipresent Catholic church and its interfering authoritarian priests and nuns, how Ireland loses so many of its best, how those that remain are always threatened by hopelessness and despair, as in some of the final fractured images of *Calvary*.

The haunting images of Eva Gore-Booth's line 'Buried the broken dreams of Ireland lie' resonate with a major scandal in contemporary Ireland, which was erupting in the world's press in late May and early June 2014 as we were beginning our visit. In London before we left for County Clare I was again struck by that line – if misremembered – when we read in the *Guardian* the devastating stories then appearing about hundreds of children who had been buried in or near a convent in the west of Ireland. The stories concerned the history of the Bon Secours Mother and Baby Home, an institution for unmarried mothers and their children in Tuam, County Galway, run for decades by the Bon Secours Sisters, a Catholic order of nuns. In 2012 a local historian Catherine Corless had published an essay suggesting the existence of mass graves containing 796 children who had died in the convent over the decades, between 1925 and 1961. She had seen and meticulously compiled the death records, but had been unable to locate the burial records; it appeared, she said, that the children were buried in unidentified mass graves.

These stories shocked the world. In London we had read an opinion piece in the *Guardian*, dated Wednesday 4 June, by Emer O'Toole, an assistant professor of Irish performance studies at the School of Canadian Irish Studies, Concordia University, Montreal. She wrote with the passionate accents and rhythms of a *J'Accuse*:

> For those of you unfamiliar with how, until the 1990s, Ireland dealt with unmarried mothers and their children, here it is: the women were incarcerated in state-funded, church-run institutions called mother and baby homes or Magdalene asylums, where they worked to atone for their sins. Their children were taken from them.

Emer O'Toole added an egregious detail that was also preoccupying the world's media coverage, that the children were dumped in a disused sewage tank, though this was to be questioned in the weeks ahead; Catherine Corless herself said in interview that she had never claimed they were so dumped, only that they must be buried in unknown unmarked mass graves.

(Looking a little way ahead, Tanya Gold wrote an article, 'The Horror of Tuam's missing babies is not diminished by misreported details', in the *Guardian*, Saturday 5 July, during our stay in Edinburgh, replying to those in the media defending the Catholic church. These apologists, she wrote, 'do not dispute the death rates in the homes or the fact that the graves of the children are unmarked'. The 'location of their graves', Gold added, remains 'a mystery, although it is probable that they are near the home')

Emer O'Toole ended her article, addressing members of the church hierarchy who said they would pray over or near the site, with a vibrant challenge:

> Do not say Catholic prayers over those dead children. Don't insult those who were in life despised and abused by you. Instead, tell us where the rest of the bodies are. There were homes throughout Ireland, outrageous child mortality rates in each. Were the Tuam

> Bon Secours sisters an anomalous sect? Or were church practices much the same the country over? If so, how many died in each of these homes? What are their names? Where are their graves? We don't need more platitudinous damage control, but the truth about our history.

It is that rage, scorn, passion and hatred that infuses the films, edges their wit, and provokes the thought (well, actually, Ann had the thought), that the claim that the children were dumped in a sewage tank was believed by the media and so many people everywhere because no cruelty, no horror, is now considered beyond a deeply distrusted church.

If the Catholic church has always put itself forward as the soul of Ireland, its centre and anchor, what now for Ireland? To quote that so quotable query from T S Eliot's *Gerontion*, After such knowledge, what forgiveness?

There were other angry articles and commentaries in the *Guardian* the week before we left for County Clare, and we wondered what the commentary might be like in the Irish press, though, as we admitted to ourselves, we knew nothing of the Irish press, not even the names of the papers. A pleasant surprise awaited us.

That Saturday of 14 June 2014, in mid-afternoon, we drove the short way from Kilkee to Kilrush, situated a little inland next to the wide Shannon river as it opens towards the Atlantic, the road from Kilkee turning into Henry Street in Kilrush, its chief commercial street, Henry Street then leading straight to the central square which we quickly came to know as Market Square. We parked the hire car nearby, and walked around the corner to Gleeson's Hardware Store in Henry Street as instructed to collect the key. Here we met the Merchant House's owner, Paul Gleeson, who took us back around the corner to the Merchant House, proudly showed us over it, and enthusiastically told us about our distant Nash relative who had stayed there. He said the Merchant House had been left in disrepair for a long time until he and his family bought it and restored it to something of its former grandeur; an historian himself, he showed us a booklet he'd written, *Kilrush: A Walking Tour*. On its inside cover, we see that the booklet, originally published in 1991, was based on a project for which he was 'awarded the *Irish Times* Young Historian for County Clare 1990/1991'; this new edition was published in 2013. A day or two later, we bought a copy from Paul Gleeson, which he kindly signed for us, 'Welcome to Kilrush'. We saw Paul Gleeson again a few times, hear him becoming voluble and excited as he talked about Irish history. It was wonderful talking with him.

It pleased us that we were self-sufficient, that we had a comfortable modern kitchen and could cook our own meals. There was no WiFi in the house, but we had noticed that WiFi was available close by at Crotty's, a hotel on the corner of Henry Street and Market Square, and we got into the way of ending every day there, sitting in what became our favourite snug, with a glass of red wine and getting out our i-pads to tune in to email and the *Guardian* UK edition, before going back to cook at the Merchant House. I loudly declared I didn't want to look at the *Guardian* Australian edition: Australian politics had become too appalling, especially the mistreatment of refugees. In the bar nearby we could see the regulars watch hurling on the large television screen. We picked up Crotty's brochure and I have it beside me now, the hotel proud that it kept its homely snugs and extensive woodwork and tasteful tiles.

We'd noticed from our front window a stylish-looking coffee shop named The Buttermarket Café across the road in Burton Street, the street we were on, but walking past it a little later we noticed that it was closed on Sundays. On the Sunday morning, we decided to visit the Vandaleur Walled Garden. I already knew of it from earlier reading of the Protestant Ascendancy Vandaleur family who had dominated Kilrush for centuries, but I was interested to see what Paul Gleeson's booklet said about their history. Gleeson writes that in the late eighteenth and early nineteenth century, a John Ormsby Vandaleur planned the town, positioning the Market Square at its centre with streets radiating out from it. There was, however, Gleeson tells us, a 'darker side to landlordism in Kilrush', particularly evident in evictions of people by the Vandaleurs during the Great Famine of 1847–51 and in the 1880s famine; in 1888 the Vandaleurs 'evicted a large number of tenants in what became known as the "Vandaleur Evictions"'. During the 1880s however, the Vandaleurs' 'influence as landlords was dying' because of the evictions: 'Their decline continued with the burning of Kilrush House in 1897.'

It was warm, and from Merchant Square we walked slowly along Moore Street, which turned into Grace Street, wondering where the Nash family might have lived. We came across what appeared to be a large and tall but now disused Protestant church, or at least apparently disused; though a Sunday, its doors were locked, and it looked like a building in decay, abandoned. In his pamphlet, Gleeson tells us that this was St Senan's Church of Ireland, built in 1813, its tower added in 1827; during the Great Famine the Sunday School, now in ruins, was used as a soup kitchen. The Vandaleur family donated stained glass windows for the church, and there are also a 'number of beautiful memorials to the Vandaleur family within the church'. The church, Paul Gleeson adds, ceased to hold services in 1990 'due to a dwindling congregation', and has 'since been deconsecrated', 'this beautiful building' now resounding to 'traditional Irish music and dancing'.

I feel pleased this Protestant church has been deconsecrated, a word I'd never heard before but rather like. Looking at it that Sunday, I felt a surge of anger at its size, its hubris, imposed on

Ireland by the English as the established church, the equivalent in Ireland of the Church of England, always striving to impress its power over the town and district. There it was, just near the large Vandaleur estate, the church of the Anglo-Protestant ascendancy, the church of the Vandaleurs, possibly the church where in the nineteenth century my Protestant family prayed and got married. My family, I reflected, walking around idly looking at the gravestones, *were* part of the Anglo-Protestant ascendancy.

We walked along a street, a long street as it turned out, looking for the main entrance of the Vandaleur Walled Garden, and on the way came across a kind of memorial in miniature next to the footpath, almost like a moment in *Gulliver's Travels*. Bending down to look at it, we could see that it was composed of a small replica of Scattery Island, a sacred isle in the Shannon with a ruined church and a tower, and a plaque with an explanation of the display, surrounded by little flowers in bloom. Ann took a photo of the words on the plaque on her i-phone, and then transferred it to my i-pad, and I'm looking at it now. Under the heading 'Scattery Island/Kilrush 1500', we read:

> The replica of the Catholic Church of St Mary's and Round Tower of Scattery Island was made in 1999 to commemorate Kilrush's 1500th Anniversary celebration as a Christian Community. The Round Tower and Churches of Scattery Island were a legacy of St Senan a local man who in the 6th Century founded a Monastic Community on Scattery (one of many in Ireland, Wales, Cornwall and Brittany). The monks of the island ministered to the people of West and Southwest Clare, north Kerry and Limerick, and in time helped found new Churches and Communities, Kilrush being one such community. The Tower and Church were the last sight that thousands of immigrants had of their homes along the Shannon Shore as they said a sad farewell on their way to America, and other parts as they left Erin in hope of a bright future.

> The Tower and Church a symbol of importance to Man and for God's Glory, is once again a symbol of the cultural richness, and our hope for better times ahead for Kilrush, and for its people.
>
> (The model was made to scale by Sean Moran, Kilrush Tidy Towns Committee)

We had read the entry on Kilrush in Lonely Planet *Ireland*, which recommended a visit to Scattery Island, though we weren't sure we would go there. Now we did feel sure. We must follow this up.

The phrases on the plaque about the 'last sight' those leaving Ireland had of their homes as a 'sad farewell' reminded me of heart-breakingly sad songs of migration.

On one side of this miniature memorial was the grass next to the footpath. On the other side there extended the long high stone wall surrounding and enclosing the Vandaleur Demesne, which, Paul Gleeson tells us in *Kilrush: A Walking Tour*, consisted of 420 acres 'laid out and planted in 1712 by the Rev John Vandaleur'.

Ann and I continue walking along the footpath beside the wall until we come to the entrance of the Vandaleur estate, then finally arrive at the Vandaleur Walled Garden. Gleeson writes that the Vandaleur house was inherited in 1882 by Hector Stewart Vandaleur, however he and his wife Charlotte rarely visited, living elsewhere including in their London house; apparently, or so it is remembered, Charlotte referred to the Kilrush house as the 'house in the bog'. After the house burned to the ground in March 1897, it was never rebuilt. (A stray thought crossed my mind that local Clare people, increasingly irked by the Anglo-Protestant presence, had burned it down; Gleeson resists any such speculation, simply noting that the 'fire started in the top floor of the main house and quickly engulfed the roof and the house'.) In 2000, Gleeson adds, the Kilrush Amenity Trust and Kilrush Town Council set about restoring the walled garden which had lain overgrown and forgotten.

Tired from our walk, Ann and I gratefully took a table in the lunch place, where we gulped down water, ordered a soup lunch, a chowder I think, drank coffee. I picked up their brochure. We read for a while. In a long white tent outside, what appeared to be some kind of birthday party was in full swing with dishes being brought out from the kitchen to them and kids running around, the Vandaleur Walled Garden clearly serving also as a function centre. We moved into the enclosed walled garden area, joining other tourists there. Because it was protected by high walls, there were many interesting tropical or sub-tropical plants, and it was indeed charming to stroll about in.

Part of the restoration of the gardens was the installing of various wooden posts and other features painted bright red, a sort of Chinese-style red, signifying good fortune. My mind went back to the Lilliputian monument of Scattery Island in the grass outside the walls of the Vandaleur estate, commemorating the sadness of migrants leaving Ireland. I wondered if it was now the unlamented destiny of the Vandaleurs to be remembered with intense dislike in County Clare for their unfeeling arrogance, evicting people during the disastrous times of famine.

There was a trifling incident of note. We came across a maze in one part of the gardens, and I foolishly said look, there's a maze, let's go into it, thinking to myself it was quite small and we could easily negotiate it, it's probably a child's maze. We went in through an entrance we spied, and almost immediately, not finding a way out, I started to panic that I would never get out, until Ann rather easily worked out how to get to an exit. Then we walked back to Crotty's pub, in need of a glass of wine after my ignominious episode in the children's maze. Settled in a snug, we took a sip and opened our i-pads to see what was happening in the world.

On Monday morning, 16 June, before leaving the Merchant

House for the day we consulted our Lonely Planet *Ireland* for tips on what newspaper to read. We decided on the *Irish Times*, Lonely Planet saying that it has 'long prided itself on being the paper of the liberal intelligentsia with a core readership in Dublin'. We hoped it might be the equivalent of the *Guardian*, which we enjoyed reading every day in London. We walked along Henry Street and found a newsagent, noticing that there were customers there in conversation with the shop person, conversations we observed in every shop we went into during the week. We bought an *Irish Times* and also a small notebook each, Ann to keep notes for her long-running diary, while I hoped I could use mine to effect when I came to write about our week in Kilrush when we got back to Sydney. Then, like coffee-seeking missiles, we arrowed back to the Market Square and a little further on, in Burton Street, entered the Buttermarket Café, which was clearly newly renovated and turned out to be very pleasant to be in. The weather was still warm, so we sat outside in the courtyard, enjoying the coffee they brought out to us. Delighted that the café had WiFi, we got out our i-pads to do emails and read the *Guardian* online.

(Spoilt by good coffee in Australia, we feared coffee would be a problem. It always is when travelling; we had, in a rather lordly way, noticed that English coffee was getting better, even adopting the Australian fashion for the flat white, though the flat whites we tried in London before we came to Kilrush were more like a café au lait, almost like a bowl of soup.)

Having had our *Guardian* fix, we picked up the *Irish Times*, shared it out, and were immediately impressed. Here is a paper, we decided that week, that looked at the world from unusual angles. Seeing the date on the paper, I guiltily remembered that 16 June is Bloomsday. During the week, I came to think of the articles and commentary of the *Irish Times* as having something of the character of Leopold Bloom, the stranger who (in Georg Simmel's terms), comes today and stays tomorrow, who by his very existence disturbs the society, makes it feel uncomfortable, regards it with a kind of unnerving detachment.[4] Does Ireland, I wondered, by its very existence disturb Britain, Europe, the West? Is Bloom to Ireland as Ireland is to the world?

Things were looking up, our week was taking shape, we could come here every morning with the *Irish Times*, Ireland's *Guardian*, though the *Irish Times*, unlike the *Guardian*, remains a broadsheet. We could look at our i-pads, drink the good coffee they served, then set off each day to look at something, and then come back to Crotty's in the late afternoon, maybe to write there notes in our new notebooks, though I was a little anxious: what, I confided to myself, if I go the whole week and don't have one worthwhile thought. What if its blank pages remain blank?

We decided that day to do the usual tourist thing, to drive north in County Clare along the coast to see the Cliffs of Moher, which I don't think I'd ever heard of but turned out to be a major stop in the world's tourist trails; there were large tourist buses everywhere and tourists from many nations enjoying the sight of the extraordinary cliffs. We could see islands across from the Cliffs which the guidebook says are the Aran Isles; I thought of a Sean O'Casey play (I think) about the Aran Isles I'd read when young, about the heartbreak of the women when their menfolk in wild seas didn't return from fishing. Today, however, as at Kilkee the day before, the wild Atlantic remained uncannily still. The cliffs are indeed remarkable, but I won't talk more about them here, my interest is in south west Clare, in Kilrush and Kilkee. In Ireland I'm a highly directed 'genealogical tourist', not a general 'world tourist'.

To our knowledge, there was no commemoration of Bloomsday that day in quiet Kilrush, which we more and more appreciated for its friendliness, people in the street always acknowledging us:

we would say hi to a person passing, and he or she would say good morning. Kilrush was once known in the 1950s for its golden era of Kilrush Opera, as Paul Gleeson tells us in *Kilrush: A Walking Tour* , but now no more; and its cinema on Frances Street was closed down, as we could see walking along it. However, the next day, having bought the *Irish Times* in Henry Street and again sat in the warmth of the courtyard at the Buttermarket Café, it was immediately clear that Bloomsday had been enthusiastically celebrated in the city in which *Ulysses* is set.

An article on page three, 'Sunshine warms Bloomsday celebrations in Dublin', by Rachel Flaherty, accompanied by large coloured photos of Dubliners in period dress on foot and riding bikes, smiling and laughing, began: 'Joycean enthusiasts in their full Edwardian costumes were dripping beads of sweat on a glorious sunny Bloomsday in Dublin yesterday.' The article evoked a packed, joyful and very cosmopolitan day, involving the politically powerful as well as ordinary Dubliners and visitors from around the world, including admirers of Joyce, who the journalist talked to and quoted, from South Korea, China, Russia and Paris; a cosmopolitanism that would have pleased Joyce himself. There was a traditional breakfast at the James Joyce Centre where, in imitation of Bloom early in his day in 1904, people could partake of 'kidneys, sheep's heart, gizzards and cod's roe'. Attending the day's events were the Lord Mayor of Dublin, and a Senator; at a reception Ireland's President Michael D Higgins acknowledged 'how much writers and artists enriched our lives'. In the afternoon there were 'readings and songs from the book'; at night there was 'interactive entertainment with James Joyce meets Rocky Horror at the Sugar Club'.

Yet, I read this article a little sourly. Were Bloomsdays now just occasions for a shallow celebration of Ireland, the land and society that Joyce and so many other Irish writers like his friend Samuel Beckett had exiled themselves from. Why, I thought to myself, had Bloomsday become a celebration of Bloom as some kind of genial Irish everyperson rather than a commemoration of Bloom as a Jewish outsider figure whose very existence might profoundly disturb Ireland or any modern society? I recalled how I evoke Bloom in my *1492: The Poetics of Diaspora*, as a non-Jewish Jew of extremely uncertain identity; a heretical Jew who visits the pork butcher in the morning for breakfast innards and walks home with a kidney in his sidepocket; an admirer of Spinoza who had been excommunicated by his Sephardic community in the seventeenth century; a connoisseur of ambiguity and ambivalence as befits a Marrano; an internationalist who rejects nationalism in its Irish and Zionist forms; a utopian who in 'Circe' declares that he stands for 'Union of all, jew, moslem and gentile' and 'Mixed races and mixed marriages.'[5]

I remembered an occasion, quite a while ago now, probably not long after *1492: The Poetics of Diaspora* had been published in 2001, when I was rung by someone who said she was helping to organise Bloomsday that year in Sydney, people in a theatre would take turns to read out passages from *Ulysses* through the day; she had heard I was interested in Joyce and had written something about the novel, maybe I could participate. Can you tell me, she said, what you wrote about? I thought, I know she won't like this, but I'll have to tell her. I said in one of the chapters of my book I focus on the evocation of Bloom as a cosmopolitan Jew whose forebears had come from eastern and central Europe, and how, especially in the 'Cyclops' episode set in Barney Kiernan's pub, Bloom is derided and violence threatened against him by the nationalist citizens in the bar as a Jew who could not therefore be a citizen of the Irish nation; his apparent friend Martin Cunningham who Bloom had arranged to meet joins in, agreeing with the nationalist men around the bar that Bloom is a 'perverted Jew... from a place in Hungary'.[6]

As I felt sure would happen, given the complacent mediocrity of the Sydney theatre and literary scene, middle-brow culture for middle-class people I occasionally note to myself, I never heard from the Bloomsday organiser again. No Joycean daring there.

In the Buttermarket Café, growling such dyspeptic thoughts to myself, I turn the page of the *Irish Times* and find myself staring at an article, 'McAleese says asking bishops to advise pope on family life "completely bonkers"', which instantly catches my attention, not to say bursting out laughing. Coming so close after the dreadful revelations of Tuam, I thought, this might be interesting, as indeed it was, exceedingly so. The journalist Joe Humphreys relates to his readers that Mary McAleese, a former president of Ireland (perhaps in the grand tradition of Mary Robinson, I wondered) had the day before on Bloomsday been awarded by University College Dublin its highest honour, a Ulysses medal. In a public interview to mark the award, McAleese, as Humphreys remarks, let go with some provocative opinions. McAleese begins by mocking a plan of Pope Francis to ask a synod of bishops in Rome to advise him on whether church teaching on the family should change.

> Commenting on a planned October synod in Rome on the issue, she said: 'The very idea of 150 people who have decided they are not going to have any children, not going to have families, not going to be fathers and not going to be spouses – so they have no adult experience of family life as the rest of us know it – but they are going to advise the pope on family life; it is completely bonkers.'

In advance of the October meeting, Humphreys tells us, the Vatican had circulated a questionnaire worldwide seeking feedback on pastoral issues of marriage and family. He reports McAleese's response to the pope: 'I wrote back and I said I've got a much simpler questionnaire and it's only got one question and here it is: How many of the men who will gather to advise you as pope on the family have ever changed a baby's nappy? I regard that as a very, very serious question.' McAleese added that though Pope Francis had raised expectations of change, the chances of this happening were 'very poor', for while the pope, she acidly observed, said he wanted a new role for women in the church, any discussion of women priests was off the table.

In this Bloomsday interview Mary McAleese then turned her attention to Joyce and *Ulysses*, leading her to reflect on the church's historical infamies in relation to Jews. McAleese said she had 'always been perplexed why he would choose a Jewish person in Dublin' as the novel's lead character. One possibility, she mischievously ponders, was that Joyce may have been affected by 'one of the big international scandals' of the latter part of the nineteenth century, the abduction of Edgardo Mortara, a Jewish boy, by the Vatican, where he was raised as a ward of the state. McAleese also scathingly notes that while 'the church has an image as a protector of children', the 'treatment of Jews in Rome was appalling' right up to the twentieth century.

These remarks on the Mortara case I found very interesting indeed, and I don't think they were idle comments, I think McAleese had a very serious purpose just as she had when she asked the pope her question whether any bishop had ever changed a nappy: to remind her contemporary Irish audience of a history that she considered was allegorical; a history enacted in nineteenth-century Catholic-dominated Italy that the Irish could apply to their own society in the present, in the twenty-first century, in the wake of the Catholic church in Ireland being disgraced by the pedophile scandals and the brutality of the Tuam convent where the babies and children had been taken away from their mothers.

In Wikipedia and other places when googling, I gleaned the following: on 23 June 1858 in Bologna in the Papal States, police arrived at the home of a Jewish merchant, Momolo Mortara and his wife Marianna, to take away Edgardo Levi Mortara, one of their eight children, who was six years old. By order of the Bologna Inquisitor, Edgardo was taken to Rome and placed in a monastery for converts. As the story became known to the world, it appears that some years before 1858, the family's Catholic serving girl, fearful that Edgardo as a little child might die of an illness, had secretly baptised him or so she claimed. When word reached the Bologna Inquisitor, he ordered that Edgardo be seized, for he was now recognised by canon law as a Christian who could not therefore be raised by non-Christians. It appears that the pope took a personal interest in the case, helping raise Edgardo himself, to the extent of regarding the boy as his own child, at the same time ignoring the distressed appeals of the parents to be reunited with their son. Meanwhile, as world public opinion turned against the Vatican, in Italy the case came to symbolise the entire revolutionary campaign of Mazzini and Garibaldi to end the historic dominance of the Catholic Church and establish a modern secular Italian state.

McAleese's own awareness of the Edgardo Mortara abduction may have been heightened by David Kertzer's 1997 book *The Kidnapping of Edgardo Mortara*, which was made into a play and performed in 2002 and 2006.

Sitting there in the Buttermarket Café's courtyard sipping coffee, it seemed to me that McAleese was suggesting to her Bloomsday audience that Mazzini and Garibaldi's vision of a modern secular Italy should be applied to contemporary Ireland. There was also a scathing op ed by *Irish Times* literary editor and social and political affairs commentator Fintan O'Toole, entitled 'Ireland's portrayal of itself as the purest, holiest or richest country has brought us lies and exclusion', directing biting sarcasm at Ireland since independence as a society that, bizarrely, against all evidence, has created an exaggerated image of itself as superior among the nations. Ireland's 'delusions of grandeur' are highly destructive: 'This place became so vicious partly because of a hysterical insistence on its unique virtue – a habit of mind that has never gone away.' The existence of those who marred the image of 'perfection', of a 'unique purity', were hidden, excluded, denied, in a vast system of coercive confinement: 'industrial schools, Magdalene laundries, mother and baby homes and mental hospitals'. Reading this op ed by O'Toole, I recalled a review by the political theorist Judith Brett, who had spent some time in Dublin teaching, of a book of O'Toole's, *Ship of Fools: How Stupidity and Corruption Sank the Celtic Tiger.*[7]

I remember Ann saying around this time in conversation about Tuam and the Irish films we had been seeing, that the men of Ireland since the early 1920s have been so hopeless, the politicians and priests so ruinous for the society, that surely now it's time for the women to have a go. I think that is what Mary McAleese was allegorically implying, that a modern secular Ireland could be created where the ethical thought and challenging insights of eloquent women like herself and Mary Robinson and young radicals like Emer O'Toole could be fully acknowledged, assisting in a profound transformation of Irish society, a desperately needed metamorphosis.

Something else I thought was clear from Mary McAleese's 16 June interview, that she talked in the freewheeling trickster spirit of Molly Bloom's wonderfully irreverent soliloquy that bookends *Ulysses*, Molly with her scorn for the men of Ireland, including Bloom and Stephen Daedalus as they micturate side by side, looking up at her luminous shadow in the window of her and Bloom's house.[8]

Tuesday 17 June was not finished with us yet – it was only getting going. Kilrush that day made us sharply aware of Irish attitudes to time and history, an awareness that grew on us as the week went on. In the introduction to *Is History Fiction?* Ann and

I had noted that in European and Western historical consciousness, time is experienced as double, as secular yet also sacred and mythic; as we put it, secular time is a line, unbroken, continuous, homogenous; but time is also as if a substance – sacred, mythic, messianic, prophetic, millennial, miraculous, nostalgic.[9] Ireland was making us aware of a dimension we could have added to time as a substance, that in Ireland, in daily conversation, traumatic events, such as the mid-nineteenth-century Great Famine or the 1916 Easter Rising, are markers of time, are woven into contemporary consciousness, into folk memory. I see now that I scribbled down this comment as the first entry of my traveler's notebook.

At the Buttermarket Café that morning, we decided that we would walk down Frances Street to the river where boats were moored, the Kilrush Marina, and see if we could book a visit to Scattery Island. We left the café and walked back along Burton Street the short distance to the Market Square. In *Kilrush: A Walking Tour*, Paul Gleeson tells us that the 'large imposing building in the centre of the Market Square was built by John Ormsby Vandaleur as the Market House in 1808', and contained weighing facilities for the markets held in front of the building. However, the 'Market House was burned down by the British Auxiliary Forces (the Black and Tans) in 1921', though rebuilt in 1931 and now houses the offices of Kilrush Town Council. On the southern side of the building, Paul Gleeson writes, is a 'memorial to the Easter 1916 Rising' built for the 50th Anniversary Celebrations in 1966.

A monument in the square in front of the Market House caught our eye, and we inspected it carefully. It was packed with historical information. Gleeson writes that this is the Maid of Erin Monument, which had been erected in 1913 as a memorial to the 'Manchester Martyrs of 1867, Allen, Larkin and O'Brien'. The inscription, Gleeson tells us, was in Irish, Classic Irish, French and English:

> Erected in 1903, by a committee of Kilrush Nationalists, through public subscription received from Irishmen the world over, to the memory of the Manchester Martyrs, Allen, Larkin and O'Brien, who were judicially murdered by a tyrannical government on the 23rd of November 1867 for their gallant rescue of Kelly and Deasy, the Fenian Chiefs from the prison van at Manchester. God Save Ireland.

The Black and Tans toppled the statue of Erin in May 1921, and it crashed to the railing below, Erin losing a hand. However, Gleeson says, the statue was 'rescued' and 'stored until after Independence when she was restored to her original position'. We were rather fascinated by this monument, reaching out to the world in different languages, and Ann took many photos.

Ann and I then walked along Frances Street a little way and entered Considine's Bakery. We'd already picked up that it is a family bakery and considered the best in Kilrush. We buy rolls for lunch and also a large round apple pie, just like what we had at the Pantry in Kilkee (perhaps that was supplied by Considine's); it would become our main dessert after dinner every night until we left, cutting a wedge each to have with fresh cream we had bought at the local supermarket.

We then walked down Frances Street and along the wharf area to an office next to the Marina where they sold tickets for Scattery Island. We booked for a 4.15 pm visit, the only time available, then walked back into town to while away the intervening hours. We spent some time visiting a large church with a very high steeple, St Senan's Roman Catholic Church, on Toler Street, which runs off Frances Street. Gleeson records that this 'imposing and fine Romanesque style Church is built of West Clare Cold Stone on a site donated by Crofton Moore Vandaleur', who laid the foundation stone for it in 1839 and also gave a sizeable donation; in 1861 the tall steeple was added 'which dominates the Kilrush skyline';

and in 1891 the main altar was installed, erected to 'the memory of Fr Dineen, the parish priest during the "Vandaleur Evictions"': 'Fr Dineen would ring the Church bell when the evictions were taking place.' Ann and I wandered around, and as usual in a Catholic church – I remember a church in Italy we once visited, on Lake Como, an ordinary church not on any tourist trail, with extraordinarily beautiful and sensuous carved robes on a statue of Mary – I was delighted by a kind of visual excess and theatricality, from the stained glass windows to coming across two figurines telling a story about Jesus.

Later in the afternoon with other tourists we boarded the little ferry that crosses the Shannon to Scattery Island. It was staffed by the ferry captain, a quiet elderly man, and his young assistant, who explained to the passengers that we first had to go through a lock, which the town was very pleased to have built not all that long ago, because before that boats could only leave Kilrush on the high tide. Now they could come and go all the time. As I write these words I recall that on returning to Sydney, still with Ireland very much in mind, I began reading Tim Pat Coogan's book *The Famine Plot: England's Role in Ireland's Greatest Tragedy* (I've already rehearsed its argument for regarding the Famine as a British-conducted genocide in Chapter 3, where he writes that nineteenth-century Ireland lacked 'infrastructure such as roads, bridges, harbors, and canals'.[10] As I see the Kilrush lock in my mind's eye now, I think again of this observation, and wonder why was Ireland so historically undeveloped by the British especially compared to Scotland, and wonder if this situation changed after Ireland gained independence in 1922. We did indeed go through the lock, watching the water rise as the young assistant made sure the boat didn't grind against its sides, and then once through the other side the captain skillfully steered the boat to the island. The captain and his assistant helped us all get out, as the boat rocked next to the little wharf.

The boat would wait for us.

At the Visitor Centre we were met by a government guide, who took our little party around various sites, all of them ruins. Scattery Island, he told us, was where St Senan came in the sixth century to start a monastery, though St Senan had first to compel the departure from the island of its resident monster, a giant serpent; the guide mentioned that this was a common story in these kinds of situations. There was a magic well, ruined churches, and the tall tower also now a ruin. The guide said it's not clear what the tower was for, though one common theory was protection for the monks, since over the centuries the island had been subject to many Viking raids; he wasn't sure about that theory, he said, as the invaders could easily have smoked the monks out. Fisher people used to live on Scattery Island in houses facing away from the Atlantic, their boats tethered to the shore in front of each home, until quite recent times, including, he said, our ferry boat's captain when he was young; but the families at some stage all moved to Kilrush so the children could go to school.

Scattery Island, a sacred isle composed of ruins, called to mind for us another sacred isle we had visited some years before, Iona, the tiny island just off the larger island of Mull, on the west coast of Scotland, which is not far by sea from Ireland, indeed its creation story is that St Colomba came from Ireland to Iona to found Christianity in Scotland in 563. When in Edinburgh we told our friend Mark Dorrian that we would be visiting the west coast and might go to Skye. He said, no, don't go to Skye, everyone goes to Skye, go to Iona. We spent a lovely day on Iona, so green, with cattle in fields, and from memory well-kept buildings run by liberal interfaith communities; in one, I was particularly pleased to see a pro-Palestinian poster. There was also a hotel for visitors on the island. By comparison, how poor Scattery Island seems, yet it's deeply moving.

On Wednesday 18 June, we join a boat with other tourists and go dolphin watching in the grey waters of the Shannon estuary.

On Thursday 19 June, sitting in the Buttermarket Café, inside now, the weather retreating from its warm spell, reading the *Irish Times*, I notice an item reporting that the new owners of Lissadell House, who had purchased it from Josslyn Gore-Booth in 2003, had now settled a long-running dispute with the local council about rights of way on the estate. It would reopen the Friday of this week, and have a room devoted to Constance Markievicz and another to W B Yeats. We discuss whether to go, but decide with regret that it's too far to drive to Sligo, we're leaving early on the Saturday morning on our return journey to London and would have to spend some of the Friday preparing for it.

We decide today to drive from Kilrush to Loop Head Peninsula, where the Shannon meets the Atlantic. On the way, not far from Loop Head, we stop for a fish-and-chips lunch in Keating's Bar at Kilbaha, then make our way to Loop Head Lighthouse, where we join a small group of tourists. A young female guide leads the way up the steep stairs of the lighthouse until we reach the top, step out onto the balcony, and look over the nearby coast and the wide Atlantic, still almost unnaturally calm. As she explains various features of the history of the lighthouses that have been at Loop Head, she talks in a way that confirms for us how much time in Ireland is measured in terms of traumatic events, especially when she says something like, *the present lighthouse was built in 1854, nine years after the Famine began*. She reminds the group that Ireland was neutral in World War II, pointing down at the grass below the lighthouse, saying words were written in large letters for American pilots when flying over to recognise that they were crossing a neutral country.

We then drove along what the Loop Head brochure we'd picked up before leaving the lighthouse complex calls the Wild Atlantic Way scenic route to Kilkee, parked and walked to the Pantry, enjoyed a coffee and discussed how the young guide spoke as if measuring time from the Famine, and how different Ireland was, being neutral in World War II, like Sweden if we remembered right, where Raphaël Lemkin the creator of the concept of genocide had found refuge from the Nazis before leaving for the US . Then, as we had a few days before, when we first got to Kilkee from Shannon airport, we had walked along the lane next to the Pantry to the beach, and this time made our way to the opposite headland, where we sat on a bench and looked over the beach and the town. With Ann being brought up in Newcastle further up the coast from Sydney, and my being brought up in Bondi, I think we like being next to the sea; appreciate its liminality, feeling that we do not belong to the land we are at the edge of, but we are certainly intensely interested in the histories that cross it and the surrounding seas.

What we were finding this week in Ireland was that Kilrush and Kilkee form a nexus, as they always historically had: Kilrush as a riverside town on an estuary leading into the Atlantic and thence to distant diasporas, and Kilkee the seaside resort facing the mystery of a moody unpredictable ocean pressing against it, hoping in summer it will be benign.

When we return to Kilrush, after parking the car, we run into Paul Gleeson, who is working on the ground floor part of the Merchant House, which had once been the merchant family's shop. On the shop front window, typed lists of names have been put up of Kilrush men who fought in the World War I, some placed with Australian Infantry. Gleeson said something like, 'we are trying to restore the honour of the men who fought for the British in the First World War', that too much time had passed for them still to be treated as outcasts. We look at the names, maybe a Nash name might be there, but no, there's not. We notice a Dan Garry listed, and wondered if he could have been part of the Garry family that my grandmother Susan Nash's older sister Sarah had married into in Kilrush in 1867, a Catholic family, Sarah having converted to being Catholic on the day of her marriage to Joseph Garry. Gleeson said there was an irony there, because at some time in County Clare history the Protestant Nash family must once have been Catholic and then converted to being Protestants; in the mid-nineteenth century, he was pretty sure, the Protestants and Catholics would have had very little to do with each other. Later, sitting in a snug at Crotty's, Ann visited Ancestry.com on her i-pad and could see no connection between a Dan Garry and the Sarah Nash/Joseph Garry family. Ann also went on the Australian War Memorial website and found that quite a few Irish soldiers are listed as part of the Australian Infantry, but no 'Dan Garry', though there is a 'David Garry' there; she emailed this information about Dan Garry to Paul Gleeson. We wondered if a Garry relative ever visited the Nash family in Sydney.

On the morning of Friday 20 June, after leaving the Buttermarket Café, Ann and I walk back to the Merchant House and enjoy a quiet as it were home day, washing and drying clothes in preparation for leaving early the next morning, to drive to Shannon airport, return the car, fly to Bristol and then by train to Cardiff to see our literary critic friend Gavin Edwards from Sydney days of the early 1970s. Then back to London.

Yet Kilrush was not finished with us, Ireland was not finished with us. In the bundle of brochures and pamphlets we had brought back to Sydney from our stay in Kilrush was a pamphlet entitled *National Famine Commemoration 2013* recording how Kilrush and

County Clare commemorated the Great Famine in a remarkable range of activities 3–12 May 2013. I'm looking at the pamphlet now, turning over its packed pages. It is a very moving document, a program listing daily events, exhibitions, music, theatre, films, reenactments, lectures and walks, that people in Kilrush and Clare, adults and school children, could see, attend and participate in. On the cover is the sadly iconic drawing – it's also on the cover of Tim Pat Coogan's *The Famine Plot* – in the *Illustrated London News* (part of a total of 18 sketches created between December 1849 and February 1850) of Miss Kennedy in a carriage distributing clothing in Kilrush, surrounded by women and children in rags and bare feet. In the Introduction we're told that Kilrush and its environs were among the worst hit areas.

I'm struck by the Australian connections to the Famine. On Friday 3 May, an 'Introductory Lecture' was given by Tom Power, entitled 'The role Australia played in the Irish Famine'. On Saturday 11 May there was a three-act play with a film prologue, *Voyage of the Orphans*, by the International Youth Theatre, 'the poignant true story of the 4,000 Irish famine orphans who were transported from Irish workhouses to Australia between 1848 and 1850'. There was a lecture and a reading by the novelist Evelyn Conlon of her forthcoming novel, *Records on Globe Street*, 'based on the lives of the Famine orphan girls' (I've just ordered it from Gleebooks, it has now been published under the perhaps more felicitous title *Not the Same Sky*), to be 'launched at the International Famine Commemoration in Sydney, Australia in August 2013'.[11] I google this reference and to my shame realise that I entirely missed the event happening in my home city, I didn't know it had occurred. Online the Irish Government News Service tells us that 'Arts Minister Jimmy Deenihan', Chair of the International Famine Commemoration, laid a wreath in Hyde Park Barracks, Sydney, on Sunday 25 August 2013: 'This is the 5th International Famine Commemoration. Previous events took place in Boston, New York, Liverpool and Canada'.

I'm also struck by the internationalism of it all, so evident in the Kilrush programme throughout its 10 days. The Introduction to the pamphlet tells us that at some venues there will be donation boxes 'for charities currently fighting famine around the world'. On Tuesday there was a reenactment of a Soup Kitchen, where soup 'from Famine times will be served by people wearing Irish contemporary dress' and a 'collection will be made for countries currently fighting Famine'. On Wednesday under the heading 'Current Famine in the World', we learn that 'Querrin National School pupils will give a short presentation about their project *Famine in Africa*'. On Wednesday 8 May and Thursday there were further soup kitchen events, with soup recipes from the Famine being made available and another collection made for 'countries currently fighting famine'.

A reenactment of great poignancy was held on Monday 6 May, a 13 – kilometre walk in memory of the '41 people drowned in the ferry disaster at Cammoge Point on 12th December 1849 after they were refused admission to Kilrush Workhouse'. On Saturday 11 May a 'Family Survival Celebration Day' included an 'open day at the Kilrush Men's Sheds, who are building traditional boats', with a display of currachs that are 'named after the Cammoge Ferry Disaster victims'. On Wednesday 8 May in Kilkee a lecture was given on the 'Failure of Famine Relief'. On Sunday 5 May there was a ceremony, 'after a short Liturgy of Prayer, at the site of nameless burials of more than 2000 victims of famine and fever', held at Old Drumcliff Cemetery, Ennis.

There was exploration of Irish historical consciousness, with the showing on Sunday 5 May of a film, *A Room in Air*, evoking the 'way in which the Famine proved to be a psychic and emotional fault line for Ireland and its people'; on Saturday 4 May there was a lecture on the 'effect of the famine on the Irish language'.

Certain places were recognisable to us, for example, on Tuesday

7 May there was a 'Bread and Potato Food Demonstration' featuring Soda Bead made by the local bakers Considine's Bakery, and a talk and tasting of soda bread and Lumper Potato at Buttermarket Café, Kilrush.

There was a strong interest in migration and diaspora experience, with a lecture on Wednesday 8 May on 'Scattering the People: the Great Famine and Irish Emigration with particular reference to County Clare', and on the same day a photographic exhibition *Messengers of Yesterday* of images exploring the 'Irish American identity' in the historical framework of the Famine. On Sunday 12 May, there was a Flotilla of Vessels on the Shannon Estuary 'symbolic of emigration during the Famine including boats from the West Clare Currach Club and *Celtic Mist*'. (Here's my ignorance of all things Irish resurfacing, I hadn't heard of the *Celtic Mist*. I google and see an online reference to it as a sailing boat donated in 2011 to the Irish Whale and Dolphin Group in recognition of their research work in the previous 21 years.)

There was a strong interest in the fate of the Famine orphans, not only those who went to Australia. On Thursday 9 May, there was a lecture on 'Children of the Famine: Irish Orphan Migration from Clare and Limerick to Canada in 1847'.

On Sunday 12 May President Michael D Higgins attends the closing commemoration ceremony, held on Frances Street in Kilrush at 2.30 pm. The president lays a wreath, while community participation in the ceremony includes 'music, readings, poetry and prayers' as well as a 'theatrical piece in remembrance of those who suffered and perished during the Famine', and then 'a minute of silent reflection'.

As I sit here in our house in Glebe, Sydney, reading this pamphlet, I feel very proud to have descended on my father's side from Kilrush, County Clare; feel very proud to have an ancestral Irish family background.

For this ego histoire, I will now cease my exploration of my father's Irish family and its contexts and intersecting histories, though for those intensely interested in Ireland and its histories as I have now become, it will always keep calling you, calling you, across the seas.

Ireland and its histories, you will have to let me go, feel confident that I will return, I always will.

I must find my mother.

Irreverently, as I write these final fragments for this diary of Ann and my 2014 Irish visit, I think of some lines from Emmylou Harris's rendition of the American folk song 'The Wayfaring Stranger' that she recorded in her 1980 album *Roses in the Snow*. Recall its familiar opening lines: 'I am a poor wayfaring stranger/ While travelling through this world of woe', hoping to cross the Jordan to 'home'. Recall too the first two lines of its final stanza:

> I'm going there to see my mother
> She said she'd meet me when I come

At night as I cook our evening meal, when the song comes round on our Sonos mix, I pause and listen intently.

1 Niall Williams, *History of the Rain* (Bloomsbury, London, 2014), p.9.

2 Niall Williams, *History of the Rain*, p.126.

3 Sonja Tiernan, *Eva Gore-Booth: An image of such politics* (Manchester University Press, Manchester, 2012), p.155.

4 See John Docker, *1492: The Poetics of Diaspora* (Continuum, London, 2001), pp.86-7.

5 Docker, *1492: The Poetics of Diaspora*, p.66.

6 Docker, *1492: The Poetics of Diaspora*, pp.68-9.

7 Judith Brett, Inside Story, 18 February 2010, review of Fintan O'Toole, *Ship of Fools: How Stupidity and Corruption Sank the Celtic Tiger.*

8 Docker, *1492: The Poetics of Diaspora*, p.261; Joyce, *Ulysses*, introduction and notes by Declan Kiberd (Penguin, London, 1992), pp.824-5.

9 Ann Curthoys and John Docker, *Is History Fiction?* (UNSW Press, Sydney, 2010), pp.9-10.

10 Tim Pat Coogan, *The Famine Plot: England's Role in Ireland's Greatest Tragedy* (Palgrave Macmillan, New York, 2012), p.31.

11 Evelyn Conlon, *Not the Same Sky* (Wakefield Press, Adelaide, 2013).

www.ingramcontent.com/pod-product-compliance
Lightning Source LLC
LaVergne TN
LVHW052344100826
845147LV00012B/745

* 9 7 8 1 8 7 5 7 0 3 3 3 3 *